Water Movement in Mirelands

Water Movement in Mirelands

(Vodoobmen v bolotnykh landshaftakh)

K. E. Ivanov, D. Geogr. Sc.

Faculty of Geography, University of Leningrad

Translated from the Russian by

Arthur Thomson, M.A., B.Phil., *and*

H.A.P. Ingram, B.A., Ph.D.
Department of Biological Sciences, University of Dundee

1981

ACADEMIC PRESS
A Subsidiary of Harcourt Brace Jovanovich, Publishers
London   New York   Toronto   Sydney   San Francisco

ACADEMIC PRESS INC. (LONDON) LTD.
24/28 Oval Road
London NW1

United States Edition published by
ACADEMIC PRESS INC.
111 Fifth Avenue
New York, New York 10003

First published as "Vodoobmen v bolotnykh landshaftakh"

British Library Cataloguing in Publication Data
Ivanov, K. E.
    Water movement in mirelands.
    1. Peat-bogs
    2. Hydrology
    I. Title II. Vodoobmen v bolotnykh
    landshaftakh. *English*
    551.48   GV621   80-42153
    ISBN 0-12-376460-2

Printed in Great Britain by
Page Bros (Norwich) Ltd

Preface

This is the first treatise appearing in the English language to deal with the general hydrology of peatlands. Its significance stems firstly from the unique character of peatland hydrology and the central role played by water relations in the establishment and maintenance of peatlands; secondly from the great importance of peatlands as objects of ecological, geophysical and geographical enquiry, as natural resources in their own right and as areas whose peculiar hydrological characteristics present a formidable challenge to agriculture, civil engineering, land management and conservation.

The author's standpoint is that peatlands are most usefully considered as mire ecosystems developed from waterlogged patches of mineral terrain. The course of development depends on the climate and morphology of the site. Mires in depressions grow differently from those in interfluves because their water supply undergoes a different sequence of changes. From this arises a system of peatland classification which combines the stratigraphy of the peat deposit with the characteristics of its present vegetation, soil and hydrology. Thus it is shown how, at every stage of development, differences in ground water flow are responsible for differentiating the soil-physical characteristics and associated vegetation types within a mire ecosystem, and enables them to form an integrated pattern so that each ecosystem behaves as a functional unit in peatland terrain. Although elements of this approach are widely accepted in the West, no general quantitative analysis based upon it has as yet been undertaken outside the Soviet Union. The author here demonstrates the use of such analysis in evaluating the effect of climate on peatlands, in the general ecological study of peatlands, and in the survey of peatlands by air photogrammetry. He also uses it to identify mechanisms that make for stability in peatlands, especially in those widely misunderstood mire ecosystems which contain pools or lakes. For this task he is uniquely qualified, having played a central part in the rapid post-war development of Soviet peatland hydrology, first at the State Hydrological Institute and latterly as Professor of Land Hydrology in the University of Leningrad.

This English edition is the outcome of collaboration between a philologist and a plant ecologist specializing in mire hydrology and its applications. The translation is preceded by an Introduction outlining the scope and history of general peatland studies and mire hydrology within and outside the Soviet Union. Several reforms and innovations to the English terminology of the subject are introduced and the author's bibliography has been supplemented to enhance its usefulness to the Western reader. The author has made minor corrections to the original Russian text and has checked and commented upon the English version.

December 1980
A. Thomson
H. A. P. Ingram

Contents

Translators' Introduction

The importance of water relations in peatland areas has long been acknowledged, both within and outside the Soviet Union. The study of these relations is one in which the provinces of hydrology, ecology and soil science overlap, posing theoretical problems of great interest. *Water Movement in Mirelands* shows how some of these problems may be solved, and solved furthermore with a rigour as yet unknown in the West. By *mirelands* the author understands regions of the earth's surface which are permanently waterlogged. If, in consequence, they are covered by a certain minimum thickness of peat, they are regarded as *mires*; if not, they are described as *swamps*. By *peat* we mean the autochthonous organic sediment which accumulates as a result of incomplete decay of mire vegetation.

Importance of Mires

Mires abound in the cool circumboreal zone. According to Hammond (1975) they cover about 150 million ha, an area equivalent to that of the nine member states of the European Economic Community. Other authors suggest a total area as much as three times this size. Mires therefore made an early impact on the development of modern economic systems in Europe. As obstacles to communication they had puzzled the traffic engineers of the bronze age and caused the Romans to embark on major drainage schemes. The agrarian revolution found them intractable—a threat to human health, dangerous to livestock, poor in forage value and impossible to till. On the other hand, their peat could be used as a fuel, their woody vegetation reduced to charcoal and their herbaceous plants harvested for animal bedding or to provide flooring or thatch for human dwellings; the wildfowl that found refuge in water-filled peat quarries also provided sport and food. Modern developments may have changed our interest in mires, but they have certainly not diminished it. Today, the civil engineer encounters mires not only when building roads but also during the installation of railways, power and telecommunication systems and pipelines, and when planning schemes of water supply or river regulation. In agriculture and now also in forestry we are still preoccupied with drainage and the regulation of water levels, as well as with the problem of low fertility. Interest in the use of peat has been sharpened by a world shortage of energy and diversified by the development of new industrial technology in soil conditioners and horticultural products, insulating materials and cellulose feedstocks, waste disposal and the control of water pollution. Where mires were once regarded as a source of respiratory and rheumatic disorders, peat now finds various therapeutic uses. Primitive interest in wildfowling may persist, but alongside it we have developed a broader concern with wildlife as a cultural and recreational resource, so that our mires are now seen as objects worthy of planned management, of conservation and of scientific study.

The study of mires is known as telmatology. As already suggested, it is rooted in several technological fields, and its problems are of interest to an equal range of scientific disciplines. Ecologists, pedologists, geophysicists, geochemists, sedimentologists and geographers have all regarded telmatology as a branch of their subject. In consequence there are now several national associations of scientists and technologists interested in promoting the study of mires and peat and 1968 saw the foundation of an International Peat Society with headquarters in Helsinki. This organization has arranged symposia in various countries, most of which have resulted in major publications, including the proceedings of a series of International Peat Congresses. The useful serial *Peat Abstracts*, published quarterly in Dublin by Bord na Mona since 1952, is further evidence of international interest in mires.

Mires as Natural Systems

An ecosystem is an ecological structure in which the physico-chemical environment interacts with a community of organisms (or biotum). It is a concept which directs the enquirer's attention to the functional relationships between organism and organism, biotum and environment. Indeed, it regards these relationships as the main links between the plants, animals and microbes of organic communities and their inorganic surroundings. The existence of such links is thought to explain how living organisms form associations which recur recognizably over large regions of the earth. It may also explain how, within any such region, particular associations occur in particular environments. Identifying these functional links in ecosystems and measuring their strength is a major objective in ecology and related branches of science. The exercise is also useful in civil engineering and the other technologies which seek to exploit the natural environment; for these links are basic to our understanding of the earth's surface and show within what limits it may safely be manipulated.

The functional links in ecosystems are of various kinds. Some involve the simple transfer of energy and matter; others, more subtle interactions.

These transfers and interactions take place both between the organisms of an ecosystem and between those organisms and their non-living environment. When studying the ecology of terrestrial vegetation it is often convenient to consider the environment as two compartments: the atmosphere and the soil. The atmospheric environment determines the energy climate of the plant cover and is the ultimate source of its carbon, nitrogen, oxygen and moisture. The soil is the proximate moisture source. It may also be the site of weathering and microbial activity, affecting the geochemistry of the eco-system and the availability to plants of sundry inorganic nutrients required for photosynthetic carbon fixation and growth. Plant growth results in the production of new organic matter. In many ecosystems this is either eaten by animals or decomposed by microbes, but in mires a large part of it accumulates in the form of peat. The process of decay is much slower in peat than in most other soils. The chief obstacle to plant decay in mires is perennial waterlogging of the soil, which prevents the growth of aerobic microbes so that only the inefficient, anaerobic forms are active. In some mires nutrient deficiency may also restrict microbial action. The resulting incomplete decay of plants has made it possible to found a science of peat stratigraphy, based on identifying the remains of peat-forming plants.

Waterlogging and nutrient availability also affect the macroscopic vegetation of mires. The plants which are characteristic of swamps and mires have evolved in adaptation to waterlogged soils. They are termed *helophytes* and are either rootless mosses and liverworts (bryophytes) or else (with very few exceptions) graminoid (grass-like) plants with frequently renewed ephemeral root systems possessing aerenchyma, tissues readily permeable to respiratory gases. Other plants, including most woody species (trees and shrubs), are not restricted to waterlogged habitats, but they only survive in mires by developing unusually shallow root systems.

The two main types of mire, namely bog and fen, differ profoundly in their vegetation, in accordance with differences in the nutrient status of the soil. In the circumboreal forest zone where mires are best developed, typical fen vegetation comprises hypnoid mosses of normal structure together with tall-growing graminoids and other herbaceous plants. Typical bogs in the same zone support vegetation in which mosses of the genus *Sphagnum* predominate. The *Sphagna* have a distinctive structure with elaborate systems of water-retaining tissue and are accompanied mainly by graminoids of low stature and by dwarf shrubs. Fen vegetation is eutrophic, with a high demand for plant nutrients, while the vegetation of bogs, having a low nutrient demand, is said to be oligotrophic. Arrested decay interrupts the recycling of nutrients incorporated in the organic material of mire soils. In these ecosystems nutrient supply is therefore largely dependent on the soil water. Fens characteristically occupy surface depressions and part of their water supply is telluric, derived by drainage through surrounding mineral ground in which it has become enriched with nutrients. Bogs on the other hand, are usually raised above the influence of telluric water. Their moisture is meteoric in origin, derived directly from atmospheric precipitation and consequently poor in plant nutrients. The topographic contrast is reflected in the German and Russian terminology, in which fen is called "low lying mire" and bog, "raised mire". Peat normally accumulates more slowly in fens than in bogs. This evidently follows from the somewhat greater microbial activity and faster decay in eutrophic soils, rather than from differences in photosynthetic productivity. Indeed fens are generally more productive than bogs. However their slower rates of peat accumulation serve to accentuate the topographic distinction between bog and fen so that, where these two types of mire are juxtaposed, the contrast between areas with telluric water supply and areas with only meteoric water is maintained during long periods of peat deposition.

Significance of Mire Hydrology

It is therefore clear that water plays a decisive role in the origin and development of mires. Perennial waterlogging of the soil causes peat accumulation, while the essential difference between fen and bog is the mineral content of their water supply. Ecologically, the influence of water relations extends beyond the gross effects already mentioned. Indeed few discernible variations in the vegetation or surface characteristics (microforms) of mires appear to escape this influence so that the literature is full of allusions to it. Recent examples include the monographs of Overbeck (1975) and Göttlich (1976) and the articles on mires in Ratcliffe's (1977) important review, while some of the earlier work has been summarized by Ingram (1967).

The water relations of mire ecosystems thus constitute a net-work of interactions or functional links whose importance is widely recognized. In the study of ecosystems there is a need to evaluate interactions of all kinds. In these terms we may venture to summarize many of the salient facts of mire ecology by regarding them as terrestrial ecosystems with hydrological links of unusual strength.

The multifarious ecological effects of water give rise, in their turn, to many of the technological problems and opportunities which mires present. Some aspects of these are considered in the treatises of MacFarlane (1969) Radforth and Brawner (1977) and Eggelsmann (1978), and in various symposium proceedings published by the International Peat Society.

xiv   WATER MOVEMENT IN MIRELANDS

History of Mire Hydrology

In the literature of land reclamation and agricultural improvement there are references to mire hydrology which date back at least to the *Moorkatechismus* of J. C. Findorff, published in 1764 (Baden and Eggelsmann, 1963; Overbeck, 1975). Several treatises on telmatology, published in Scotland between 1807 and 1826, lay emphasis on those aspects of the hydrology of mires which were thought relevant to their drainage (Rycroft *et al.*, 1975). From the standpoint of pure science, the earliest interest seems to have concerned aspects of water storage in mires. Early speculation that mires were sponge-like reservoirs with significant power to regulate river flow is attributed either to A. von Humboldt or F. Hochstetter. This notion became established before 1860 and still persists despite much contrary evidence (Ingram, in press). The hydrological basis of the differences in mineral nutrition between fen and bog was first suggested by C. A. Weber (1908), who perceived that fens occur below, and bogs above, the level of drainage from mineral surroundings. Weber (1856–1931) worked at the mire research station which was established at Bremen in 1877. He occupies a unique position in the history of telmatology, since he first applied the terms eutrophic and oligotrophic in their modern ecological sense. His hydrological conclusions were confirmed by further descriptive research, published before 1935 by A. K. Cajander in Finland, by C. Malmström, H. Osvald and E. Granlund in Sweden, and by H. Godwin in Britain. Most of the bogs studied by these workers occurred in raised mire systems. In these, peat deposition begins either in a basin or on a level platform and the system often passes through lacustrine and fen stages before eventually a dome-like massif is formed, generally with an intricately-patterned surface expanse. This expanse is ombrotrophic, being fed by direct precipitation alone. It drains centrifugally towards a marginal eutrophic fen, or *lagg*, that also receives drainage from the mineral hinterland.

Detailed attention to the differences in ground water quality between fens and bogs lent further support to Weber's conclusions. Begun by M. Kotilainen in Finland before 1930, these geochemical studies culminated in Sweden after 1945 with the work of Margaretha Witting, H. Sjörs and N. Malmer. By analysing the chemical composition of peat and mire water it became possible to trace the influence of enrichment by the mineral surroundings and to establish the position of a geochemical *limit of mineral soil water*. In mire complexes (or macrotopes, see p. 26), this was often found to coincide with the phytosociological boundary, established by vegetation analysis, between eutrophic and oligotrophic plant communities; that is, between fen and bog vegetation. The geochemical approach has since been used to evaluate mires in the context of public water supply, notably in Czechoslovakia by Ferda and Pasák (1969).

A subsequent outcome of descriptive research was the realization that the high nutrient demands of fen vegetation can largely be satisfied by rapid seepage of water through mire soils, even when the quality of the moving water would otherwise be unfavourable to fen development (Ingram, 1967). The effects of such water movement on mire vegetation were described from Sweden by Sjörs (1948) and from Minnesota by Heinselman (1963), but the most detailed analysis is that of Kulczyński (1949), whose consideration of mire stratigraphy and vegetation in relation to the headwater hydrology of the Bug and Pripet gave the first extensive, quantitative confirmation of this view. This investigation was one of several studies on the physical hydrology of mires which were begun after 1930. Other notable pioneers included K. Prytz of Denmark and L. Tinbergen of Belgium, who studied evapotranspiration. Catchment studies by W. Baden and later R. Eggelsmann at Bremen, and in Finland by L. Heikurainen, enabled all items of the mire water budget to be evaluated. Their work suggests that, at least in the short to medium term, drainage for forestry or agriculture increases temporary water storage capacity in mires and thus enhances their power to regulate stream flow, incidentally emphasizing how small is the "sponge" effect in intact bogs.

This approach was later extended by Verona M. Conway, A. Millar and W. Burke to the *blanket mires* of the climatically moist seaboard of western Europe. In contradistinction to raised mires, these are formed on sloping substrates, independently of level areas or basins, so that hilly terrain becomes covered with a mantle of wet peat. Though now generally treeless, blanket mires may often have replaced forests. They thus present the clearest possible contrast to the mires of northern Minnesota, where tree cover often persists. Data on the water balance and soil physics of these mires show the effect of forest cover and demonstrate the potential complexity of water interchange between peat and adjacent fluvio-glacial deposits (Boelter and Verry, 1977).

From this widespread scientific attention some generalizations about the overall hydrological role and behaviour of mires are beginning to emerge (Ingram, in press). However, western observers have been reluctant fully to exploit this new knowledge. There have been few attempts either to understand the detailed hydrological relationships of particular types of mire surface and vegetation or to develop a general theory of mires as ecosystems in which hydrological interactions form important functional links. Not only has this retarded the development of telmatology as a scientific discipline of relevance to ecology and geomorphology; it has greatly hindered the technical use of hydrological findings in the planning and efficient execution of engineering projects concerned with farming, forestry, wildlife conservation, transport, flood control, water supply, waste disposal and peat extraction over large tracts of the cool circumboreal zone. Moreover, neglect of the details of hydrological processes and their operation in large tracts of mire has made it impossible to devise methods of interpreting aerial photographs in terms of hydrodynamics. Until this has been done, interpretive schemes such as the one developed in Canada by N. W. Radforth must remain predominantly descriptive.

The Soviet Contribution

Despite the activities of the International Peat Society, it is still true to say that on the whole Soviet telmatologists are more aware of western research than *vice versa*. Ignorance of the Soviet effort in the west has been unhelpful to the progress of telmatology and one result has been the development of two different approaches to the subject.

Hammond (1975) estimates that 64 % of the world's total area of mires is to be found in the Soviet Union, chiefly concentrated in the north-west European territories and in western Siberia. Mires are a feature of the Soviet scene that cannot be ignored, for they are accessible to the point of obtrusiveness. From obtrusiveness has come technological difficulty and hence funding for research. From accessibility has come intensive scientific attention. This, in turn, has been shaped by a philosophical tradition which became established early in two relevant fields of enquiry: a tradition laying emphasis on function rather than physical structure. In pedology, V. V. Dokuchaev considered that the fundamental circumstance of a soil is not its geological origin or chemical composition, but the climatic regimen under which it has developed. He realized that stratified soil profiles develop and persist because the different layers are involved in different processes whose details change with climate. In ecology, V. N. Sukachev developed a concept, kindred to that of the ecosystem, in which were comprehended the processes of interaction between organic communities and their physico-chemical environment, and to which he gave the name *bio-geo-coenose*.

Soviet telmatology, however, began long before this time, for the earliest recognition of Russian mires as a natural resource is generally credited to M. V. Lomonosov, who died in 1765. In parallel with western endeavour, the first mire drainage manual appeared early in the following century. Systematic study of Russian mires as natural objects was begun during the Dokuchaev period by G. I. Tanfil'yev (about 1890), but it is thanks to the work of V. S. Dokturovskiy that telmatology became a well-established study in the Soviet Union. As a botanist and geographer, Dokturovskiy realized the advantages of attacking the problems of mires simultaneously from many sides. Thus between 1915 and 1935 he succeeded in establishing plant sociology, peat stratigraphy, geophysics, geochemistry and palaeobotany as disciplines essential to the successful development of Soviet mire science.

Sukachev was himself especially active in the ecological study of mires during the 1920s and it is interesting to note that early, systematic hydrological studies by D. A. Gerasimov, on evapotranspiration from a raised mire, date from this same period. These were quickly followed by the related work of S. N. Tyuremnov, who studied the physics of the atmospheric boundary layer in order to evaluate the energy balance of the raised mire surface. Further research by A. D. Dubakh resulted in the publication in 1936 of what seems to have been the world's first treatise on mire hydrology. Thus, in contrast to the fragmented Western effort, a readily discernible school of physical mire hydrology became established in the Soviet Union by about 1940. The foundation of a Department of Mire Hydrology within the State Hydrological Institute at Leningrad provided a further stimulus to the development of this science after the second world war. In addition to the establishment of a network of permanent stations, where components of the water balance of mires are observed in different parts of the Soviet Union, detailed physical studies of hydrological processes have been an important feature of the research programme. A basic innovation was V. D. Lopatin's extension of Dokuchaev's principle of functionally differentiated soil horizons to embrace mires, whose soils have been all too often regarded by traditional pedologists as embarrassingly intractible (Ingram, 1978). It is the physics of the superficial horizon or acrotelm (p. 16, note 6) which has received most attention. Among others, P. K. Vorob'ev has studied moisture storage in this layer; K. K. Pavlova and S. A. Chechkin have considered its participation in freezing and thawing; and V. V. Romanov and L. G. Bavina its general energy relationships, with particular reference to evapotranspiration. Several monographs have resulted from this work, including those of Shebeko (1970) on drainage applications and Romanov (1961, 1962) on general physical properties and evapotranspiration. Romanov's books have appeared in English (see Bibliography).

The Work of K. E. Ivanov

Konstantin Evgen'evich Ivanov, the most prominent of Soviet mire hydrologists during the post-war period, was born at St. Petersburg in 1912. Before the second world war he received undergraduate and research training in hydraulic engineering. The war was a major influence on his subsequent career, for military operations in northern Russia posed technical problems on an unprecedented scale, and it was at this period that he first became concerned with the physical properties of ice and of peat deposits. In 1946 he joined the high-latitude marine expedition of the Arctic Institute to study the physical properties of ice floes, but in 1948 he returned to Leningrad as head of the Department of Mire Hydrology at the State Hydrological Institute (GGI). In this capacity he led several expeditions to study mires and directed the research work of permanent mire stations. Early investigations in the north-west European territories were concerned with water storage in mires and its effect on their runoff regime. This induced him to elaborate, with V. V. Romanov, the diplotelmic (two-layer) concept of Lopatin and to establish the acrotelm as the horizon of primary functional significance. He also became interested in the throughflow or horizontal seepage of water in the acrotelm and showed how the relevant transfer functions could be measured.

Ivanov's association with Leningrad University began in 1949, when he started to give lectures in mire hydrology, hydraulics and hydraulic engineering. He was accorded the rank of Professor in 1957 and in 1963 he became Deputy Scientific Director of the State Hydrological Institute. In 1969 he became a full-time member of staff of the Geographical Faculty of Leningrad University and head of the Department of Land Hydrology.

Mires may be classified either according to their vegetation, or to the amount and quality of their water supply, or to their developmental history and the stage which this has reached. In Ivanov's hands, the ecological, geophysical and historical approaches become united into a single taxonomic scheme, which we have called the genetico-geotopic system. This advances from major geographical units, such as the water divides between great river systems, to minute components like moss-covered hummocks, pausing in its advance to characterize the intermediate taxa by the way in which they receive and dispose of their water supply and by the stage attained along the path of development prescribed for them by the geographical and climatic details of the site. Any facies of the mire surface, with its particular combination of microrelief and plant community, posesses a special water regime that prevails throughout the region where the facies or microtope occurs (see note 12 to p. 33).

Ivanov's conclusions have been set out in three monographs (see Bibliography). The first (1953) is an introduction to the physical hydrology of mires. The second (1957b) is a large work which has been very influential in countries where Russian is well understood but has, like the first, been neglected elsewhere through lack of a translation. The third book, of which this is the English edition, summarizes and brings up to date the author's earlier work and may thus serve as a general introduction to the more advanced Soviet thinking in this field. Much of the book can be regarded as continuing E. A. Galkina's work in the classification of mires and that of Dubakh on their hydrology, but the author also shows his ability to pioneer new lines of research.

In the Soviet Union the climatic conditions are so severe and the area of mireland so vast that there is no prospect of surveying more than a small fraction by ground methods. Ivanov has therefore addressed himself to the theoretical problems involved in interpreting air photographs in terms of mire hydrology. Different microtopes can be identified from the air. When their hydrological behaviour has been ascertained by studying a limited number of similar mires on the ground, it becomes possible by using climatic data to predict from air photographs the salient hydrological properties of other mires, knowing only the regional climate. For this purpose flow-nets are superimposed upon the photographs or on maps constructed by photogrammetry. Effective calculations of water movement cannot be made without simplifying conventions which reduce all flow nets to a limited variety of simple geometrical forms, substituting statistical artifacts for the cruder data of observation. Having thus set up the equivalent mire massif as an abstract conceptual entity, the author is able to treat the supply and transfer of water as integrals over the area or across the boundary of this entity.

The most original part of the book is Ivanov's attempt to apply these methods of analysis to lake–mire systems. He is especially interested in the stability of these systems and their capacity for surviving changes in water supply. For stability, when conditions become wetter, water transfer must increase; when they become dryer, it must decrease. The element which most readily adjusts its water transfer is the vegetation and associated acrotelm surrounding the lake, especially if these contain components with different hydrological properties, such as hummocks and hollows. The mathematical framework for this study of the stability of lake–mire systems is to be found in equation (2.80). This is central to Ivanov's analysis of the hydrology of mires in terms of flow-lines, gradients, hydraulic conductivity and water supply. Consideration of the hydraulic relationships between the various microtopes within a particular mire suggests how one might interpret these ecosystems analytically, using dynamic system models whose components behave according to biophysical and geophysical principles of wide applicability. Large mire systems may contain numerous microtopes of several kinds, showing a diversity of vegetation and soil physical characteristics. Thus the author's approach is not only an important contribution to land capability surveying; it also affords insight into the stability and functional ecology of an important class of complex ecosystem.

Terminology

In previous English translations from the Russian literature of mire hydrology the rendering of technical terms leaves much to be desired. In this respect the translator's problems are aggravated by differences of tradition, particularly in the field of vegetation science, and by the great progress of Soviet mire hydrology in recent decades. The borrowing of technical terms direct from the Russian is impracticable, if only because the Russian terms are often themselves borrowed from western sources. Nor are these sources helpful, since one cannot conveniently derive from them the cognate adjectives, adverbs and compounds to which their Russian derivatives so readily give rise. For instance the Russian word *landshaft* is derived from the same source as our word "landscape", but this source yields no equivalents for the Russian adjective *landshaftnyy*, the adverb *landshaftno* or the prefix *landshaftno-*. The equivalents used here are explained in footnotes where they are introduced in the text. For convenience they are also listed below in the Glossary (p. xxiv). Other useful Russian mire terms will be found in the works of Masing (1972), Bick *et al.* (1973) and Bick *et al.* (1976).

Bibliography and Transliteration

The bibliography is arranged by author according to the Roman alphabet. Besides the entries appearing in the original, it includes items mentioned by the author but omitted from his bibliography, together with references cited only in the Preface to this edition or in the translators' notes. Cyrillic entries have been transliterated in full according to the conventions described below. Each of these entries is followed either by the translators' rendering of the title or, where we have been able to trace an English translation or abstract, by a reference to this subsidiary source which includes the title proposed there. We have found the serial *Meteorological and Geoastrophysical Abstracts* to be the best guide to subsidiary sources in English for the Cyrillic references in this work. Periodical titles are abbreviated according to the conventions of the *World List of Scientific Periodicals*.

Except for geographical names, where a more phonetic scheme has been adopted, the aim in transliterating from Cyrillic has been to make the identification of personal names and titles in the original Russian publications as easy as possible from their Roman transliterations. To this end the letter *e* has been used in the bibliography to indicate both the jotated Russian *yĕ* and the unjotated *čŏberŏ'tnŏyĕ*. *i* is used only for the Russian *ē*, while *y* represents both the diphthongal *ēkrǎ'tkŏyĕ* form of this character and also the non-diphthongal *ĭ*. (For phonetic equivalents of the Cyrillic alphabet, see the *Concise Oxford Dictionary*, 1976.) Although not given here, stress is of the greatest importance in pronouncing Russian words. It should be noted that Professor Ivanov's name is pronounced with the stress on the last syllable.

Method, Responsibilities and Acknowledgements

The aim of the translators has been to convey the author's meaning in the clearest idiomatic English compatible with an accurate rendering of the original. The senior partner (A.T.), who had extensive experience of literary and scientific Russian, prepared the first English draft. This and three subsequent drafts were annotated by the junior partner (H.A.P.I.) who used his knowledge of ecology, telmatology, hydrology and soil physics to bring the text into conformity with accepted Western scientific usage. Both partners discussed the annotations until agreement on the final version was reached. So far as possible they followed the author's own mathematical notation rather than western practice (but see note 2 and 12 to pp. 47 and 105).

Minor errors detected in the original were few in number and have usually been corrected without comment. In still fewer cases, where we have found ourselves in disagreement with the author, we have left his version as it stands and indicated our misgivings in notes. In other notes we have explained our terminological innovations, set out the reasoning behind some more difficult amendments of mathematical notation which the author's use of Cyrillic subscripts has forced upon us, and ventured to indicate certain sources of background material which, in conjunction with H.A.P.I.'s preface, may make good the inaccessibility of much Soviet literature. Translators' notes are followed by the symbol (T) to distinguish them from those present in the original. In much of this editorial work we have been assisted by Dr I. T. A. C. Adamson of the Department of Mathematics and Mr A. M. Coupar, Department of Biological Sciences, both in the University of Dundee, while Professor J. W. L. Adams, Department of Education, University of Dundee, sometime Craven Fellow of the University of Oxford, has advised on questions of classical philology, enabling us to avoid some of the barbarisms in which ecological literature abounds.

Our bibliographical difficulties have been much eased by Mr E. H. Armstrong and his colleagues at the Dundee University Library and by the staffs of the Library of the University of Strathclyde, the National Library of Scotland and the Macaulay Institute Library at Aberdeen. Mr R. A. Robertson of the Macaulay Institute's Peat Section and the secretariat of the International Peat Society in Helsinki have helped in various ways. This edition owes much to the influence of Professor V. Masing of Tartu, who first drew H.A.P.I.'s attention to the book and whose knowledge of Soviet mires is invaluably combined with an appreciation of literary English. He may be said to have prepared the ground in which germinated the idea of this project, but its fruition was made possible by Miss Ruth Gadsby and her colleagues at Academic Press, who have negotiated copyright and given us their advice and encouragement throughout. We are grateful for the secretarial and technical assistance of Miss Anne Pringle, Miss Angela McKay, Mr Iain Tennant (Department of Biological Sciences) and the staff of the Photographic Department (University Library) in the Univesity of Dundee. We thank

Mr A. W. K. Ingram, of Rugby, who cheerfully undertook the arduous task of preparing the index.

Finally, we should like to thank Professor Ivanov for writing the book, for encouraging us to proceed and for very practical help in supplying three copies of the Russian edition and revising the final English draft.

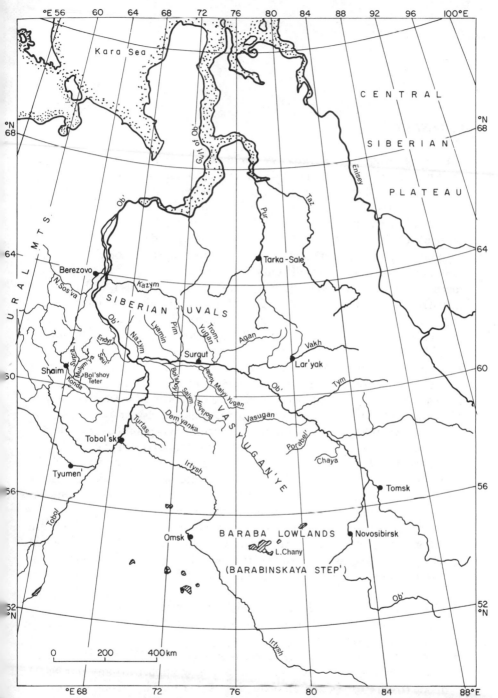

Map of Western Siberia, showing the principal hydrological features of the lowlands, including rivers mentioned in this book. (Compiled from various sources with the assistance of Mr. Alastair Cruikshank and Mr. C. Hallstead, Department of Geography, University of Glasgow.)

Glossary

aktivnyy gorizont (also **deyatel'nyy gorizont**) = *acrotelm*. Uppermost layer of peat deposit, with variable water content, high hydraulic conductivity, periodic aeration and intense biological activity (from ἄκρος, topmost; τέλμα, marsh). A mire with both acrotelm and catotelm is said to be *diplotelmic* (from διπλοῦς, two fold).

element rel'efa = *microform* (or *element of relief*). Individual feature of the microrelief of the earth's surface, e.g. a hummock or pool, 0·1–200 m^2 in area (from μικρός, small; Latin *forma* form).

inertnyy gorizont = *catotelm*. Lower portion of a peat deposit, with constant water content, low hydraulic conductivity, an absence of aeration and slight biological activity (from κάτω, down). The catotelm of an intact mire is overlain by the acrotelm. If the acrotelm is missing the mire is said to be *haplotelmic* (from ἁπλοῦς, single).

landshaft = *geotope*. Any distinguishable portion of the earth's surface and its plant cover (from γῆ, earth; τόπος, place).

landshaftnyy = *geotopic*. Cognate adjective of geotope. **landshaftno** = *geotopically*. Cognate adverb of geotope. **makrolandshaft** = *macrotope*. Distinguishable portion of the earth's surface and plant cover of 10–500 km^2 in area and comprising two or more mesotopes (from μικρός, large). **mooolandshaft** = *mesotope*. The same, but 0·1–10 km^2 and comprising two or more microtopes (from μέσος, intermediate). **mikrolandshaft** = *microtope*. The same, but 0·01–1 km^2 and with uniform environmental conditions and vegetation structure (from μικρός, small).

lentochnogryadovaya struktura = *strip-ridge structure*. Used of a mire surface, generally sloping, in which very elongated pools (water-filled flarks) are separated by narrow ridges. (The equivalent German term *Strangmoor* has give rise to the infelicitous English expression *string-mire*.)

mochazhina = *flark*. An elongated hollow on a mire surface (from Swedish *flark*). This word originally denoted an elongated hollow fed by mineral-enriched ground water.

plakor = *placotope*. Originally an elevated plateau forming a water divide between two or more river systems, but now applied to any flat water divide (from πλάξ (πλακός), plain; τόπος, place). The second part of the Russian word was derived from ὄρος, mountain.

plakornyy = *placotopic*. Cognate adjective of placotope.

travyanoy = *graminoid*. Adjective to describe plant communities in which narrow-leaved monocotyledonous species (grasses, sedges, rushes) are dominant (from Latin *gramen*, grass). The alternative expression *herb-rich* admits the possibility that in fens such species may be accompanied by dicotyledonous herbs.

Author's Introduction

All kinds of economic and technical activity involve the development of wetlands—the use of mires and mirelands for agriculture, the building of towns and factories, the making of roads and pipelines, afforestation and hydrotechnical engineering, the mining of peat as a raw material of industry or a fertilizer and many other such activities.

The greater part of the world's reserves of peat is concentrated in the Soviet Union. The development of mirelands and the study of their properties is therefore a very urgent matter in our country, and has great practical and economic significance. Mires are produced by nature, and scientific interest in them cannot be limited to considering how useful they are for this or that branch of the economy. Like other productions of nature which go to make up the geophysical mantle of the globe, they are an important link in the chain of interconnected and interacting parts that compose our environment, and any interference with them starts a process of transformation. The study of mires ought not then to be approached from a narrowly utilitarian point of view. They should not be regarded as features of the earth's surface that militate against land use and the life and activities of man. Investigation of them should not be treated as of value only when it is a basis of methods and schemes for the improvement and economic development of wetlands.

It is no exaggeration to say that there is a big gap between the little that is known about the quantitative relations between natural formations, including the predictable effects of interfering with nature, and the vast scale on which technology can affect separate components of the geophysical environment. If research into matters of theory and method lags behind the power to act upon and transform nature, that means that much needed scientific information is not being gathered and that proper arrangements are not being made to obtain the necessary observations and to carry out the necessary programmes of theoretical, experimental and expeditionary research. It has now become obvious that rational plans for land use and the development and exploitation of natural resources involve economic and geographical calculations which cannot be carried out without correct geophysical predictions and quantitative application of them to individual regions, localities and features of the landscape.

In our country, territories of considerable size have not as yet been exposed to intensive economic activity and are still almost in their pristine state. Here nature should be treated with caution. Their special peculiarities should be allowed for in planning their transformation, and rational schemes of land use should be employed. Mirelands in this condition are the dominating components of the geosystems of the northern half of the West Siberian lowlands whose natural conditions are unique, the northern part of European Russia, and many territories in the east of the country. This is why it is now necessary to devote more attention to investigation of the physical conditions and processes that affect the structure of natural geotopes and the factors that transform them.

The most active and important exogenic factor in the transformation of geotopes[1] is, of course, water. Interaction on land between water and the biosphere, in the synthesis and decay of organic matter, plays an exceptionally important part in moulding the features of existing geotopes in regions of the globe where there is an excess of moisture. There they are responsible for the accumulation of organic material on the surface of mineral strata, which we can observe to be a feature of this as well as past geological epochs. The processes that resulted in the formation of organic strata, like coal and peat, from the incomplete decay of moribund plants are represented by the swamping of huge areas of mineral soil, and the formation on them of the kind of geotopes that are characteristic of mires.

The formation of peat deposits and mire geotopes reacts upon their surroundings so as to alter and transform them, and is, in that way, part of the whole geophysical process by which our environment is moulded and developed. From the point of view of energy, peat storage is an accumulative process on the surface of the earth—a storing up of that part of the sun's energy which is absorbed through photosynthesis by the earth's plant cover. From the mechanical point of view, the effect of peat accumulation and mire formation on the surface of the earth is counter-erosional. It tends on the whole to reduce the erosive action of surface water and the displacement of the solid inorganic matter on the surface of the earth. Peat accumulation, as a geophysical process, has a stabilizing effect on the original forms of the earth's relief. This, as will become clear, is a factor of some importance in the development of the features that are peculiar to mires and mirelands. A third important feature of peat accumulation and mire formation, considered as a unidirectional geophysical process, is the change they produce in the discharge of surface water and the maintenance of subterranean water supply. The deposition of peat on top of permeable mineral strata and the clogging of the pores of subjacent mineral soils with organic colloids have the general effect of reducing the seepage of water into the deeper layers of mineral strata, and increasing the horizontal flow of water (above, below and through the soil) into the river network.

From this it follows that peat accumulation and mire formation, as a large-scale geophysical process, tends, on the one hand, to reduce the erosion of the original relief of mineral strata (through accumulating on their surface organic deposits that are highly resistant to erosion), and, on the other hand, to increase the quantity of surface runoff, which in turn increases the destructive mechanical action to which the surface covering is exposed. These two opposed processes play an important part in the making and development of mire formations, and especially in the development of such distinctive forms as lake–mire systems.

It is perfectly obvious that no transformation of the components of a natural geotope, which involves large-scale changes on extensive territories for some kind of production or land use, can be carried out without taking into consideration the part these components play in the total geophysical process. Neglect of this part inevitably leads to unforeseen and often unhappy consequences, which cause great damage to industry, agriculture and the environment. This applies in the first place to such an important component of the geophysical environment as water supply, as well as to any other natural formation on the earth's surface, including mires and mirelands.

For this reason, chief attention in this work is given to quantitative analysis of the relations between the structural and physical properties of mirelands and the movement of water in them and their surroundings. The basis of this analysis is a hydromorphological theory of mire systems, which is used in the relevant sections of the work to elucidate certain fundamental questions and practical principles involved in the calculation of water movements in mire systems. The last chapter deals exclusively with the stability of mire systems and calculations of its limits, when the water regimes of areas under development are exposed to natural or artificial changes.

1

Peat Accumulation and Mire Formation as a Geophysical Process. The Classification of Mires

1.1 Mire Formation

The immediate cause of mires is the accumulation of organic material saturated with water on the surface of mineral strata. This material, which we call "peat", is formed under certain conditions through the partial decomposition of each year's vegetation and possesses physical and chemical properties that distinguish it sharply from mineral soils. Peat accumulation and mire formation are a geophysical process which takes place on the earth's surface under very diverse conditions. Its intensity depends on two main causes: the wetness of the area and the quantity of heat it receives. Though the process occurs in arctic, subtropical and tropical climates, it reaches its maximum development in regions of excess moisture in the temperate zone. There the relation of heat and moisture is optimal for the accumulation of peat, which is determined by the difference between the annual increment of vegetable matter and the amount of decomposing organic material. In these areas, mires cover most of the land, and the average thickness of peat deposits reaches its maximum—in some cases 8–9 m.

The chief cause of the accumulation of organic matter on land is a constant excess of moisture in the soil and on its surface, when there is little seepage and other water-removing processes are slow. The surplus of moisture in the soil and on its surface gives rise to a deficiency of oxidation in the soil and impedes the entry of air into the pores of the subsoil. This results in incomplete oxidation of the organic remains of plants, the formation of humic substances, and the conservation of organic matter. This last slowly becomes denser and changes its form under the influence of its own weight and the capillary pressure of the moisture in its pores. It gradually turns into peat, an organic material characterized by a great capacity to retain water and an exceptionally high moisture content.

Numerous researches have established that peat in its natural state contains by volume 88–97% water, 2–10% dry matter and 1–7% gas. For this reason, peat accumulation also involves the accumulation of significant volumes of water on the surface of the land and a change in the composition of its plant cover and its chief physical properties.

Differences in the extent and duration of climatic, geomorphological and hydrological conditions affect the scale of peat accumulation and mire formation. In arid conditions, mires are rare. They occupy very limited areas in deep hollows and depressions, lake basins and river valleys, where ground water, lakes and rivers provide the surface of the soil with an abundant supply of water and surface moisture. In the zone of excess moisture within the temperate belt, mires occupy huge territories, often covering vast level interfluves and water divides with a continuous mantle of peat and forming the mire geotopes that are typical of this zone. The distinctive characteristic of mires in this area, which is due to climatic conditions, is their confinement to elements of mesorelief. Here they are formed, not only on concave surfaces (hollows, basins and depressions), but on absolutely level areas, and even on complex elements with relatively gentle slopes. The so-called "hanging mires" that form on mountain slopes as a result of an abundant and steady water supply from cuneiform subterranean reservoirs are an extreme manifestation of mire formation on slopes and convex surfaces. An extremely wet climate may also give rise to an analogous kind of mire formation, when an area with a hilly or mountainous relief is completely covered by a peat mantle of up to 1 m in thickness with a corresponding mire vegetation.[2] It is therefore true, despite certain contrary opinions, that mire formation is not necessarily connected with negative forms of relief. It may take place on any part of the earth's surface where the dynamic equilibrium between the total influx and efflux of moisture results in saturation of the soil or the emergence of groundwater on its surface. In that case, the climate, the relief, the soil and the hydrological structure of the locality may combine to form mires in very different ways.

Most existing mires were formed by the swamping of dry land; only a few were formed by the swamping of lakes or abandoned parts of river beds. The present geotopes of mires often do not reflect their origin, for it is only in the early stages of peat accumulation that the transformation of dry land and water into mire can be distinguished through the character and composition of the plant cover and the surface relief. The later stages of the process, the laws of which are fundamentally the same for mires of terrestrial and aquatic origin, level off the original differences in the structure of their geotopes. For this reason, it is often impossible to establish the original conditions in which a mire arose from the appearance of a mire massif and its vegetation at a later stage of its development.

Most existing large mire massifs were formed through the fusion and growth of small, isolated mire massifs. This is why one part of a large system of mires may have been formed on the site of vanished water bodies, and another one by the swamping of dry land.

To establish the origin of any large and complex mire massif, it is necessary to investigate, not only the general structure of its geotope, but also the stratigraphy of its peat deposits, i.e. the age and floristic composition of the peat deposited there at different times. Establishing their origin, however, whether terrestrial or aquatic, is not usually of much importance for deciding the many practical and scientific problems posed by the calculation of the water regime of mires and the hydrological properties of peat, except where we are concerned with the hydrophysical characteristics of the very lowest horizons of peat. Such cases occur, for example, in the construction of roads over mires, when the stability of embankments and erections made without the removal of peat depends on the water regime and hydrological properties of the peat through its entire thickness, including the zone where it is in contact with the underlying mineral strata. In hydrological calculations for soil improvement, water supply and hydrotechnical construction, it is usually enough to know the hydrophysical properties of the upper part of the peat deposit, which is the active zone for the transmission of water and heat.

1.2 General Laws Affecting the Transformation of Land into Mire and the Extension of Mires

The amount of mire in any area is immediately connected with the relation between the items in its water budget (precipitation, evaporation, efflux), the quantity of heat it receives, and the mechanism whereby excess moisture finds its way into the river network that constitutes the natural drainage of the area. The combined action of these factors at every point on the earth's surface determines the water and heat regime in the soil and on its surface, whether it be favourable or unfavourable for mire formation. The volume of efflux is mainly determined by climatic conditions, but the amount of mire also depends on the relief of the area, the natural drainage of its river network, and the permeability of its strata. Let us consider these relations as exemplified by a very simple case of mire formation in an interfluvial area.

If we make a somewhat schematic plan of a river network (Fig. 1a), consisting of a section of the main river R–R and two parallel tributaries 1 and 2, then, for any cross-section A–A running across the watershed at right angles to the tributaries at a sufficient distance from the river, it is possible to write

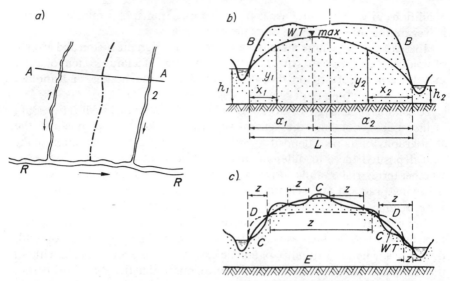

Fig. 1. General scheme of the natural drainage of an interfluvial region and a zone of mire formation in relief. a)—plan of region; b) and c)—sections along the line AA.

a general equation for the curve of the water table WT situated above the aquiclude E and drained by the river beds.[3] If the drainage pattern approximates to that of parallel planar flow, this equation has the following forms (Kamenskiy, 1935).

For the left-hand side of the curve (Fig. 1b):

$$y_1 = \sqrt{\frac{w}{k}(2a_1 x_1 - x_1^2) + h_1^2}. \tag{1a}$$

For the right-hand side (Fig. 1c):

$$y_2 = \sqrt{\frac{\bar{w}}{k}(2a_2 x_2 - x_2^2) + h_2^2}. \tag{1b}$$

In the above equations, y_1 and y_2 are the elevation of the water table above the horizontal plane where the soil becomes impermeable, and x_1 and x_2 are the distance from the left and right river beds, which drain the interfluvial massif; k is the coefficient of seepage of the water-permeable soils composing the interfluvial massif above the waterproof level; h_1 and h_2 are the levels of water in the rivers above the waterproof level; $\bar{w}$ is the mean long-term supply of moisture on the surface of the interfluvial massif, which in turn is equal to the difference between the mean amounts of precipitation and evaporation.

The curve of the water table, calculated according to the equations (1a) and (1b) for mean annual norms of precipitation and evaporation, gives a mean value for the position of the water table, from which its actual downward curve varies in wet and dry periods. The position of the water table, as determined by equations (1a) and (1b), depends on certain particular values—the mean long-term meteoric supply of moisture $\overline{w}$, the distance between the rivers L, and the permeability of the soil k. A free surface of this kind cannot exist, unless all points on the profile of the earth's surface in the interfluvial massif have elevations exceeding those of the water table's downward curve. The line B–B in Fig. 1b depicts a profile of this sort. If the surface of the earth is lower in certain parts than the water table as defined by condition (1) (for example, lines CCC or DD in Fig. 1c), then the points between the intersection of the downward curve and the surface of the earth (those marked Z in Fig. 1c), must represent areas in which the water table comes to the surface. In these areas, surplus moisture cannot be removed by seepage through the soil, and a superficial and internal flow of water arises, which is accompanied by continuous or very prolonged oversaturation of the upper horizons of the soil. In these areas, therefore, hydrological conditions favour the process of peat accumulation and they are exposed under natural conditions to an intensive process of mire formation. It is easy to see that equations (1a) and (1b) define the minimum elevation and surface profile for the avoidance of mire formation in an interfluvial massif. From this it follows that for every particular combination of the values k (permeability of the soil), $\overline{w}$ (the difference between precipitation and evaporation) and L (the distance between the rivers), there is a certain critical profile for the surface of the earth at which mire formation as a result of climatic conditions becomes impossible. If the actual profile is higher than the critical profile, natural mire formation does not take place in the interfluvial area. On the other hand, natural mire formation will take place wherever the surface is lower than the critical profile. The above equation is therefore the most general law for mire formation on land under the influence of climatic factors (atmospheric precipitation). From this it follows first of all that the process of mire formation has no necessary connection with a low level of permeability in the mineral strata underlying the peat deposits and the original form of its relief. Mires may be formed in equal degree on soils of high and low permeability and on sectors with a convex relief, provided the relief at that point is lower than the critical profile. If, however, all points on the surface of the land are higher than the critical profile for drainage, a mire cannot be formed, even on strata whose permeability is very low.

Under natural conditions, the drainage network is usually more complex than in the scheme described by equations (1a) and (1b). Naturally also, the permeability of the strata above the waterproof level is not always sufficiently uniform to be described by a single mean coefficient k. Lastly, these equations only hold good, strictly speaking, when the waterproof layer is horizontal (see Fig. 1), which of course is by no means always the case. For these reasons, the factors governing the drainage of interfluvial areas are more complex in fact than those described by equations (1a) and (1b). Nevertheless, from the physical point of view, the gist of the problem remains the same and can be more conveniently considered in its simplest and most obvious form. It should be noted that in a special test comparison of the actual boundaries of mire formation with its boundaries as calculated on the basis of the above hypotheses has amply confirmed their correctness (Ivanov and Shumkova, 1967).

1.3 The Intensity of Mire Formation

The intensity of mire formation is measured by the rate of peat accumulation in a vertical direction and the rate of advance of the frontiers of a mire along the mineral surface of the ground, i.e. the speed of the advance of the mire massif over the surrounding mineral soils. In every geological era, the increase or decrease of the area of mire is the result not only of gradual changes of climate, but of tectonic movements of the earth's crust. Under the influence of the latter, some parts of the earth's surface are raised or lowered, and improvements or deteriorations in the drainage of the area result from changes in the depth of the channels of the river network (see section 1.2). In the present Quaternary Era one can observe the advance of mires into intact areas in many northern regions of the Soviet Union. For example, in many parts of the basin of the Northern Dvina one can observe the expansion of mire massifs through the swamping of mire free forests and agricultural lands, which lie on the periphery of mire massifs. Analogous processes are taking place in the West Siberian plain, where the intensity of swamping is affected by tectonic movements. There it is increased when drainage deteriorates through the sinking of the earth's surface and reduced when natural drainage is improved by its elevation. The average speed at which mire massifs spread may oscillate between very wide limits—from a few tens of centimetres to tens of metres in a year. The rate of advance into dry land is not uniform in such cases. In wet periods of several years' duration, when precipitation is high and evaporation low in the warm part of the year, enormous areas on the periphery of the mire may be suddenly subject to swamping through a temporary, but sufficiently prolonged, reduction in the convexity of the water table (see section 1.2, Fig. 1c). On the other hand, in dry, warm periods of several years' duration, the water table falls and the growth of mire massifs may be completely stopped. One peculiarity of this process, however, is its irreversibility. Acceleration of the process of swamping, when precipita-

tion is high and evaporation low, is not followed in dry periods by a disappearance of the signs of swamping.

The horizontal spread of mire massifs stops when the zone of swamping
reaches its limiting magnitude, which is determined by the relief of the interfluvial area and the shape of the convex curve that defines the water table.
This last, as has been pointed out, is determined by climatic parameters
(the norms of precipitation and evaporation) and by the permeability of the
underlying strata. Vertical peat accumulation on a swamped area may continue even after the natural stabilization of its boundaries, and may cause a
gradual rise of the whole surface of the peat above the surrounding unswamped areas. In such cases, the rate of peat accumulation in different parts of
the swamped area is not identical. It is reduced by an increase in seepage
and the aeration of the peat-making layer, but increased by a reduction of
seepage and a rise in the level of the water table. Through different combinations of these factors each mire massif develops its own special relief, in which
the thickness of the peat deposit may vary widely. In the forest mires of the
temperate zone, where conditions are optimal for mire formation and the
accumulation of peat, the average growth in the thickness of peat deposits
is approximately 1 mm per year. North and south of this zone, the average
growth decreases correspondingly, and there is a gradual diminution in the
average thickness of peat deposits.

1.4 Mires and Geographic Zones

Mires are a zonal phenomenon. As biogenic formations on the surface of
mineral strata, they are affected by local differences in natural conditions,
among which climate and relief play a leading part. The chief characteristic
of mire formation is the accumulation of organic deposits as a result of the
operation of two opposed processes—the rate of decomposition of those
parts of the vegetation which die off each year and the yearly increase in the
mass of living vegetation. For this reason, there are four important and mutually connected criteria that make it possible to distinguish the zone to which
a mire belongs:

(1) Association with certain definite morphological elements on the
    earth's surface.
(2) The predominance of one type in its plant cover and one structure
    in its mire facies.
(3) The average thickness of peat deposits in mire massifs and the forms
    of relief that are characteristic of them.
(4) The extent to which mineral soils are covered over by peat deposits,
    or, what is the same thing, the extent to which the terrain has become
    mire.

The orographical peculiarities of a locality affect mire formation, both through the climatic conditions they create, and through the direct effect of its relief. In this way, orography determines the sources from which mires draw their water supply and the association of these with definite elements of the mesorelief.

In the climatic zone of excess moisture (the temperate belt), where precipitation significantly exceeds evaporation, mires may be situated in any elements or forms of relief—on plateau-like water divides, on the gentler slopes of interfluves, on the terraces of rivers and lakes, and on the flood plains of rivers. The criterion of zonality for mires situated in the zone of excess moisture is their association with every kind of positive and negative relief. The criterion of zonality for mires situated in the zone of deficient moisture is their exclusive association with negative elements of relief—hollows, depressions, lake basins, the flood plains of rivers and the lowest parts of river terraces, which are all places where surface and underground tributaries, not meteoric precipitation, provide them with most of their water supply.

In the plains of Eurasia, which lie within the climatic zone of excess moisture, Kats (1971) distinguishes four main zones in respect of the structural peculiarities of their mire formations and the average thickness of their peat deposits. These are:

(1) The zone of arctic mineral-sedge mires.
(2) The zone of small-hummock mires.
(3) The zone of large-hummock mires.
(4) The zone of convex oligotrophic mires.

In the climatic zone of deficient moisture the following zones are situated:

(1) The zone of eutrophic *Hypnum*–sedge and sedge mires.
(2) The zone of saline reed mires.

In level regions within the intermediate zone of unstable moisture, whose average precipitation does not exceed evaporation by more than 100 mm, there is a zone of eutrophic and oligotrophic pine–*Sphagnum* mires. In mountainous and upland terrains, the latitudinal pattern of mire zones is no longer observable. The structure of mire facies and their plant cover become more varied. This circumstance convinced Kats that, in the case of the mountainous and upland territories of central and eastern Siberia, as well as in central, western and southern Europe, it is necessary to distinguish groups of areas, where mires differ materially in the structure and composition of their plant cover. In this connection, it should be noted that in most of the countries of western Europe very few mires have survived in their natural state, and the demarcation of mire areas is more a matter of theoretical than of practical interest.

In what follows, we shall consider the properties and physical characteristics of mires and methods of hydrological calculation based upon determining their physical properties and structures. In this we shall deal mainly with zones of convex oligotrophic mires, of eutrophic and oligotrophic pine–*Sphagnum* mires, and of eutrophic *Hypnum*–sedge mires. These are areas where mires either cover the greatest amount of territory or have real economic value, despite their inconsiderable extent. In the questions dealt with below nothing is said about the two zones of hummocky mires, about the zone of arctic mineral-sedge mires, nor about the zone of halophytic reed mires, because the hydrological properties of such mires have as yet been hardly studied.

1.5 The Indicator Properties of the Plant Cover of Mires. Mire Facies or Microtopes

Much use is made of plant indicators in contemporary soil science in order to discover the physical properties of the place where they grow and the processes that take place in it. The possibilities of this method are of very wide application. They depend on how much knowledge one has of the connection of the properties and characteristics of the whole plant cover and individual species of plants with the properties of the external environment, upon which the existence of plant communities of different taxonomic ranks depends. By the indicator properties of the plant cover we understand established and known connections between the characteristics of the plant cover (e.g. the floristic composition of its plant associations, the performance of the individual plants of which they are composed, their compactness, their density of occurrence and the distribution of the various plant associations or individual species over the area), and the characteristics of their habitat and terrain (soil composition, chemical content of the subsoil, the level of the water table, seepage, inundation by rivers, and so on). The indicator properties of plants are studied and usually established in reference to some definite part of the environment or some group of physical properties that characterize it. Thus one can speak separately of the plant indicators for climates, soils, rocks, valuable minerals, water resources, forms of relief and so on (Vinogradov, 1964). One can also speak of plant indicators for different processes, including the intensity of water exchange, the seepage of groundwater, the fluctuation of the water table, the temperature regime, variations in the saturation of soils, etc. There are differences in the amount we know about the connections between plant communities and the properties and processes of the environment, but every plant community reflects a property that interests us or a process in its habitat that affects many other factors. For these reasons, the reliability and unambiguity of the pointers received from plant cover vary with the different groups of phenomena indicated.

This fact must be borne in mind in efforts to establish quantitative relations between the properties of plants and the peculiarities of their environment. The occurrence of any plant association and its constituent species is always a result of their adaptation to the whole external environment. Individual species and plant associations as a whole may therefore have a greater or lesser amplitude as indicators of the physical conditions of their environment. If, for example, we make use of plants to determine the depth of the water table, different species of plants or plant associations as a whole will be found to vary in accuracy as indicators of depth. It is obvious that to attain the most accurate results we must choose that one of the plant indicators which has the narrowest ecological amplitude in relation to the property of the environment under investigation. That is why, according to Vinogradov (1964), a distinction must be drawn between *constant* and *variable* *indicators* in the ecological evaluation of plant indicators.

By *constant indicators* are understood plants, plant associations or individual botanical criteria with a narrow ecological amplitude, which provide evidence of the necessary accuracy and fullness of detail (Vinogradov, 1964). *Variable indicators* are plants, plant associations or individual botanical criteria with a wide ecological amplitude, which in some cases have the necessary accuracy, and in other cases do not. Neither category is immutable. Through the inevitable increase in the accuracy of observations, of the scrutiny to which indicators are submitted and of our knowledge of ecology, the number of indicators in the variable group keeps growing at the expense of those that were formerly regarded as constant. One important group of indicators are those which point, not to the whole spectrum of change to which a given factor is subject, nor to a whole complex of natural conditions, but permit one to identify some narrow range of a changing magnitude, or, for example, the presence of certain objects or properties in the environment. Vinogradov divides these indicators into positive and negative. A positive indicator is one which points to the presence of certain natural conditions in a given site, in relation to which they are said to be "topophilic" (i.e. adapted in the best possible manner). For example, plants are said to be halophilic if they are adapted to salinity, hydrophilic, if they are adapted to moisture, acidophilic, if they are adapted to soil acidity and so on. A negative indicator is a plant, plant association or individual criterion which is incompatible with the existence of certain conditions or processes in its habitat.

Finally we distinguish between *direct* and *indirect indicators*. Direct indicators are functionally connected with the factor they indicate, which is an indispensable condition of their vitality. Indirect indicators are not immediately connected with the conditions that they indicate, but are indicators of other factors which are linked to these conditions, and are therefore correlated or hypothetically connected with them.

In considering the indicator properties of mire vegetation, attention should be paid first of all to the following two circumstances.

Firstly, the number of fundamental physical factors affecting the habitat of mire plants is less than in the case of those that grow in mineral ground and soils. This is explained chiefly by the greater uniformity in their water regime and mineral supply, by the greater homogeneity of their sources of water supply over the immense territories that they occupy, and by the fact that changes of habitat are much more closely connected with alterations in the water regime than is the case when the land is unswamped and the water table well below the surface. The relatively small number of fundamental factors affecting their habitat inevitably produces a sharper reaction in plants and plant associations to slight alterations in each of these factors. The indicator properties of plants in relation to the mineral content of their water supply are more reliable in these circumstances, and their sensitivity to particular phenomena is more acute.

Secondly, another important peculiarity of mire plants is that the soil in which they grow consists of the remains of these same plants and a dense carpet of living plants belonging to lower levels of the same plant association, while the microrelief of the mire's surface is a complex combination of different plant associations. It follows that the microrelief, which has so much effect on the water regime, on the mechanism of efflux and on the plant climate, turns out to be immediately linked to the floristic composition and spatial arrangement of plant associations, some of which are composed of species having a very narrow ecological amplitude as indicators of the water regime.

We shall now give a short description of the most important indicator properties of mire vegetation. In his theory of "biogeocoenosis", Sukachev (1947) divided the factors affecting the habitat of plants into four ecological spheres: the atmosphere, the pedosphere, the hydrosphere and the lithosphere. In the case of mire vegetation, our primary interest is in its hydrological significance, which is immediately connected with its use as an indicator both in relation to the microrelief of mires and in relation to the relief of mire massifs as a whole.

The hydrological factors that affect the habitat of mire vegetation are: the level of the water table, the amount of seepage[4] and the chemical quality of the water that supplies that part of the mire massif.

Trees and mosses are constant indicators of the long-term level of the water table, and the most sensitive of all plants in this respect. In Fig. 2,

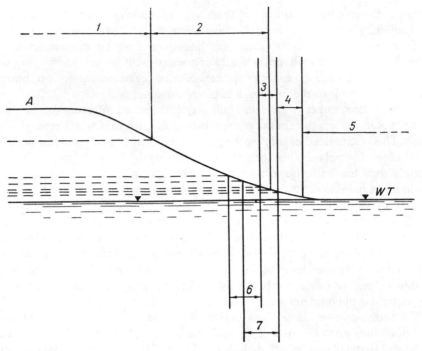

Fig. 2. Arrangement of different species of *Sphagnum* mosses in the microrelief of a mire above the water table. *A*—surface of moss cover making microrelief. *WT*—water table. 1—*Sphagnum fuscum.* 2—*S. magellanicum.* 3—*S. angustifolium.* 4—*S. balticum.* 5—*S. dusenii* and *S. cuspidatum.* 6—*S. subsecundum.* 7—*S. apiculatum.* See Table 1.

we show the characteristic differences between the height of the surface and the height of the water table for moss covers composed of different species. Among oligotrophic *Sphagnum* mosses, *Sphagnum cuspidatum* and *Sphagnum dusenii* occupy the lowest position in relation to the water level. They grow submerged in water with their tops either at the water level or elevated 1–2 cm above it. *Sphagnum fuscum* occupies the highest position in the microrelief. Its ecological range measured from the mean level of the water table is from 24–30 cm. *Sphagnum magellanicum* may exist at a wide range of different levels—from 24–4 cm above the mean level. *Sphagnum angustifolium* and *Sphagnum balticum* have narrow ecological ranges in respect of level: 3–5 and 1–3 cm respectively. Table 1 shows the distances between the surface of the moss cover and the water table which are indicated by different species of oligotrophic and eutrophic *Sphagnum* mosses. As the above data show, not all species of moss indicate the level of the water table with sufficient accuracy, and many have a wide ecological amplitude. That is why one

Table 1. Ecological amplitude and long-term mean level of water table associated with different species of moss in mire phytocoenoses belonging to the moss formation

Species of *Sphagnum* moss	Amplitude (cm)	Height of moss surface above mean level of water table (cm)
S. fuscum	12	37–25
S. magellanicum	20	25–5
S. angustifolium	2	5–3
S. balticum	2	3–1
S. dusenii	1	2–1
S. cuspidatum	1	0–1
S. subsecundum	5	10–5
S. apiculatum	2	5–3

must use combinations of species of moss in a plant association, not individual species, to determine by this method the mean long-term level of the water table, for this enables one to obtain more accurate indications of it.

Figure 2 makes it plain that the area of mire covered by any species of moss depends directly upon the slope and shape of every element of the microrelief On abrupt slopes in the upper part of an element of the microrelief, and on gentle slopes in its lower part, the area covered by *Sphagnum fuscum* and *Sphagnum magellanicum* may be very small, despite their wide ecological spread, while species with a narrow spread may in this case cover a wide area. On the other hand, abrupt slopes at the bottom of elevations may completely exclude coverage by a species of moss with a narrow ecological spread.

Wooded vegetation in mires also serves as a good indicator of the mean long-term level of the water table. Its presence in plant associations itself indicates that the mean level is lower than in cases where it is absent. The role of wooded vegetation as an indicator of mean levels is however different in oligotrophic conditions from what it is in eutrophic conditions. In oligotrophic parts of mires, changes in the mean level of mire water in relation to the surface of the moss cover show up clearly in the morphological peculiarities of pine trees (or cedars and larches in Siberian mires). The mean height of pines increases sharply as the water table sinks. Density of afforestation also increases up to a point with corresponding changes in plant associations. Observations and researches carried out at a number of mire stations and posts of the Hydrometeorological Service, which are presented in Fig. 3, show the dependence of the mean height of pine trees in mires on the mean long-term level of the water table. From this it is plain that between the limits of 20 to 46 cm below the level of the moss cover the average height of trees

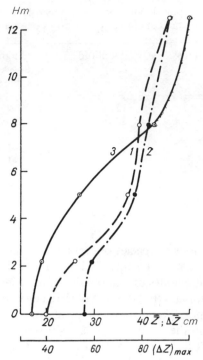

Fig. 3. Dependence of mean height (H) of stands of pine in mires with meteoric supply of water upon: (1) depth of long-term mean level of water table—Z; (2) mean amplitude of fluctuation of water table—Z; (3) maximum amplitude of fluctuation of water table—$(\Delta Z)_{max}$.

increases by 1 m for every fall of 2 cm in the level of the water table. At a mean level of 20 cm, conditions for the growth of pine trees become so unfavourable that they are practically eliminated from plant associations. In the graph reproduced in Fig. 3, the average height of trees at this level is zero. In eutrophic mires, when there is no compact moss cover and the tree layer is represented by different species of birch and black alder, the use of trees as an indicator of the mean level of the water table is complicated by the fact that, where the average height of the timber is great, the microrelief is strongly developed and the surface of the mire under the crowns of trees takes the form of an alternation of deep holes and tree-trunk elevations. To carry out a comparative analysis of the level of the water table in such cases, one must measure distances from a plane coinciding with the mean height of the surface of the mire, including in the calculation the elevations that surround tree-trunks.[5]

There is no practical method of finding the mean annual and the maximum long-term variation of the level of the water table from the plant cover of a mire, except through its plant associations, for every individual species of plant has a wide ecological spread in relation to such variations. This peculiarity of mire vegetation is explained by the fact that the water table is always near the surface of a mire, so that, however low its level may be (1 m is the maximum), the supply of moisture to the root systems by capillary rise from the water table is not interrupted. For this reason, the same plant association and the same mean level of the water table may be associated with oscillations of very different magnitude. The value of plant cover as an indicator depends on differences in the amount and direction of groundwater seepage, and is therefore found in their structural forms, which are derived from the different principles that govern the alternation and spatial distribution of plant associations and complex groups of plant associations. These structural forms are also closely connected with the microrelief of the surface of the mire. That is why mire plants cannot be used as indicators of the amount and direction of groundwater seepage, unless one remembers that the structure of any plant cover depends not only on the composition of its plant associations, but also on the form of relief that is bound up with it. The following group of criteria, which describe the structure of the plant cover, also serve as indicators of the amount and direction of groundwater seepage.

(1) The floristic composition of the plant cover and the spectrum of plant associations that go to make up the given phytocoenosis.
(2) The horizontal distribution of the plant associations, including the size and shape of the areas occupied in turn by the different plant associations.
(3) The type of microrelief peculiar to any given combination of associations and the dimensions (in plan and cross-section) of the higher and lower elements of the microrelief.
(4) The orientation in plan of the elements of microrelief and the position of the plant associations that belong to each of these elements.

Obviously, judgements concerning the amount and direction of seepage can only be made on the basis of a whole complex of criteria, which define the structure of the plant cover. Roughly the same complex of criteria makes it possible to determine how mire waters flow in the different parts of the mire, i.e. to draw conclusions as to where surface currents periodically occur, where water flows away only through filtration, and where surface current always predominates.

It is obvious that one cannot through these criteria determine the structure of the plant cover, nor use it as an indicator of seepage or the efflux of water, unless the areas of mire are sufficiently large in comparison with the separate structural elements, and unless the number of these last elements is sufficient to enable one to find the statistical mean of the different parameters applicable to the structural elements of the area. To make full use of the indicator properties of the plant cover of mires in studying their water regime and hydrological properties it is also necessary to use the smallest territorial unit of mire for which the values of the structural criteria enumerated above will remain unchanged.

These demands are satisfied by what is called the "facies" in physical geography, where it means a part of the earth's surface characterized throughout its whole extent by the same physico-geographical conditions, the same physical properties, and the same flora and fauna. The general description "identical physico-geographical conditions" needs further elucidation, when it is used in relation to mires. The elementary geographical unit in the case of mires is a *mire facies* or *mire microtope*, by which we mean a part of a mire where the plant cover and all other physical components of the environment connected with it are uniform. Later on, when we consider the fundamental properties of the acrotelm and catotelm of mires,[6] these physical components will be considered in greater detail (see section 2.8). Changes in the structure of the plant cover and in the corresponding properties of its environment are also evidence of changes in the type of microtope composing the mire. In this way, any mesotope, whatever its size or origin, may be described in terms of one or several types of microtope.

The principles governing the distribution of different types of microtope in the terrain of a mire not only characterize in turn the different types of larger-scale mire formations,[7] but also provide criteria which enable one to determine their physical properties, manner of construction and hydrological characterisation.

The best criteria for investigating the hydrology of mires, the physical and mechanical properties of peat deposits and the plant cover that is dependent on them are those which are reflected and can be easily recognized in aerial photographs. With the aid of these, we can determine the characteristics of different parts of mire massifs which interest us and study the structure of mire formations as a whole. These criteria will be considered later (section 1.8) along with the method and principles used in analysing mires by means of aerial photography.

1.6 Laws Governing the Formation of Mire Massifs. Phases and Stages in Mire Development

The originating centres of mire formation are portions of the land or water bodies in which the deposition and accumulation of peat have begun. In the zone of excess moisture, any of the lower places in the relief of the locality may serve for this purpose—small depressions with gentle slopes, basins, hollows, abandoned river channels, river flood plains and depressions in river terraces, lakes, abandoned river beds and slow-flowing water bodies.[8] The huge horizontal tracts of level land, which function as the water divides of rivers, are, it seems, transformed simultaneously into mires, and recent investigations of the stratigraphy of peat deposits show that this often happens without there being any clearly defined original centre of mire formation.

Let us here introduce the concept of a "mire massif". By this we understand a part of the earth's surface occupied by a mire whose boundaries form in plan a closed outline or figure. We shall define the boundary of a mire as the zero-depth of its peat deposit. The process of peat accumulation, which begins at the lowest points in the relief of a locality, gradually evens out the surface of the terrain it occupies, and, at the same time, raises the level of groundwater on the higher parts of the dry land which surrounds it. In Fig. 4, two typical patterns of peat accumulation and alteration of mire

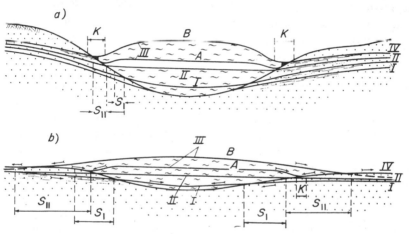

Fig. 4. Diagram showing how in an oligocentral system the relief of a mire massif develops and how its water table changes in the different phases through which the accumulation of peat and the water supply pass. a) in deep depressions; b) in shallow depressions; I, II, III, IV—phases of development; S_I, S_{II}—successive stages in swamping; K—zone receiving external water supply in Phase III.

massif relief are presented: (a) the formation of mire in a deep depression with steep slopes, and (b) the formation of mire in a shallow depression with very gentle slopes. In both cases, the swamping of the higher portions of land round the mire massif begins at a later stage, when the thickness of the peat is such that the level of the mire approaches that of the surrounding unaffected land, which supports the mire's water table. As soon as this last attains the level of the soil in the zone of support, a zone of water-logged soil is formed around the boundaries of the original mire massif, and this leads to a farther extension in the swamping of mineral soils and subsoils (see zones S_I and S_{II} in Fig. 4). In this way, the vertical accumulation of peat is accompanied by a simultaneous spreading of the mire massif and the advance of mire into the surrounding land.

The speed of peat accumulation in the original centre of mire formation is subject to variation. In the lowest part of an insulated hollow or depression (Fig. 4), where seepage is least—i.e. where the water is practically stagnant—the rate of decomposition of plant remains is at its least, and the rate of peat accumulation correspondingly at its greatest. In those parts of the original hollow where there was still a slope at the bottom, when mire formation began, a high rate of seepage is for some time maintained, and the rate of peat accumulation correspondingly reduced. In this way, owing to differences in the rate of peat accumulation, the concave relief of the original depression is gradually evened off, and the concave surface of the mire massif in the early stages of peat accumulation (Phase I, Fig. 4) is gradually transformed into a horizontal one (Phase II, Fig. 4). In the second phase of peat accumulation, seepage is practically uniform throughout the whole area of the mire and is very low everywhere, except in the zone where there is contact with the surrounding mineral soil. Here, because of the survival of local gradients, seepage and the mineral content of the water is high. In contrast with the rest of the area of the massif, where the rate of peat accumulation is uniform, it remains very low in the marginal sectors near the edge of the massif. In this phase of its development, the general surface of the mire massif is raised above the surface of the marginal strip. When there is surplus water in these marginal areas, water runs off from them in the direction of the outer boundaries of the mire (see reliefs A and B in the third phase of development in Fig. 4.). The occurrence of seepage at the periphery of the massif retards peat accumulation at this place compared with the central part. This is why the surface of the central part begins gradually to rise above the edges, thereby also increasing the efflux of water. The massif assumes by degrees the definitely convex relief that is characteristic of the third phase of the second stage of development.

With the entry of the mire massif into its third phase of development, a fundamental change takes place in the balance of its water supply. In the first and second phases of development, the main surface of the mire is below that of the boundary between the peat deposit and the surrounding mineral strata, and its water supply is composed of meteoric precipitation and an influx of surface and ground water from the surrounding mire-free terrain. From the moment of the appearance of a convex relief, however, the main part of the massif begins to receive its water supply exclusively from meteoric precipitation. Groundwater and surface influx from the surrounding terrain begin to supply only the edges of the mire massif (see the strips marked K in Fig. 4a). It follows that the formation of a convex relief in the third phase of the development of a mire massif creates a sharp contrast between the water supply of its different parts. This change affects the whole subsequent development of the massif.

The speed of vertical peat accumulation and the composition and distribution of the plant cover over the greater part of the mire massif comes to depend only on the relation between the quantity of precipitation and the rate of efflux. This last depends in turn upon the distribution of slopes over the surface of the massif, i.e. on the relief and the dimensions of the mire. Changes in the relief of this surface, once a mire's development is no longer dependent upon that of neighbouring centres of mire formation, are due to the rate of peat accumulation and the depth and steepness of the slopes of the original hollow in which the massif was formed. It is on these factors that the relation between the vertical rise and horizontal extension of the surface of the mire massif depends.

When the surface of a mire becomes convex, the hydrological conditions that result in the transformation of surrounding lands into mires are altered. When the relief of a mire massif is concave or flat, as in the first and second phases of development, the swamping of adjoining lands proceeds, as we have seen, through a change in the supporting surface and a rise in the water table, as the original depression is filled up with peat (see zones S_I and S_{II} in Fig. 4). Transition to a convex relief provides the surrounding area with an additional supply of water which flows into it from the mire itself. In this way, peripheral sectors of the mire and the unaffected lands adjoining it receive the greatest amount of water, and the advance of mire onto mineral soils is accelerated.

When the relief of the massif is convex, the rate of its horizontal spread depends, other things being equal, on the relief of the strip joining the mire to the mineral soil, whose formation coincides with the moment when the massif enters the third phase of its development. If the original depression is still not completely filled with peat up to the level of its edges (Fig. 4a), the horizontal growth of the mire is limited and proceeds slowly, all the more so if the sides of the depression are steep. Swamping of the surrounding lands can then come about, as in the first and second phases of development, through a raising of the level and of the supporting base of the water table. When these conditions obtain on the boundaries between mires and mire-free slopes, what are called "marginal depressions of efflux"[9] are formed, which give rise to streams and perfluent swamps that carry away the water that enters them along the edges of the mire to the nearest water-collecting rivulet. The relief of the massif then becomes markedly convex, and its edges attain gradients that are sometimes as steep as 0·05–0·1.

If, at the moment when the relief becomes convex, the original depression is filled with peat up to its edges (Phase III in Fig. 4b), farther spread of the massif proceeds rapidly. The swamping of adjoining ground takes place, both because it is soaked by waters running off the massif, and because its natural drainage deteriorates through the raising of the water table (Fig. 4b). The slopes that the convex relief of the massif then assumes are usually very long and gentle, with gradients of the order of 0·0004–0·003, while the strip of swamp round the mire massif becomes very broad, often attaining 1–2 km (see Phase IV on Fig. 4).

In the diagrams of Fig. 4, the symbols S_I and S_{II} show the different dimensions of the zones of mire formation in the first and second phases of peat accumulation. Whether the slopes of the original depression be steep or gentle, these are wholly due to the raising of the water table. In the same diagrams, it can be clearly seen that, when the mire massif enters the third phase, the breadth of the zone of mire formation does not significantly increase, if the slopes of the depression are steep; whereas, when the surface of the mire becomes higher than that of the area surrounding it, the zone of mire formation may attain very large dimensions (Fig. 4b).

The schemes of mire formation so far considered all involve an original centre round which the mire massif is formed. Such schemes are of very wide, but not universal application. They are applicable in full measure only to the zone of excess moisture, and represent cases where the mire massif developing at the original centre of swamping is not united at any stage of peat accumulation with mire massifs being formed in neighbouring depressions and hollows. It is obvious that the gentler the slopes at the original centre of swamping, the more the separate and originally isolated mire massifs will be fused at the earlier stages into those larger and more complex formations which are known as "systems of mire massifs" (see Fig. 6). From the causes of mire formation considered above and from the extension in plan of the boundaries of mire massifs, it follows that the fusion of several massifs into one may take place, not only in the later stages of peat accumulation, when they have a convex relief, but also in the first and second phases, when the depressions which were the original centres of swamping are shallow and poorly developed. If fusion occurs in the early stages, it is difficult, if not impossible, to identify the special peculiarities of its component massifs in the existing geotopic structure and plant cover of a system of mire massifs. Such systems after formation pass through a succession of stages comparable to those of single mire massifs with a complex interior relief. Owing to this, all the characteristic marks of the hydrological regime and plant cover of the separate massifs at the time of fusion are gradually obliterated.

In the climatic zone of deficient moisture, where the index of dryness $R_x > 1$, it is physically impossible for mire massifs to develop a convex relief, where points on the surface of the mire are higher than the level of its boundary with surrounding mineral soils, because under these circumstances the meteoric water supply is always less than evaporation.[10] Consequently, mires cannot exist and peat accumulation cannot continue, unless all points on the surface of the mire are situated lower than the boundary between the mire and the dry land, so that surface and groundwater coming from the surrounding unswamped terrain may enter the mire and compensate for the deficiency of meteoric moisture. For this reason, the final stages in the development of the relief of mire massifs must be characterized either by concave or by flat surfaces. This means that they must belong to the first or second phase of development.

Distinguishing between the three phases in the development of the relief of mires from one original centre of mire formation is indispensable for hydrological calculations, for the analysis and calculation of the water regime of mires, and for the study and determination of the mutual relations between the laws that govern the development and determination of the plant cover of mires and the composition and balance of their water supply. In section 1.5 it was already noted that the plant cover and its structure are sensitive indicators of the water regime of mires, and particularly of the depth of the water table, of the mineral content of their water supply and of the amount of water movement within them. Every one of the three fundamental phases is characterized by one definite type of water supply and water balance and by a type of vegetation that corresponds ecologically with it.

In the first phase, the mire massif's water supply is almost always composed of three constituents: a quantity of precipitation falling directly upon the surface of the mire, a quantity of water entering the mire massif from the aquifers of the surrounding land, and a quantity of water entering it by surface flow from surrounding terrains at a higher elevation. Owing to the concave relief typical of the first phase, ground and surface water reaching the boundaries of the massif may, through horizontal seepage and surface flow, reach any point in the massif, and in this way help to supply water to the plant cover on all parts of the mire massif. When there is groundwater with a head of pressure, this may not only enter the massif along its boundaries, but emerge at any point from subjacent aquifers into the peat deposit.

In the second phase, when the relief of the mire is level and has a flat surface whose altitude coincides with that of the boundary between the mire massif and the mineral soil, the components of the water balance may be the same, but the proportion of water from the different sources of supply will be different from the initial proportion. It is obvious that surface water flowing to the boundaries of the mire, and unpressurized groundwater emerging from aquifers in a cavity at the edge of a mire, cannot make their way to every point in the mire for lack of the necessary gradients. They will concentrate mainly at the periphery, reaching the centre of the mire only in insignificant quantities, which will compensate for a difference in the amount of meteoric moisture falling directly on that part of the surface of the mire. It follows that unless pressurized groundwater emerges into the peat deposit, different parts of a mire in its second phase will not be uniform in the chemical quality and mineral content of their water supply, and this fact finds expression in the increased variety of their plant cover.

In the third phase, the relief is convex and all points on the mire's surface are higher than the level of its boundary with the mire-free land around it. Surface streams and unpressurized groundwater cannot therefore contribute to the water supply of the massif (see Stage B, Phase III in Fig. 4b), or can do so only along a narrow strip on the boundary between the peat and the mineral soil, where the level of the surface of the mire is lower than the level of the surrounding mire-free land and the gradient is zero (see K in Stage A, Phase III, Fig. 4b and Fig. 4a). This is why the third phase may be characterized by the greatest differentiation, not only in the plants that cover the surface of the mire, but in the ecological types to which they belong. These may extend from eutrophic vegetation, which is the most demanding with regard to the mineral content of its water supply and is found only on the boundary between the mire and the mineral soil, to the extremely oligotrophic, which is undemanding in this respect and is found in other parts of the mire whose supply of water and minerals is derived only from precipitation.

It is plain that the most uniform ecological conditions prevail in the first phase of development, when the mire is usually occupied completely by eutrophic or mesotrophic plants. The second phase has in this respect an intermediate position. Here combinations of eutrophic and mesotrophic plants make their appearance, or combinations of mesotrophic and oligotrophic, with a tendency toward the less eutrophic as one passes from the periphery to the centre of the mire massif. The course of development from the original centre of mire formation, in which there is initially a transition from eutrophic to mesotrophic and then to oligotrophic vegetation in the central parts of the massif followed by an extension of this process to the periphery, is called the central-oligotrophic course of development. This is the commonest way in which mires develop from an original centre of mire formation (Galkina, 1946; Ivanov, 1957b). Another course of development, the periphero-oligotrophic, is encountered in cases where mire formation and peat accumulation take place in valleys and elongated depressions, along the bottom of which flow streams and rivulets.[11]

In this last case, the strip of mire contiguous with the stream has a lower rate of peat accumulation, and, having better conditions with regard to natural drainage and a mineral-rich water supply, retains a eutrophic and mesotrophic vegetation longer than anywhere else. The transition from the first phase to the second, and then to the third, shows itself here in the fact that on both sides of the stream the relief of the massif may change from concave to flat and then convex without losing its overall slope towards the stream. In this case, the transition from eutrophic to mesotrophic and then to oligotrophic vegetation occurs at first in parts of the mire at a distance from the bed of the stream. Near the stream, this transition occurs later, when peat has been deposited on its bed, so that seepage and drainage capacity have been reduced.

It should, however, be noted that the oligoperipheral course of development may also be regarded and theoretically represented as the formation of two independent massifs, divided in the early stages by the bed of a stream, but later fused into one, as the bed of the stream is covered with peat. This produces a complicated relief consisting of two convexities and a depression between them in the place of the former stream, which is usually occupied by a sluggishly flowing swamp.

As we have seen, these three principal phases in the development of isolated mire massifs coincide with periods in which the relief of the mire and the conditions of its water supply undergo a change. Contemporary investigators distinguish in each phase successive stages that are characterized by different plant groups, different patterns of distribution over the area and a distinctive form of relief (Galkina, 1959, 1964; Ivanov, 1957b). As was pointed out in section 1.5, the floristic composition and structure of plant communities reflect corresponding properties of their habitat, and therefore the laws governing the distribution of different microtopes enable us to form judgements concerning the physical properties and hydrological regime of different parts of a mire massif. Plant communities therefore provide us with one of the most important criteria for determining the phase and stage of development of a mire massif. This criterion is also widely used in studying the hydrological properties of particular mire massifs and calculating their water regime by aerial photography.

The different stages in each phase of the development of mire massifs have been distinguished in a number of fundamental works on telmatology by Tsinzerling (1938), Galkina (1946, 1959, 1963) and Bogdanovskaya-Gienev (1969), as well as in the work of many foreign investigators, especially those of the Scandinavian school. On the basis of these researches, it is possible to form one general conclusion. Passage through any stage of development in any phase depends significantly on the particular geomorphological conditions of the place where the massif occurs. In every region with a special geomorphology and climate, one can observe typical sequences in the stages of development of mire massifs and distinguishing features for each stage. Despite this, the most widely distributed types of mire massif occurring on level ground (in the temperate zone) retain pretty well the same type of relief at the original centre of mire formation. For that reason, isolated mire massifs in each phase of their development pass through a series of stages, in each of which the different microtopes are distributed over the area in a stable and clearly expressed general pattern. It is because of this fact that isolated mire massifs formed from one original centre, and possessing at each stage of their development a pattern of microtope distribution that conforms to clearly defined principles is called a "mire mesotope". By the structure of a mire mesotope we understand the type or types of mire microtope of which it is composed and the pattern of their distribution over the area of the massif (Fig. 5).

The clearest examples of this way of treating mires as complex natural formations are found in the works of Galkina and her school (Galkina, 1946,

Fig. 5. Examples of structure of mire mesotopes of a) oligocentral type, b) oligoperi-pheral type. The signs used are explained in Fig. 7. For meaning of +, *AOB* and A_1, O_1, B_1 *see section* 2.13.

1959, 1963; Kiryushkin, 1964; Kozlova, 1954; Lebedeva, 1959, etc.), which are devoted to the study and classification of mire geotopes by air-to-ground methods of investigation, an approach that has also been widely used in works on the hydrology of mires (Ivanov, 1963a,c, 1957a,b, 1963). It should be noted in this connection that the sources and balance of the water supply of mire mesotopes, which are immediately linked to the relief of their place of origin and their phase and stage of development, are the chief and ever-changing factor in the process of peat accumulation, which in turn deter-

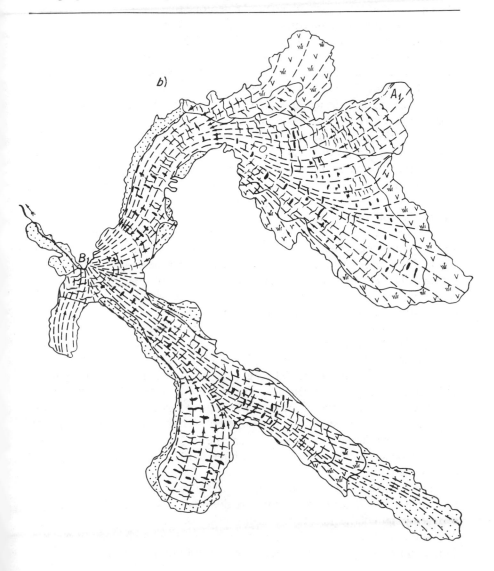

mines the sequences of mire microtopes and the pattern of their distribution in mesotopes. Changes in plant cover produce changes in the types of peat deposit found in stratigraphical sections of mire massifs. This circumstance makes it possible to relate the geomorphological method of classifying peat deposits (Tyuremnov and Vinogradova, 1953) to the genetico-geotopic approach (Galkina, 1963). As can be seen, a mire mesotope is a natural unit of physical geography identical in significance with what is called in Russian a *bolotnoye urochishche* (a mire locality).

By a mire macrotope we understand a geotope that has been formed by the fusion of isolated mire mesotopes which, up to a certain stage in their development, were formed round a single original centre of mire formation. A mire macrotope is therefore a complex mire massif (Bogdanovskaya-Gienev, 1969) consisting of several simple mire massifs that have become merged into one. This is why we may also call a mire macrotope a system of simple mire massifs, or, for brevity, a system of mire massifs (Ivanov, 1957b; Romanova, 1961).

Investigations of the macrotopes of various parts of Eurasia, which differ in their present orography and their geological structure, show that there are differences of type in these very complex mire formations. These types reflect the morphological peculiarities of huge geographic areas which now have identical, or nearly identical, climates. Just as the course of development of simple mire massifs and the types of mesotope they form depends on the relief of the original sites of mire formation, so the types of mire systems and the macrotopes they form are closely related to the still larger forms of relief of the places where they occur. They also repeat and combine in a regular manner smaller forms of relief across vast interfluvial expanses. In them can be traced the shape, size and structure of river valleys, the structure of river systems, the outline in plan of these territories and their general tilt in this or that direction. Account must be taken of the fact that macrotopes may be formed from the fusion of mesotopes, which since uniting are at different stages and even different phases of development, but were at the time of fusion at closely related stages of the same phase of development. This circumstance is also reflected in the present structure of mire macrotopes. Besides that, mire mesotopes, which have formed a system, may have followed the same course of development (oligocentral, oligoperipheral or mixed), or different courses, as when one part of the system was formed from oligocentral mesotopes, and another part from mesotopes of mixed development.

The two chief criteria for determining the type to which a system of mire massifs or a mire macrotope belongs are therefore, firstly, the phase and stage of development of the mesotopes at the time of their unification, and secondly, the course of development of the mesotopes after they had formed the system. This enables us to distinguish four fundamental types of macrotope.

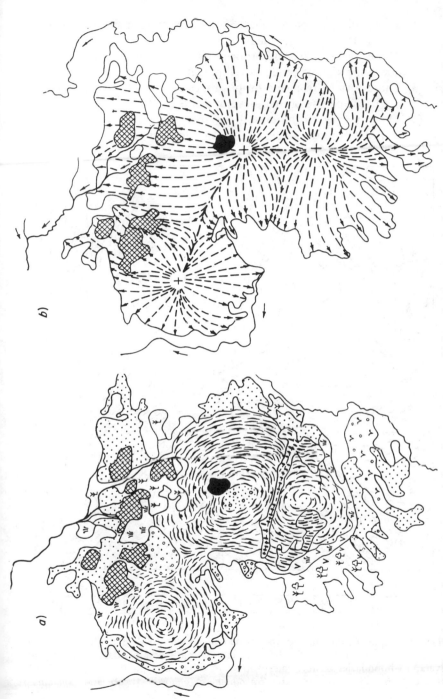

Fig. 6. Example of a mire macrotope consisting of two mesotopes which are homogeneous in the course and stages of their development. The signs used are explained in Fig. 7.

(1) Those formed from mesotopes that are uniform in the course and stages of their development.

(2) Those formed from mesotopes that are uniform in the course, but not in the stages of their development.

(3) Those formed from mesotopes that are uniform in the stages, but not in the course of their development.

(4) Those formed from mesotopes that are uniform neither in the course, nor in the stages of their development.

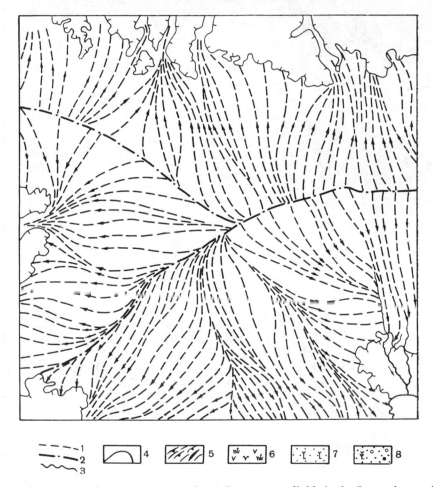

Fig. 7. Example of a mire macrotope formed on a water divide in the first and second phases of development. 1—flowline; 2—endotelmic water divide; 3—streams and rivers; 4—boundaries of mire microtopes; 5—ridge–flark microtopes of strip-ridge structure; 6—microtopes of the *Sphagnum–Eriophorum*–shrub and *Sphagnum–*

Study by combined air and ground methods of large systems of mire massifs, of the structure of the macrotopes that compose them and of the texture of peat deposits has shown that, where such systems are formed in the early stages of their constituent mesotopes, the features of these mesotopes are not clearly distinguished in their contemporary structure. This is because the system has developed for a long time as a single complex mire massif after the union of the original massifs. Where the mesotopes were united into a system at later stages in their development, the structures of

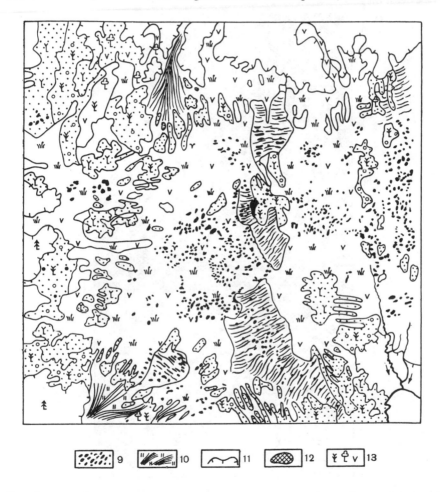

Eriophorum–sedge groups; 7—*Sphagnum*–pine–shrub microtopes; 8—pine–shrub microtopes; 9—ridge–pool (unorientated) microtopes; 10—*Sphagnum*–sedge swamp microtopes; 11—boundaries of mire system (at zero depth of peat deposit); 12—islands of mineral soil in mire systems; 13—pine–birch–sedge microtopes.

the component mesotopes can be clearly traced in the present macrotopic structure. Examples of mire massif systems are given in Figs 6 and 7. The system in Fig. 6 has preserved, in the structure of its plant cover, all the main criteria of its component mesotopes, which were fused together at stages of development characterized by convex forms with ridge-flark microtopes.

In the structure of the macrotope in Fig. 7, however, it is impossible to discern the traces or distinguish the outlines of the original mesotopes.

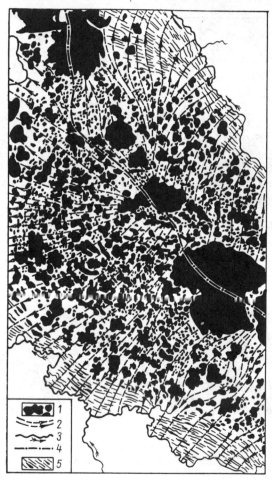

Fig. 8. Fragment of mire macrotope representing a very large lake–mire system. 1—endotelmic lakes among microtopes of the *Sphagnum*–pine–shrub, *Sphagnum*–*Eriophorum* and ridge–flark groups; 2—flowlines; 3—rivers bounding system; 4—water divides; 5—ridge–pool microtopes of strip-ridge structure.

To determine the stages during which such a system was formed one must analyse the stratigraphy of its peat deposit.

We have already mentioned that in the case of huge flat interfluves with a very low relief, like the northern part of the West Siberian plain, or the northern regions of European Russia, mire formation may take place over vast areas without involving, even at the beginning, any clearly defined centre of origin. In such cases, there may be no clearly defined basins or depressions such as would have served for this purpose. Such mire massifs, occupying areas measured in thousands, tens of thousands and even hundreds of thousands of square kilometres, developed simultaneously like single systems through mire formation and peat accumulation over the whole area without previously forming isolated mesotopes. Despite this fact, it is impossible to call them mesotopes because of their size, the complexity of their structure and the way in which microtopes are arranged within them. They must be treated as macrotopes with a different course of development from that previously described. From the first, the structure of such macrotopes reflects large-scale forms of relief which are determined by the structure of the present river network and its drainage potential. We may take as an example of such large-scale mire macrotopes the whole of the Surgut Polesie, a territory that comprises all the land between the Siberian Uvals and the west-flowing reaches of the river Ob, as well as the left bank of the Nazym and the lower reaches of the Vakh. The mires of the Ob-Irtysh water divide are another example of the same huge kind of macrotope. They are in reality a single mire massif comprising all the basins and water divides that are bounded to the west by the Irtysh, to the north and east by the Ob, and to the south by the northern frontier of the Baraba steppe. Macrotopes of similar proportions are encountered in the basin of the Konda, to the east of the middle reaches of the Ob, and in many other regions within the temperate zone of the northern hemisphere. In Figs 7 and 8, we show the structure of certain fragments of such macrotopes, using for this purpose only the main types of mire microtope.

1.7 The Classification of Mires

In the preceding section, we gave a brief account of the chief causes of mire massifs of different degrees of complexity and of the laws that govern their formation. If, however, we wish to find qualitative relations and equations that describe the connections between the water regimes and the structure of mire massifs as a basis for hydrological calculations, we must evaluate the biophysical properties of mires in terms that can be expressed mathematically. To do this we must find a suitable way of classifying mires.

At the present time there are many ways of approaching this problem.

Scientists have classified mires in different ways according to their aim in studying them and their manner of describing them as natural phenomena— botanically, by the type and floristic composition of their plant cover; hydrologically, by the conditions of their water supply; mineralogically, by the type and structure of their peat deposits; genetically, in terms of their origin; geomorphologically, in terms of their connection with different elements of land relief, etc. Each of these ways of analysing mires seems to call for a different classification.

From the point of view of the scientist and engineer, however, such an approach is one-sided and cannot reflect the many-sidedness of mires as natural phenomena. For that reason, any classification that groups them according to isolated criteria cannot in general satisfy the varied demands of engineering and has only a limited scientific use. The assignment of a mire to any type cannot contain a maximum of useful information, or be used to solve the complex problems of science and technology, unless it is based on genetic principles, i.e. upon the most important aspects of its origin and development which are responsible for its present condition, structure and properties.

The plant cover of mires and its association with different forms of surface irrigation is the prime index of their biophysical properties. It is therefore understandable that the most general and fruitful approach to the classification of mires as natural phenomena is to divide them up into types according to geotopic principles. This approach permits one to use the structure of the surface and the vegetation of mires to classify them into taxonomic units which comprise in their different types the maximum number of criteria and maximum information about their properties.

It should also be remembered that classification should not be rigid. The appearance or discovery of a new attribute or characteristic that must be included in the description of an individual should not make its categories unsuitable, and call for a new classification. Taxonomic units should be chosen so as to provide for the inclusion of new information. In this respect also, the genetic principle is the best, because categories chosen in this way are not restricted to any limited number of criteria. Finally, no classification can have a broad range of application, unless it makes use of modern methods of studying nature and gives full scope to their possibilities. Aerial photography is the modern method of investigating mires and obtaining information about their properties, as well as of studying other natural features of the surface of the earth. For that reason, the general classification of mires must involve criteria that are easily detected in aerial photographs and should make use of geotopic categories. The genetico-geotopic method of classifying mires is the best way of meeting these requirements. It analyses the different geotopic structures of mires and uses taxonomic units that reflect the stages and phases in the development of mire massifs and peat accumulation under different geomorphological conditions. The system of classification developed in the above-mentioned works of Galkina and her disciples, which is widely used in modern hydrological research into mires, singles out the mesotope as the fundamental unit in the typology of mires (Ivanov, 1953a, 1957b, 1963).[12]

As was mentioned in section 1.6, the mesotope reflects the morphology of the site of a massif, the nature of its water supply at different stages in its development, and the type and structure of its vegetation. It also reveals the physical properties of the acrotelm of the massif through the distribution of different types of microtope over its area. In equal degree, the macrotope, as a more complex phenomenon arising from the uniting of a number of mesotopes, is characterized by distinctive types of microtope with distinctive patterns of arrangement, which reflect the physical properties of its acrotelm. It follows that there must be four elements in a genetico-geotopic classification of mires.

(1) The *geomorphological element*. This is a classification of mires according to the elements of relief in which they are situated. It involves consideration of the surface relief and plan of mire massifs, the components of their water supply and the direction of efflux.

(2) The *mesotopic element*. There is a series of types of mesotope for every type of place where mire massifs are formed. These types are the successive stages in the development of an isolated mire massif from a single centre of mire formation (see Fig. 9).

(3) The *macrotopic element*. There is a series of types of macrotope, reflecting in structure the large-scale morphological peculiarities of their territory and the conditions under which originally isolated mire massifs were merged into one system (see Figs 7 and 8).

(4) The *microtopic element*. Microtopes (facies) are classified according to ecological conditions, life-form and floristic composition. These are the elementary units out of which meso- and macrotopes are built (Table 2).

The logical result of uniting the first three elements into a single scheme is the genetico-geotopic classification of mires presented in Table 3. From this it follows that every particular mire mesotope or macrotope has its own characteristic combination of microtopes, i.e. a selection of microtopic types and definite rules for their arrangement over the area it occupies. At the same time, there remain within this classification unlimited possibilities of incorporating into it new and as yet unknown meso- or macrotopes and the types they exemplify, without changing the principles of classification upon which it is based. Herein lies the great practical and scientific value of

a)

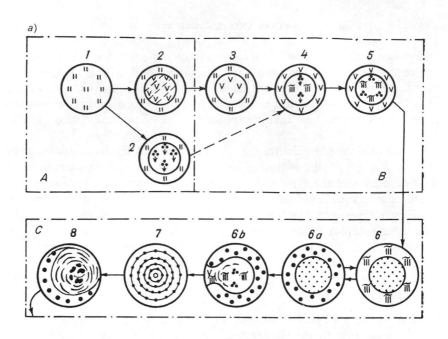

b)

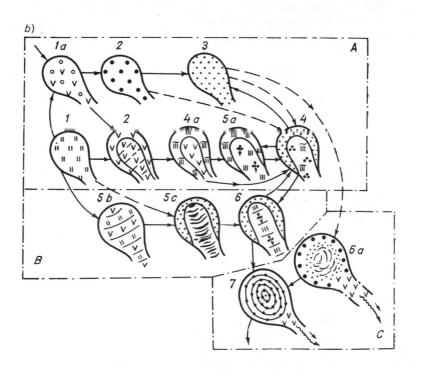

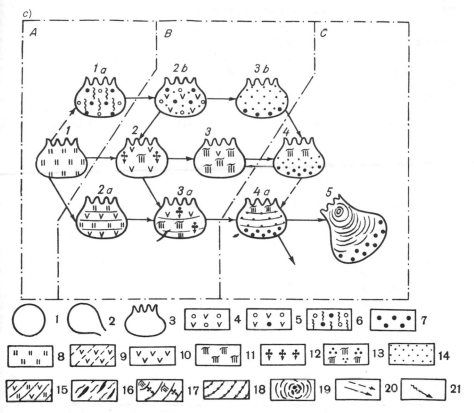

Fig. 9. Scheme of the structures of successive stages in the development of mesotopes of Class I(a), Class III (b) and Class V (c). (From E. A. Galkina.) 1, 2, 3—outlines symbolizing mesotopes of Classes I, III and V respectively. 4–19—Mire microtopes (facies) of different types: 4—birch with black alder or birch of mosaic structure. 5—birch–sedge or birch–pine–sedge. 6—birch–sedge–reed. 7—pine–shrub–*Sphagnum* (or with moss cover of *Sphagnum* and forest mosses). 8—herb-rich (reed, bog bean, horsetail, sedge), or homogenous structure. 10—sedge–*Sphagnum*, of homogeneous structure. 11—*Eriophorum–Sphagnum*, of patchy structure. 12—*Scheuchzeria–Sphagnum* of patchy structure. 13—*Eriophorum*–shrub–*Sphagnum* forested with patchy stands of pine (Litvinov form). 14—pine–*Sphagnum*, of patchy structure. 15—complex (grass–sedge, or sedge on low ridges and sparsely graminoid in flarks). 16—complex (pine–shrub–*Sphagnum* on ridges with algae and sparse herbs in flarks). 17—complex (*Eriophorum–Sphagnum* or shrub–*Eriophorum–Sphagnum* on ridges, *Scheuchzeria* in flarks). 18—complex (pine–shrub–*Sphagnum* on ridges, *Sphagnum–Scheuchzeria* in flarks). 19—complex regressive (lichens and *Sphagnum* on elevations of the first-order microrelief, liverworts in flarks, sometimes with isolated specimens of deer's hair sedge). 20—possible sequences in the transition of mesotopes from one structure to another. 21—Direction of channelled runoff. *A,B,C,*—Phases I, II and III respectively. (See general scheme of genetico-geotopic classification of mires in Table 3 and diagrams of phases in Fig. 4.)

Table 2. Classification of mire microtopes

Ecological type of vegetation	Mire formations (plant life forms)		
	Ligneous	Graminoid-ligneous	Muscoid-ligneous
Eutrophic fen	Alder Birch Fir Pine Osier	Wooded sedge Wooded reed	Wooded sedge– *Hypnum* Wooded sedge– *Sphagnum*
Transitional mesotrophic	Wooded transitional	Wooded sedge transitional	Wooded *Sphagnum* transitional
Raised-mire oligotrophic	Pine–shrub	Pine–*Eriophorum*	Pine–*Sphagnum*

the genetico-geotopic classification of mires in contrast with all less comprehensive schemes of classification.

The second exceptional merit of this classification is that it permits one at a glance to relate the different taxonomic units (types of micro-, meso- and macrotope) and their structure to their causes and the different items in their water supply. By this means one can establish quantitative relations between the structure and plant cover of mire geotopes and the most important ecological factors. Figure 9 makes it plain that the successive stages in the development of a mesotope are represented in the area it occupies by consecutive arrangements of different mire microtopes. The shape of the mesotope's outline reproduces schematically the form that is typical of an isolated mire massif developing in the given geomorphological conditions. When we come to deal with hydrological calculations and the analysis of the general relation between the physical properties of mires and the type

...minoid	Graminoid–muscoid	Muscoid	Complex
...etail ...-sedge ...e	Fen sedge–*Hypnum* Fen sedge–*Sphagnum*	Fen *Hypnum* Fen *Sphagnum*	Ridge–flark with eutrophic vegetation both on ridges and in flarks
...sitional ...chzeria ...sitional	Transitional *Sphagnum*–sedge	Transitional *Hypnum* Transitional *Sphagnum*	Aapa complexes (ridge–flark with differences of ecological plant types between ridges and flarks)
...horum	*Sphagnum–Eriophorum*	*Sphagnum fuscum* *Sphagnum*–shrub forested with pine	Ridge–flark with plants of oligotrophic types both on ridges and in flarks Ridge–pool–flark Ridge–pool Pool–flark Islet–flark

and composition of their plant cover, we shall find that this method of classification, founded no longer on a qualitative, but on a quantitative basis,
is both necessary and sufficient for solving many scientific and practical
problems.

1.8 The Structure of Mire Geotopes and their Investigation by Aerial Photography

If any mire massif has the dimensions of a macrotope (i.e. is formed of several
mesotopes), we shall understand by its structure the quantity, types, dimensions and mutual arrangement of the mesotopes and water bodies of which
it is composed. A mire massif consisting of only one mesotope is a special
case of mire massif structure (Fig. 5). By the structure of a mire mesotope
we shall understand in turn the microtopes and water bodies of which it

Table 3. General Scheme of the Genetico-Geotopic Classification of Mires

Geomorphological conditions of deposit		Genetico-geotopic structure of mire massif	
In macrorelief	In mesorelief	Mire macrotopes	
		Mesotope classified by original morphological centre of mire formation	Stage and course of development
On water divides	Placotopic deposits on horizontal water divides	Only found in macrotopes	
	Placotopic deposits on sloping water divides		
In river valleys, lakeside depressions and basins	Basin deposits	Insulated basins (I)	11, OC
		Effluent basins (III)	12, OC
		Effluent depressions (IIb)	16, OP
		Perfluent basins IV) Perfluent depressions (IIa)	5, Mixed
			16, OP
	Sloping terraces and slopes adjoining terraces	Gentle slopes (Vb)	Mixed, OC
		Foot of slopes (Va)	11, Mixed, OC
		Deltoid slopes (VIII)	3, Mixed, OC
	Floodplain deposits and river backwaters	Lakeside and riverside floodplains (VII)	OP, OC
		River backwaters (VI)	OP
	Mires in dry river courses	Dry beds (IX)	?

Notes: OC—Oligocentral; OP—Oligoperipheral; Mixed—Partly OC, partly OP; Early, Late—Stage at which mesotopes were fused into macrotope. The numbering of types according to stage and course of development is derived from Galkina (1959).

is composed, together with particulars as to their number, type, area, outline and arrangement.

In section 1.5, we considered and defined the concept of a mire microtope (or mire facies) as the smallest unit of mire formation in which the plant community structure and the physical properties connected with it are uniform. Two conditions must be fulfilled, if researches into the physical properties of plant covers and peat deposits are to serve as a basis for the

Mire macrotopes			
ɔmogeneous in course of development		Heterogeneous in course of development	
ɔmogeneous in phase	Heterogeneous in phase	Homogeneous in phase	Heterogeneous in phase
rly, late	Early and late	Early, late	Early and late

Only found in mesotopes			
rly, late	Early and late	Early, late	Early and late

(See also Fig. 19. In the light of Fig. 19, the Russian word *log* is translated "depression", and not "ravine"—T)

study of hydrological processes, and the calculation of their water and tem-perature regimes under natural conditions. Firstly, experimental data must be presented in the form of functional or statistical dependencies applying to specific types of microtope and their structural elements. Secondly, means must be found of determining with sufficient speed and accuracy the types of mire microtope that make up any given meso- or macrotope. The fulfilment of these conditions makes it possible to construct a theoretical programme for the analysis and calculation of water conditions in mires on a biophysical basis.

Aerial photography is at the present moment the best and most objective method of investigating natural objects on the surface of the earth (Smirnov, 1967). Soundly based methods of map interpretation have now been so fully worked out that they can serve as the chief sources of quantitative, as well as qualitative, information concerning natural objects and processes.

The technique for obtaining by aerial photography all the necessary quantitative and qualitative information for hydrological calculations, especially about the runoff from mires, was worked out as early as the late 1940s and early 1950s (Galkina, 1949; Ivanov, 1953a; Kalyuzhnyy, 1970). In a number of subsequent works (Ivanov, 1957b, 1960, 1963; Romanova, 1961; Anon., 1971c), methods were evolved for making hydrological calculations and generalizations which made use of experimental data about hydrological characteristics in combination with the results of aerial survey. Further improvements in the completeness and accuracy of calculations about water conditions in mires depend to an equal degree on the accumulation of the relevant experimental data, and the perfecting of methods of obtaining the necessary information from aerial photographs of mires, when there is a necessary link between new experimental data and the types and structures of microtopes detectable directly or indirectly by aerial photographs.

The interpretation and processing of aerial photographs for hydrological research and calculations therefore involves the following requirements:

(1) Clear and complete information about the structure of particular mire massifs and about the types of meso- and microtopes of which they are composed, so that the results obtained by observing and analysing the physical characteristics of their peat deposits and plant cover can be linked to their structural elements.

(2) Sufficient information about mire massifs that have not been studied from the ground to enable one to attribute to them also physical characteristics that have been shown by measurement to belong to other similar mire massifs.

(3) All the data necessary to enable one to simulate mire massifs.

The data obtained from an aerial photograph which is to be used to calculate the water and temperature conditions of undrained mires must contain the following information:

(1) The types of microtope that go to make up the given massif.

(2) The position and boundary of the different types of microtope.

(3) Maps of endotelmic streams and rivulets, especially of those that have outlets beyond the external boundaries of the massif, and consequently carry away some of the water that leaves the mire in channelled water courses beyond its boundaries.

(4) Maps of endotelmic water bodies (lakes), especially those that have a channelled run off beyond the external boundaries of the mire massif.

(5) Maps of endotelmic swamps and an indication of their types.

All this information can be entered by means of symbols on a plan of the mire massif (see Figs 5–7), which is compiled directly from an aerial photograph of the required scale, and is itself on the same scale. In the hydrology of mires, plans of this kind with indications of the types of microtope have been called "typological plans of mire massifs".

The above information is not enough to enable one to compute the runoff and water balance of mire massifs, nor to investigate their genesis or the relation between biophysical properties and the manner in which they receive and dispose of their water supply. For these purposes, a flow-net is constructed by aerial survey. This last is a system of lines entered on a plan of the mire (or on a survey photograph), each showing at one and the same time the rate of flow in different directions of the water which filters into deposits or flows over the surface of the mire (see Figs 5–8), and the maximum gradient of the water table at any point in the massif. Methods of constructing flow-nets and the direct and indirect criteria for them are considered in section 2.9, as is also their use for hydrological calculations.

The recognition of types of mire microtope by aerial survey, the delimitation of their boundaries, the technique of compiling typological plans and the interpretation of the features found in them are all considered in special manuals and instructions on method (Kudritskiy et al., 1956; Anon., 1971c). They cannot here be dealt with in detail.

The data gathered by the aerial survey of drained mires chiefly deal with the components of the drainage network and the changes that took place in the mire massif and the surrounding geotope since drainage was introduced. Aerial survey is not usually employed in such cases to calculate the components of their water balance nor their water regime, since the conditions that would supervene after the introduction of drainage were planned and calculated beforehand. Even so, aerial survey can be useful in such cases to check whether the condition of the area drained corresponds with prior calculations and presuppositions.

Experimental methods of determining the physical properties of the plant cover and peat deposit of a mire depend to a great extent on the structure of mire microtopes, which is also the chief criterion for many of the hydrological and physical properties of microtopes. By the structure of a mire microtope we therefore understand the floristic composition of the plant associations of which it is composed, the number of such associations and the pattern in which they are arranged, the type of microrelief associated with them, and the position of those parts of it which have an open water surface. *Descriptions of any type of microtope must therefore include four main criteria:*

(1) The floristic composition and grouping of its plant associations.
(2) The type of microrelief and the scale of its elements.
(3) The orientation in plan of the elements of its microrelief.
(4) The relation between the areas occupied by the different elements of the microrelief, by corresponding plant associations and by parts with an open water surface.

Certain criteria must also be used to describe plant associations in their most complete form, if they are to provide reliable clues to the physical characteristics with which they are associated. These criteria are:

(1) The quantitative relations between different plant species (the relation between the number of specimens and the weight of plant matter per unit area).
(2) The density of plant matter per unit area (the weight of the whole mass of vegetation per 1 m^2).
(3) The vertical distribution of the density of plant material.

At the present moment, however, it is customary to indicate structure by the cruder method of naming groups of plant associations. First place in the naming plant associations goes to the "edificator", the second to dominants and the third to codominants.[13] This is sometimes supplemented by the mention of species of plants in the group which are indicators of environmental conditions, in particular of the water regime.

In this process, all microtopes must be broken down into one or other of two important groups according to the structure of their microrelief and the variety of their plant cover. These are, firstly, microtopes with a mosaic or patchy, but uniform structure, and secondly, complex microtopes combining markedly different plant associations confined to higher or lower parts of the microrelief, and often associated with different formations. The former are characterized by a hummocky or slightly undulating relief with differences in vertical development and in the relative areas covered by elevations and depressions, or by an even and compact covering of moss or of muscoid and graminoid species.[14] Here the plant cover consists of a group of associations with a low degree of variety. Microtopes of the latter type are characterized by a very broken microrelief, whose surface is divided into large-scale elevations (ridges) and depressions (flarks or pools)[15], which may vary greatly in their area and in the amount of the massif that they cover.

Complex microtopes, which occupy a predominating position in the wooded mires of the zone of excess moisture, must be divided into two groups.

(1) Microtopes with an orientated ridge relief (predominantly in the wooded zone).

(2) Microtopes with an unorientated relief, which are of lesser extent and are, for the most part, retrogressive sectors of mire massifs.[16]

In both groups, a division is made between ridge-flark and ridge-pool microtopes, although there is no fundamental distinction between their structures. This is done because it enables one to apply to them descriptions that provide a suitable basis for calculations (see section 2.8).

In characterizing types of microrelief, the following gradations may be provisionally recognized:

(1) Small-hummock relief, where hummocks and elevations do not exceed 50 cm in cross section.

(2) Hummock relief, where they measure from 50–100 cm.

(3) Large-hummock relief, where most exceed 1 m.

In complex microtopes, one must distinguish two orders of microrelief in accordance with their different physical properties. Firstly, there is the microrelief of the large elements of microtopes (ridges and flarks), which are occupied by different groups of plant associations and make up the second-order microrelief. Then there is the microrelief of the whole microtope—the size, shape and orientation of the group of ridges and pools (flarks) of which it is composed and which constitute the first-order microrelief of the microtope.

2

The Hydrodynamics of Mires

2.1 Introductory Remarks

In the preceding chapter, we considered many of the general properties of mires as natural phenomena. All sorts of calculations relating to the water and heat regimes of mires, in their natural state and after they have been drained and developed, are required for such practical purposes as the construction of engineering works, the construction of factories and towns, road-making, the laying of telegraph wires, electric cables and pipelines for gas and petrol, the installation of drains and the working of plants and drainage networks. Most of the practical principles involved in such calculations are based on the general theory of the movement of moisture in mire massifs, the interchange of water and heat between them and their surroundings, and the experimentally ascertained values of the physical constants involved in such processes.

The active zone of water and heat exchange in natural mires is a relatively thin upper layer of peat together with its plant cover and the skeletal remains of it which have not yet decomposed. This layer, which is called the active horizon or acrotelm of the mire, contains the peat-making part of the deposit. Its thickness varies from 7–8 cm in herb-rich fen microtopes to 60–70 cm in moss-rich raised-mire microtopes with a well-developed microrelief. All the relatively rapid processes of water and heat exchange in undrained mires are connected with the physical properties of the acrotelm and the plant cover which it supports. In contrast, the main thickness of the deposit, which is composed of peats in different stages of decay and with different botanical components, is called, in the case of undrained mires, the inactive zone or catotelm, and plays only a secondary part in the changing vicissitudes of the mire's hydrometeorological processes. The physical character of the catotelm and the nature of the water movements occurring within it can only be estimated by studying the age-long processes and transformations that take place in the water regime of natural mires and by calculating the long-term average quantity of the different items in their water supply.

Draining adds to the acrotelm a significant part, and sometimes even the whole thickness of the peat deposit. As a rule the natural plant cover is artificially removed some time after the beginning of drainage operations. What then happens to its surface depends on its future use. It may become a peat surface devoid of vegetation. It may be transformed into agricultural land and used to grow crops. Its surface may be utilized for the drying and extraction of peat, or to provide a site for building.

No matter what its subsequent use, the process of draining allows oxygen to enter the deeper layers of the peat deposit. This leads to the oxidation of organic substances and activates the biological processes of decomposition down to a considerable depth. In this way, layers of peat which fall within the zone of aeration after draining begin and continue to change their physical properties owing to changes in the physico-chemical composition of the peat and two mechanical factors—precipitation and the increased compaction of the solid phase.

If mires that have been drained are later put to agricultural use, the upper horizons of the peat are subjected to farming operations, which keep on altering their properties. As they are gradually transformed into fertile soil, the upper layers of peat bring about changes in the physical properties of all the remaining thickness of the deposit down to the mineral soil. In this way, the draining of mires destroys their stability. It not only changes the mechanism and paths of water transmission, but starts a continuous transformation of their hydrophysical character, which lasts for a very long period.

For this reason, the physical characteristics of peat in drained mires are not stable, but change in the course of time under the influence of numerous factors, whereas, in the case of natural mires, the main physical constants that determine how moisture is transmitted are virtually stable and are determined by the composition of their plant cover, the acrotelm which it forms and the stratigraphy of their peat deposits. This fact compels us at the present time to use approximate, adjusted averages for the physical parameters of drained mires, since the complicated changes produced in time by drainage and subsequent use have not been sufficiently studied.

For most hydrological processes that have to be dealt with in practical calculations, the important physical characteristics are the hydraulic conductivity[1] and water yield of the peat deposits of mire massifs. In the case of undrained mires, it is important to know about the incidence of these properties in the acrotelm. Changes in them over the area of a mire massif are subject to definite laws, which give rise to differences in the rate at which water is moved or exchanged in different sectors of the massif and between the massif and its surroundings. Hydraulic conductivity and water yield depend in turn upon the water level regime, the wetness of the peat, the external load on the solid peat matrix and its own compaction. They may therefore change in the course of time under the influence of the swiftly changing hydro-meteorological regime. We shall now survey briefly the chief factors that affect the hydraulic conductivity and water yield of mire massifs.

2.2 The Total Water Content of Mire Massifs. The Moisture Content and Moisture Capacity of Peat in its Natural Location

The total quantity of water contained in peat (without dividing it into free and bound moisture) is determined by the ratio of the volume of water V_w contained in a given volume to the total volume of the peat V_p:

$$\eta = \frac{V_w}{V_p}. \tag{2.1}$$

η is called the *volumetric moisture content* of peat and is expressed in fractions or percentages.

To define the total quantity of water contained in peat use is also made of the concept of *gravimetric moisture content*, which can be expressed in two ways:

$$\delta = \frac{G_w}{G_p} \tag{2.2}$$

or

$$\vartheta = \frac{G_w}{G_{nm}}, \tag{2.3}$$

where G_w = weight of water, G_{pm} = weight of peat matrix, G_p = total weight of natural peat (water plus dry material in given volume of peat).

These two ways of expressing gravimetric moisture content, (2.2) and (2.3), can be converted into each other in the following manner:

$$\delta = \frac{\vartheta}{1 + \vartheta}; \qquad \vartheta = \frac{\delta}{1 - \delta}. \tag{2.4}$$

The conversion of volumetric into gravimetric moisture content, and vice versa, is carried out by means of the following equations, whose derivation is too simple to be given here:

$$\delta = \frac{\eta \gamma_w}{\eta \gamma_w + \gamma_{pm}(1 - \epsilon)} = \frac{\eta \gamma_w}{\eta \gamma_w + \gamma_{pm} \Theta}, \tag{2.5}$$

$$\vartheta = \frac{\gamma_w \eta}{\gamma_{pm}(1 - \epsilon)} = \frac{\gamma_w \eta}{\gamma_{pm} \Theta}, \tag{2.6}$$

$$\eta = \frac{\gamma_{pm}(1 - \epsilon)\delta}{\gamma_w(1 - \delta)} = \frac{\gamma_{pm}\delta\Theta}{\gamma_w(1 - \delta)},$$ (2.7)

$$\eta = \frac{\gamma_{pm}}{\gamma_w} \vartheta(1 - \epsilon) = \frac{\gamma_{pm}}{\gamma_w} \vartheta\Theta,$$ (2.8)

where γ_w and γ_{pm} are the densities of water and the solid peat matrix re-spectively, ϵ is the total porosity of natural peat, and Θ is the compaction of the solid peat[2]. Total porosity[3] is expressed by the simple equation:

$$\epsilon = \frac{A}{A + B},$$ (2.9)

where A is the total volume of voids and B the volume occupied by solids.

In soil mechanics, (2.9) is often replaced by the equation

$$\epsilon_v = \frac{A}{B},$$ (2.9')

where ϵ_v is called the void ratio. The relation between these two terms is given by the equation

$$\epsilon = \frac{\epsilon_v}{\epsilon_v + 1}.$$ (2.9'')

The compaction of peat Θ stands for that part of a volume of natural peat which is occupied by peat in its solid phase. It is obvious that Θ is connected with the total porosity ϵ and the weight/volume ratio of solid phase peat, $_vG_{pm} = G_{pm}/V_p$, by the equation:

$$\Theta = 1 - \epsilon = \frac{_vG_{pm}}{\gamma_{pm}}.$$ (2.10)[4]

The moisture content of peat, both in natural and in drained mire massifs, may vary greatly, and a change in water content is accompanied by a change in all its fundamental properties: its capacity to discharge and absorb water (i.e. water yield and water storage), its water conductivity below the water table (coefficient of filtration), its capillary water conductivity in the zone of aeration (above the water table), its mechanical strength or capacity to resist external loads, and its reaction to compression.

The content of moisture in the peat deposits of natural mire massifs below the water table (i.e. when almost all voids are filled with water) is, as a rule, very large. According to numerous researches carried out by different authors, it varies from 91 to 98% of their volume (Dubakh, 1944; Lundin, 1964; Romanov, 1961).

In undrained peat deposits, the volume occupied by solid matter is not usually greater than 10%. In layers above the water table, including the horizon which is composed of living plants, a considerable number of pores are occupied by air. For that reason, peat deposits in the zone where the water table fluctuates have no constant water content, and vary greatly in wetness as the water table fluctuates.

Even when the level of the water table is constant, the static (or equilibrium) distribution of moisture in the zone of aeration is by no means uniform. This is due to a decrease in the compaction of the solid matrix and an increase in the total porosity and size of pores as one passes from horizons composed of peat to the living plant cover as well as to the different height of capillary action in pores of different sizes.

Below the water table, the wetness of peat depends on the compaction of the solid matrix, and is always near to the maximum for the given degree of compaction, i.e. the wetness corresponding to complete saturation of the interstices between the particles of solid-phase peat. The maximum water content for any given degree of compaction is called the *moisture capacity of peat*. In contrast with mineral soils, however, peat does not have a constant moisture capacity. It changes greatly according to the compaction of the solid matrix.

Unfortunately, the literature of the subject up to now does not contain sufficiently accurate and generally accepted determinations of the moisture capacity of peat. The subject is differently treated in different works, and in most cases the concepts of "moisture capacity", "full moisture capacity" and "maximum moisture capacity" are transferred unthinkingly from corresponding branches of soil science to the peat deposits of mires. None the less, moisture capacity is assuming significance of the first order for establishing the varying march of the water content of peat deposits in natural mire microtopes. It is also important for determining the water yield, water conductivity and water storage capacity of undrained mires and the changes that drainage produces in these properties, as well as for calculating the water balance of mires. For these reasons we must treat it in greater detail.

When the compaction of the solid matrix remains constant, peat reaches its maximum moisture content at the moment when it passes from a three-phase to a two-phase condition, to which the name *soil mass* is given in soil mechanics. When the compaction of the solid matrix remains constant, changes in the water content of peat, right up to the point of complete saturation, take place through water filling up that part of its pores which was occupied by the atmosphere. In contrast to this, changes in the moisture content of *soil mass* (i.e. in the full moisture capacity of the peat) can only occur through the drawing apart or closing together of the particles of the solid matrix (i.e. through changes in the size of the pores and the compaction of the solid matrix). The closeness of the particles to each other and the resulting moisture capacity depend on the external pressure applied to the peat matrix, the specific gravity of the solid-phase particles which are in a suspended state, and the hydrodynamic pressure exerted on the solid-phase particles by the seepage of water through them. The relation between external compression and total porosity or the moisture capacity of peat of different degrees of humification and different floristic composition is one that can be expressed by compression curves (Fig. 10).

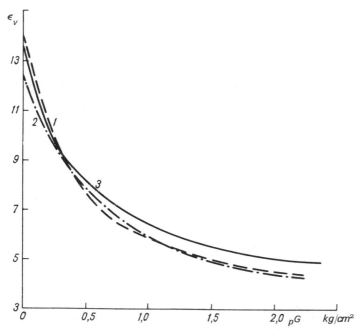

Fig. 10. Compression curves. 1 sedge peat (degree of decomposition 20%); 2—sedge-*Sphagnum* peat (degree of decomposition 25%); 3—*Eriophorum-Sphagnum* (bog) peat (degree of decomposition 30%); ϵ_v—coefficient of porosity.

In the natural peat deposits of undrained mires and in those of drained mires whose structure has remained undamaged, the forces of external pressure exerted on the solid matrix which change the moisture capacity of layers of peat below the water table are the weight of water suspended by capillary forces, the weight of moisture bound to the solid matrix and the weight of solid matter in the layers of peat above the water table.

In addition to this external load, the following forces act upon the particles of the solid matrix: the weight of the particles suspended in water and the hydrodynamic pressure exerted through seepage. Other things being equal, the moisture capacity of a peat deposit will be less when water seeps through it from top to bottom, and greater when it seeps through it from bottom to top, as when there is a vertical discharge of groundwater under pressure.

Since gases are formed in and discharged from peat deposits through the action of biochemical processes, there is always below the water table a greater or lesser quantity of gas bubbles compressed between the solid phase particles, which impart additional buoyancy to the peat matrix.

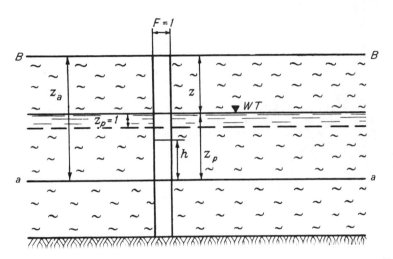

Fig. 11. Measurement of water content of a peat deposit in natural conditions. B—surface of acrotelm; WT—water table; $F = 1$—unit breadth; aa—plane surface below water table; z—depth of WT below B; z_a—depth of aa below B; z_p—depth of aa below WT; $z_p = 1$—unit depth below water table; h—piezometric pressure at aa represented by height of column of water.

From all this it follows that in natural mire massifs consolidation of the peat matrix in any layer aa (see Fig. 11) below the water table takes place under the action of the following forces:

(1) The dead weight of the solid phase particles in an absolutely dry state below the water table

$$G_{pm} = \gamma_{pm} \overline{\Theta} z_p .$$

(2) The weight of capillary moisture and moisture bound to the solid matrix

$$G_{wc} = \gamma_w \bar{\eta}_1 z,$$

where γ_{pm} is the specific weight of solid phase peat in compact form ($\gamma_{pm} \cong 1{\cdot}6$); γ_w is the specific weight of water ($\gamma_w \cong 1$); $\bar{\eta}_1$ is the mean volume of moisture in a layer of the acrotelm above the water table; z is the thickness of the peat deposit between the water table and the surface of the plant cover; and $\overline{\Theta}$ is the mean compaction of the solid matrix in the layer z_p below the water table.

(3) The weight of solid matrix above the water table

$$G'_{pm} = \gamma_{pm} \overline{\Theta}_1 z,$$

where $\overline{\Theta}_1$ is the mean compaction of the matrix in the layer z.

(4) The buoyancy of solid phase particles below the water table

$$G_{wb} = \gamma_w \overline{\Theta} z_p.$$

(5) The buoyancy exerted on the solid phase by bubbles of gas below the water table

$$G_{gb} = \gamma_w (1 - \bar{\eta} - \overline{\Theta}) z_p = \gamma_w (\bar{\epsilon} - \bar{\eta}) z_p,$$

where $\bar{\eta}$ is the mean volumetric moisture content in the layer z_p.

It follows that a layer of peat of unit thickness lying at a depth z_p below the water table, in the absence of vertical seepage, is consolidated under the action of the following resultant pressure upon it:

$$_pG = G_{pm} + G_{wc} + G'_{pm} - G_{wh} - G_{qb} = \gamma_{pm} \overline{\Theta} z_p +$$
$$+ \gamma_w \bar{\eta}_1 z + \gamma_{pm} \overline{\Theta}_1 z - \gamma_w \overline{\Theta} z_p - \gamma_w (1 - \bar{\eta} - \overline{\Theta}) z_p. \qquad (2.11)$$

Since the average moisture content $\bar{\eta}$ and compaction $\overline{\Theta}$ change as the thickness of the layer z_p changes, there are differences in the amount of compression $_pG$ acting upon the solid matrix at different depths below the water table. When the movement of water by seepage in the pores of the peat has a vertical component, a vertical hydrodynamic pressure $_pG_\phi$ is exerted upon the peat matrix, which is directed upwards or downwards according to the direction of seepage:

$$_pG_\phi = {_pG_1} - {_pG_2} = \gamma_w(z_p - h) = \gamma_w \frac{v}{k} z_p = \frac{vz_p}{(\alpha g/\mu)R^2 \epsilon_a}, \qquad (2.12)$$

where $_pG_1 = \gamma_w z_p$, the piezometric pressure in a layer of peat at the level of the water table ($z_p = 0$); $_pG_2 = \gamma_w h$, the piezometric pressure at the level *aa*, *h* being the height of the column of liquid at that level (see Fig. 11); k = coefficient of seepage; v = the rate of seepage; R = hydraulic radius of pores; μ = coefficient of viscosity; α = a dimensionless coefficient dependent upon the form of pores; ϵ_a = active porosity.

Thus the total pressure on the solid matrix at depth z_p below the water table may by means of (2.11) be expressed as follows:

$$_pG = \gamma_{pm}(\overline{\Theta}z_p + \overline{\Theta}_1 z) + \gamma_w(\eta_1 - \overline{\Theta}z_p) - \gamma_w(1 - \bar{\eta} - \overline{\Theta})z_p + \gamma_w(z_p - h). \tag{2.12'}$$

It is obvious that, when $h < z_p$, the hydrodynamic pressure is directed downwards and enters the equation (2.21') with a positive sign, increasing the pressure on the solid matrix. When $h > z_p$, seepage is directed upwards and the hydrodynamic pressure reduces the pressure on the matrix. The dependence of the pressure exerted on the solid matrix upon the total porosity ϵ (or the void ratio ϵ_v) is expressed, when pressure is along one axis, by experimentally determined curves, and may be written in the form

$$\epsilon = \epsilon_0 - a_p G, \tag{2.13}$$

where a is the coefficient of compaction of the soil, or the modulus of deformation of the solid state, usually expressed in $\mathrm{cm}^2\ \mathrm{kg}^{-1}$, and ϵ_0 is a dimensionless constant whose magnitude is dependent upon the degree of humification and floristic composition of the peat.

Since the total porosity ϵ is numerically equal to η_w, the moisture capacity or maximum possible moisture content at a given pressure, we may insert the value $_pG$ from equation (2.12') in the expression (2.13), and obtain an equation for the moisture capacity of a layer of peat at a given depth from the surface of the peat $z_a = z_p + z$ (see Fig. 11):

$$\eta_w = \epsilon_0 - a[\gamma_{pm}(\overline{\Theta}z_p + \overline{\Theta}_1 z) + \gamma_w(\bar{\eta}_1 z - \overline{\Theta}z_p) -$$
$$- \gamma_w(1 - \bar{\eta} - \overline{\Theta})z_p + \gamma_w(z_p - h)]. \tag{2.13'}$$

Expressing z_p in terms of the distance of the water table from the surface $(z_p = z_a - z)$, we obtain

$$\eta_w = \epsilon_0 - a\gamma_{pm}[\overline{\Theta}(z_a - z) + \overline{\Theta}_1 z] - a\gamma_w[\bar{\eta}_1 z - \overline{\Theta}(z_a - z)] +$$
$$+ a\gamma_w(1 - \bar{\eta} - \overline{\Theta})(z_a - z) - a\gamma_w[(z_a - z) - h]. \tag{2.13''}$$

From this last expression it is plain that the moisture capacity of a unit layer of peat at a given depth z_a changes with the depth of the water table z. As this approaches the surface $(z \to 0)$, the moisture capacity of the layer approaches the limit

$$\eta_{w, z=0} = \epsilon_0 - a(\gamma_{pm} - \gamma_w)\overline{\Theta}z_a - a\gamma_w(1 - \bar{\eta} - \overline{\Theta})z_a + a\gamma_w(z_a - h), \tag{2.14}$$

and may in the most general case increase or diminish as changes occur in the relative values of the second, third and fourth terms on the righthand side of equation (2.14).

We shall call the normal moisture capacity of a layer of peat at a depth z_a that which obtains when the solid matrix is fully compacted at $z = 0$, when vertical seepage is non-existent ($h = z_a$), and when the gas content of the layer z_a is zero ($1 - \bar{\eta} = \Theta$). In that state, compaction of the matrix takes place exclusively through the weight of solid particles. Writing $\eta_{w.n}$ for the normal moisture content, we obtain from (2.14)

$$\eta_{w,n} = \epsilon_0 - a(\gamma_{pm} - \gamma_w)\overline{\Theta}z_a. \tag{2.14'}$$

To describe the relative wetness or moisture saturation of mire massifs, sectors of mire massifs and layers of peat, use is made of the concept of water saturation, which is the relation between moisture capacity at a given pressure and the normal moisture capacity:

$$\beta = \frac{\eta_w}{\eta_{w.n}}. \tag{2.15}$$

When $\beta = 1$, the given layer of peat at the depth z_a has a normal moisture saturation. When $\beta > 1$, it is supersaturated. When $\beta < 1$, it is below normal. Inserting the values η_w and $\eta_{w.n}$ from (2.13'') and (2.14') in equation (2.15), we obtain a general expression for the moisture saturation of a layer of peat at the depth z_a:

$$\beta = 1 + \frac{a[(\gamma_{pm} - \gamma_w)\overline{\Theta} - \gamma_w\bar{\eta}_1 - \gamma_{pm}\overline{\Theta}_1]z + {} }{ \epsilon_0 - a(\gamma_{pm} - \gamma_w)\overline{\Theta}z_a}$$
$$\frac{{} + a\gamma_w(1 - \bar{\eta} - \overline{\Theta})(z_a - z) - a\gamma_w[(z_a - z) - h]}{\epsilon_0 - a(\gamma_{pm} - \gamma_w)\overline{\Theta}z_a}. \tag{2.15'}$$

From this it is plain that moisture saturation is equal to normal moisture capacity ($\beta = 1$), when $z = 0$ and there is neither seepage ($h = 0$) nor gas ($\bar{\eta} + \overline{\Theta} = 1$) in the peat.

It follows from equation (2.12') that, when there is a vertical component of seepage directed upwards ($h > z_p$), the pressure on the matrix is negative, i.e. is directed upwards, when

$$\gamma_w(1 - \bar{\eta} - \overline{\Theta})z_p + \gamma_w(h - z_p) > \gamma_{pm}(\overline{\Theta}z_p + \overline{\Theta}_1 z) + \gamma_w(\bar{\eta}_1 z - \overline{\Theta}z_p). \tag{2.16}$$

Here the particles of the peat matrix will be observed to draw away from each other, and there will be an increase in porosity ϵ and a simultaneous decrease in the compaction of the matrix Θ. An extreme manifestation of this process is the lamination of peat deposits often observable in supersaturated parts of natural mires, and the formation within them of horizontal layers of water. As will be shown in section 2.9, these phenomena are observed in places where the seepage flowlines to the acrotelm converge. These are the sectors of mires where there are breaks in the horizontal lines of seepage. The lamination of solid peat and the formation of layers of water exemplify one of the ways in which the forces acting upon the peat matrix are brought into balance and the peat deposits in undrained mires are built up.

We must therefore regard the moisture capacity of the peat in undrained mires as a quantity varying according to its situation, the thickness of the peat and fluctuations in the level of the water table z. In any given region it is determined by a balance between the forces which arise in the solid and liquid state as a result of buoyancy on the one hand and vertical seepage on the other.

2.3 The Combination of Water with the Peat Matrix. Bound and Free Water

Most of the water contained in mire massifs is located in the pores of the peat that constitutes the catotelm. Only a small part is located in the acrotelm, in open and covered water bodies (lakes, swamps and "lenses" of water in peat beds), and in layers of water formed through the displacement and floating away of peat deposits in areas that are supersaturated with moisture.

The moisture contained in the pores of peat which can be displaced through gravitation or through a pressure gradient due to the liquid's own weight is called *free water*. Moisture which remains immobile and does not seep out when a relatively small pressure gradient is applied to it is said to be bound. According to modern researches into the properties of peat, the forces that immobilize this part of the water in peat differ in their physical nature. The smaller part of this immobile water is physically or molecularly bound. The weight of this water (W_b) is 50–100% of that of the solid matrix. The larger part is what is called *immobilized water*. This consists of intracellular water filling up the cell cavities of incompletely decayed plants and water retained within the structure of the peat matrix through being shut off in sealed or single-ended pores or in very small capillaries.

As Churayev (1960) points out, it is difficult to determine the amount of immobilized water, for it does not differ much in its properties from free water. Yet, despite the fact that this water does not seep, like other forms of immobile water, at the low pressure gradients encountered in natural mires and in the draining of peat deposits, the water yield of peat deposits and the water-retaining capacity depends upon its amount. As peat becomes more dispersed, the interface between the solid and liquid particles increases. This increases the amount of energy in the system, which is due to interaction between the surface forces present in the solid and liquid phases, and this in turn increases the water-retaining capacity of the peat. For that reason, the quantity of bound water and the quantity of water that flows out of a volume of peat under the influence of gravity may vary greatly, although the moisture content of the peat be the same. The higher the dispersity or degree of decomposition, the smaller the quantity of water that circulates in a given time interval, and the smaller likewise the water yield in free flow under the action of gravity (at normal atmospheric pressure).

Recent researches into the physical nature of peat as a three-phase system show that it is difficult to establish strictly quantitative frontiers between the above indicated categories of moisture; all the more so, because many of the properties of the water contained in the pores of the organic matrix depend greatly upon the chemistry of colloids and of the solutions which they form, which depend in turn on the degree of humification and floristic composition of the peat.

Making use of the theory of inactive residues worked out by B. V. Deryagin, Churayev has proposed a method of determining the quantity of immobilized water in peat by using the radioactive tracer Na_2SO_4 labelled with the isotope S^{35} (Churayev, 1960). These researches show that the quantity of immobilized (non-solvent) water (W_{im}) is 300–400% of the weight of the solid matrix for various samples of peat. Correspondingly, the moisture locked up in cells or in sealed and one-ended pores $W_{cp} = W_{im} - W_b = 200$–300% of the solid matrix. Knowledge of the quantity of immobilized water in peat is important as the physical basis for calculations of seepage at low pressure gradients, such as we have to deal with in natural and drained mire massifs. The hydraulic conductivity or coefficient of filtration (seepage) of peat is determined not by its total porosity ϵ, but by its active porosity ϵ_a, which is always less than ϵ by the volume of immobilized water:

$$\epsilon_a = \epsilon - W_{im}\frac{G_{pm}}{\gamma_w} = \epsilon\left(1 + \frac{\gamma_{pm}}{\gamma_w}W_{im}\right) - \frac{\gamma_{pm}}{\gamma_w}W_{im}, \qquad (2.17)$$

where all symbols are as before (see section 2.2).

The average hydraulic radius of the active pores R_a may be determined by the equation

$$R_a = \frac{\epsilon_a}{s_a}, \qquad (2.18)$$

where s_a is the specific kinetic surface of water-saturated peat, which can be determined by trial on samples and evaluated by the Kozeny–Carman equation[4a]

$$s_a = 970\sqrt{\frac{\epsilon_a^3 d^2 I}{Q}}$$

in which d is the diameter of the sample, Q is the loss through seepage and I is the pressure gradient.

Using the well-known formula of Poiseuille for the average rate of laminar flow in fine tubes of a radius R

$$u = \frac{\gamma_w}{8\mu} R^2 I,$$

and replacing the radius of the tube by the product of the pore's hydraulic radius (R_a) and a coefficient of shape (α), and expressing the rate of flow (u) in terms of the rate of seepage and active porosity $(u = v/\epsilon_a)$, we obtain the following expression for the coefficient of seepage of peat k_p:

$$k_p = \frac{v}{I} = \frac{\gamma_w}{\mu} \alpha \epsilon_a R_a^2 = \frac{\gamma_w}{\mu} \alpha \frac{\epsilon_a^2}{s_a^2}, \tag{2.19}$$

where γ_w is the specific weight of the liquid in dyne/cm^3, μ is the coefficient of viscosity in poise[5], and α a dimensionless coefficient characterising the shape of the pores.

For circular models of pore α is 0·5, for square ones 2, for narrowly slitted ones 0·125, and for equilateral-triangular ones 0·77. Allowing for the fact that the structure of the active pores of peat is a random assortment of the most varied shapes, we may average out the value of α at about 1, and then equation (2.19) takes the form:

$$k_p = \frac{\gamma_w}{\mu} \epsilon_n R_a^2, \tag{2.20}$$

or, using equation (2.17),

$$k_p = \frac{\gamma_w}{\mu} R_a^2 \left(\epsilon - \frac{W_{im} G_{pm}}{\gamma_w} \right) = \frac{\gamma_w}{\mu} R_a^2 \left(\epsilon - \frac{\gamma_{pm}}{\gamma_w} \Theta W_{im} \right). \tag{2.21}$$

The equations (2.20) and (2.21) permit us to determine the coefficient of seepage of peat through the quantity of immobilized water and the volumetric weight $({}_v G_{pm})$ of natural peat or the compaction of the solid matrix (Θ). The results of these laboratory researches into the quantity of bound water and the compaction of the solid matrix may therefore be used to determine the hydraulic conductivity of peat.

The quantity of immobilized water in the acrotelm of different types of microtope has been accurately studied in recent years by Vorob'ev (1965, 1969). Because the structure of the acrotelm is very different from that of the solid matrix (see section 2.1), the major part of its immobile water is locked up in cells or one-ended pores located in the undecomposed stems of *Sphagnum* and *Hypnum* mosses. The quantity of water physically bound by molecular forces in the acrotelm of mires is very small, because little of its solid part consists of small dispersed particles. In most cases it can therefore be ignored.

For practical calculations of the water regime of mires, it is important to establish, even approximately, the total quantity of bound water in peat, and to divide off that which is bound by capillary forces from that which is immobile under low pressure gradients, for these are the categories that determine the water yield of peat under natural conditions (and usually when peat massifs are being developed). They also account for the dependence of water yield upon the degree of humification and the floristic composition of the peat.

2.4 The Structure of Peat Deposits in Natural Mires and the Changes Produced by Drainage

A series of researches carried out in the last three decades (Vorob'ev, 1965, Ivanov, 1948, 1953b; Lopatin, 1949; Lundin, 1964; Romanov, 1961, etc.) has shown that the organic accumulations of mire massifs are divided in respect of their biophysical properties into two horizons: a relatively thin layer (less than 1 m) representing the transition from the peat deposit to the living plant cover, and the main thickness of organic accumulations, which constitutes what is in the strictest sense the peat deposit of the mire. The chief differences between these layers lie in the intensity of the physical and chemical changes that take place in them and in their reaction to changes in the hydrometeorological conditions above the surface of the mire.

The upper layer and its plant cover is in reality a frontier zone, where there is an intensive exchange of moisture and heat between the atmosphere and the lithosphere or peat deposit. In this layer there are rapid changes in the quantity of moisture, heat and air owing to hydrometeorological conditions, such as the pattern of precipitation and the intensity of solar radiation, evaporation and runoff. Below this layer, in the main body of the peat deposit, changes in the content of heat, moisture and gas as well as in the biochemical processes connected with them, take place more slowly and do not reflect swift changes in hydrometeorological conditions. This last fact enables us to regard peat deposits in their natural condition as a moisture-saturated soil of organic origin with mechanical, physical and hydrological properties that vary little in the course of time.

As was pointed out in section 2.1, it is necessary in the case of natural mires to distinguish two horizons; an upper one which is called the acrotelm, and a lower one which is called the catotelm. This division, which was introduced by Lopatin (Konstantinov and Sakali, 1967), and has been shown to have a physical basis in other researches (Ivanov, 1948, 1957b; Romanov, 1961), has proved very important in the study of the hydrological processes of undrained mires and of the part they play in the origin and development of mire systems. In this connection it must be mentioned that the acrotelm is in reality the peat-forming layer, i.e. the layer in which there is incomplete decomposition of dying vegetation and in which a soil of peat is formed.

The acrotelm of a mire has the following characteristics:

(1) An intensive exchange of moisture with the atmosphere and the surrounding area.
(2) Frequent fluctuations in the level of the water table and a changing content of moisture.
(3) High hydraulic conductivity and water yield and a rapid decline of these with depth.
(4) Periodic access of air to its pores with the effect of clearing them of water and lowering the water table.
(5) A large quantity of aerobic bacteria and micro-organisms facilitating the rapid decomposition and transformation into peat of each year's dying vegetation.
(6) The presence of a living plant cover, which constitutes the top layer of the acrotelm.

The catotelm has the following characteristics:

(1) A constant or little changing water content.
(2) A very slow exchange of water with the subjacent mineral strata and the area surrounding it.
(3) Very low hydraulic conductivity in comparison with the acrotelm (a difference of 3–5 orders of magnitude).
(4) No access of atmospheric oxygen to the pores of the soil
(5) No aerobic micro-organisms and a reduced quantity of other kinds in comparison with the acrotelm.

Because the surface of mires in most microtopes is not even, but has a well-differentiated microrelief (see section 1.8), the elevations and depressions of the acrotelm are not of uniform depth and vary greatly in different types of microtope. Any exact definition of the frontier between the acrotelm and the catotelm must always be to some extent artificial, because the changes in all physical and biochemical properties accompanying changes of depth are continuous. It must be remembered, however, that the chief factors affecting the intensity of biochemical processes in the acrotelm are the periodic fluctuations of the water table, the amplitude of these, and the resulting access of atmospheric oxygen to the main thickness of the organic strata. This is why the acrotelm must be regarded, on the one hand, as the zone of aeration of peat soils in their natural state, and, on the other, as the peat-forming layer, where organic material derived from the dying plant cover is oxidized and decomposed, and so transformed into peat of varying degrees of humification and compaction. Accepting this as our starting point, the thickness of the acrotelm for any given type of microtope may be taken as equal to the distance from the surface of the mire to the average minimum level of water in the warm season. Here we are taking into account the fact that the lower positions of periodically repeated minimum levels (in years when there are hot, dry spells during the summer), in comparison with the average positions, do not have much influence on peat formation. In microtopes with a markedly differentiated microrelief (hummocks, large hummocks and especially elongated ridges), the thickness of the acrotelm must be taken as the distance from the mean level of the higher elements of the microrelief to the top of the mean minimum level of the water table in the summer. In the case of the lower elements of the microrelief (depressions and flarks), the thickness of the acrotelm must be correspondingly less, roughly by the size of the difference between the levels of the elevations and depressions. Since the top of the plant cover in the lower elements of microrelief (especially in muscoid and musco-graminoid formations) is unstable and subject to considerable vertical displacement through changes in the water table, measurement of the thickness of the acrotelm through these elements of the microrelief is inconvenient and useless for the physical explanation of the phenomena. It must therefore be conceded that in the case of microtopes with markedly differentiated microreliefs the depth of the acrotelm has to be measured in terms of the stable elements of the microrelief, whose surface is not subject to any significant variation through fluctuations in the water table, i.e. by reference to elevations and ridges, not depressions and flarks. If it is remembered that microtopes with a ridge-pool structure generally have an open surface of water between the raised elements of their microrelief, this approach to the problem of determining the thickness of the acrotelm is that much easier to justify.

In microtopes with a completely even plant cover, which is characteristic of certain associations of muscoid and musco-graminoid types of vegetation, which have only one layer of vegetation, the depth of the acrotelm remains the same at every point of the microtope. Analysis of observations made above the minimum level of the water table in different microtopes (Ivanov, 1957b) has shown that the thickness of the acrotelm in most types of microtope varies from 30 to 70 cm, reaching from 7–8 cm to 1 m in exceptional cases. The greatest thicknesses are characteristic of certain ligneous microtopes, e.g. 94 cm for firwood microtopes and 82 cm for pine–sedge–*Hypnum* types. The minimum thicknesses are found in the reed-sedge group.

The catotelm has no characteristic thickness and is not immediately connected with any of the types of plant association that compose our present mire microtopes. It may change from zero at the boundary between the mire massif and mineral soils to the greatest depths of peat deposits known to us, i.e. from 18 to 20 m. For that reason, the distribution of the thickness of the catotelm over the area of a mire massif corresponds as a whole to the general distribution of the depth of organic accumulations within the borders of the mire massif (i.e. within the borders of the macro- or mesotopes), and may be determined by stratigraphic cross-sections and profiles of the surface and bottom of mire massifs as the difference between the total depth of the peat deposit and the thickness of the acrotelm of the corresponding microtope.

The draining of a mire, involving as it does the destruction of its plant cover and the lowering of the average water table, leads to a radical change in the structure and physical properties of peat deposits. As a result of the lowering of the average water table, a significant part or the whole thickness of the natural peat deposit falls within the zone of aeration. Peat begins to settle and grow more compact, at first only in the upper levels, and its hydro-physical properties become significantly more uniform through the thickness of the deposit. The acrotelm disappears in drained mires used for agriculture, peat production or building. In shallow sectors with a thin layer of peat, the whole deposit is periodically aerated through seasonal variations in water levels.

Owing to these fundamental changes in the water regime and structure of the peat deposit of mires, methods of calculating the transmission of water in drained mires, especially where water balance relationships are considered, differ materially from those applied to undrained mires. Natural mires differ from drained mires in their physical properties and the structure of their peat deposits. This must be taken into account in evaluating and computing the influence of drainage on the water regime of the swampiest lands, and on the condition of land masses and river basins in which drainage works are carried out.

2.5 The Structure of the Microrelief of Mires

In section 1.8 we surveyed briefly the types of structure that are typical of different orders of mire geotopes—the microtopes of mire facies, the meso-topes of mire localities, and the macrotopes of systems of mire localities or physico-geographic geotopes of the mire type. The varied nature of the structure and plant cover of mires makes it necessary to find a stricter defini-tion of what we mean by the surface of a natural (undrained) mire. Otherwise it would be impossible to use experimental determinations of the physical characteristics of the acrotelms of mire massifs to compute their water and heat regimes, or to investigate the connection between their plant cover and their ecology.

As already mentioned, most mire microtopes have an uneven surface, which may be characterized by small, medium or large hummocks, by undulations or by elongated ridges. Our first task in all such cases is to decide what we mean by the "surface" of the mire. It is agreed that an integrated plant cover or plant community has a many-tiered structure (Khil'mi, 1966): an upper tier represented by ligneous vegetation (if present) and large shrubs like willow, an intermediate tier represented by small mire shrubs or herbs, and a lower tier represented by different species of moss. The vegetation of different types of microtope may include in their associations plants belonging to all three tiers, or plants belonging to two of them (e.g. the *Sphagnum–*

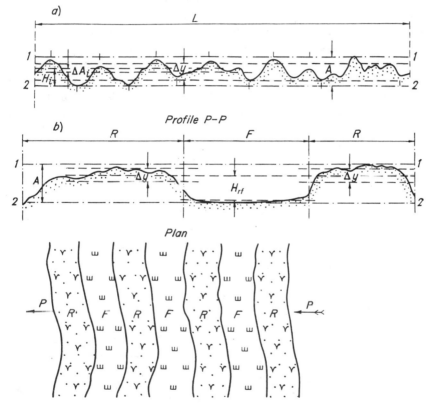

Fig. 12. Mire surfaces (a) with a hummocky microrelief (b) with a complex strip-ridge structure. A—zone of microrelief; R—ridge; F—flark; H_{rf}—elevation of mean surface of ridges above mean surface of flarks (in ridge pool complexes—above mean level of pools); ΔA_i—thin layer of microrelief; H_i—height of A_i above lowest level of microrelief; L—length of sector of microrelief; P–P—profile of sector of microrelief; Δy—difference between mean levels of elevations and depressions in microrelief of the second order.

Eriophorum–Carex group), or plants belonging to only one of them (e.g. the *Hypnum* or the *Carex* group). In all cases where the lowest tier of plant cover takes the form of moss, it is assumed that the surface of the mire is composed of compact moss capitula of different species (in uncrushed condition). If the lowest tier (the moss cover) is missing, as for example in *Carex*–reed, reed and pure *Carex* associations, the surface of the mire is taken to be the compact surface formed by the interlacing of the rhizomes of sedges, reeds and other plants and by the saturated or solid peat that fills up the space between them. This last depends on the amount of moisture on the surface of the mire. The same considerations apply to many microtopes of the ligneous type: the black alder, alder–sedge, birch–willow–reed–sedge and other such types which have no moss in their lower tier. When we are speaking of the type and scale of the elevations and depressions of a mire microrelief, we must bear in mind the above concept of the surface of a mire.

Let us now consider a certain sector of a mire microtope whose length is L and whose microrelief is shown in cross-section in Fig. 12. Lines 1–1 and 2–2 represent horizons between which all points on the surface of the mire are situated. The distance A between the horizons 1–1 and 2–2 is called the zone of development of the natural surface of the mire.[6] We divide the distance A

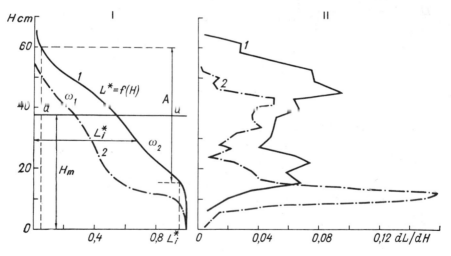

Fig. 13. *I*—curve showing proportion of first-order microrelief occupied by vegetable matter—$L^* = f(H)$. II—curve showing frequency of different elevations above lowest level of microrelief—dL^*/dH. 1—in fully developed complex microtope of strip-ridge structure; 2—in developing complex microtope of strip-ridge structure. $L^* = L_i^*/L$; L—length of microrelief; L_i^*—length of microrelief occupied by vegetable matter; H—height in cm; H_m—mean height of microrelief; A—zone of microrelief; a–a—median dividing off equal areas ω_1 and ω_2 above and below the curve L^*–$f(H)$.

into a series of thin layers ΔA_i, and in each layer we add up the total length of the space filled with vegetation and peat L_i and the length of the space filled with air $(L - L_i)$. Expressing L_i as a fraction of L, we may construct a graph showing the dependence of the function $L_i^* = L_i/L$ upon the height of the layer H_i above the horizon 2–2 (see Fig. 13). A graph of this kind shows the degree to which different zones of the microrelief are filled with plant material, for the shape of the curve $L^* = f(H)$ depends on the type of microrelief and the pattern of its positive and negative elements. In other words, the shape of the curve $L^* = f(H)$ is one of the quantitative parameters of the structure of the microrelief. We shall call such curves *the curves of occupation of the development zones of mire microreliefs*. The function $L^* = f(H)$ may be transformed into a curve showing the frequency of particular differences of elevation between summits of the microrelief and the lowest horizon of the development zone (2–2). This is done by graphing the dependence of dL^*/dH upon H, i.e. d^2L^*/dH^2.

Using curves of occupation of the zone of microrelief for different types of microrelief, it is possible to establish a characteristic average surface for each type of microtope, taking as median a line like a–a (Fig. 13), which divides the function $L^* = f(H)$ into two equal areas ω_1 and ω_2. It is then obvious that, if we designate by H_m the distance from the lower level of the zone of microrelief to the average surface in the given microtope,

$$H_m = \frac{\Omega}{L^*} = \frac{\Omega}{1} = \Omega,$$

where Ω is the area bounded by the curve $L^* = f(H)$ expressed in linear units.

Figure 13 gives first-order curves of occupation of the zone of microrelief for two different types of mire microtope. Curves of occupation and distribution for pine–*Sphagnum* microtopes and *Sphagnum*–shrub microtopes containing pine have a shape approximating to symmetrical (normal) distribution. For well-developed ridge–flark microtopes with a strip-ridge structure, the curves of occupation along the flowlines (perpendicular to the elongations of the ridges and flarks) have a complicated shape with three points of inflection corresponding to the two maxima in the curve of distribution. The curves of occupation of developing ridge–flark microtopes have an analogous, but less definite form. The second-order curves of occupation and distribution of ridge–flark microtopes show that ridges with a hummocky structure and *Sphagnum*–pine–shrub or *Sphagnum*–shrub–*Eriophorum* vegetation also have an almost symmetrical form. The distribution curve of *Sphagnum*–*Scheuchzeria* flarks fluctuates little in height and has a well-marked maximum between 5 and 10 cm.

The distance between the lower horizon of the zone of microrelief (2–2) and the mean elevations of its summits and valleys is an important characteristic of microreliefs (see Fig. 12). In determining the position of these levels, one must take into account the peculiarities of the plant cover of each type of microtope under investigation and the connection of various species of plant with positive or negative elements of microrelief. To obtain a statistical mean for the elevations in such cases, one should not take into account every little fall or rise in the microrelief, but only those that are connected with the structure and composition of the plants making up a plant association of the given type. For example, in *Sphagnum–shrub–Eriophorum* microtopes one should accept as top measurements for mosses only those found on hummocks with shrubs, and for bottom measurements only those found in hollows where the moss cover is not associated with shrubs or *Eriophorum*.

In microtopes composed of *Sphagnum, Eriophorum*, shrubs and pine, it is necessary to average out separately the top levels of hummocks formed by the shrub–*Eriophorum* components of the association and those formed by tiers of moss on tree-trunks of pine. Similarly, for the average top position of depressions one accepts only the average elevation of mosses found in depressions which are not associated with shrubs or *Eriophorum*. Thus three average surfaces may be found in ligneous microtopes of the moss group: an average surface for tree-trunk elevations, an average surface for the elevations connected with the shrub and *Eriophorum* components of the plant association, and an average surface for the depressions containing a tier of moss without any other components.

The analogous characteristics for microtopes with a ridge–flark or ridge–pool structure are somewhat more complex. In these microtopes, the ridges (elevations covering an enormous area) and the depressions that correspond to them (flarks or open pools) are elements of microrelief of the first order (see section 1.8). But every individual ridge and flark combination characterized within its area by its own plant associations also possesses its own microrelief—a microrelief of the second order. The character of this microrelief depends on the composition of the plant associations found in it. Accordingly, in the case of complex microtopes, one must distinguish between, firstly, the overall difference between the heights of the average surfaces of ridges and the heights of the average surfaces of flarks (H_{rf}), and secondly, the individual difference between the average surfaces of particular ridges and flarks (Δy) (see Fig. 12). Since in most cases the surface of the moss in flarks is pretty even, the microrelief of ridge–flark microtopes may be described in terms of only three surfaces: the mean surface of the tops of ridges, the mean surface of the bottoms of ridges and the mean surface of the flarks. It must be remembered, however, that the surface of a flark does not as a rule have a stable elevation and fluctuates with changes in the level of the water table.

When physical parameters relating to the acrotelm are used in hydrological calculations, they should be based upon stable elements of the microrelief, which do not fluctuate under natural conditions with changes in the water table. This restriction is based upon the ideas we have just been considering concerning the characteristic surfaces of the microrelief of mire microtopes, which must be defined as statistical averages based upon an adequate number of measurements for each type of microtope.

At the present time, many types of microtope have not been elucidated by the construction of curves of occupation for the development zone of their microrelief, but work is in progress on the construction of such functions. For that reason, calculations of the water regime, runoff and items in the water balance of mires have so far been based upon those physical constants of the acrotelm which are connected with the average depressions and elevations of the stable elements of microrelief in each particular type of microtope (Anon., 1971c). As we have to compare the degree of difference between the microreliefs of different types of microtope, we can hardly hope to obtain empirical curves of occupation and distribution without first determining the corresponding coefficients of variation and irregularity. To ensure that these statistical parameters are not purely artificial quantities, but possess physical meaning and admit of comparison, their mean square deviation must be computed either in relation to the height of the zone of microrelief A (see Fig. 12), or in relation to the average heights of elevations and depressions.

This makes it necessary to determine the magnitude of A more exactly. To eliminate the influence upon the magnitude of A of large or small values of H_i which are accidental and of rare occurrence, when the number of measurements is small (being limited statistical samples), it is necessary to make A the difference between two values of H_i, one with a probability not exceeding p and the other with a probability not exceeding $1 - p$ (e.g. $p = 0.05$ and $1 - p = 0.95$). A will then be the magnitude expressed by the equation (see Fig. 13):

$$A = H_{p=0.05} - H_{1-p=0.95}.$$

The values of $H_{p=0.05}$ and $H_{1-p=0.95}$ must be determined by means of the empirical curve $L^* = f(H)$, which was constructed from data obtained by measurement. In doing this, one ought not to accept values of H_i with too low a degree of probability p in order to increase the stability and comparability of the values of A. When the number of measurements of H_i is limited, and especially when the number of measurements is different for different types of microtope, the accuracy of measurements with a low probability may be insufficient.

We must therefore call the height of the development zone of the microrelief A the distance between two surfaces having the given degree of probability of not exceeding in height points on the microrelief of the given type of microtope. It is important that in comparative researches into the structure and development zone of a microrelief calculations of A should be based upon identical probabilities of not exceeding points on the microrelief.

2.6 The Water Yield of Undrained and Drained Mires

The water yield of a mire is the quantity of water discharged under the action of gravity from a peat deposit saturated up to or beyond its normal moisture capacity. The coefficient of water yield is a quantitative expression of the above property. The overall coefficient of water yield ξ is the ratio of the volume of water discharged from a layer of peat above the water table to the bulk volume of this layer, when the water table is lowered from the surface of the mire to a given horizon z. The layer coefficient ξ_z is the ratio of the volume of water discharged from a layer to the total volume of the layer, when the water table is lowered from its initial position z_1 to a final position z_2. The relation between the overall and layer coefficients of water yield is expressed by the equation

$$\xi_z = \frac{(\xi + d\xi)(z + dz) - \xi_z}{dz},$$
(2.22)

which follows immediately from the definition of the coefficients of water yield, when the water table is lowered by a small amount dz.

Replacing dz by Δz for practical calculations, we obtain an expression for the conversion of overall into layer coefficients:

$$\xi_z = z\frac{\Delta \xi}{\Delta z} + \xi + \Delta \xi.$$
(2.23)

The overall coefficient expresses the so-called *specific water yield*, by which is understood the quantity of water freely discharged per unit volume from a fully saturated soil lying above the water table (Lundin, 1964).

The quantity of water yield from the peat deposits of mire massifs depends upon the following factors:

(1) The initial moisture capacity of the different layers of peat, which is determined by the coefficient of saturation of the peat (2.15), and depends on the hydrodynamic equilibrium of the layers (2.13″ and 2.14′).

(2) The distance through which the water table declines from its initial position z_1, measured from the surface of the mire, to its final position z_2.

(3) The distribution of active porosity in the peat above the water table, which in turn is determined by the structure and dispersity of the solid peat matrix and the quantity of immobilized water in it (2.17).

(4) The compressibility of the kinds of peat which compose the deposit (2.13).

Theoretical calculations of water yield and determinations of the coefficients of water yield by functions allowing for all the enumerated physical factors involve complicated practical problems. They demand exact data about the floristic composition and degree of humification of the species of which the deposit is composed, about the differences between one part of a mire massif and another, and about the amount of water in the peat before the lowering of the water table. For that reason, practical calculations of the water yield of peat deposits are based upon a multitude of experimental data derived from numerous investigators concerning the coefficients of water yield of peat in natural and undrained mires and also for different types of microtope making up the acrotelm of undrained mires.

All these recent experimental determinations of the water yield of peat of undamaged structure making up the peat deposits of mires have been carried out by the use of four fundamental methods:

(1) Measuring moisture in the zone of aeration above the water table before and after lowering the water table by a certain amount.

(2) Testing samples in the form of tall columns of intact soil under laboratory conditions where the water yield is estimated from the volume of water discharged by the sample when the water table is lowered a certain distance Δz from its initial position z.

(3) Measuring rises in the water table of peat deposits when precipitation takes place under natural conditions (Vorob'ev, 1965; Ivanov, 1957b).

(4) Testing short samples in capillarimeters (tension cells), where samples are taken from different layers of a peat deposit or acrotelm so as to determine the quantity of capillary and bound (immobilized) water as a result of capillary suction in the matrix, which is modelled by the negative pressure created in the apparatus. From the point of view of studying the process of water yield and for obtaining data about the physical changes that depth produces in peat this last method is the most comprehensive, but when water distribution is stable supplementary calculations and data-processing are necessary for determining by this method the coefficients of water yield and their dependence on the position of the water table (Vorob'ev, 1969).

The general conclusion that emerges from this multitude of experimental data is the construction of empirical relationships between overall and layer coefficients and the depth of the water table z. This last is reckoned from the surface of the mire. In undrained mires, the mire surface is equated with the surface of the acrotelm (see section 2.5), but in drained mires (as in those used for agriculture, peat extraction and building sites), it is equated with the surface of the peat deposit or the cultivated soil.

This way of conceiving these empirical relations has a firm theoretical basis. The physical state of the peat deposit in undrained and drained mires (the compaction of the solid peat matrix above and below the water table, active porosity and the quantity and distribution of capillary and immobilized water) depends in the last resort on the vertical pressure and hydrodynamic forces acting on the solid matrix and on the compressional properties of each given kind of peat (see sections 2.2 and 2.3). Both in natural and in drained mires, the pressure on the solid matrix in each layer and the changes it undergoes are determined by the position of the water table relative to the surface. In this case, the moisture capacity of individual layers below the water table and the changes resulting from changes in the water table are determined by equations (2.13″) and (2.15′). On the other hand, except when all water is in the form of ice, the equilibrium distribution of capillary and immobilized water above the water table is determined by the distribution of active porosity through the whole height of the zone of aeration and the size of the pores in each of these layers, and is therefore a function of the position of the water table.

It follows that the theoretical expression of the layer coefficient of water yield as a function of the lowering of the water table by Δz from its initial horizon z_1 to any final position $z < h_p$ under equilibrium conditions, taking into account equations (2.13″) and (2.15), has the form

$$\xi_z = \frac{1}{\Delta z}\left[\int_{h_p}^{z_1} \eta_{w1}(z)\,\mathrm{d}z - \int_{h_p}^{z_2} \eta_{w2}(z)\,\mathrm{d}z + \bar{\eta}_1 z_1 - \bar{\eta}_2 z\right], \qquad (2.24)$$

where $z = (z_1 + z_2)/2$, h_p is the full depth of the peat deposit, $\eta_{w1}(z)$ is the function expressing the layer distribution of moisture capacity throughout the depth z, when the water table was at its original depth z_1, $\eta_{w2}(z)$ is the same when the water table is at $z_2 = z_1 + \Delta z$, $\bar{\eta}_1$ is the mean volumetric moisture content in the zone of aeration when the water table was at z_1, and $\bar{\eta}_z$ is the same, when the water table is at z_2.

Taking into account (2.14), we obtain in place of (2.24) an expression for the overall, as opposed to the layer, coefficient of water yield

$$\xi = \frac{1}{z}\left[\int_{h_p}^{0} \eta_{w,\,z=0}(z)\,\mathrm{d}z - \int_{h_p}^{z} \eta_{w,\,z}(z)\,\mathrm{d}z - \bar{\eta}_1 z\right], \qquad (2.25)$$

where $\eta_{w, z=0}$ is a function expressing the layer distribution of moisture capacity when the water table is at the surface—in undrained mires it is at the estimated surface of the microrelief of the acrotelm (see section 2.5)—and $\eta_{w, z}$ is a function expressing the layer distribution of moisture capacity throughout the depth of the deposit when the water table is at a given level z.

If we take into consideration changes in the compaction and active porosity above and below the water table due to changes in its level and the resulting alterations in the dynamic equilibrium of the deposit, then it is plain from these last equations (2.24) and (2.25) that the quantity of water discharged by a peat deposit above and below the water table is a function of the initial level of the water table and the amount by which it is lowered. By determining the quantity of discharge for each unit by which the water table is lowered (e.g. $\Delta z = 1$ cm), it is clearly possible to establish reliable empirical relationships between the position of the water table and, first of all, the layer, and then the overall coefficient of water yield. In some cases, the fall in the level may be large, and there may be a thick aerated zone below the surface of the acrotelm, or, in drained mires, below the surface of the peat. In such cases, these relations only reflect a difference in the moisture content after equilibrium has been established in the distribution of capillary and immobilized moisture above the water table and in the forces acting upon the solid matrix below the water table. For that reason, such empirical relationships can only be used in practical calculations when certain conditions are fulfilled. Firstly, the water yield of the mire massif must be measured over sufficiently long periods. Secondly, over these periods a static equilibrium of forces must be established between the solid and liquid phase both above and below water table, or, alternatively, the input and discharge of moisture at the surface must be subject to little variation. When the level of the water table is high in undrained mires, the amplitude of its fluctuations is relatively small, and in most cases does not much exceed the thickness of the acrotelm, whose pores are large and whose hydraulic conductivity is high. In such cases, a balanced distribution of moisture above the water table is quickly established, and static equations for water yield can be used even for calculations relating to short periods, e.g. 24 h.

Many investigators have measured the water yield of the acrotelm for different microtopes in undrained mires and for the peat deposits of drained mires, and have derived from them empirical functions relating the overall (2.25) and layer (2.24) coefficients of water yield to the position of the water table. The results of these measurements and the functions derived from them are given in their works (Aver'yanov, 1956; Vorob'ev, 1963, 1965, 1969; Ivanov, 1957b, 1963; Korchunov and Mogilevskiy, 1961a; Lundin, 1964; Maslov, 1970; Anon., 1971c).

In these researches it was assumed that the compression of the solid peat matrix in the acrotelm was little altered by changes of level and that this could be overlooked in practical calculations of $\xi_2 = f_1(z)$ and $\xi = f_2(z)$. In the case of massifs that had been or were being drained, the effect of compression and shrinkage on water yield and the accompanying changes in physical properties were allowed for indirectly in the empirical functions.

The very thorough researches of Vorob'ev (1969) were based on testing short samples in capillarimeters. This made it possible to determine the dependence of moisture distribution upon the position of the water table in the following way:

$$\eta_{H_0} = \rho \exp(n - k \log {}_p G) = \rho \exp(n - k \log H_0), \qquad (2.26)$$

where η_{H_0} is the moisture content (volumetric moisture expressed in percent) of a layer of peat of thickness Δz at the height H_0 above the water table, ρ is the density of the solid matrix in the layer Δz, n and k are coefficients dependent on the humification and floristic composition of the peat in the acrotelm, and dependent therefore on the type of microtope. In complex microtopes n and k are determined separately for the different microforms in the microrelief.

If H_0 is expressed in cm and ρ in gm/cm^3, then n and k for slightly humified peat (less than 10%) have the values shown in Table 4.

Table 4.

Botanical composition of layers of acrotelm (in natural deposits)	n	k
Sphagnum fuscum and *angustifolium*	8·33	0·87
Supersaturated sectors composed of *Sphagnum cuspidatum* and S. dusenii peat	8·96	1·165

The advantage of this relationship is its universal applicability. The moisture content of any given type of peat in different layers of the zone of aeration depends on the density of the solid matrix, or, in other words, on its degree of compaction. This relationship can be recommended for all calculations of the equilibrium water content of the acrotelm of natural mires, and of the coefficients of water yield of different kinds of peat. These were directly investigated in the above-mentioned experiments of Vorob'ev, whose results are given in Table 4. General physical principles and what we know about the plant cover of mires and about slightly humified peat of undamaged structure entitle us to assume that this relationship can also be used in calculations of the water yield from the acrotelm of all muscoid and muscoid-ligneous microtopes in undrained mires. In Fig. 14 we show the relationship

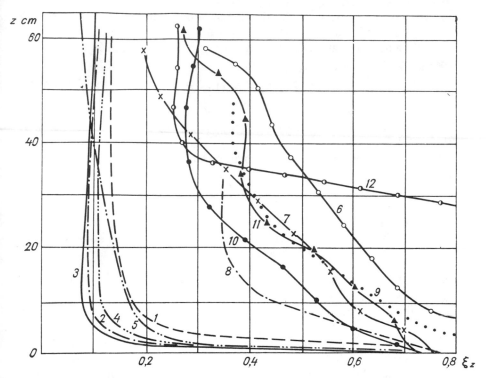

Fig. 14. Dependence of layer coefficients of water yield ζ_z upon level of water table z for different types of eutrophic microtopes (grass and grass-moss groups) and for oligotrophic moss microtopes. 1—*Hypnum*–sedge. 2—sedge–reed. 3—*Calamagrostis*–sedge–reed. 4—reed. 5—sedge-*Hypnum*. 6—pine–*Sphagnum*–shrub. 7—*Sphagnum*–shrub forested with pine. 8—*Sphagnum*–shrub–*Eriophorum* forested with pine. 9—*Sphagnum*–*Eriophorum*. 10—*Sphagnum*–shrub–*Eriophorum* ridges forested with pine in ridge–flark microtopes. 11—*Sphagnum*–shrub–pine ridges in ridge–pool microtopes. 12—*Sphagnum*–pine–*Scheuchzeria* and *Sphagnum*–*Scheuchzeria* flarks in ridge–flark microtopes.

of coefficients of water yield to the level of the water table for various types of bog and fen microtopes. Special investigations of the value of $\xi_z = f_1(z)$ for the same type of microtope in mires situated in regions far removed from each other show that they are practically identical. This justifies the use in calculations of empirical functions for water yield $\xi_z = f_1(z)$ obtained from different types of oligotrophic (bog) and eutrophic (fen) microtopes without reference to their geographical position.

The coefficients of water yield given in Fig. 14 may be used in dealing with complex ridge–flark microtopes of the muscoid group. We may then calculate the coefficients of water yield of the acrotelm of the whole microtope by means of the following equations:

(1) When the water table is at the surface of the flarks or lower $(z_1 > y)$, the equation used is

$$\xi'_z = \xi_{zr}P_r + \xi_{zf}(1 - P_r), \qquad (2.27)$$

where P_r is the fraction of surface of the microtope occupied by ridges, ξ_{zr} is the water yield of ridges at the level z, and ξ_{zf} the water yield of flarks at the same level.

(2) When the water table is above the surface of the flarks $(z_1 < y)$, the equation used is

$$\xi'_z = \xi_{zr}n_zP_r + \xi_{zf}(1 - n_zP_r), \qquad (2.28)$$

in which (compare (1a), (1b))

$$n_z = \sqrt{\frac{4}{L^2_{r_{max}}}(yz_1 - z_1^2) + \frac{z_1}{y}}. \qquad (2.29)$$

In this last expression, $L_{r_{max}}$ is the breadth of the ridge at its base, i.e. at the level $z_1 = y$, which is also the level of the flark, and z_1 is the distance from the top of the ridge to the water table. All other symbols have the same meaning as before.

Equation (2.29) is entailed by the equation of the cross-sectional profile of the mean surface of the ridge, if we take this as a segment with $L_{r_{max}}$ as its base, which field researches have shown to be very near the actual profile (Ivanov, 1957b). The value of $(4/L^2_{r_{max}})(yz_1 - z_1^2)$ is always small in comparison with z_1/y, and may therefore be disregarded. The factor n_z may then be expressed by the simple function;

$$n_z = \sqrt{\frac{z_1}{y}}. \qquad (2.30)$$

For example, to find the value of the coefficient of water yield for a layer in a ridge–flark microtope, when the ridge quotient (P_r) is 0.3 (30%) and the level of the water table from the CSM (Calculated Surface of the Microtope) is equal to -32.5 cm, we obtain from equation (2.27) on the basis of the data given in Fig. 14:

$$\xi_{z=-32.5} = 0.29 \times 0.3 + 0.55(1 - 0.3) = 0.47$$

With the same ridge quotient $(P_r = 0.3)$, $z = +12.5$ cm from the CSM, $y = 40$ cm, $z_1 = 0.5\,H_{rf} - z = 17.5 - 12.5 = 5$ cm, and $\xi_{zr} = 0.93$, the coefficient of water yield by equations (2.28) and (2.30) will obviously be:

$$\xi_{z=+12.5} = 0.93\sqrt{\frac{5}{40}} \times 0.3 + 1\left(1 - \sqrt{\frac{5}{40}} \times 0.3\right) = 0.99.$$

In the case of natural mires, the value of functions relating to the distribution of moisture capacity η_{w1} and η_{w2} and moisture content $\bar{\eta}_1$ and $\bar{\eta}_2$ in the zone of aeration, which are made use of in general expressions for the coefficient of water yield, is determined in the last resort by the position of the water table. This is due to the fact that changes in the load on the solid matrix and in active porosity are confined within limits set by the amplitude of seasonal fluctuations of level. When however peat massifs are drained and developed, the natural dynamic equilibrium of the deposit is completely destroyed. Increase in the depth of the zone of aeration and the amplitude of fluctuations of level, which in years of drought may fall below the interface between peat and mineral soil, if the latter is sandy, leads to a break in the continuity of capillaries and the formation of suspended capillary moisture, when the water table is lowered. For this reason, there is no clear correspondence between the layer coefficients of water yield and the level of the water table, and the correlation between them becomes extremely low.

Extensive researches into the water yield of drained peat deposits (both in the field and in the laboratory) have been carried out by Lundin (1964) and many others (Ivanov, 1957b; Maslov, 1970, etc.). According to these researches, the capillary rise for fen deposits in the zone of aeration is 50–110 cm with a maximum height of 175 cm. This last value is for sectors exposed to heavy precipitation and situated near the edge of drainage canals or peat quarries. Lundin has analysed data from 10 different mire massifs. This has enabled him to recommend for calculations of specific water yield (i.e. the overall coefficient of water yield), when $z > h_{c\,max}$, the following function:

$$\xi = 0.20\left(1 - \frac{0.7h_{c\,max}}{z}\right),\tag{2.31}$$

where $h_{c\,max}$ is the maximum capillary rise and z is the depth of the water table below the surface. When the depth of the water table $z < h_c$, the value of ξ varies from 0.06 to 0.10, depending upon the nature of the peat and its degree of humification and compaction after draining.

Lundin has calculated the relation of the overall coefficient of water yield (expressed as a fraction of its maximum value ξ/ξ_{max}) to the level of the water table for different degrees of compaction resulting from drainage and development. According to Lundin, the height of complete capillary saturation above the water table h_{0c} is an indication of the degree of compaction of the deposit. h_{0c} is obviously less than h_c, and the greater they both are, the greater the compaction and the less the active porosity. Calculations made from an empirical graph of $\xi/\xi_{max} = f(z)$ show that, on the basis of equation (2.31), we may take $\xi \cong 0.20$ as the maximum value, which occurs as $h_{c\,max}/z \to 0$. According to the experiments and data of Lundin, the value of ξ_{max} for various drained mires with fen peat deposits and differences in the intensity and period of draining to which they have been subjected varies between 0·13 and 0·26. For peat from raised mires that have been drained $\xi_{max} \cong 0·1$.

Maslov (1970) has compared the values recommended by various authors for the relation between water yield and seepage in the case of drained peat deposits. From them it appears that according to all formulae there is little change in the overall coefficient of water yield from a 1 m layer of peat (i.e. when the water table is lowered 1 m from the surface) for values of the coefficient of seepage between 0·001 and 0·01 cm/s. If we exclude the results of P. A. Betsinskiy of Hungary, which show the greatest deviations in the value of water yield, all the remaining results give values of ξ for a 1 m layer of peat within the limits shown in Table 5.

Table 5. Comparison of coefficient of seepage with extreme values of overall coefficient of water yield (ξ) from 1m layer of peat deposit

Coefficient of seepage, cm/s	0·0001	0·0005	0·001	0·005	0·01
Extreme values of ξ	0·5–0·01	0·025–0·08	0·05–0·12	0·09–0·18	0·17–0·24

The data we have considered about the water yield of drained mires shows greater variability in its values, because it is subject to the influence of many factors. This makes it difficult to compare the results of different authors and to avoid mistakes in selecting values for the purpose of calculation.

In approximate calculations of water balance carried out in compiling plans for draining or in estimating the effects of draining on areas that are being drained or those surrounding them, it is possible to make use of suitably adjusted functional relations and data.

2.7 The Hydraulic Conductivity of Peat in Natural and Drained Mires

The hydraulic conductivity of a peat deposit, as of any porous medium or soil, is the quantity of water flowing across a unit area whose surface is at every point perpendicular to the gradient of the forces acting upon the flow of liquid, when the gradient of these forces is equal to unity. The field of forces acting upon liquid enclosed in the pores of the soil is a potential one, since the movement of liquid within the pores is so small that forces of inertia can be overlooked and the magnitude of the forces acting upon the flow of liquid shows itself to be exclusively a function of the coordinates.

This implies that the movement of moisture at any point in a peat deposit is in the direction of the gradient of some potential function Φ which depends on the moisture content and moisture capacity of the peat (i.e. the nature and degree of compaction of the solid matrix). The moisture potential Φ, which describes the potential energy of the forces acting within the medium of dispersal as a function of the volume of water, is equal to the total energy attaching films of water at maximum distance from the soil matrix. It is therefore expressed numerically by the hydrostatic pressure of water in the pores of the soil (Korchunov, 1956; Lykov, 1954).

Symbolizing the flow of moisture across a unit of area by the vector $\mathbf{q}$, and the gradient of moisture potential by[6a]

$$\text{grad } \Phi = \mathbf{i}_1 \frac{\partial \Phi}{\partial x} + \mathbf{i}_2 \frac{\partial \Phi}{\partial y} + \mathbf{i}_3 \frac{\partial \Phi}{\partial z}, \qquad (2.32)$$

we shall write the general expression for the flow of moisture at a given point in a peat deposit in the form

$$\mathbf{q} = \lambda_w \text{ grad } \Phi, \qquad (2.33)$$

where λ_w is the general coefficient of hydraulic conductivity, which is a statement about the quantity of water flowing through a unit area with an equipotential surface when grad $\Phi = 1$.

Choosing the water table as the plane of comparison for levels of energy, we can write expressions for the moisture potential in the following form:

(a) Above the water table (in the zone of aeration)

$$\text{grad } \Phi = \frac{1}{C_w} \text{ grad } \eta = \text{grad}(\gamma h_a + \gamma h_{os} + \gamma h_c). \qquad (2.34)$$

(b) Below the water table[6b]

$$\text{grad } \Phi = - \text{ grad } \gamma h, \qquad (2.35)$$

where η is the volumetric moisture content of the peat, C_w the coefficient of change of water content per unit change of moisture potential, γ the specific weight of water, $(\gamma h_a + \gamma h_{os} + \gamma h_c)$ the negative hydrostatic pressure consisting of the potential energy of the forces of absorption (γh_a), osmosis (γh_{os}) and capillarity (γh_c) acting in the triple-phase medium above the water table, and γh the positive hydrostatic pressure below the water table.

The flow of moisture in the zone of aeration $\mathbf{q}_a$ will then be expressed by the equation

$$\mathbf{q}_a = \lambda_w \text{ grad}(\gamma h_a + \gamma h_{os} + \gamma h_c) = \frac{\lambda_w}{C_w} \text{ grad } \eta, \qquad (2.36)$$

in which permeability is numerically expressed by the coefficient λ_w.

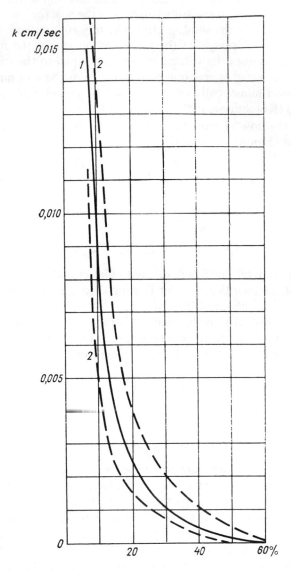

Fig. 15. General dependence of coefficients of seepage of peat upon its degree of humification (%) in natural deposits of undamaged structure. 1—curve of mean value of coefficient of seepage (k) of peat bed. 2—maximum deviation of value from point to point in a peat bed.

For layers of peat situated below the water table, in which water movement is the result of a gradient due to the force of gravity, the flow of moisture is

$$\mathbf{q} = k \operatorname{grad} \gamma h. \tag{2.37}$$

Here the permeability of peat is expressed by the coefficient of seepage k, and (2.37) is an expression of Darcy's law [6c].

As was shown earlier (see sections 2.2 and 2.3 and equations (2.19), (2.17) and (2.13)), the coefficient of seepage depends on the active porosity of peat, which in turn is determined by the pressure on the solid matrix and the immobilized water that is united to it. For that reason, hydraulic conductivity, which is expressed numerically by the coefficients of seepage and permeability, changes when the pressure on the solid matrix is altered by fluctuations in the water table.

It is now possible, with the help of numerous researches into the coefficient of seepage of peat (Dubakh, 1944; Ivanov, 1953b, 1957b; Lundin, 1964, etc.), to define the general conditions upon which this coefficient depends in the acrotelm and catotelm of natural mires and in the peat deposits of mires that have been drained and developed. In the catotelm of undrained mires, the coefficient of seepage of peat depends on the degree of dispersion of the solid matrix and on the degree of saturation of the peat (below the water table). Growth in the number of small and very small particles in the peat, i.e. in the degree of humification, and correspondingly in the area of interface between the liquid and the solid phase, leads to a diminution of the coefficient of seepage, whose value ranges from $10^{-2} a$ to $10^{-6} a$ cm/s, where a is a positive number from 1 to 10.

Since the floristic composition of the peat, the volumetric weight or compaction of the solid matrix and the moisture saturation of peat deposits are all closely connected with the degree of humification, the fundamental physical criterion for determining the coefficient of seepage is the degree of humification. At any given degree of humification, floristic composition makes little difference to the coefficient. In determining the coefficient of a natural peat bed of a given degree of humification, differences in the floristic composition of the peat have less effect on seepage than differences in position within the peat bed. The right-hand column of Table 6 shows the limits within which the filtration coefficient k fluctuates in a natural deposit, and the effect of small changes of position in a peat bed at the same stage of humification. Figure 15, in agreement with Table 6, shows the general relationship between the average coefficient of seepage and the degree of humification in a natural peat deposit. In compiling it, average values of k for all kinds of peat and all degrees of humification were used.

As the hydraulic conductivity of peat depends on its active porosity, and not on its full physical porosity, changes in the coefficient of seepage are due

Table 6. Calculated values of coefficient of seepage of different kinds of peat in catotelm of undrained mires (excluding flooded sections of mires)

Type of peat in natural deposit and degree of humification	Coefficient of seepage (cm/s)	
	Average value	Limits of variation
Fen peat (*Hypnum*–sedge, sedge, sedge–*Sphagnum*)		
Slightly humified (25–30%)	0·005	0·002–0·01
Moderately humified (40–55%)	0·0008	0·0002–0·002
Bog peat		
Very slightly humified (up to 10%)	0·015	0·01–0·025
Slightly humified (10–20%)	0·004	0·002–0·007
Moderately humified (35–45%)	0·0005	0·00025–0·001
Much humified (55–65%)	5×10^{-5}	2×10^{-6}–8×10^{-5}

to two main factors—external pressure on the solid matrix, which determines how closely the organic particles of peat and the bound water they contain are compacted, and the quantity of immobilized water in the particles of peat, which determines the size, or (to simplify the physics of the phenomenon) the "swollenness" of the particles. When peat is drained, these two factors have opposite effects upon the coefficient of seepage. On the one hand, pressure on the solid matrix is increased by lowering the water table because of the increased weight of material and capillary moisture lying above the water table. The solid matrix becomes more compact and so reduces the free and active porosity of the material, which must reduce its coefficient of seepage. On the other hand, the partial dehydration of the peat above the new level of the water table and the process of evaporation reduces the size of the particles and increases the porosity of the material, thereby increasing the coefficient of seepage.

Because these two processes partly compensate each other, the change in active porosity produced by drainage is relatively small. According to the researches of numerous authors, it is reduced 1·2 to 100 times, which means that at its maximum it is two orders of magnitude less than in undrained peat deposits. Numerous measurements made by different researchers (Dzektser, 1959; Lundin, 1964, Maslov, 1970; Boelter, 1965, etc.) under different conditions go to prove this. The changes produced by draining in the coefficient of seepage are not uniform. They may be quite insignificant, or they may reduce its original value by two orders of magnitude, according to whether one or other of the two above-mentioned causes predominates. Each of them in turn is a product of the original degree of saturation of the mire massif and the source of its water supply, which may come from below under pressure, from the side in the form of free-flowing groundwater, or from the atmosphere.

Lundin (1964) and Maslov (1970) are responsible for the most careful researches and the best analyses of previous work on the coefficient of seepage of drained peat deposits. The best established formula for the coefficients of drained mires is that recommended by Lundin. According to this, they depend on the depth of the water table after drainage and the time that has elapsed since draining and the lowering of the water table. After draining, time brings about a change in the physical state of everything, both through the increased compaction of the peat and through the improved access of oxygen, which results in increased oxidation and activation of biochemical processes. Lundin's equation takes the form

$$k = k_0 e^{-tz}, \tag{2.38}$$

where k_0 is the initial coefficient of seepage, which is that obtaining when the water table is at or near the surface and corresponds to conditions in undrained mires ($z = 0$), and t is the coefficient expressing the influence of the time elapsed since draining, or the age-of-drainage coefficient.

Table 7 cites Lundin's values for this coefficient. As one would expect, the values of t begin to increase immediately after the draining of the mire and reach their maximum in 10–12 years. Consequently, the coefficient of seepage of drained peat deposits reaches its minimum in 10–12 years. After that, the values of t decline somewhat, and the coefficient of seepage increases correspondingly.

Table 7. Values of parameter t

Number of years after draining	Up to 1	2	5	10	15	20	25	30
Values of t, when depth of level z is expressed in metres		1·0	2·8	4·0	4·5	4·4	4·0	3·6	3·4

The discovery of this temporal pattern in the changes of the coefficient of seepage of drained peat deposits seems to show that in the first 10 years the chief factor in the modification of hydraulic conductivity is the process of compaction, whereas after that physico-chemical changes in the composition of peat, including those due to agricultural technology, begin to play the predominating role.

It should be noted that the time-dependence of k, as investigated by Lundin, is based upon data obtained from observations in drained mires that had been used after draining for agricultural production. When mires are drained for any other use, such as cutting peat, the effect of time on the value of k may very naturally be different. Such observations are not available, however, for at the present time there are no cases where land has been drained for 25 years or more, except where this has been done for agricultural purposes.

Despite this, there is no reason to expect any great error, if we accept Lundin's data and recommendations as a basis for calculations relating to drained mires, even where drainage has taken place for some different kind of operation. On the basis of existing data and observations, Lundin calculates that, when fen deposits are drained, their hydraulic permeability is reduced from 10 to 70 times according to their condition before draining, and that it is reduced almost 100 times when raised mire deposits of *Sphagnum–Eriophorum* peat are drained. Making use of equation (2.38), the expected reduction of the coefficient of seepage produced by drainage can be expressed by the relationship

$$\frac{k_1}{k_2} = e^{t(\bar{z}_2 - \bar{z}_1)}, \tag{2.39}$$

where k_1 and k_2 are the coefficients of seepage before and after draining, and z_1 and z_2 are the mean levels of the water table before and after draining without allowance for seasonal fluctuations.

Despite the large amount of experimental material upon which the deduction of the above relationships is based, the physical changes produced by drainage are so complex and due to so many different factors that it is impossible at this stage to evaluate them and obtain by calculation exact figures for the coefficient of seepage of drained peat deposits. As Lundin rightly points out, this work involves a study of the influence of drainage on the seepage properties of peat, in which a distinction must be drawn between the changes occurring in layers that lie below the mean water table and those occurring in layers that lie above it. Engineering practice has shown that the best way to determine the coefficient of seepage after draining and the physical changes produced by the development of a drained massif is to deduce the coefficient of seepage from the volumetric content of the solid peat matrix. Lundin has worked out the following functions for this on the basis of his experimental investigations:

For fen peat deposits: $k = \dfrac{16\cdot8}{\exp[0\cdot98(V_p^{pm} - 4\cdot5)]}$,   (2.40)

For raised mire peat deposits: $k = \dfrac{1\cdot75}{\exp[2\cdot3(V_p^{pm} - 4)]}$,   (2.41)

in which k is the coefficient of seepage in metres per day and V_p^{pm} is the volume of the solid matrix per unit volume of peat deposit expressed in percentages.

To calculate V_p^{pm} after draining from the known depth of the water table and the time elapsed since draining, Lundin recommends the relationships:

For fen deposits: $$V_p^{pm} = 4\cdot5 + 2\cdot35 \times \log\frac{16\cdot8}{k_0} + 1\cdot02tz_{dr}. \qquad (2.42)$$

For bog deposits: $$V_p^{pm} = 4\cdot26 + 2\cdot1tz_{dr}, \qquad (2.43)$$

in which z_{dr} is the average depth of the water table after draining, k_0 the coefficient of seepage before draining (i.e. when $z = 0$), and t the age-of-drainage coefficient as defined in Table 7. For practical calculations of the coefficient of seepage according to equations (2.40) and (2.41), it is best to base values of V_p^{pm} upon data drawn from laboratory tests in the field of samples of peat of undamaged structure taken from drained deposits.

According to the data of Maslov, after the draining of fens in the Meshchera lowlands and the flood plain of the river Yakhroma, the coefficient of seepage was reduced only 1·2 to 5 times, which is significantly less than in Lundin's researches. These results, like the data of many other authors, show that the researches carried out to date are far from enough to establish a general relation (obviously a very complex one) between changes in the hydraulic conductivity of peat deposits and the chief factors that affect it when draining takes place, which are the initial degree of humification and botanical composition of the peat, the initial saturation and water supply of the massif, the type of drainage used and the level of drainage achieved, the time elapsed since draining, and the use to which the massif is subsequently put.

The effects of the passage of time after draining must be different in different climatic conditions, since the speed at which peat is consolidated and transformed biochemically depends on how the temperature and wetness of the area change with the seasons.

The hydraulic conductivity of the acrotelm of undrained mire massifs exceeds by thousands and tens of thousands of times that of the beds of peat that make up the catotelm. The limits of change in the acrotelm are from $10^{-2}a$ to 10^2a cm/s. If, however, we treat the speed of flow in the zone of semi-superficial runoff as a linear function of the slope (the pressure gradient) according to Darcy's law, which is perfectly legitimate at low velocities (Ivanov, 1957b), then the maximum values of the coefficient of seepage in the acrotelm of undrained mires may reach as high as 10^3 cm/s.

Seepage in the acrotelm of undrained mires differs materially in its physical nature from the seepage of ground water in the catotelm. This is due to the large size of the pores found in the living and the dead, but undecayed, plant cover of the acrotelm, which changes sharply with depth and causes the changes in seepage to which we drew attention earlier. On the other hand, the presence of a relatively hard, elastic matrix of undecayed plants belonging to the plant associations from which the peat is formed gives rise to a relatively constant distribution of active porosity through the whole depth of the acrotelm, which changes little when fluctuations of the water table alter the pressure on the solid matrix. This applies in the first place to those structural elements of microtopes and their microrelief, whose moss cover is reinforced by trees and shrubs belonging to the same plant associations. In herb-rich microtopes the rhizomes of sedges, like *Eriophorum* and deer's hair, of grasses, of reeds, etc. play the same reinforcing role and increase the stability of the acrotelm. Owing to these biophysical peculiarities of the acrotelm's structure, its hydraulic conductivity can be adequately characterized by stable empirical functions relating values of the coefficient of seepage to distance from the surface of the mire. The nature of these depends upon the type of plant associations which make up the microtopes or the large structural elements of which they are composed (in the case of complex microtopes). Figure 16 gives examples of relationships connecting the values of the coefficient of seepage k_z with depth z in the acrotelm of microtopes of the herb-rich group (sedge–*Hypnum* and *Calamagrostis*–birch) and of large structural elements of complex microtopes of the *Sphagnum*–pine–shrub group.

Research carried out over the years in the mireland hydrological stations of the Hydrometeorological Service into the relationship $k_z = f(z)$ for different types of microtope has made it possible to obtain the necessary physical foundation for hydrological calculations relating to the water regime of mires and the horizontal exchange of water between them and the areas of land and water that surround them (Ivanov, 1957b, 1963; Anon., 1971c), as well as to make the generalizations that are necessary for a scientific hydrology of mires.

2.8 Mire Microtopes and Massifs. Their Basic Hydrodynamic Properties

Any mire massif which forms a meso- or a microtope is a systematically constructed whole consisting of a number of microtopes (or facies), which differ from each other in the composition and structure of their plant cover, and, correspondingly, in the physical properties of their acrotelms. Calculations of their hydrometeorological regimes cannot be based upon the results of research into the physical properties of their plant cover and peat deposits, unless experimental descriptions of their properties are linked to definite types of microtopes, which are the elementary geographical units out of which mires are built. This makes it possible to construct wide generalizations from the data, and to extend the results of experimental research to other types of mire massif, making use of aerial survey for this purpose (see

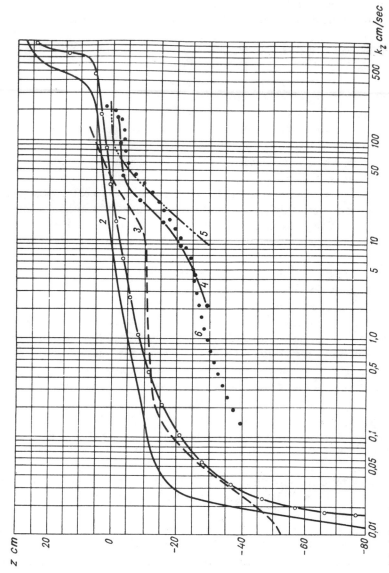

Fig 16. Empirical functions connecting changes in the layer coefficients of filtration with depth in the acrotelm of various types of microtope—$k_z = f(z)$, 1—sedge–*Hypnum*; 2—*Calamagrostis*–birch; 3—pine–*Sphagnum*–shrub on elevated element of microrelief; 4—complex microtope of strip-ridge structure with *Sphagnum*–shrub–pine ridge element of microrelief forested with pine; 6—*Sphagnum*–shrub microtope forested with pine on elevated element of microrelief.

sections 1.7 and 1.8). In this way, theoretical relationships for calculating the water regimes of mire massifs may be deduced which are based upon the general laws of their formation and development.

A hydrodynamic description of a mire massif necessarily includes:

(1) The level of the water table, and the amplitude of its fluctuation and variations of level over the area of the mire massif.

(2) Laws relating changes in the hydraulic conductivity of the acrotelm and the peat deposit to position in the mire massif and depth below its surface.

(3) Laws relating changes in the water yield of the acrotelm and the peat deposit to changes in the water table.

(4) The thickness of the acrotelm and how this varies over the area of the massif.

(5) The amount of seepage in the acrotelm and the peat deposit and how it varies at different points and at different depths below the surface of the massif.

(6) A modulus of seepage and its variations over the area of the massif.

For any given type of microtope, the above characteristics, so far as they relate to the acrotelm, must remain unchanged within the part of the mire massif which this type occupies. Hence changes in these characteristics over the area of the mire massif are in general determined by the number of microtopes and their situation within it. There are well-defined laws for the distribution of microtopes in different types of mesotope, and corresponding laws also for changes in their hydrodynamic characteristics.

In muurotopes the component mesotopes may be more varied and their mutual relations more complex. Territorial changes in their hydrodynamic characteristics should be considered along directions with clearly defined properties, such as the direction of the greatest slopes perpendicular to the contours of the mire (see section 2.9), which can easily be determined by aerial photography (see section 1.8).

In this way, mire systems of any degree of complexity can be described by appropriate laws describing changes in hydrological characteristics as between one area and another.

These same characteristics, considered now in their relation to the peat deposit, and not to the acrotelm, do not change over the area of the massif in complete correspondence with the location of the different types of microtope since the present vegetation and structure is not a reliable guide to the stratigraphy of peat deposits, nor to the degree of humification and floristic composition of the layers of peat of which they are composed. In fact, the connection between different types of mire microtope and the types of peat in their catotelm is by no means a necessary one and has varying degrees of intimacy (Romanova, 1960).

Let us now define certain important concepts. We shall call the *water table* in mires the position of the boundary which, at a given atmospheric pressure, divides the zone where the peat deposit is completely saturated and contains both free gravitating water and water bound to the solid matrix from the zone of aeration, which contains only bound water (see section 2.3).[7] Here the position of this boundary is determined by means of dip wells. In each microtope the datum plane is taken to be *either* the average surface of the zone of development of the microrelief *or* the suitably adjusted average surface of the elevated and depressed microforms in the place where the dip well is situated (see section 2.5).

As the researches of Korchunov and Mogilevskiy (1961b) have shown, determination of the true level of the water table in mires by means of the usual dip wells is subject to certain errors through the influence upon the water level in the well of the distribution and magnitude of the water potential in the zone of aeration. The divergence of the level in the dip well from the true position of the water table in the deposit increases with the degree of humification and the diameter of the well. When the degree of humification is low and the pores of the acrotelm are large, these errors are small and can usually be overlooked. When, however, arrangements are being made to measure the water table in deeper layers of the catotelm, which are composed of peat of an intermediate degree of humification, it is necessary to allow for this by reducing the cross-section of the dip well as much as possible and making the necessary corrections to the readings.

The difference between the highest and lowest levels in the interval of time with which one is concerned is called *the amplitude of oscillation of the water table.* We may therefore speak of the annual, monthly, ten-day and daily, as well as of the secular (multi-annual) amplitude of its fluctuation. This last is the difference of level between the highest and lowest positions that have been observed in a period of many years. Since the amplitude of oscillation of the level is an important physical characteristic of the water regime of mires and its quantitative expression is unconnected with the artificially chosen datum plane used in reading levels, application of the fundamental principles of hydrological statistics and the construction of frequency and probability curves give an idea, not of the artificial variation of this magnitude, but of its special values in different microtopes for each type of plant association and in different parts of the mire massif. In the very same way, deviations in the level readings from the average surface of the mire make it possible to estimate correctly changes in the aeration of the acrotelm and in the ecological conditions of the vegetation.

By the seepage of a mire massif we understand the flow of moisture or discharge of water which filters through the catotelm or acrotelm below the water table across a unit area of surface at right angles to the pressure gradient in that place. Seepage will be expressed in general by equation (2.37).

Let us consider a section of a mire massif (Fig. 17) along any arbitrarily chosen line 0–s where the slope of the surface is greatest (see Fig. 18). This we shall take as the direction of the horizontal coordinate with 0 as the point of origin. The vertical axis y is drawn downwards from 0. As before, we shall indicate the flow of moisture at a certain point $s_0 y_0$ of the massif by the vector $\mathbf{q}$. We shall break this down into its vertical and horizontal components ($\mathbf{q}_y$ and $\mathbf{q}_x$), which we shall describe as the vertical and horizontal seepage of the massif at the given point. Taking into account the facts that there are no impermeable layers in a peat deposit and that there is only one water-bearing horizon where the distribution is subject to hydrostatic principles, changes of pressure h in a horizontal direction in every layer of the deposit must be determined by the slope of the free surface of the water table i_g (i.e. the ground-water gradient—GWG). In a vertical direction, however, such changes are determined by the position of the layer in the peat deposit. Each of these has its own coefficient of filtration, its own thickness and a pressure that may vary from what obtains at the water table to what obtains in the layer of subjacent soil in immediate contact with the peat.

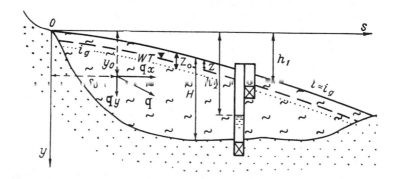

Fig. 17. Section along the flowline of a mire massif. The lower dotted line at a depth z_0 below the surface of the mire represents the boundary between the acrotelm and the catotelm (T).

Under these conditions, the horizontal seepage in the jth layer of the deposit $\mathbf{q}_{xj}$ is expressed by the relationship

$$\mathbf{q}_{xj} = i_g k_j, \qquad (2.44)$$

and will be different for every given layer j because of its dependence upon the hydraulic conductivity k_j.

Because water flows continuously and is not compressible, vertical seepage q_y must be identical for any given layer and is expressed by a well-known relationship derived from ground water hydraulics (Kamenskiy, 1935):

$$q_y = KI = \frac{K(h_1 - h_2)}{H} = \frac{h_1 - h_2}{\sum\limits_{1}^{n} \dfrac{H_j}{k_j}}, \qquad (2.45)$$

where n is the number of layers of peat deposit (soil) with different coefficients of seepage, H_j the thickness of the jth layer, H the thickness of the deposit $(H = \sum\limits_{1}^{n} H_j)$, $(h_1 - h_2)$ the difference of capillary head or fall of pressure in a vertical direction between the level of the water table h_1 and the piezometric level h_2 at the boundary of the deposit with the mineral soil (see Fig. 17), I the average gradient of vertical pressure, and K the hydraulic conductivity of the peat in a vertical direction. From this it follows that

$$K = \frac{H}{\sum\limits_{1}^{n} \dfrac{H_j}{k_j}}. \qquad (2.46)$$

It also follows that q_y has a positive value when $h_1 > h_2$, i.e. where the pressure at the bottom of the deposit is greater than at the surface. In that case, the vertical filtration (seepage) of the mire massif is directed upwards, which means that it has a pressure supply of water from the subjacent aquifers. When $h_2 > h_1$, vertical seepage is directed downwards, which means that the mire massif loses part of the water it contains to the subjacent horizons.[8]

The piezometric pressures $h_1, h_2, \ldots$ at different points of the peat deposit of a mire massif are determined by means of dip wells with filters placed at various levels to measure the pressure in the corresponding beds of peat. The total horizontal seepage at a given place in a mire massif, or, in other words, the unitary horizontal filtrational discharge is

$$q_z = i_g \sum\limits_{1}^{n} k_j H_j, \qquad (2.47)$$

where q_z is the horizontal filtrational discharge across a vertical cross-section, whose height is $(H - z)$ and whose breadth is unity, z is the distance of the water table below the surface of the mire in the given microtope (see Fig. 17), and n is the number of layers of peat with different coefficients of seepage in the thickness $(H - z)$.

When the coefficient of seepage changes continuously with depth, (2.47) may be replaced by the expression

$$q_z = i_g \int_z^{H-z} k_z \, dH, \tag{2.48}$$

where k_z is the value of the coefficient of seepage in a layer at a distance z from the surface of the mire.

Dividing the whole thickness of the peat deposit into a catotelm or inactive horizon $(H - z_0)$ and an acrotelm or active horizon z_0 (see Fig. 17), we may write this last expression as the sum of two quantities:

$$q_z = i_g \int_z^{z_0} k_z \, dH + i_g \int_{z_0}^{H-z_0} k_z \, dH. \tag{2.49}$$

The first term expresses the part of the horizontal discharge of water that seeps through the acrotelm, and the second the part that seeps through the catotelm. In view of the high hydraulic conductivity of the acrotelm in comparison with the catotelm (see section 2.7), it is possible to disregard the part that seeps through the catotelm in calculating the total horizontal seepage. As was shown in an earlier work (Ivanov, 1953a), the size of the second term in expression (2.49) constitutes less than one tenth of a per cent of the first. It follows that in calculating the unitary discharge q_z, when the water table lies within the acrotelm $(z < z_0)$, we may omit the second part of (2.49) and suppose, since $dH = dz$, that

$$q_z \cong i_g \int_z^{z_0} k_z \, dz . \tag{2.50}$$

In this equation the relationship $k_z = f(z)$ is determined through the data considered in section 2.7.

Since the relief of the mean surface of mire massifs (see section 2.5) practically coincides with the relief of the water table (Ivanov, 1957b), one can replace the values of the slopes of the water table i_g with equivalent values of the slopes of the average surface of the mire i in all expressions for horizontal seepage (2.47–2.50).

When the water table is at z, the relation of the unitary horizontal discharge q_z *to the slope of the mean surface of the mire i is called the modulus of horizontal seepage, and is symbolized by* M_z.

It follows from equation (2.50) that there are two ways of expressing the modulus of seepage:

$$M_z = \frac{q_z}{i} = \int_{z_0}^z k_z \, dz, \tag{2.51}$$

and that it can be calculated for each type of mire microtope by known empirical relationships of the form $k_z = f(z)$ (Table 1 of the Appendix). The modulus of seepage is therefore a function of the water table and describes the horizontal seepage of the acrotelm of mire microtopes of different types at a given level z of the water table. The relation of values of M_z to values of z for different types of microtope is given in Appendix 1. Knowing the values of M_z and the slope of the mean surface of a given microtope i, it is possible to calculate the horizontal seepage for any level of the water table z:

$$\mathbf{q}_z = M_z i. \tag{2.52}$$

The modulus of vertical seepage M_y, as is plain from equations (2.45) and (2.46), is equal to the hydraulic conductivity of the peat in a vertical direction, and, when the coefficient k_z changes continuously with depth, it is expressed in accordance with equations (2.45) and (2.46) in the form

$$M_y = \frac{\mathbf{q}_y}{I} = \frac{H-z}{\displaystyle\int_0^{H-z} \frac{\mathrm{d}z}{k_z}} \tag{2.53}$$

The values of the moduli of seepage in a horizontal and a vertical direction describe the intensity of water movement in the given place, and are comparable physical parameters for different types of mire microtope and peat deposit. We now introduce the concept of an average modulus of seepage $\overline{M}_z$. This is the relation of the average long-term horizontal seepage $\overline{\mathbf{q}}_z$ to the slope of the surface of the mire massif at the given point. In this case, we have on the basis of (2.51)

$$\overline{M}_z = \frac{\overline{\mathbf{q}}_z}{i} = \int_{z_0}^{\overline{z}} k_z\, \mathrm{d}z, \tag{2.54}$$

where $\overline{z}$ is the average level of the water table corresponding to the average seepage $\overline{\mathbf{q}}_z$.

We now introduce the concept of a mean coefficient of seepage $\overline{k}_0$ in the acrotelm corresponding to a mean long-term level of the water table $\overline{z}$.

$$\overline{k}_0 = \frac{\displaystyle\int_{z_0}^{\overline{z}} k_z\, \mathrm{d}z}{z_0 - \overline{z}}, \tag{2.55}$$

where z_0 is the thickness of the acrotelm. In place of (2.54), we now obtain another expression for the average modulus of seepage in the form

$$\overline{M}_z = \overline{k}_0(z_0 - \overline{z}). \tag{2.56}$$

Using equations (2.54) and (2.56), we obtain a relationship for the mean horizontal seepage of the acrotelm:

$$\bar{\mathbf{q}}_z = i\bar{k}_0(z_1 - \bar{z}). \tag{2.57}$$

A similar expression can obviously be found for seepage at any level of the water table z:

$$\mathbf{q}_z = ik_0(z_0 - z), \tag{2.58}$$

where k_0 is the mean coefficient of seepage in the layer where the seepage occurs $(z_0 - z)$, when the water table is at z.

This last equation describes the curve relating horizontal seepage, or the unitary discharge of water, in the acrotelm to the level of the water table at a given point in the mire massif.

The definitions of mire microtope or facies (p. 16) and acrotelm (p. 58) preclude any change in the physical properties of an acrotelm in the area occupied by one and the same microtope. Therefore within the limits of the area occupied by a given type of microtope, the following elements must remain constant: the function $k_z = f(z)$, which describes the distribution of the coefficient of seepage in the acrotelm; the function $\xi_z = \xi(z)$, which relates water yield to the level of the water table (see section 2.6); the values of z_0, z, k_0 and $\mathbf{q}_z$; and the chemical quality of the water. That being so, it follows from (2.57) that the slope in one and the same type of microtope must also be constant.

The hydrological description of a mire microtope involves a conjunction of constant values for the above parameters. Two important consequences flow from this: firstly, a change in any of these parameters entails a change in the composition and structure of the plant cover, i.e. of the type of mire microtope, and secondly, the function that related the unitary discharge $\mathbf{q}_z$ to the level of the water table z (2.58) must remain unchanged within the limits of one and the same type of microtope.

We shall now go on to consider the hydrodynamic characteristics of a mire massif, which it is always possible to treat as a well-ordered system constructed out of microtopes. As was pointed out in section 1.7, a mire massif may represent either a single mesotope or a system of mesotopes, i.e. a mire macrotope. In both cases, the fundamental structural unit is the mire microtope. A hydrological description of a mire massif must therefore reflect the properties of an entire group of mutually connected microtopes. To convince ourselves of this, let us consider expressions relating to the average modulus of seepage like (2.56) and (2.54). From these equations it is plain that all the three hydrological parameters of a mire microtope, z_0, $\bar{z}$ and $k_z = f(z)$, may change without involving any change in $\bar{M}_z$. It follows that any particular value of the modulus of seepage $\bar{M}_z$ represents a group of mutually related microtopes, such that, if suitable changes occur in the values of z_0, $\bar{z}$ and k_0, the product $(z_0 - \bar{z}) \times \bar{k}_0$, or the integral $\int_{z_0}^{z} k_z \, dz$, may continue to be equal to the given value of the modulus. In other words, the expressions (2.56) and (2.54) are a condition defining a group of microtopes possessing the given value of the average modulus of seepage $\overline{M}_z$. Consideration of the different principles affecting changes of the moduli of seepage $\overline{M}_z$ and $\overline{M}_y$ over the areas of mire massifs (whether they be mesotopes or macrotopes) should produce comparable characterizations of the different meso- and macrotopes.

Let us begin by considering the rules relating to changes in the average modulus of horizontal seepage $\overline{M}_z$ along the lines of maximal slope s, which we regarded earlier as having a curvilinear set of coordinates along the horizontal plane (see Fig. 17). Since the slopes of the water table coincide with those of the average surface of the mire, we may obviously lay it down that along any line s in a mire massif

$$i = i_g = \frac{dy}{ds}, \tag{2.59}$$

where y is the ordinate of the points on the surface of the mire in the given system of coordinates.

The direction of the lines of maximal slope s also defines the direction of the greatest velocity of horizontal seepage in the acrotelm and peat deposit and, in accordance with equations (2.50) and (2.52), the direction of horizontal seepage $\mathbf{q}_z$ at any given point in the area of the massif. In that way, the s-lines taken together define the rates of horizontal seepage, and are known as the flow-net or network of lines of flow of the horizontal movement of mire waters (Ivanov, 1953a, 1957b). The law of the change of the average modulus of seepage $\overline{M}_z$ along any line of flow s is subject to variation. For that reason, the hydrological description of a mire massif is in its general form a conjunction of functions

$$\overline{M}_{zi} = f_i(s_1), \tag{2.60}$$

expressing a multiplicity of changes of the modulus of seepage along flowlines covering the whole area of the massif.

As will be shown later (see sections 2.13, 2.14), any particular mire massif can be broken down into a finite number of fragments or sections with an identical law for the change of $\overline{M}_z$ along any flowline within this fragment. This makes it possible to characterize any particular mire massif by means of a few different functions $\overline{M}_{zi}$ equal to the number of simple fragments, into which the complicated flow net of a mire macrotope can be broken down. Mire massifs of symmetrical form, having, for example, in plan the form of a circle or a rectangle with parallel flowlines, are sufficiently characterized by a single function $\overline{M}_z$ since they consist of only one fragment, and the law of the change of $\overline{M}_z$ remains the same along any flowlines in such massifs. From this it follows that the complexity of the hydrological structure of any particular mire massif can be quantitatively estimated.

Let us suppose that the total number of fragments, into which a mire massif can be broken down, is equal to N. Let the number of these fragments having different functions $\overline{M}_z$, i.e. the variety of fragments, be $N_p \leqslant N$. It is then obvious that the relation

$$\frac{N_p}{N} = N_p^*　　　　　　(2.60')$$

will express the relative magnitude of the variety of the fragments of the massif, i.e. the amount of variety per fragment, and may be a measure of the complexity of the structure of a massif containing a given variety of fragments N_p.

Let us consider an example. Let two different massifs have the same multiplicity of different fragments, say 5; but let one of them contain 20 fragments, the other 5. In the first case $N_p^* = 0.25$, and in the second $N_p^* = 1$. Taken together the two magnitudes N_p and N_p^* may obviously serve as a full measure of the complexity of the structure of the system. In the first of the two cases considered the conjunction has the value:

$$N_p = 5, N_p^* = 0.25;$$

in the second:

$$N_p = 5, N_p^* = 1.$$

It will be noted that in the second case, where the number of varieties is 5, the massif has the simplest possible structure, since it contains the minimum number of fragments compatible with this degree of variety. In the first case, where the number of varieties is again 5, the arrangement of the different fragments is much more complex. From the above argument and example, it is plain that the less N_p^* is and the greater N_p, the more complex the structure of the massif. Thus in the case of large mire systems it is always possible to estimate the relative complexity of their structure without making use of particular values of the function $\overline{M}_{zi} = f_i(s_i)$. These last will be considered, as already mentioned, in sections 2.13 and 2.14.

Table 8 gives the values of the average seepage, the average moduli of seepage and the characteristic slopes for the commonest types of mire microtope.

Table 8. Hydrological characteristics of mire microtopes

Groups of types of mire microtopes	Mean long-term amount of seepage $\bar{q}_z$ (l/s/km)	Mean long-term modulus of seepage $\bar{M}_z$ (cm²/s)	Characteristic slope of mire and water table surface along flowline i_s
1. Pine–shrub (stand height 9–13 m)	0·5–1·5	0·5–0·7	0·01–0·02
2. Pine–*Sphagnum*–shrub (stand height 4–6 m)	0·7–2	1·4–2·5	0·005–0·008
3. *Sphagnum*–shrub and *Sphagnum*–shrub–*Eriphorum*, forested with pine (in central parts of convex massifs)	1–2·5	8–16	0·00125–0·0015
4. Ridge–flark of strip-ridge structure and ridge–pool:			
(A) Ridge–flark complexes with *Sphagnum*–shrub microtopes having pine on ridges and *Sphagnum*–*Scheuchzeria* in flarks with open water surface:			
(a) Ridges—80%; Flarks—20%; y_{max} = 30 cm	0·8–2	2·2–5	0·0037–0·004
(b) Ridges—70%; Flarks—30%; y_{max} = 26 cm	0·8–2	2·7–5·7	0·0030–0·0035
(B) Ridge–flark complexes with *Sphagnum*–shrub microtopes having pine on ridges and *Sphagnum*–*Eriophorum* in flarks:			
(a) Ridges—80%; Flarks—20%; y_{max} = 22 cm	1·2–2·5	3·4–7	0·0030–0·0037
(b) Ridges—70%; Flarks—30%; y_{max} = 22 cm	1·3–3·0	4·3–10	0·0025–0·0035
(c) Ridges—60%; Flarks—40%; y_{max} = 22 cm	1·5–3·0	7·5–15	0·0018–0·0025
(C) Ridge–flark complexes with *Sphagnum*–shrub microtopes having pine on ridges and *Sphagnum*–*Scheuchzeria* in flarks:			
(a) Ridges—60%; Flarks—40%; y_{max} = 22 cm	2·2–4	9–16	0·0022–0·0030
(b) Ridges—50%; Flarks—50%; y_{max} = 22 cm	2·9–4	13–18	0·0020–0·0025
(D) Heavily inundated ridge–flark and ridge–pool complexes with *Sphagnum*–shrub and *Sphagnum*–shrub–*Eriophorum* microtopes on unforested or rarely forested ridges and *Sphagnum*–*Scheuchzeria* flarks partly with open water surface or pools:			
(a) Ridges—60%; Flarks—40%; y_{max} = 24 cm	3–6	18–22	0·0017–0·0027
(b) Ridges—50%; Flarks—50%; y_{max} = 22 cm	2–6	22–40	0·0009–0·0015
(c) Ridges—30%; Flarks—70%; y_{max} = 22 cm	6–9	40–50	0·0015–0·0018
(d) Ridges—20%; Flarks—80%; y_{max} = 22 cm	9–11	60–110	0·0010–0·0015
(e) Ridges—10%; Flarks—90%; y_{max} = 22 cm	11–15	140–170	0·0008–0·0010
5. Sedge–*Hypnum*	5–9	230–240	0·0001–0·0004
6. *Hypnum*–sedge	5–9	170–190	0·0003–0·0005

2.9 The Flow-net and its Construction by Aerial Survey

A set of lines drawn on the plan of a mire massif at right angles to the contours of the surface is called a network of lines of flow or a flow-net (Ivanov, 1953a, 1957b).

Being also a system of lines expressing the direction of the greatest slopes of the water table, the flow-net is the fundamental hydrodynamic means of describing undrained mire massifs in their natural state. It defines for any point in the plan of a mire massif the direction of the horizontal components of the rates of seepage in the acrotelm and catotelm of the peat deposit, and of surface flow when the water table is high. Because there is only one water-bearing horizon in the peat deposit of a mire massif, the general direction of seepage in the acrotelm and catotelm coincides with the direction of surface runoff, and is determined by the slopes of their common piezometric surface, which is the free surface of the mire's groundwater and periodically rises higher than the surface of the acrotelm.[9]

Repeated observation has shown that the slopes and outline of the average surface of the plant cover in the zone of microrelief of mires coincides almost completely with the slopes and outline of the water table. Moreover, fluctuations in the level of the water table take place simultaneously at different points with only small differences of amplitude in different types of microtope. Owing to this peculiarity, vertical change in the water table through runoff and evaporation causes no change in the shape of the mire's relief nor, as a consequence, in the shape of its flow-net, which may therefore be used as a basis for calculation, whatever be the level of water and the resulting rates of seepage and discharge. In other words, the shape of the flow-net does not change, a fact that greatly simplifies the solution of many hydrological problems.

It follows then that, both in calculations of maximal seepage and discharge, when levels are highest, and in calculations of minimal seepage and discharge, when levels are lowest, the slopes of the water surface remain unchanged at any point in the mire massif. The practical coincidence of the relief of the water table with the average surface of the microrelief of the plant cover also makes it possible to use the flow-net to trace accurately the contours of the surface of the mire as a system of lines at right angles to the lines of flow.

Every line of the flow-net, as was said earlier, depicts the direction of the maximal slope of the water table or gradient of piezometric pressure. In this it is assumed that the distribution of pressure in the peat deposit is either wholly or nearly subject to the law of hydrostatics. Discharges of pressure water at separate points in the peat deposit can cause only local disturbances, which do not affect the general direction of the horizontal components of the rates of flow. Where there is a supply of water at an even pressure over the whole surface of the mire, the graph of pressure distribution deviates from the hydrostatic along the horizontal axis, but the horizontal gradient of pressure must still remain unchanged and equal to the maximum slope.

Since the flowlines determine at each point of the mire massif the direction of horizontal seepage and surface runoff, it is always possible with their help to determine the degree of convergence or divergence of flow along any flowline. The unitary horizontal discharge at the given point in the mire massif can be determined from the known discharge at some other point in the flowline, using equations that allow for continuity of flow and other items contributing to the water supply. The feasibility of the above methods provides a basis for many kinds of calculation, and more especially for general inferences about the connections between the form of flow in plan, the hydraulic conductivity of the acrotelms of different microtopes and the shape of the relief of mire surfaces (Ivanov, 1965).

For a number of reasons it is better to speak of a "flow-net", rather than of a "network of streamlines". Lines at right angles at every point to the water-flow contours on the plan of a mire and tangential to the vectors of the horizontal components of the rates of seepage in the acrotelm and peat deposit cannot be regarded, strictly speaking, as streamlines. They only indicate the direction of the horizontal component of seepage and the surface flow over a vertical cross-section equal in breadth to unity and in depth to the thickness of the acrotelm and the peat deposit. The term "streamline" is reserved for trajectories tangential at every point in a stream to the vector of its total velocity.[10]

Typological plans with flow-nets for mire massifs are constructed on the basis of a simple visual interpretation of aero-photographic plans according to rules and principles set forth in special manuals.[11] Typological interpretation of such plans for hydrological calculations is now a well-established discipline giving very reliable results. The air survey materials that can serve as a starting point for the construction of typological plans and flow-nets are as follows: photographic plans, diagrams constructed from aerial photographs with details added by drawing, and, in many cases, contact printing. This last is used when calculations need not be very exact, as in those carried out to illustrate methods.

In place of a typological plan, calculations may be based directly on a photographic plan with a flow-net and boundaries between mire microtopes superimposed upon it. The determination of types of mire microtope and of the composition and structure of plant cover may prove a relatively simple task that can be mastered after a short period of work with aerial photographs; but the construction of a flow-net to serve as a basis for calculations, and not as a merely qualitative characterization of the general direction of flow, demands a much more profound knowledge of the structure of mire systems.

For that reason, we shall take time to deal with this question in greater detail, and to consider the physical bases of the indirect criteria portrayed in aerial photographs which must be used to construct quantitative, as opposed to qualitative, flow-nets.

Types of mire microtope can be determined from pictures of their plant cover and its structure obtained with a degree of precision dependent upon the altitude and scale of the survey; but the flow-net and the direction and rate of seepage cannot, of course, be portrayed on an aerial photograph. Though we do undoubtedly possess a large number of criteria for types and structures of microtopes, information about their properties which is derived, not from how they are portrayed in aerial photographs, but from general principles that we know to apply to the given object, must be treated as strictly supplementary.

In constructing a flow-net, use is made, not of the picture immediately before us at the time, but of a whole system of previously established relations between the structures of micro-, meso- and macrotopes and the direction of seepage and runoff. Indeed the sole criterion for determining the direction of seepage and surface flow is the reaction of the plant cover to the direction, quantity and chemical quality of the water that flows through it as expressed in the vegetation structure, not only of microtopes, but of meso- and macrotopes. The degree of precision appertaining to a flow-net varies according to the size of the mire system that is being investigated. The larger the size of the mire system and the smaller the scale on which it is represented, the greater the area for which one must construct a flow-net on a drawing of a given size. There must therefore be an element of approximation in the direction of flow portrayed by each particular line of flow. To some extent this takes place naturally in the process of interpretation. As one passes from small objects to larger and larger mire systems, the scale of the photographs diminishes and the directions of flow indicated by the flow-net become less precise. In this process, a change takes place in the structural criteria used to determine the flowlines. The small structural elements disappear from the picture, and one must be guided by the large structures that are peculiar to meso- and macrotopes.

Let us begin by considering the first group of criteria for superimposing flowlines on an aerial photograph. These are derived from the structure of microtopes, i.e. from the smallest structural formations. They include the orientation of the microforms, or elements of microrelief, in microtopes of complex structure, such as ridge–flark and ridge–pool microtopes with their ribbon-like ridge structure. Ridges, flarks and pools situated between ridges are portrayed in aerial photographs as parallel strips of different tone and breadth, whose general direction in each part of a mire massif coincides with the contours of the mire and is perpendicular to the direction of maximum slope and of seepage and surface flow. Use of this criterion makes it possible to determine very precisely the position and orientation of flowlines in these microtopes; but supplementary criteria are necessary to determine the direction of water movement.

To do this one must consider elements of another order which define the structure of meso- and macrotopes, as well as the position of these last with respect to the external hydrographic (river and lake) network. This second group of criteria includes the following:

(1) The shape in plan and the position in mire mesotopes of cuneiform, perfluent swamps originating in lakes.
(2) The shape in plan and the position in mire macrotopes of perfluent swamps.
(3) The shape in plan and the orientation of swamps formed behind mineral islands located inside mire systems.
(4) The position of the sources and channels of streams and rivulets that originate in mires and cross the boundaries of mire massifs.

If any of these criteria is combined with the ribbon-like structure of ridge–flark and ridge–pool microtopes, the position of the flowlines and the direction of flow is unambiguously defined. In the case of the mire systems in the zone of excess moisture, criteria of the first and second groups are usually combined and often superimposed one upon the other. That is why the construction of a flow-net is a clearly defined and uncomplicated task, if the aerial photograph covers a sufficiently large area of mire massif and contains structural criteria of the first and second groups. Cases may be encountered, however, where, because of the huge area covered by the mire massifs, the aerial photograph covers only a part of that area, in which there are only criteria of the first group relating exclusively to the structure of microtopes. In this part of the massif, it is possible to superimpose flowlines making use for this purpose of the orientation of the ridges, flarks and pools; but because of the absence of criteria connected with the structure of meso- and macrotopes, it is impossible to determine with confidence the direction of slope and flow along the flowlines. Consequently, it is necessary to study the area in a photograph on which there may be found at least one criterion of the second group, which will make it possible to determine the direction of flow. This may be the position of the source of a stream, or of a wooded strip running along the channel of an endotelmic rivulet carrying water from this part of the mire massif to beyond the boundaries of the system, the orientation of swamps as shown by dark strips behind mineral islands, etc. Then the direction of flow on the rest of the photograph is determined by passing successively from one flowline to another.

The best scales for the visual construction of flow-nets are those that permit one to use simultaneously the structural criteria of microtopes and macrotopes. These scales lie between $1:17\,000$ and $1:50\,000$. In smaller scale photographs, the structural criteria of microtopes disappear, and criteria of the second group have to be used to draw flowlines. Different degrees of generalization and correspondingly different scales of photography are required to solve different hydrological problems. Scales between $1:20\,000$ and $1:50\,000$ are the best for obtaining from aerial photographs the necessary data about projected fronts of flow (Chapter 3), for calculating the runoff from mires and the discharge into drains, for the movement of water between mire microtopes and endotelmic lakes, and for calculations of water balance dealing with vertical movements of moisture. These scales are sufficiently accurate to portray the type and structure of microtopes with the detail necessary to define and apply to them the calculable seepage functions $k_z = f_1(z)$ and $M_z = f(z)$. They also give a sufficiently large picture of the dimensions of different microtopes to make it possible to superimpose on them flowlines, to distinguish the boundaries between microtopes, and to analyse them into projected elements so as to determine the equivalent length of their fronts of influx and efflux. In many hydrological problems, however, significantly smaller or larger scales may be required. For example, the structure of very large macrotopes includes complete interfluves, and in investigating the connections of these with their water supply and relief considerable generalization of the flow-net is necessary. The reason for this is that the smallest structural elements in such macrotopes are microtopes and the areas they occupy, so that physically they play the same part in calculations relating to such systems as, for example, ridges and flarks do in calculations relating to complex ridge–flark microtopes, where general functions for water yield $\xi_z - f(\sigma)$ and hydraulic conductivity $(k_z = f_1(z)$ or $M_z = f(z)$ have to be calculated from the special functions that apply to ridges and flarks.

Investigation of the connection between the structure of a lake–mire system and its water supply and drainage is an example of such a problem, as is also the group of problems dealing with the stability of lake–mire and mire systems, to which some consideration is given in Chapter 4.

Aerial photographs on a scale larger than $1:20000$ must be used, for example, in constructing a flow-net for calculating the water balance of individual endotelmic lakes from the water yield and hydraulic conductivity of the acrotelm of the microtopes contiguous to the lake. These problems are explained in section 3.5. Large scales may also be required in calculating the water balance of small areas in mire massifs.

In Table 9 we shall enumerate and describe the chief criteria for constructing flow-nets by means of aerial photographs. In doing this, it is always necessary to make use of more than one criterion. By analysing and putting together the information they contain it is possible to determine correctly the orientation and direction of flowlines in any part of a mire system. The ultimate purpose of constructing a flow-net is to obtain a basis for calculation in diagrammatic form, which will enable one to determine the length of the

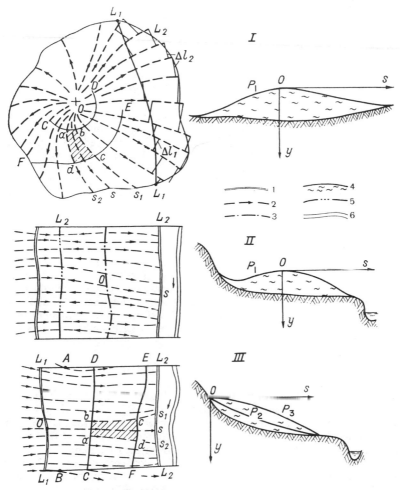

Fig. 18. General scheme of the horizontal efflux of water from mire massifs. I and II—cases of efflux without perfluence. III—case of perfluent efflux across a mire-massif. P_1—massif with first-order convexity. P_2—massif with concave profile. P_3—massif with second-order convexity. 1—boundaries of massif in plan. 2—flowlines. 3—water divide in mire massif. 4—peat deposit. 5—axis of marginal hollow in mire massif. 6—river. L_1, L_2—fronts of influx and efflux respectively. Δl_1, Δl_2—projections of sections of the front of efflux on the normal to flowlines.

Table 9. Structural criteria for the construction of flow-nets from aerial photographs of mires

Main criterion	Relation of criterion to structural characteristics of taxonomic units of mire geotopes	Manner of representation in photographs
1	2	3
1. Strip-ridge structure of ridge–flark microtopes	First-order microrelief of complex microtopes	(a) Striped pattern formed of slightly wavy strips of dark tone depicting ridges with *Sphagnum–shrub–pine* groups against background of lighter tone depicting furrows with *Sphagnum–Eriophorum* groups (b) Striped pattern formed by wavy strips of lighter tone, sometimes with marked granularity, depicting ridges with *Sphagnum–shrub–pine* and *Eriophorum* groups against background of darker tone depicting swamped furrows with *Sphagnum–Scheuchzeria*–sedge and sedge–deerhair groups
2. Strip-ridge structure of ridge–flark microtopes	First-order microrelief of complex microtopes	Striped pattern formed of wavy strips of bright tone with marked granularity depicting ridges, alternating with strips of darker tone depicting pools with an open water surface situated between ridges. The breadth of both strips fluctuates greatly according to the breadth of the ridges and pools
3. Direction of elongation and shape of strips of swamped microtopes formed behind dry islands (composed of mineral soil) situated in mire massifs	Element of structure of a mesotope or a macrotope	Strips of darker tone beginning at mineral islands on the brighter background of the main microtope. In most cases, the strip is broader near the island and grows narrower at increasing distance from it, until it gradually disappears. Sometimes, however, it has the same breadth throughout its whole length and extends as a narrow band for a significant distance along the line of the mire's maximum slope

ientation of flowlines in relation to photographs	Degree of reliability and adequacy of criterion	Physical basis of criterion
4	5	6
›wlines perpendicular to general direction of the ·y strips in the given ıll part of the ːrotope	Criterion completely reliable, but only determines the orientation of the streamlines. Supplementary criteria relating to the structure of the mesotope or macrotope are necessary to determine the direction of flow	Biological reaction of plant communities to the direction of flow of water in the rooting layer of the acrotelm. Scale: 1:15 000–1:50 000
ᵥvlines directed ›endicularly to the ːral direction of the ›s in the given small of the microtope ᵤout taking its waviness account		
ᵥlines are drawn: ᵥhere the strip grows ᵤarrower, along its axis nd parallel to it in ▬djacent sections; ᵥhere the strip is of ᵤniform breadth, along ·s direction and parallel › its direction in ▬djacent sections	Criterion is completely reliable. It determines the direction of the current in the given section and the orientation of the streamlines in the immediate neighbourhood through position of the strips of swamped microtopes	Change in chemical composition of water or concentration of current when filtered through mineral soils of islands with increased coefficient of seepage compared with peat. Both causes produce changes in plant cover behind islands, increased swamping and formation over certain distance of another type of microtope, usually a swamp with mesotrophic and oligotrophic vegetation. Scale: 1:25 000–1:70 000

Table 9.—*continued*

Main criterion	Relation of criterion to structural characteristics of taxonomic units of mire geotopes	Manner of representation in photographs
1	2	3
4. Wedge-shaped swamps with diverging or converging flow formed on slope of mire mesotopes	Element of structure of a mesotope taking the form of mire massifs with a convex surface	Sharply diverging or converging outlines depicting the edges of swamped microtopes against the background of a main microtope with a different structure, e.g. strip-ridge
5. Transitional swamps intersecting the whole mire massif and receiving water supply from beyond its bounds and from adjoining microtopes	Element of structure of macrotope	Broad strips of a dark tone, sometimes with blurred edges, on which there are separate bright sections (spots) of brighter strips along the general direction of the swamp. They usually divide off mesotopes in a mire macrotope
6. The relative position of the boundaries of mire microtopes of different types within the territory of mesotopes of symmetrical or nearly symmetrical form	Element of structure of mesotope	In mesotopes, whose form in plan is round and has a symmetrical relief, the boundaries of the microtopes are almost concentric circles. In mesotopes with a slope to one side and a cylindrical shape the boundaries of the microtopes are parallel lines

Orientation of flowlines in relation to photographs	Degree of reliability and adequacy of criterion	Physical basis of criterion
4	5	6
Flowlines are drawn along the edges of the diverging or converging outline of the swamped microtope, and along the line of its axis: a) *in diverging forms*, from the point of emergence to the middle of the line where the criteria of a swamped microtope disappear;) *in converging forms*, from the middle of the wedge to its apex, where the source of an endotelmic stream is often situated	Criterion determines with complete certainty the orientation of streamlines. The direction of flow is reliably determined by the use of supplementary, linked criteria: (a) *in diverging wedge-shaped swamps*, by the presence at the beginning of the swamp of points of the darkest tone with a gradual lightening of tone in the direction of the diverging current; (b) *in converging wedge-shaped swamps*, by the presence at the narrow end of the source of a stream	The emergence of layers of peat with low coefficients of seepage in the acrotelm on the slopes of a convex mire massif, and, in consequence, an abrupt change in the seepage of the acrotelm and a change in the structure of the microtope. Scale: 1:25 000–1:50 000
Flowlines directed along the edges of the swamp microtope and the axis of the dark strip. The density of flowlines across the breadth of the swamp is proportional to its breadth at a given place, indicating the divergence or convergence of the current	Reliable criterion for the orientation of the flowlines. To determine their direction one must use other connected criteria: the place where streams are formed in the swamp, and their emergence beyond the limits of the massif; the position of the outside rivers, which receive water from the mire	The concentrated filtrational or surface current of water from the mire (when the water table is high among mesotrophic and eutrophic vegetation). Scale: 1:25 000–1:70 000
Flowlines are perpendicular to the boundaries of the different types of microtope	Reliable criterion for the orientation of the flowlines. Supplementary criteria are used to determine the direction of flow: position of streams (rivers) draining area, of wedge-shaped and transitional swamps, of swamps behind mineral islands, of backwater (stagnant) swamps	Reaction (adaptation) of plant communities to changes in seepage and the water table in the direction of the maximum surface slope. Scale: 1:25 000–1:70 000

Table 9.—*continued*

Main criterion	Relation of criterion to structural characteristics of taxonomic units of mire geotopes	Manner of representation in photographs
1	2	3
7. The relative position, alternation and outline of microtopes of different types in mire macrotopes	Elements of structure of macrotope	(a) Alternation of very elongated oval sections or strips of darker tone, depicting microtopes of moss–tree group with dividing strips of bright tone, depicting microtopes of the grass–moss group (b) Very elongated strips of a darke tone with blurred edges on a brighter background, depicting microtopes of the moss–grass and moss–tree groups. In this case, the dark strips depict the wetter microtopes of these same groups
8. Position and shape of dense aggregations of small endotelmic pools and pool-like flarks	Element of structure of macrotope	Multitude of very small patches of dark tone of an irregular or round shape on brighter background forming a clearly distinguished stri with definite form and breadth

projected fronts of influx and efflux of any given mire massif. It is therefore essential that the distances between the superimposed flowlines, at the points where they intersect the fronts of influx and efflux, should not be too small to permit exact measurement of projected sections of these fronts, nor too large to permit one to draw sections of a curvilinear front at right angles to the flowlines. In practice, they must be from 5 to 10 mm, according to the curvature of the front and the scale of the aerial photograph. In Fig. 18, there is an example of an equivalent flow-net with equivalent fronts L_1 and L_2 delimiting the areas of the mire massif which are zones of influx and zones of efflux

Orientation of flowlines in relation to photographs	Degree of reliability and adequacy of criterion	Physical basis of criterion
4	5	6
Flowlines directed along the long axis of alternating sections of dark and bright tone. The lines of flow are general, and do not depict the orientation of flowlines within each microtope	Reliability of the criterion depends upon the degree of comprehensiveness of the macrotope studied and the possibility of using other criteria, which characterize the general structure of the macrotope and its constituent mesotopes. Use may be made of small-scale copies to construct generalised flow-nets	Reaction of plant communities to changes of seepage and water table. Scale: 1:50000–1:70000
Flowlines run along the main direction of the dark strips, disregarding changes in their breadth and the waveness of their blurred edges	Criterion reliable for orientation of flowlines. Other criteria are necessary to determine the direction of flow	
Flowlines have an opposite direction or meet at right or acute angle, expressing a break in the continuity of the filtrational current in the acrotelm at the interface of different mesotopes	Criterion reliable for determining the direction of contrary currents in contiguous mesotopes	Degradation of the plant cover through overwetting of acrotelm, leading to formation of an open water surface and a denuded surface of peat

2.10 A General Equation for the Water Balance of Mire Massifs and Particular Cases of it[12]

Let us begin by considering in the most general terms the water balance of the mire massif depicted in Fig. 18(III). We shall introduce the following symbols: L_1—the length of the front of influx from areas adjacent to the massif and situated higher than it; Q_1—the total recharge of water across the front of influx; L_2—the length of the front across which efflux from the massif occurs; Q_2—the total discharge of water across the front of efflux; P_{gr}—the net transfer resulting from exchanges of water between the peat deposit and the subjacent mineral soils over the whole area of the massif ω; P_p—the total amount of precipitation; and P_e—the total amount of evaporation over the whole area of the massif. The points A and B mark the places where areas of influx and efflux respectively cross the boundaries of the massif. The letter s denotes flowlines on the area of the massif. Change in the water storage of the massif dW in time dt will obviously be expressed by the following equation:

$$\frac{dW}{dt} = Q_1 - Q_2 + P_p + P_{gr} - P_e, \qquad (2.61)$$

in which differences in the transfer of water across the boundary of the massif $(Q_1 - Q_2)$ express the so-called external (or horizontal) water exchange between the massif and surrounding lands, and the sum $(P_p + P_{gr} - P_e)$ expresses the internal water exchange within the boundary of the massif. On the basis of equation (2.50), Q_1 and Q_2 may be expressed in terms of the seepage of the acrotelm $q_z = f(z)$, that is to say, of the microtopes adjacent to the external boundary of the mire. The components of the internal water exchange are the flux density of precipitation, the exchange of water between the peat deposit and soil, and the evaporation per unit area of the massif— p_p, p_{gr} and p_e, which usually vary from place to place in the massif.

Equation (2.61) may then be written in the following form:

$$\frac{dW}{dt} = \oint_{L_1} q_{zn}\, dL - \oint_{L_2} q_{zn}\, dL + \int_{\omega} (p_p + p_{gr} - p_e)\, d\omega, \qquad (2.62)$$

where q_{zn} is the normal component of seepage or unit of discharge in the direction of the boundary at every point on it. In later expressions, we shall for the sake of brevity express the amount of internal water exchange per unit area by a single symbol

$$p = p_p + p_{gr} - p_e, \qquad (2.63)$$

and we shall call it *the internal balance of the water supply of a mire massif at a given point*. When p_p, p_{gr} and p_e are constant over the whole massif, the following equality holds good

$$p\omega = (p_p + p_{gr} - p_e)\omega = P_p + P_{gr} - P_e.$$

From this it is possible, knowing the components of the water balance P_p, P_{gr} and P_e, to calculate the mean value of internal water supply for the area of the massif:

$$p_m = \frac{P_p + P_{gr} - P_e}{\omega}. \qquad (2.64)$$

As follows from expression (2.63), the balance of internal water supply may be positive or negative according to the climatic and geomorphological conditions of the mire massif and the season of the year, for the sign is determined by the relation between precipitation and evaporation and the amount and direction of groundwater exchange.

Let us consider some special cases where the composition of the water balance of mire massifs is affected by their type, their own relief and the relief of the place where they are situated. Figure 19 shows all the different possible ways in which a mire may arise in a locality with some or other type of relief and how these are related to the classes of mesotope recognized by the genetico-geotopic classification of mires (see Table 3). As is obvious from these cases, the general equation (2.62) expressing the factors affecting the water balance of all types of mire massif whose external water balance involves both influx and efflux (mire massifs with a transit flow) applies to all mire massifs in river valleys or lake basins (floodplain and terrace deposits) having a concave relief or a convex relief of the second order (see P_2 and P_3 in Fig. 18), and also to those of the basin type with a concave or flat relief. All these are types of mire massif with transit flow.

Equation (2.62) takes a simplified form in the case of mire massifs of the terrace or basin type with first-order convex reliefs (see P_1 in Fig. 18), and in mire massifs of the placodic[13] type, whether they be situated on flat water divides, or on water divides which slope, but possess a first-order convex relief. Massifs of this category only have a front of efflux. Their external water exchange is an efflux due to a positive balance in their internal supply. In the case of all such massifs, we put $L_1 = 0$ in equation (2.62) and obtain the following:

$$\frac{dW}{dt} = \int_\omega p \, d\omega - \oint_L q_{zn} \, dL, \qquad (2.65)$$

where $L = L_2$, i.e. the whole external boundary of the mire massif is a front of efflux.

Pressure water from the subjacent soil is practically unknown in mire massifs of the placodic type with a convex relief. For that reason, the balance of their internal water supply, as expressed by equation (2.63), can take only two forms. The first is where, on the interface between the peat and the mineral soil, an impermeable layer is formed (owing to the clogging of sandy soils by organic colloids carried down by currents from the peat deposit), or the soil below the deposit is a clay of low permeability. In this case $p_{gr} \cong 0$. The second form is where there are losses through seepage into permeable subjacent strata. Therefore, in the case of convex mire massifs of the placodic type, the ground water component of equation (2.63) is either equal to zero or has a minus sign. Obviously there cannot be seepage into the subjacent strata in the case of convex mire massifs unless

$$p_p > p_{gr} + p_e.$$

Class of Mesotope	Course of development	Phase I (concave relief)	Phase III (convex relief)
Isolated Basins (I)	Oligo-central		
Effluent Basins (III)	Oligo-central		
Effluent Hollows (IIb)	Oligo-peripheral		
Perfluent Basins (IV)	Mixed		
Perfluent Hollows (IIa)	Oligo-peripheral		
Gentle Slopes (IVb)	Mixed		

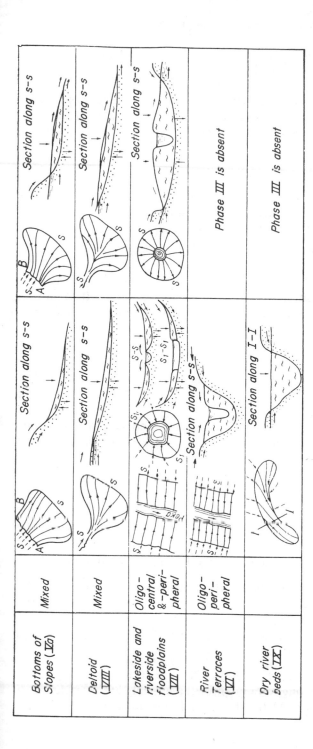
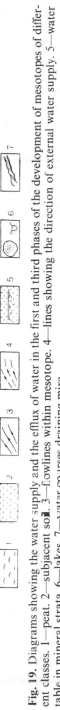

Fig. 19. Diagrams showing the water supply and the efflux of water in the first and third phases of the development of mesotopes of different classes. 1—peat. 2—subjacent soil. 3—flowlines within mesotope. 4—lines showing the direction of external water supply. 5—water table in mineral strata. 6—lakes. 7—water courses draining mire.

This condition specifically excludes the possibility of the formation of convex mire massifs in the zone of deficient moisture, for in such circumstances p_p is always less than $(p_{gr} + p_e)$, if p_{gr} is negative, and the internal water exchange p must be negative. The formation of mires in the zone of deficient moisture is therefore possible only when the balance of external water exchange is positive, i.e. $Q_1 > Q_2$. In that case, when $dW/dt = 0$, the average long-term water balance must satisfy the equation

$$\bar{Q}_1 - \bar{Q}_2 = \bar{P}_p \pm \bar{P}_{gr} - \bar{P}_e. \tag{2.61'}$$

If we put $L_2 = 0$ in equation (2.62), where L_2 is the front of efflux, we obtain an equation of water balance for mire massifs in arid regions with no outlet, which have as a rule a concave or flat relief,

$$\frac{dW}{dt} = \oint_{L_1} q_n \, dL - \int_{\omega} p \, d\omega. \tag{2.66}$$

The existence of such mire massifs is plainly possible only if the following conditions are satisfied (at least in the case of mean long-term values):

$$\left.\begin{array}{l} \bar{P}_e > \bar{P}_p; \\ \bar{P}_e = \bar{P}_p + \bar{P}_{gr} + \bar{Q}_1. \end{array}\right\} \tag{2.67}$$

If the last condition is not satisfied, the balance of the massif will be disturbed, and it will either begin to dry up gradually ($\bar{P}_e > \bar{P}_p + \bar{P}_{gr} + \bar{Q}_1$), or will receive an excess of moisture and expand ($\bar{P}_e < \bar{P}_p + \bar{P}_{gr} + \bar{Q}_1$). This process will continue until an external runoff arises to compensate for the surplus of moisture, and a new balance, expressed in terms of equation (2.61'), is established.

Finally, when the internal water exchange of a massif is equal to zero, the equation of balance for average, long-term quantities takes the form

$$\oint_{L_1} \bar{q}_n \, dL = \oint_{L_2} \bar{q}_n \, dL, \tag{2.68}$$

since it is obvious that in that case $dW/dt = 0$. This situation occurs:

(1) In the zone of unstable moisture, i.e. when $\bar{P}_e = \bar{P}_p$ and $\bar{P}_{gr} = 0$.
(2) In the zone of deficient moisture, i.e. when $\bar{P}_e > \bar{P}_p$ and the internal water supply $\bar{P}_{gr} = \bar{P}_e - \bar{P}_p$.
(3) In the zone of excess moisture, i.e. when $\bar{P}_p > \bar{P}_e$ and seepage from the massif (internal drainage) $\bar{P}_{gr} = \bar{P}_p - \bar{P}_e$.

It should be noted that the equation of balance in the form (2.68) can be applied only to average long-term quantities, and really has no meaning for short intervals of time, in which the above conditions are not usually satisfied.

On the other hand, equations (2.65) and (2.66), although they also express special cases, hold good for any interval of time whatsoever, like equations (2.61) and (2.62).

2.11 Hydrological Equivalence as Applied to Mire Massifs

Every particular mire massif and, more particularly, every mire macrotope has its own peculiarities and a distinctive structure which, as explained in section 2.8, can be described by the application of a quantitative criterion of absolute or relative variety to the simple elements into which it can be analysed, and each of which can be described by one determinate form of the function $\overline{M} = f(s)$. This variety of structure makes it difficult to discover the general biophysical and hydrological properties of mire massifs as natural systems. To establish and express these in quantitative form a somewhat different approach is necessary.

We shall begin by defining what we mean by *equivalence* in the case of mire massifs. We shall call those mire massifs equivalent which have one and the same external and internal water exchange, however they may differ in their outline in plan, their form of relief and the distribution of their plant cover. In other words, hydrologically equivalent mire massifs must be identical in the quantity and proportions of the items in their water balance. Let us now consider what conditions such mire massifs must satisfy.

The condition of equivalence and the corresponding rule for the transformation of mire massifs can be obtained by application of the well-known theorem of Gauss, according to which the flux of a vector across a closed boundary is equal to the integral of the divergence of the vector's field over the area defined by the boundary.[14] Taking L, the external boundary of the mire massif (which is where the depth of the peat deposit becomes zero), as this boundary, the condition of equivalence for the average long-term value of seepage $\bar{q}$ is written in the terms used above in the following way:

$$\oint_L \bar{q}_n \, dL = \int_\omega \operatorname{div} \bar{q} \, d\omega \qquad (2.69)$$

where $\bar{q}_n$ is the normal component of the average seepage with respect to the boundary at every point on it.

It is obvious that at every point within the boundary of the mire massif the divergence of the vector of the average unit discharge is equal to the average intensity of the internal supply $\bar{p}$:

$$\operatorname{div} \bar{q} = \bar{p}. \qquad (2.70)$$

Taking into account the fact that the left-hand side of equation (2.69) is the complete long-term average discharge of water $\bar{Q}_L$ flowing out of the massif, and making use of the equality (2.70) we have

$$\bar{Q}_L = \oint_L \bar{q}_n \, \mathrm{d}L = \int_\omega \bar{p} \, \mathrm{d}\omega. \tag{2.71}$$

It is not difficult to see that this same relation follows immediately from the equation of balance (2.62) when $\mathrm{d}W/\mathrm{d}t = 0$, i.e. in cases where the intervals of time are sufficiently large.

From equations (2.69) and (2.71) it follows that, if $\bar{p}$ is constant within the boundary of the massif, or is a function solely of its size $\bar{P} = \bar{p}(\omega)$, the average long-term discharge of water flowing out of the massif $\bar{Q}_L$ does not depend upon the outline of the massif in plan, and remains constant for all massifs of the same area. It follows from this that, where the internal water supply $\bar{p}$ is determined by the same climatic and geomorphological conditions, all mire massifs with the same area have the same norm of efflux $\bar{Q}_L$, whatever be the shape of their boundaries in plan.

Investigations of evaporation from mires (see Chapter 3) show that in the zones of excess or adequate moisture, the average quantity of evaporation from the different types of mire microtope making up a given mire massif changes only within narrow limits, by 10–15%. In arid regions, where differences in evaporation may be greater, there is significantly less difference in the composition of plant cover and the wetness of surface in the different microtopes of the fen type, from which mire massifs are composed in this region. This offsets increases in the differences of evaporation which might arise when the supply of thermal energy is excessive

This means that it is possible to assume that in the same climatic and similar geomorphological conditions the average intensity of internal water supply $\bar{p}$ remains practically constant and independent of the area of the massif. The sign of integration may then be removed from $\bar{p}$ in equation (2.71):

$$\bar{Q}_L = \oint_L \bar{q}_n \, \mathrm{d}L = \bar{p}\omega. \tag{2.72}$$

The relation will be invalid only in those cases where there are sources of pressure water at separate points in the mire (or analogous losses through seepage[15]), which must be allowed for under the term p_{gr} in the equation describing the balance of internal supply (2.63). In these cases a supplementary condition is added to maintain the validity of the relation expressed by (2.72): all sources in the form of concentrated discharges of groundwater under pressure (or similar losses) must remain within the boundary of the massif, whatever be the deformation of it that they involve.

Conditions (2.71) and (2.72) make it possible to consider, in place of individual massifs with an infinite variety of shapes, generalized forms of mire massif, which are equivalent in water balance and equal in area. These we shall call *equivalent mire massifs*. In selecting a geometrical form for modelling real mire massifs in all their variety account should be taken of the conditions of external water supply as reflected in the form of their flow-net. All mire massifs having no external supply in the form of an influx of surface or ground water from surrounding areas have flow-nets with centres or lines of divergence inside their boundary (see Fig. 19). Mire massifs with an external influx, i.e. a transit flow, have flow-nets with fronts of influx and efflux situated on the boundary between the massif and the surrounding mire-free terrain.

It is therefore advisable to use a circular massif as the geometrical model for all mire massifs which have no external water supply, and a rectangular massif as the model for all mire massifs having an external water supply or transit flow. For a circular mire massif we have (see (2.72))

$$\bar{Q}_L = \int_0^{2\pi} \bar{q}_r r_0 \, d\phi = \bar{p}\omega, \tag{2.73}$$

where $\bar{q}_r = \bar{q}_n$, the unit discharge along the radii of the circle, which is normal to its circumference; ϕ is the angle at the centre of divergence of the flow $(dL = r_0 \, d\phi)$ and r_0 is the radius of the massif. Since the massifs must be equal in area to satisfy the condition of equivalence, the middle parts of equations (2.72) and (2.73) may be equated to give

$$\int_0^{2\pi} \bar{q}_r r_0 \, d\phi = \oint_L \bar{q}_n \, dL, \tag{2.74}$$

where $r_0 = \sqrt{(\omega/\pi)}$ is the radius of the equivalent mire massif or *equivalent radius*.

On the assumption that the outline of the massif is circular and that the divergent flow is evenly distributed along every segment with a radius r, the average unitary discharge $\bar{q}_r$ is obviously a constant quantity (see section 2.13). From equation (2.74) it therefore follows that

$$2\pi r_0 \bar{q}_r = \oint_L \bar{q}_n \, dL,$$

from which in turn it follows that

$$\bar{q}_r = \frac{1}{2\pi r_0} \oint_L \bar{q}_n \, dL = \frac{1}{2\sqrt{\pi\omega}} \oint_L \bar{q}_n \, dL. \tag{2.75}$$

This last expression shows that, if a real mire massif with an internal water supply and any outline whatsoever is replaced by an equivalent circular massif, there will be situated along the boundary of the latter an equivalent microtope (see sections 1.7 and 2.8) with a seepage $\bar{q}_r$ equal to the ratio of the flux of the vector of unit discharge across the boundary of the real mire massif to a quantity dependent upon the area of the massif $2\sqrt{\pi\omega}$. From equations (2.75) and (2.72) we obtain

$$\bar{q}_r = \frac{\bar{Q}_L}{2\sqrt{\pi\omega}},$$

or, dividing both sides by ω,

$$\frac{\bar{Q}_L}{\omega} = \frac{2\bar{q}_r\sqrt{\pi\omega}}{\omega} = \frac{2\bar{q}_r}{\sqrt{\omega/\pi}} = \frac{2\bar{q}_r}{r_0}.$$

Since $\bar{Q}_L/\omega$ is the average modulus of efflux $\bar{m}$ from a mire massif of area ω, we obtain the following simple relationship:

$$\bar{m} = \frac{2\bar{q}_r}{r_0}. \tag{2.76}$$

Equation (2.76) is an important deduction, which can be verbally expressed as follows: the average modulus of horizontal efflux[16] from a mire massif of any shape having an internal water supply is equal to twice the unit discharge on the boundary of an equivalent massif divided by the radius of the equivalent massif. This equation is important in all calculations of the efflux from mire massifs.

In future we shall call the average unitary discharge $\bar{q}_r$, expressed by equation (2.75), the equivalent unitary discharge (or the equivalent average seepage).

For a mire massif with transit flow, for which there is a rectangular massif of equivalent area, $d\bar{W}/dt = 0$, and, with the help of (2.62) and (2.72), we may write

$$\mathcal{U}_{L_2} - \mathcal{U}_{L_1} = \oint_{L_2} q_{2n}\,dL - \oint_{L_1} q_{1n}\,dL = p\omega, \tag{2.76'}$$

and

$$Q_{L_2} - Q_{L_1} = L_2\bar{q}_2 - L_1\bar{q}_1 = \bar{p}BL = \bar{p}\omega, \tag{2.76''}$$

where B and L are respectively the breadth of its equivalent massif and the length of its front of efflux, which is equal to its front of influx.

Putting $L = (L_1 + L_2)/2$, we find that the equivalent breadth of the massif

$$B = \frac{\omega}{L} = \frac{2\omega}{L_1 + L_2}. \tag{2.76'''}$$

Since the right-hand sides of equations (2.76') and (2.76'') are identical, we obtain from them an equation for calculating equivalent seepages across the fronts of efflux and influx:

$$\bar{q}_2 - \bar{q}_1 = \frac{2(\oint_{L_2} \bar{q}_{2n}\,dL - \oint_{L_1} \bar{q}_{1n}\,dL)}{L_1 + L_2}. \tag{2.77}$$

Here the average modulus of efflux from a mire massif with transit flow is expressed in terms of equivalent seepages by the simple relationship:

$$\overline{m} = \frac{\overline{q}_2 - \overline{q}_1}{B}.$$ (2.77')

2.12 The Deducible Consequences of Hydromorphological Relations

As has already been shown, mire vegetation, which is the living plant cover of mire massifs, reacts with great sensitivity to the environment in which it grows. The fundamental factors that determine the composition of plant associations at any point in a mire massif are: the amount of seepage, the level of the water table, the amplitude of its fluctuations and the chemical quality of the water. Changes in these factors at any point in a mire massif are attended by corresponding changes in the composition of its plant cover and the rate of peat accumulation. This last leads in turn to changes in the relief of the massif's surface, both in particular places and in the massif as a whole. The resulting changes in the composition of the plant cover produce changes in the structure of the acrotelm, and so lead to corresponding changes in the hydraulic conductivity and water yield of the peat producing layer. Changes in the relief of a massif are followed in turn by corresponding changes in the distribution of seepage or "density of flow". This then alters the whole regime of the mire—the level of the water table, the amplitude of its fluctuations, the chemical quality of the water, the concentration of solutions, and the water balance of the different parts. In this way, the environment gradually changes and corresponding changes occur in the composition of the plant cover, which in turn alters the physical properties of the acrotelm, the speed of peat accumulation, and after that the relief and so on. It is the continuous operation of these mutually dependent processes, with sometimes one, sometimes another playing the dominating part, that constitutes the biophysical reality underlying the origin and development of mire massifs.

These processes, however, are relatively slow. Their speed is determined by the rate of peat accumulation, which is on average 1 mm per year. At any given time, a mire massif can therefore be regarded as an unchanging natural formation possessing a definite relief, an ordered distribution of vegetation over its expanse due to differences in seepage, a certain average level of water table, and water of a certain chemical quality. For every period in the history of a mire massif it is therefore possible to establish general relationships between local variations in fundamental hydrological properties, the relief of the massif and ordered changes in the composition of its plant cover associated with correlative changes in the properties of the acrotelm. The establishment of such relationships for mires in our own age is one of the chief tasks of the general theory of mire hydrology.

Hydromorphological functions are mathematical expressions that establish relations between the water supply of mires (as determined by the climatic and hydrological conditions of their situation), the distribution patterns of their plant cover, the relief of their surface and the physical properties of their peat-producing layer.

The chief value of such functions is that they permit one to analyse the course of development of mires and the dynamics of their growth. This, like every other theoretical analysis, makes it possible to consider in a wide variety of combinations the different natural factors and conditions which explain the origin and development of mire massifs, however often or rarely such circumstances may be encountered in nature. Hydromorphological functions also provide a theoretical basis for the calculation of the efflux, the water balance and the water table regime of mires.

Figure 20 depicts in diagrammatic form the mutual relations between hydromorphological factors and the course of development and states of a mire massif (or some individual part of it). Continuous lines with arrows indicate the chief direct and inverse relations; dotted lines the secondary relations, which play a significantly smaller quantitative part in this process of interaction, especially when one is dealing with relatively short periods of time. In working out this diagram with the help of theoretical and empirical functions, the inverse secondary relations may be disregarded, provided one is only considering interactions over periods of time that are short in comparison with the time required for any substantial change in the relief of the massif.

In the diagram of Fig. 20, the double lines show the connections expressed by hydromorphological functions. These obviously do not include the system of direct and inverse relations that affects the rate of peat accumulation, the changes that time produces in the relief of a mire, or the influence of temperature and the physical properties of the acrotelm. The exclusion of these relationships from hydromorphological functions is due to the fact that in them the relief of a mire massif is regarded as an independent, already given factor, whose features are nowadays determined by aerial survey. This approach is justified by the fact that the cycles of interaction expressed by relationships 1–15 are measured in decades (or even shorter periods), and can therefore be regarded as processes taking place against the background of an unchanging relief.

In contrast to this, the periods of time that must elapse before relationships 16–25 can exercise a substantial influence upon the relief of a mire are measured in many hundreds or thousands of years, i.e. periods as long as those associated with a change of climate. When we use the concepts of

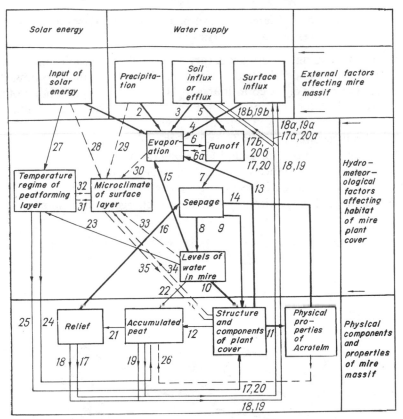

Fig. 20. Diagram of the interaction of hydrometeorological factors with processes and situations occurring in the development of a mire system.

average long-term efflux, evaporation, seepage, water table, precipitation, thermal input, etc., in order to deduce hydromorphological functions relating to mires, it should be borne in mind that these describe relatively permanent conditions affecting the external environment and the relief of mires.

In fact, if we remember that in two neighbouring sections of a mire, which differ in seepage, water table level and the physical properties of the acrotelm, the difference in the rate of peat accumulation amounts to no more than 0·5 mm/year, then 200 years are required to produce any noticeable difference of level (e.g. 10 cm) between the surfaces of these two sections. From this it follows that for a relatively short period of time it is perfectly possible to consider separately one part of an interacting system where the speed of the processes involved is of one and the same order (see Fig. 20).

2.13 The Fundamental Hydromorphological Equation for a Mire Massif and an Analysis of it

We begin by dividing off an elementary section abcd in a mire massif (see Fig. 18). This is bounded by two horizontals CD and FE and two flowlines bc and ad. For origin of the coordinates we shall take the highest point of the mire massif which lies on a profile of its surface drawn along a flowline. As horizontal axis we shall take the flowline s, which passes through the centre of the chosen section. We now introduce the following symbols (Fig. 21): s—the distance from the horizontal CD along the average flowlines; b_s—the length of the arc at a distance s from CD; b_0—the breadth of the arc ab made by CD at the beginning of the section; q_0—the unit discharge in the acrotelm at the beginning of the section; q_s—the unit discharge at the distance s.

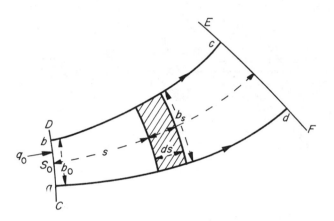

Fig. 21. Section of mire massif treated as analytic element.

Let us now put together an equation to describe a state of continuous flow in this section on the supposition that we know the seepage regime of the acrotelm and the input of moisture to the section. The discharge of water into the section abcd along the acrotelm is obviously equal to $q_0 b_0$, and that which flows out of it to $q_s b_s$. The difference between these two amounts under the established conditions is equal to the quantity of water accruing to the area per unit of time:

$$q_s b_s - q_0 b_0 = \int_0^s p_s b_s \, ds, \qquad (2.78)$$

where p_s is the intensity of internal supply (i.e. $p_0 - p_{gr} - p_e$) as defined by equation (2.63), which is in general a function of s.

Applying this last equation to the average long-term values $\bar{q}_s$, $\bar{q}_0$ and $\bar{p}_s$, and using it to find the value of $\bar{q}_s$, we get a general equation for the average seepage of the acrotelm at any point in the mire massif:

$$\bar{q}_s = \frac{\bar{q}_0 b_0 + \int_0^s \bar{p}_s b_s \, ds}{b_s}. \tag{2.79}$$

Supposing then, according to expression (2.54), that $\bar{q}_s = \overline{M}_s i$, and expressing the slope i of the surface of the massif along the flowline in the accepted system of coordinates (y, s) in the form $i = dy/ds$, we obtain the equation

$$\frac{dy}{ds} = \frac{\bar{q}_0 b_0 + \int_0^s \bar{p}_s b_s \, ds}{\overline{M}_s b_s}. \tag{2.80}$$

This last expression is the fundamental differential equation connecting the relief of a mire massif along any flowline s with the type of microtope (as defined by the average modulus of seepage $\overline{M}_s$), with the form of flow in plan (b_0, b_s), and with the intensity of the external $(\bar{q}_0)$ and internal $(\bar{p}_s)$ water supply. In this equation, the quantities y, $\bar{p}_s$, b_s and $\overline{M}_s$ are in the most general case functions of the distance s measured along the flowline.

The intensity of all the biophysical and biochemical processes which regulate the speed of peat accumulation and the formation of a mire massif depends upon the flux density of water exchange (seepage) and the aeration of the peat-forming acrotelm (i.e. the level of the water table) at any given point in the massif. The problem under review is then a physical one and the equation that describes the hydromorphological relations involved in it will be suitably expressed in terms of a system of coordinates whose horizontal axis is the actual flowline[17] and whose origin is that particular point on the surface of the massif which is the centre of its convexity (see Figs 5a and 6), or the boundary between the massif and the adjacent mire-free soil (see Fig. 5b). Vertical sections along any flowline (e.g. AOB in Fig. 5a or $A_1 O_1 B_1$ in Fig. 5b) we call hydrodynamic profiles of a mire massif.

Let us consider certain special cases resulting from equation (2.80). If within the external boundary of any mire massif there are one or more points (centres of convexity) or lines where waters divide (see Figs 6 and 8), for which $s = 0$ and the external water supply $q_0 = 0$, then it follows from equation (2.80) that in these cases the slope of the surface

$$i = \frac{dy}{ds} = 0,$$

which, of course, is in full accord with the physical meaning of these concepts.

For massifs in river valleys or perfluent basins with an external water supply from aquifers, which grow thinner where the peat deposit joins the original mineral bank, the value of $\bar{q}_0$ at this point, where $s = 0$, is obviously equal to the discharge of seepage from the aquifer per unit length of this front. Putting $\bar{q}_0 = \bar{q}_{gr}$ to describe this case, we find from equation (2.80) that the slope of the surface of the mire along the flowlines on the boundary between the mire and the bank is

$$i_{s=0} = \left\{\frac{dy}{ds}\right\}_{s=0} = \frac{\bar{q}_{gr}b_0}{\overline{M}_{s=0}b_{s=0}} = \frac{\bar{q}_{gr}}{\overline{M}_{s=0}} = \frac{\bar{q}_{gr}}{\bar{k}_0(z_0 - \bar{z}_{s=0})}, \qquad (2.81)$$

which means that the slope is determined only by the intensity of the external supply and the properties of the acrotelm of the microtope adjacent to the bank $(\bar{k}_0, z_0 - \bar{z}_{s=0})$ (see Fig. 17).

When the external supply of a massif consists of surface water flowing down from mineral banks at a higher altitude and of groundwater derived from aquifers, we shall understand by the quantity $\bar{q}_0$ in equation (2.80) on the boundary of the massif the sum of the two components of the external supply:

$$\bar{q}_0 = \bar{q}_{gr} + \bar{q}_{sf}, \qquad (2.82)$$

where $\bar{q}_{gr}$ is the average seepage per unit length of the front of groundwater input at the boundary of the massif, and $\bar{q}_{sf}$ is the average input of surface water per unit length of the front of external supply. The values of $\bar{q}_{gr}$ and $\bar{q}_{sf}$ are in general quantities that vary along the front of external supply, and are therefore functions of points on the boundary of the massif.

Supposing that, when $s = 0$, $dy/ds = 0$ and $\bar{q}_0 = 0$, we obtain from equation (2.80) an expression for the hydrodynamic profiles of mire massifs with centres of convexity or water divides within their boundaries:

$$\frac{dy}{ds} = \frac{1}{\overline{M}_s b_s} \int_0^s \bar{p}_s b_s \, ds. \qquad (2.83)$$

As is plain from equations (2.80) and (2.83), the outline of the hydrodynamic profiles of a mire massif along a given line of flow is determined by changes in the slope dy/ds along the length s, and depends upon three functions: $\overline{M}_s = \overline{M}(s)$, $\bar{p}_s = \bar{p}(s)$ and $b_s = b(s)$. $\overline{M}(s)$ characterizes changes in the average modulus of seepage along the flowline, $\bar{p}(s)$ changes in the average intensity of internal supply, and $b(s)$ changes in the length of the front of flow.

When the supply of moisture is purely meteoric, the average intake at the surface of the mire $\bar{p}_s$ cannot change along the flowline, except through differences in the norm of evaporation owing to changes in the character of the microtopes along the flowline. Overlooking these relatively small changes (see section 2.11) in a first approximation, we may take the value of $\bar{p}_s$ to be constant along any flowline of a massif with a meteoric water supply. In the case of massifs with a significant exchange of water with the subjacent soil (as is usually the case only in fens that occupy river valleys and lakeside depressions), the value of $\bar{p}_s$ may change very substantially along the flowline. When the volume of moisture seeping from the peat deposit into permeable layers of the subjacent soil is greater than the meteoric supply, $\bar{p}_s$ may even have a negative value. Substantial changes in $\bar{p}_s$ along the flowline may also be caused by large-scale local intrusions of pressure water from subjacent layers into the peat deposit, or by periodic downcutting in the level of a river draining a mire situated in its flood-plain or terrace. In the most general case, the value of $\bar{p}_s$ at any point in the flowline is equal to the algebraic sum of meteoric supply, evaporation and water exchange with the subjacent soil in accordance with equation (2.63). In this, the water exchange between the peat deposit and the subjacent soil at a point in the massif must be thought of as an intrusion of pressure water from subjacent aquifers, or, on the other hand, as a seepage from the peat deposit into subjacent horizons. Change along a flowline may be continuous, or, as has been pointed out, discrete.

Let us now differentiate equation (2.80) with respect to s. Keeping in view the fact that the sign of $\bar{p}_s$ is determined by the values of $\bar{p}_p$, $\bar{p}_e$ and $\bar{p}_{gr}$, and supposing that $\bar{p}_s$ remains constant within the limits of the flowline under consideration (from $s = 0$ to s), we obtain the equation

$$\frac{d^2y}{ds^2} = \left(\bar{q}_0 b_0 + \bar{p}_s \int_0^s b_s \, ds \right) \frac{d}{ds}\left(\frac{1}{\overline{M}_s \, b_s} \right) + \frac{\bar{p}_s}{\overline{M}_s}. \tag{2.84}$$

Let us now suppose that $\bar{p}_s > 0$ in the section of the flowline under consideration. As is plain from equation (2.63), this can be satisfied in the following ways:

(1) When $\bar{p}_{gr} = 0$, and the norm of precipitation $\bar{p}_p$ is greater than that of evaporation $\bar{p}_e$. This occurs when a mire massif is situated in the climatic zone of excess moisture and there is no water exchange with the subjacent soil.

(2) When the norm of precipitation $\bar{p}_p$ is greater than that of evaporation $\bar{p}_e$, and the intake of moisture from the subjacent horizons $\bar{p}_{gr} > 0$ (i.e. there is a pressure supply), or there is an efflux into the subjacent horizons ($\bar{p}_{gr} < 0$), but the absolute value $\bar{p}_{gr}$ remains less than the difference ($\bar{p}_p - \bar{p}_e$).

(3) When the norm of precipitation $\bar{p}_p$ is less than that of evaporation $\bar{p}_e$, but the pressure supply from the subjacent soil $\bar{p}_{gr} > (\bar{p}_e - \bar{p}_p)$.

This last case occurs only in the zone of deficient moisture, when the amount of external water supply from soil or surface, as expressed by the term $\bar{q}_0 b_0$, must always be either positive or equal to zero.

It follows that, when there is a positive balance in the internal water supply of a mire massif, the second term on the right-hand side of equation (2.84) $\bar{p}_s / \overline{M}_s$ will always be positive, as well as the first expression in brackets on the right-hand side of the equation. The sign of the whole of the first term on the right-hand side of equation (2.84) is therefore determined by the sign of the derivative $(\mathrm{d}/\mathrm{d}s)(1/\overline{M}_s b_s)$, which depends on the law governing changes in the product $\overline{M}_s b_s$ along the flowline s. It is obvious that if the flowlines diverge and b_s increases $(\mathrm{d}b_s/\mathrm{d}s > 0)$, the sign of the derivative will be negative, if it be also the case that the modulus of seepage $\overline{M}_s$ also grows, or remains constant, or diminishes less rapidly than the reciprocal of b_s. In that case, the sign of $\mathrm{d}^2 y/\mathrm{d}s^2$ depends on the relation between the numerical values of the terms on the right-hand side of equation (2.84). When

$$\frac{\bar{p}_s}{\overline{M}_s} > \left| \left(\bar{q}_0 b_0 + \bar{p}_s \int_0^s b_s \, \mathrm{d}s \right) \frac{\mathrm{d}}{\mathrm{d}s}\left(\frac{1}{\overline{M}_s b_s} \right) \right| = |A|, \qquad (2.85)$$

the sign of $\mathrm{d}^2 y/\mathrm{d}s^2$ in (2.84) will be positive, and consequently, in the accepted system of coordinates (see Fig. 17), the curve of the surface of the mire massif along any flowline must be convex. When

$$\frac{\bar{p}_s}{\overline{M}_s} < \left| \left(\bar{q}_0 b_0 + \bar{p}_s \int_0^s b_s \, \mathrm{d}s \right) \frac{\mathrm{d}}{\mathrm{d}s}\left(\frac{1}{\overline{M}_s b_s} \right) \right| = |A|, \qquad (2.85')$$

the sign of the derivative $\mathrm{d}^2 y/\mathrm{d}s^2$ will be negative. Consequently, the curve of the surface along the flowline must be concave.

From this it follows that, if there is a positive balance of internal water supply and the product of the modulus of seepage and the breadth of the front of flow increases along the flowline, the hydrodynamic profile of the massif may be either convex or concave.

If, when the flowlines diverge, the decrease in the modulus of seepage along the flowline is faster than the increase in the front or flow, i.e.

$$\left| \frac{\mathrm{d}\overline{M}_s}{\mathrm{d}s} \right| > \frac{\mathrm{d}b_s}{\mathrm{d}s}, \qquad (2.86)$$

then $(\mathrm{d}/\mathrm{d}s)(1/\overline{M}_s b_s)$ will be positive, and therefore $\mathrm{d}^2 y/\mathrm{d}s^2$ will be greater than zero, and the hydrodynamic profiles will always be convex.

Let us now consider the case of a convergent flow. Here b_s must decrease as s increases, i.e. $\mathrm{d}b_s/\mathrm{d}s < 0$. The sign of $(\mathrm{d}/\mathrm{d}s)(1/\overline{M}_s b_s)$ must be positive, if the modulus of seepage along the line of flow decreases, remains constant or increases slower than b_s decreases. It is then clear that $\mathrm{d}^2 y/\mathrm{d}s^2$ will always be positive, and that the surface of the massif along the line of flow must be convex.

If the flowlines converge, and the modulus of seepage $\overline{M}_s$ increases faster than b_s decreases, the sign of the derivative $(d/ds)(1/\overline{M}_s b_s)$ will be negative, i.e. we shall be dealing with an instance of the first kind, where the curve of the hydrodynamic profile depends on the factors dealt with in (2.85) and (2.85′).

We have now reviewed the changes that can occur in the relations between $\overline{M}_s$ and b_s along the flowline s, when there is a positive balance in the internal water supply (Table 10). They show that there are three main groups of hydrodynamic profile:

(1) Convex profiles along the whole length of the flowline s. These answer to the condition that the product of the modulus of seepage and the breadth of the front of flow $(\overline{M}_s b_s)$ decreases along s, i.e. $d(\overline{M}_s b_s)/(ds) < 0$.

(2) Complex profiles, whose shape may change along the flowline from convex to concave, or *vice versa*. Their shape is determined by the relation between the factors dealt with in (2.85) and (2.85′) as the distance s increases, and answers to the condition $d(\overline{M}_s b_s)/(ds) \gtrless 0$.

(3) Concave profiles along the whole length of the flowline s. This occurs when $d(\overline{M}_s b_s)/(ds) > 0$ and the condition (2.85′) is satisfied for all values of s from zero upward.

In similar fashion, one can analyse the hydrodynamic profiles of mire massifs with a negative balance in their internal water supply ($\bar{p}_s < 0$), a class of cases that is characteristic for the most part of mires in the zone of deficient moisture. Table 10 gives all the relations between the shape of the hydro-dynamic profile and the quantities that determine it—$\bar{p}_s$, $\overline{M}_s$ and b_s. It is important to note that mires cannot exist when the balance of internal supply is negative, except when the following condition is satisfied:

$$\bar{q}_0 b_0 > \left| \int_0^s \bar{p}_s b_s \, ds \right|. \qquad (2.87)$$

This means that the external water supply must exceed the total loss of moisture in a section whose length is s.

If the external water supply $\bar{q}_0 b_0$ proves to be less than $\left| \int_0^s \bar{p}_s b_s \, ds \right|$, then it is obvious that there can be no mire. It is therefore pointless to consider forms of relief where $\bar{p}_s < 0$, unless they satisfy the inequality (2.87) (see Table 10). This condition defines a relationship which enables one to determine the maximum size of a mire massif along a flowline, once one knows the form

Table 10. Tabulated conspectus of the relation of the shape of the relief of a section of a mire massif to the components of the water supply, its flow characteristics and its geotopic structure

Sign of internal water balance $\bar{P}_s$	Relation between components of water balance giving rise positive or negative value of $\bar{P}_s$	Shape of flow in plan	Change in modulus of throughflow $\bar{M}_s$ (speed of replacement of mire microtope) along streamlines	Sign of magnitude $A\left(\dfrac{d^2y}{ds^2}\right)$ in (2.84)	Relation of members of right-hand side of equation	Shape of relief of surface of mire
1	2	3	4	5	6	7
$\bar{P}_s > 0$	In zone of deficient moisture: $\bar{P}_0 < \bar{P}_e$ and (1) $\bar{P}_{gr} > 0$ and $\bar{P}_{gr} > (\bar{P}_e - \bar{P}_0)$	Divergent b_s increases along s	$\bar{M}_s$ decreases and $\left|\dfrac{d\bar{M}_s}{ds}\right| > \dfrac{db_s}{ds}$ ($\bar{M}_s$ decreases faster than b_s increases)	$+$	$\dfrac{\bar{P}_s}{\bar{M}_s} \gtreqless |A|$	Convex
	In zone of excess moisture: $\bar{P}_0 > \bar{P}_e$ and (1) $\bar{P}_{gr} = 0$ / or (2) $\bar{P}_{gr} > 0$ / or (3) $\bar{P}_{gr} < 0$ and $|\bar{P}_{gr}| < |\bar{P}_0 - \bar{P}_e|$ /	Divergent b_s increases along s	(1) $\bar{M}_s$ decreases and $\left|\dfrac{d\bar{M}_s}{ds}\right| < \dfrac{db_s}{ds}$ / ($\bar{M}_s$ decreases slower than b_s increases) or (2) $\bar{M}_s = $ constant / or (3) $\bar{M}_s$ increases /	$-$	$\dfrac{\bar{P}_s}{\bar{M}_s} > |A|$	Convex
			$\bar{M}_s b_s = $ constant / ($\bar{M}_s$ decreases in inverse proportion to b_s)		$\dfrac{\bar{P}_s}{\bar{M}_s} < |B|$	Concave
					$A = 0$ $\left.\dfrac{\bar{P}_s}{\bar{M}_s}\right\}$ may have any value	Convex
		Convergent b_s decreases along s	(1) $\bar{M}_s$ decreases / or (2) $\bar{M}_s = $ constant / or (3) $\bar{M}_s$ increases / and (3.1) $\dfrac{d\bar{M}_s}{ds} < \left|\dfrac{db_s}{ds}\right|$ / ($\bar{M}_s$ increases slower than b_s decreases)	$+$	$\dfrac{\bar{P}_s}{\bar{M}_s} \lesseqgtr |A|$	Convex
			or (3.2) $\dfrac{d\bar{M}_s}{ds} > \dfrac{db_s}{ds}$ / ($\bar{M}_s$ increases faster than b_s decreases)	$-$	$\dfrac{\bar{P}}{\bar{M}_s} > |A|$	Convex
					$\dfrac{\bar{P}_s}{\bar{M}_s} < |A|$	Concave
			or (3.3) $\bar{M}_s b_s = $ constant /		$A = 0$	Convex

Condition		$\bar{M}_s$ behaviour	Sign	Relation	Form
$\bar{p}_0 < \bar{p}_e$ and (1) $\bar{p}_{gr} > 0$ and $\bar{p}_{gr} < (\bar{p}_e - \bar{p}_0)$ / or (2) $\bar{p}_{gr} = 0$ / or (3) $\bar{p}_{gr} < 0$ /	(b_s increases along s)	M_s decreases and $\dfrac{\cdots}{ds} > \dfrac{\cdots}{ds}$ (M_s decreases faster than b_s increases)	$+$	$\left|\dfrac{\bar{p}_s}{M_s}\right| < A$ — Convex; $\left|\dfrac{\bar{p}_s}{M_s}\right| > A$ — Concave	
In zone of excess moisture: $\bar{p}_0 > \bar{p}_e$ and $\bar{p}_{gr} < 0$ and $|\bar{p}_{gr}| > (\bar{p}_0 - \bar{p}_e)$	Divergent (b_s increases along s)	(1) $\bar{M}_s$ decreases / and (1.1) $\dfrac{d\bar{M}_s}{ds} < \dfrac{db_s}{ds}$ / ($\bar{M}_s$ decreases slower than b_s increases) +			Concave
		or (1.2) $\dfrac{d\bar{M}_s}{ds} = \dfrac{db_s}{ds}$ / ($\bar{M}_s b_s$ = constant and $\bar{M}_s$ decreases in inverse proportion to b_s)		$A = 0$	Concave
		or (2) $\bar{M}_s$ = constant / or (3) $\bar{M}_s$ increases /			
	Convergent (b_s decreases along s)	(1) $\bar{M}_s$ decreases / (2) $\bar{M}_s$ = constant / (3) $\bar{M}_s$ increases		$\left|\dfrac{\bar{p}_s}{M_s}\right| < A$	Convex
		and (3.1) $\dfrac{d\bar{M}_s}{ds} < \left|\dfrac{db_s}{ds}\right|$ / ($\bar{M}_s$ increases slower than b_s decreases) +		$\left|\dfrac{\bar{p}_s}{M_s}\right| > A$	Concave
		or (3.2) $\dfrac{d\bar{M}_s}{ds} > \dfrac{db_s}{ds}$ / ($\bar{M}_s$ increases faster than b_s decreases) −		$\left|\dfrac{\bar{p}_s}{M_s}\right| \lessgtr A$	Concave
		or (3.3) $\dfrac{d\bar{M}_s}{ds} = \dfrac{db_s}{ds}$ / ($\bar{M}_s b_s$ = constant and $\bar{M}_s$ increases in inverse proportion to b_s)		$A = 0$	Concave

NOTES (1) Alternative states are followed by an oblique stroke (/).
(2) When $\bar{p}_s > 0$, the relation between $q_0 b_0$ and $\int_0^s \bar{p}_s b_s \, ds$, which determines the sign of A, may have any value.
(3) When $\bar{p}_s < 0$, $q_0 b_0$ must be greater than $\int_0^s \bar{p}_s b_s \, ds$.
(4) When $\bar{q}_0 b_0 < \int_0^s \bar{p}_s b_s \, ds$, the existence of a mire is impossible.

of flow in plan, i.e. $b_s = b(s)$ and the intensity of water exchange within the massif $\bar{p}_s$. This relation is written in the following form:

$$\int_0^{s_{max}} \bar{p}_s b_s \, ds = \bar{q}_0 b_0, \tag{2.88}$$

where s_{max} is the greatest possible length of the massif along the flowline.

From this last equality it is easy to see that massifs with a high degree of divergence in their flowlines must be the shortest, and massifs with a convergent flow the longest. $\bar{p}_s$ and $\bar{q}_0 b_0$ being constant, the greater the convergence of flow the longer the massif must be along the flowline.

Looking at all the cases in Table 10 where $p_s < 0$, it is not difficult to see that in most cases the relief of the massif along the flowline is concave, and only in two cases convex. Where the internal balance of the water supply of a mire massif is negative, the characteristic form of its relief is concave.

This analysis of the relation between the hydrodynamic profile of a mire massif and its form of flow in plan and internal water balance enables one to deduce the direction of the water exchange between the soil and the massif and the balance of its internal water supply, provided one knows the form of relief along the flowlines, the successive changes in its microtopes as reflected in the values of $\bar{M}_s$ as a function of s and the form of flow in plan $b(s)$. If one knows the forms of relief, the sign and amount of the balance of internal supply, and the order in which the different types of microtope are arranged, it is possible to infer the form of flow in plan and the order of magnitude of its external water supply. Relationships for calculating these will be considered in the sections of the book which follow.

2.14 Plotting the Hydrodynamic Profiles and Relief of a Mire Massif with the help of Aerial Photographs and Hydromorphological Equations

The starting point for all hydrological and hydromorphological calculations based on equation (2.80) is a flow-net constructed by aerial survey and superimposed on the map of a mire massif with indications of the boundaries between the different types of microtope. Flow-nets are often very complex (see Figs 6 and 7), but any flow-net for a complete mire massif, however complex it may appear at first sight, can be broken down into a set of fragments, in each of which a single and reasonably simple law can be found to describe changes in its form of flow $b_s = b(s)$.

To carry out calculations in terms of equation (2.80), one must discover from the flow-net the form of the function b_s which describes the form of flow in plan along the direction one has selected. The function b_s may be given either graphically (see Fig. 22) or analytically. Real mire massifs

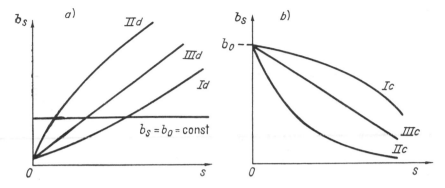

Fig. 22. The connection between changes of b_s and the line of flow s: a). In the case of parallel-flowing and divergent flowlines d; b) In the case of convergent flowlines c.

usually have a complicated flow-net, in which the functions b_s along any flowline cannot be represented by any simple mathematical function. It is therefore advisable to break it down into a set of fragments, in each of which b_s does change along any flowline according to some definite law. For this purpose, it is always possible, however varied and complicated the forms of flow in the plan are, to divide the flow-net into separate fragments and to reduce them all to no more then seven basic forms (Fig. 23):

(1) Divergent flow of type I (Fig. 23a).
(2) Divergent flow of type II (Fig. 23b).
(3) Divergent flow of type III (Fig. 23c).
(4) Parallel (including level) flow (Fig. 23d).
(5) Convergent (centripetal) flow of type I (Fig. 23e).
(6) Convergent flow of type II (Fig. 23f).
(7) Convergent flow of type III (Fig. 23g).

Within the limits of any such fragment, the degree of convergence or divergence can obviously be characterized by the increase or decrease of the length of the arc of the front of flow contained between two neighbouring flowlines measured against the length s of the average flowline, i.e. by the derivative db_s/ds. In the case of divergent and convergent flows of the first type, the numerical value of the derivative $|db_s/ds|$ will obviously increase continuously with s (see Fig. 23a and e). In the case of divergent and convergent flows of the second type, the value of $|db_s/ds|$ will decrease as s increases (see Fig. 23b and f). When finally the directions of divergence and convergence are at right angles to the average flowline, $|db_s/ds|$ will be constant, i.e. independent of s.

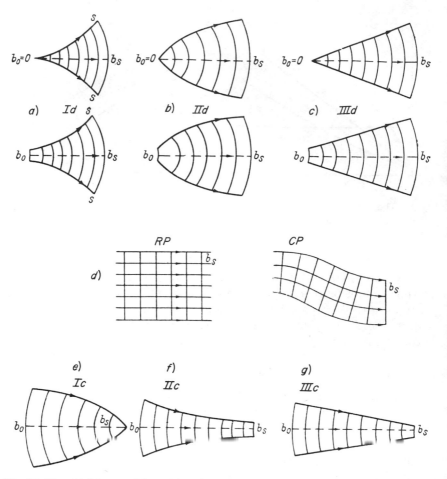

Fig. 23. The chief forms of flow. *Id, IId, IIId*—divergent flows of the 1st. 2nd and 3rd types. *Ic, IIc, IIIc*—convergent flows of the 1st, 2nd and 3rd types. *RP, CP*—rectilinear-parallel and curvilinear-parallel types of flow. b_s—variable front of flow. b_0—initial front of flow.

For a divergent flow of the first type, a graph of b_s as a function of s will then be a downward directed convexity (see Fig. 22a, curve Id), for one of the second type, an upward directed convexity (IId), and for one of the third type, a straight line (IIId). For parallel flow $db_s/ds = 0$. In all three types of convergent flow (Fig. 22b), we have to deal with analogous functions involving a decrease in b_s as s increases.

All expressions relating changes in the breadth of the arc (or front of flow) to increases of s in fragments of all the types indicated can be represented approximately by exponential or logarithmic functions:

$$b_s = as^n + b_0, \qquad (2.89)$$

$$b_s = b_0 e^{as}, \qquad (2.89')$$

where b_0 is the breadth of the front of flow between two neighbouring flow-lines at the beginning of the fragment, a and n are constants and e is the base of natural logarithms. In expression (2.89):

$a > 0$ for all divergent flows and $a < 0$ for all convergent flows;
$|n| > 1$ for all divergent and convergent flows of the first type;
$|n| < 1$ for all divergent and convergent flows of the second type; and
$|n| = 1$ for all divergent and convergent flows of the third type.

For simplicity's sake, the forms of divergent and convergent flow shown in Fig. 23 have rectilinear axes. In real mire massifs, flow-nets often cannot be broken down into fragments without the use of curvilinear axes; but even in such cases the types of divergent and convergent flow are identical. Fragments with curvilinear axes of flow may be called curvilinear-divergent flows of the Ist, IInd and IIIrd types and curvilinear-convergent flows of the Ist, IInd and IIIrd types. It is often difficult to determine by direct inspection to which type a given fragment belongs. In such cases, it is always possible to transform the curvilinear axis of flow into a straight line, and, marking off the distances to neighbouring flowlines, obtain forms of flow with a rectilinear axis. After this it is not difficult to determine with the aid of the forms shown in Fig. 23 the type to which the given curvilinear fragment belongs. It is still easier to identify the characteristic form of a curvilinear fragment by making a graph of the function $b_s = \phi(s)$.

When one wishes to identify the form of flow in a given fragment, it is better to express equation (2.80) in dimensionless quantities, because in that case the value of the term $\int_0^s b_s \, ds$, which describes the divergence or convergence of flow, does not depend on the size of the fragment, but only on its form, and is identical for all similar fragments of any size. We take as our unit of measure the length of the first arc b_0. Then the distances s_* along the flowline, the arc lengths b_s, and the altitudes y_s must be expressed as follows:

$$s_* = \frac{s}{b_0}; \qquad b_{s_*} = \frac{b_s}{b_0}; \qquad y_* = \frac{y}{b_0}. \qquad (2.90)$$

Substituting the dimensionless values s_*, b_{s_*} and y_* in equations (2.79) and (2.80), and supposing that the intensity of the internal water supply remains constant within the limits of the fragment ($\bar{p}_s = \bar{p}_c$), we obtain

$$\bar{q}_{s*} = \frac{1}{b_{s*}}\left(\bar{q}_0 + \bar{p}_c b_0 \int_0^{s*} b_{s*}\,ds_*\right), \tag{2.91}$$

$$\frac{dy_*}{ds_*} = \frac{1}{\bar{M}_s b_s}\left(\bar{q}_0 + \bar{p}_c b_0 \int_0^{s*} b_{s*}\,ds_*\right). \tag{2.92}$$

Expressions (2.89) and (2.89′) will take corresponding forms:

$$b_{s*} = a_* s_*^n + 1, \tag{2.93}$$

where $a_* = ab_0^{n-1}$, and

$$b_{s*} = e^{a_* s_*}, \tag{2.94}$$

where $a_* = ab_0$.

It will be noted that the expressions (2.93) and (2.94) reduce to (2.89) and (2.89′), if we make the initial breadth of flow b_0 in the fragment (a breadth that can be chosen at will) equal to one unit in the given system of measurements (e.g. 1 km or 1 m). It should be remembered that the coefficients a_* and a depend upon the chosen system of measurement.

Substituting the values of b_{s*} given in (2.93) and (2.94) in equation (2.92), and then integrating, we obtain the following differential equations:

$$dy = \frac{\bar{q}_0 + \bar{p}_c b_0\left(\dfrac{a_*}{n+1} s_*^{n+1} + s_*\right)}{\bar{M}(a_* s_*^n + 1)}\,ds_*, \tag{2.95}$$

$$dy = \frac{\bar{q}_0 + \bar{p}_c b_0 \dfrac{1}{a_*}(e^{a_* s_*} - 1)}{\bar{M}_s e^{a_* s_*}}\,ds_*. \tag{2.96}$$

For fragments with a divergent flow, when the origin of the flowline (where $s = 0$) is the centre of a convexity (i.e. $b_0 = 0$), equation (2.89) for finding b_s has the form

$$b_s = as^n. \tag{2.89″}$$

Substituting this last expression in equation (2.80), and supposing that $p_s = p_0 = $ constant and $b_0 = 0$, we obtain

$$dy = \frac{\bar{p}_c s}{(n+1)\bar{M}_s}\,ds. \tag{2.97}$$

The final forms of the relationship $y = f(s)$, i.e. of the equations of the hydrodynamic profiles within the boundary of each fragment considered, must be determined by the form of the function $\overline{M}_s = \psi(s)$, which is the law governing changes in the modulus of seepage along the flowline. That in turn is identical with the law that governs changes in the mire microtopes along the flowline, and with the values of the power n and the coefficient a_* which define the divergence or convergence of the form of flow.

Taking the upper boundary of the fragment as the origin from which are measured the distances s and the elevations y, and confining ourselves to finite differences, we obtain empirical formulae for constructing the profiles of a mire massif by aerial survey and physical assessment of the properties of the acrotelm of mire microtopes:

$$y_N = \sum_{j=0}^{j=N} \frac{\bar{q}_0 + \bar{p}_c b_0 \left(\dfrac{a_*}{n+1} s_{*j}^{n+1} + s_{*j} \right)}{\overline{M}_j (a_* s_*^n + 1)} \Delta s_j, \qquad (2.98)$$

$$v_N = \sum_{j=0}^{j=N} \frac{\bar{q}_0 + \bar{p}_c b_0 \dfrac{1}{a_*} (e^{a_* s_{*j}} - 1)}{\overline{M}_j e^{a_* s_{*j}}} \Delta s_j, \qquad (2.99)$$

where y_N is the height of the surface of the massif at s_N compared to its height at the origin of the fragment, N is the number of intervals into which the distance s_N has been analysed, and j is the ordinal number of the given interval.

When flow-nets are worked out for different mire massifs and they are broken down into fragments, they show that in the case of divergent and convergent flows of the first type the value of n does not exceed 2, and is not lower than 0·5 in those of the second type. The value of a_* very naturally varies widely. For that reason, acutely divergent flows, which conform with the logarithmic law (2.89′) are relatively rare, and are usually confined to profiles running along the flowlines of a water divide (see Figs 6 and 7).

Hydrodynamic profiles with a complex network of flowlines can also be constructed without breaking them down into fragments and finding analytic expressions for the form of flow in each fragment. To do this it is necessary to make direct use of the relationship (2.80), adapting it to the finite differences Δy and Δs in the form

$$\Delta y_j = \frac{\bar{q}_0 b_0 + \sum_1^m \bar{p}_{s_j} b_{s_j} \Delta s_j}{\overline{M}_{s_j} b_{s_j}} \Delta s_j = \frac{(\bar{q}_{j-1} b_{j-1} + \bar{p}_{s_j} b_{s_j} \Delta s_j) \Delta s_j}{\overline{M}_{s_j} b_{s_j}}, \qquad (2.100)$$

where Δy_j is the difference between the levels of the profile at the beginning and end of the measured interval Δs_j, into which the whole length of the flowline has been broken down, and j is the ordinal number of the interval counted from the beginning of the flowline where $s = 0$. In writing (2.100) it is assumed that the modulus of seepage $\overline{M}_s$ and the internal water supply $\bar{p}_s$ change along the flowline, and that $\bar{q}_{j-1}b_{j-1}$ is the discharge of water flowing across the front of influx into the jth interval.

When equations (2.98) and (2.100) are used, choice of the most suitable method of calculating profiles depends on the particular form of the flow-net of the mire massif under consideration, on the number of profiles that are to be calculated and constructed and on the means available for calculating and abstracting data from an aerial plan of the mire. When use is made of computers and graph-reading devices (in this case, the graphs are flow-nets), it is to be noted that equation (2.100) is the more convenient relationship. Exact integration in analytic form of equations (2.95) and (2.96) is only possible in the case of certain definite forms of the function $\overline{M}_s$. Even when $\overline{M}_s$ is a simple linear function of s, having, for example, the form

$$\overline{M}_s = Bs + \overline{M}_0,$$

where $\overline{M}_0$ is the modulus of seepage at the beginning of the flowline and B is a constant, integration produces very complex expressions. In general, integration is only possible for certain values of n, in particular for radially divergent or convergent flow (type III), when $n = 1$. When $n = 2$, a general integral for equation (2.95) can no longer be written, and a solution can be looked for only in the case of particular numerical values of $\overline{M}_s$, B and a_* (Ivanov, 1965). Table 11 gives the equations for cases where b_0 and q_0 are equal to zero and $\overline{M}_s$ is variable. The very important cases involving integration of equations (2.95) and (2.96) are however those where the values of the modulus of

Table 11. Equations of hydrodynamic profiles where there is divergent flow from a centre of convexity $(b_0 = 0, q_0 = 0)$ and parallel flow with change along the streamline of the modulus of seepage $\overline{M}_s$

Law of change of $\overline{M}_s$	Equation
Linear change: $\overline{M}_s = Bs + \overline{M}_0$ (where B is a constant and $\overline{M}_0$ is the value of M_s when $s = 0$)	$y = \dfrac{\bar{p}_c}{(n+1)B}\left(s + \dfrac{\overline{M}_0}{B}\ln\dfrac{\overline{M}_0}{\overline{M}_0 + Bs}\right)$
Non-linear change: $\overline{M}_s = Bs^2 + \overline{M}_0$	$y = \dfrac{\bar{p}_c}{2(n+1)B}\ln\left(1 + \dfrac{Bs^2}{\overline{M}_0}\right)$

NOTE   The value of n depends on the form of flow (see Table 13).

seepage along the line of flow $\overline{M}_s$ are constant ($\overline{M}_s = \overline{M} = $ const., see Tables 12 and 13).

In accordance with section 2.8, hydrodynamic profiles whose equations entail constancy in the modulus of seepage along the flowline will be called *normal profiles of the outline of a mire massif*. In such cases, the shape of the profile, as follows from equations (2.95) and (2.96), will depend only on the law which governs the extent to which the flowlines of the massif diverge or converge, i.e. on the values of n and a, and on those of its water supply $\overline{p}_s$ and $\overline{q}_0$. Integrating equation (2.95) from 0 to s with $\overline{M}_s$ constant, and taking 1, 2 and 3 as values of n, we obtain a set of equations for normal profiles when there is an external water supply $\overline{q}_0$ (see Table 12).

If we take a set of particular values, like $\overline{q}_0 = 10 \ \text{l.s}^{-1}.\text{km}^{-1}$; $\overline{p}_s = 200 \ \text{mm/year}$; $\overline{M}_s = 120 \ \text{cm}^2/\text{s}$, $40 \ \text{cm}^2/\text{s}$, and $10 \ \text{cm}^2/\text{s}$; and $a = 0.5$, 1.0 and 2.0, we

Table 12. Equations for the normal hydrodynamic profiles of a stream with an external water supply ($q_0 \neq 0$), whose divergence is expressed by the exponential function ($b_{s_*} + a_* s_*^n + 1$)

Values of n in function $b_{s_*} = a_* s_*^n + 1$	Type of diverging stream	Equation
1	III	$y_* = \dfrac{\overline{q}_0}{a\overline{M}} \ln(as_* + 1) +$ $+ \dfrac{\overline{p}_c b_0}{2\overline{M}}\left[\left(\dfrac{s_*^2}{2} + \dfrac{s_*}{a}\right) - \dfrac{1}{a^2}\ln(as_* + 1)\right]$
2	I	$y_* = \dfrac{\overline{q}_0}{\overline{M}\sqrt{a}} \operatorname{arctg}\sqrt{a \cdot s_*} +$ $+ \dfrac{\overline{p}_c b_0}{3\overline{M}}\left[\dfrac{s_*^2}{2} + \dfrac{1}{2a}\ln(as_*^2 + 1)\right]$
3	I	$y_* = \dfrac{\overline{q}_0}{\overline{M}a^{1/3}}\left(\dfrac{1}{6}\ln\sigma + \dfrac{1}{\sqrt{3}}\operatorname{arctg}\dfrac{2as_* - 1}{\sqrt{3}}\right) +$ $+ \dfrac{3\overline{p}_c b_0}{4\overline{M}a^{2/3}}\left(\dfrac{1}{6}\ln\dfrac{1}{\sigma} +\right.$ $\left. + \dfrac{1}{\sqrt{3}}\operatorname{arctg}\dfrac{2a^{1/3} - 1}{\sqrt{3}}\right),$ where $\sigma = \dfrac{1 + 2a^{1/3}s_* + a^{2/3}s_*^2}{1 - a^{1/3}s_* + a^{2/3}s_*^2}$

find that when divergence is acute ($n = 3$) the normal hydrodynamic profiles have a concave shape. When divergence is small, as when $n = 1$ and divergence is radial, the shape is convex. Finally, when $n = 2$, the profile is concave at the beginning, but becomes convex as s increases.

In the case of a circular mire massif with radially divergent flow (type III), the equation of the normal profile is obtained from equation (2.97) by putting $n = 1$ and $s = r$, since the flowlines of such a massif are the radii of a circle (see Table 13):

$$y = \frac{\bar{p}_c r^2}{4\bar{M}}. \tag{2.101}$$

The equation for the normal profile of parallel planar flow diverging from a water divide within a massif is obtained from equation (2.95) by putting $\bar{q}_0 = 0$, $n = 0$ and $b_0 = 1$, and integrating from 0 to s (see Table 13):

$$y = \frac{\bar{p}_c s^2}{2\bar{M}}. \tag{2.102}$$

Table 13. Parameters of the equation of normal hydrological profiles of parallel flowlines ($q_0 = 0$) and flowlines diverging from a centre of convexity ($b_0 = 0$, $q_0 = 0$)

Type of flowlines	n	β
Parallel flowlines	0	2
Divergent flowlines of type II	$0 < n < 1$	$2 < \beta < 4$
Radially divergent flowlines of type III	1	4
Divergent flowlines of type I	> 1	> 4

NOTE   The general form of such equations is: $y = \dfrac{\bar{p}_c s^2}{\beta \bar{M}} = \dfrac{\bar{p}_c s^2}{2(n + 1)\bar{M}}$.

When the massif has an external water supply, the equation of the profile for parallel-planar flow has a corresponding form:

$$y = \frac{\bar{p}_c s^2}{2\bar{M}} + \frac{q_0 s}{\bar{M}}. \tag{2.103}$$

Equations (2.101), (2.102) and (2.103) deal therefore with the simplest planar projections of mire massifs, to which all actual massifs can be reduced by application of the already considered principle of hydrological equivalence (see section 2.11). This permits one to use these equations to discover resemblances between mire massifs that differ in the quantity of their water supply, and to find analogies between massifs that differ in their physico-geographic and climatic circumstances.

If in equations (2.101), (2.102) and (2.103) we replace the norm of internal supply $\bar{p}_c$ with an equal norm of efflux $\bar{m}$, raise the ordinates of the profile y to their maximum, and put r_o and s_o for r and s (see section 2.11), we find that

$$\bar{m} = \frac{4\bar{M}y_{max}}{r_o^2}, \tag{2.104'}$$

$$\bar{m} = \frac{2\bar{M}y_{max}}{s_o^2}, \tag{2.104''}$$

$$\bar{m} = \frac{2\bar{M}y_{max}}{s_o^2} - \frac{2\bar{q}_0}{s_o}. \tag{2.104'''}$$

From these last equations it follows that mire massifs with an internal water supply cannot have the same norms of efflux if they are situated in regions with a different climate (i.e. with a different relation between their norms of precipitation and evaporation), unless:

(a) Having the same morphology, as defined by y_{max}/r_o^2 or y_{max}/s_o^2, they have different values of $\bar{M}$, i.e. are composed of different microtopes.
(b) Having the same values of $\bar{M}$, they have the same morphology.
(c) They have a different internal water exchange with the subjacent soil.

In the case of convex massifs, this entails different losses by seepage into the subjacent soil, since discharges of pressure water into the peat deposit of convex massifs are practically unknown.

When massifs are identical in their projected area and the composition of their microtopes, but have different norms of efflux (or of internal supply), their convexity (y_{max}) must change. When, however, they have the same convexity and microtopes, a change in the norms of efflux must result in a change in the projected area of the massif. Equation (2.104''') is an analogous relationship for simulating mire massifs with an external water supply. In this relationship, the modulus of efflux $\bar{m}$ describes the actual efflux from the mire massif. This may be called the partial efflux in the same way as, in the case of river basins, the relation between the increase of discharge at two successive weirs to the difference between their catchment areas is called the partial modulus of efflux. Obviously, a mire massif cannot have an actual efflux in this sense, unless the term $2\bar{M}y_{max}/s_o^2$, which depends on the intensity of the internal water supply, is greater than $2\bar{q}_0/s_o$, which represents the external water supply. If this is not the case, equation (2.104''') expresses the modulus of absorption by the massif of part of the water received by it from outside. In other words, the massif would deliver across its boundary a smaller quantity of water than it had received. This phenomenon is also observed in mires situated in regions of deficient moisture, i.e. with a long-term average index of aridity > 1. The modulus of absorption of efflux by a mire massif is therefore expressed by the equation

$$\overline{m}_{abs} = \frac{2\overline{q}_0}{s_o^2} - \frac{2\overline{M}y_{max}}{s_o^2}.$$ (2.105)

It must be emphasized that, since all actual mire massifs can be reduced to very simple equivalent forms (circular with radially divergent and rectangular with parallel flow), expressions (2.104′), (2.104″), (2.104‴) and (2.105) have a completely general character. They can therefore be used to compare the water balance of different mire massifs, to look in hydrological calculations for analogous massifs in different geophysical conditions, and to solve problems about the effect of mire transformation upon their water balance and the condition of the surrounding countryside. It goes without saying that the principle of hydrological equivalence is not in itself a sufficient basis for generalizations about the internal structure of mire systems and the items in their water regime that are connected with it.

The introduction of the concept of a normal profile for mire massifs (Ivanov, 1957b) makes it possible to evaluate more strictly from a physical point of view the whole spectrum of existing profiles. These may differ from the normal ones, and are described by telematologists in purely qualitative terms as "acutely convex" or "slightly convex" according to the arrangement of the different types of microtope on the mire massif (Romanova, 1961). A profile combination may undoubtedly be called acutely convex when the function $B_s - \phi(s)$ changes in such a way that the modulus of seepage $\overline{M}_s$ decreases as s increases, i.e. the water saturation of the microtopes decreases along the flowline. On the other hand, a profile combination should be called slightly convex when changes in b_s along the flowline s are associated with an increase in the modulus of seepage $\overline{M}_s$ and in the water saturation of the microtopes. If we accept this definition, it is plain that for every function of the form $b_s = \phi(s)$ there is set of normal profiles, each with its own norm of seepage $\overline{M}_s = $ const., by reference to which sets of actual profiles with the known values $\overline{M}_s = \psi(s)$ can be classified as acutely or slightly convex.

In actual fact, mire massifs cannot usually be referred as a whole to any one class, like the acutely convex or the slightly convex, even when they have a symmetrical (circular or rectangular) shape, or consist of fragments of a single type (see section 2.14). Real mire massifs (even when they make up only a single mesotope) usually have a slightly convex or normal profile along the direction of one group of flowlines, and an acutely convex one along the other. Unless a mire massif has one of these types of profile along its whole length, it cannot properly be said to have an acutely convex, slightly convex or normal profile. Obviously this can occur only in massifs that consist of a single mesotope, and is totally excluded in the case of those that make up macrotopes. Ivanov and Kotova (1964) cite examples of profiles of mire massifs with a very simple structure—the moss-mires (*ryams*) of Siberia, each of which makes up a single mesotope. These show that one and the same hydrodynamic profile may have one branch that is acutely convex, and another one that is slightly convex or has a complex structure, i.e. part of the profile changes from being acutely convex to being slightly convex. Such massifs often have either completely or incompletely developed normal profiles. In most cases, however, the profiles encountered are of complex structure, containing one part that is acutely convex and another that is slightly convex or normal. The application of the terms "acutely convex" or "slightly convex" to mire massifs as a whole is often impossible. They have physical meaning and practical significance only when they are used in relation to hydrodynamic profiles along particular flowlines and their constituent parts.

3

Calculation of Water Exchange in Mires by Water Balance Methods

3.1 Fundamental Problems

The water exchange of mires and wetlands with their surroundings (the atmosphere and the lithosphere), and within their own peat deposits, is one of the fundamental processes that determine the development of mire systems and the formation of the biogenic components of the geotopes of low-lying areas in the zone of excess moisture. All engineering and economic measures directed at the development and use of wetlands must be carried out in conformity with the need to conserve and permit the renewal of natural resources. This implies that the development of large mire massifs and wetlands must be based upon a correct control of the natural water regime which guarantees optimal conditions, not only for the use of the developed areas, but for the condition of the geotopes of surrounding and adjacent lands. It also poses the problem of predicting the effects of reclamation and calculating the best way to control the natural regime. In every case, this involves soundly based calculations of water exchange under natural conditions and investigation of the two-way relationship between the processes of water exchange and the state of the elements of which the natural geotope is composed.

For this reason, calculations of water exchange and the water balance methods used for this purpose may be directed at very different goals. Of these we shall enumerate only a few connected with the development of wetlands and the hydrological basis of land improvement which are of special importance under modern conditions. In this number we must include:

(1) Evaluation of the part played by rivers and wetlands in the water supply of rivers and lakes, in the water balance of river catchments and in the actual flow of rivers.

138

(2) Investigation of the influence of large-scale drainage works and economic activities on the water regime of areas that have been re-claimed and those adjoining them (on the water table, runoff and the balance of water bodies), as well as on the condition of nature in the lands that surround them. In recent years this problem has become especially important from a practical point of view because of the large-scale works that have been planned and are being carried out, like the drainage and reclamation of huge areas of wetland in certain regions of our country (the Byelo-Russian Polesie and the West Siberian plain).

(3) Establishment of how the water regime and geotopes of wetlands are affected by rises of water level resulting from hydrotechnical works and large-scale transfer of the flow of rivers across water divides from one basin to another.

(4) Calculation of water exchange and water reserves in the rooting layer of the soil, from which plants draw their water supply in drained mire massifs used as agricultural land. This is done to establish a regime for draining or irrigating in periods of excessive humidity or drought (both in yearly cycles and over long-term periods), and also when one is using drainage-irrigation systems to regulate the water regime according to the anticipated meteorological conditions.

(5) Calculations of the regime of water exchange in the upper layers of the peat deposit and the zone of aeration of mires that have been drained for the production of peat or some kind of construction: roads, pipe-lines for oil and gas, houses and factories.

Calculations of water exchange with these varied tasks in view must be carried out for different types of mire massif, and for large-scale mire systems and wetlands of more complex structure, differing in their conditions of origin, in their relief, in their plant cover, in the structure of their peat deposits, and, above all, in their water supply and exchange of water with the subjacent soil. The structure of equations of water balance and the magnitude of the terms contained in them must therefore correspond to the peculiarities of the object with which they deal and the requirements of the problem to be solved. For this reason, we consider below the different methods of calculation and the stock of information required, using examples that are closely connected with the solution of the above enumerated problems.

3.2   Calculation of Water Exchange in Swampy River Catchments Containing Undrained Mire Massifs

Swampy catchments may have three different types of structure according to the size and situation of the mire massifs they contain.

(1) A mire massif with a convex surface (corresponding to the third phase of development of mire massifs—see sections 1.6 and 1.7) may be situated wholly within the catchment of a river. Water discharged from the massif flows first to the boundaries of the mire, to which also flows the discharge from the unswamped part of the catchment, which surrounds the massif on all sides like a ring and has a surface sloping down from the water divide to the boundaries. The water discharged from the swamped and unswamped parts of the catchment is therefore concentrated at first in its lowest part— a ring-shaped bordering strip of peat and mineral soil where the swamps and streams are formed which will carry the discharge on to the catchment mouth of the basin.

(2) A mire massif may be situated completely within a river catchment, but have a concave or flat surface with a general slope toward the river channels in the catchment. This case is typical of catchments containing mire massifs originating on river terraces or flood plains. Such massifs are usually found in the first (fen) or second (transitional) phase of development, and are exemplified by various types of sedge, reed, *Hypnum*–sedge or ligneous microtopes (with eutrophic plant associations).

(3) A mire massif, or group of mire massifs, may be a water divide, and some parts of it may lie within the terrain of two or more adjacent river basins (see Fig. 7).

It is important to note that these three "synthetic" cases of swampy catchment structure are directly deducible from the general principles that govern the geotopic structure of level areas in the zones of excessive, unstable and deficient moisture and the zoning of mires according water supply and the mesorelief of the site (see section 1.4). In the zone of excessive moisture there are also many catchments where mires are situated on level water divides, flood plains or broad river terraces. This kind of structure is characteristic of river catchments of the forest zone, which cover a great area in Western Siberia and the north-east of the East European plain.

Some swampy catchments in the zone of deficient moisture have a peculiar structure. This is the presence on level water divides of slight depressions occupied by concave or flat mire massifs with no runoff (the first phase of development). Such catchments are found, for example, in the middle and southern zone of the Baraba lowlands.

In each of the classes of catchment considered above we must of course distinguish between those river-drained swampy catchments where the amount of runoff measured at the catchment mouth is practically equivalent to the total runoff, and those where the total runoff is greater than that which is recorded at the catchment mouth because of leakages into deeper water-bearing layers of soil that are not drained by the river network.

For the purpose of constructing an equation of water balance, this last case is the more general one, and therefore, in dealing with all variants in the structure of swampy catchments, we shall proceed on the assumption that river catchments are not insulated. Equations for the water balance of insulated catchments will then be treated as special cases of a more general expression. We shall formulate two equations for water balance—one for swampy river catchments as a whole, whose area is determined by the position of the point of discharge of the river, and the other for mire massifs that are situated inside the boundary of the catchment.

We shall now introduce the following symbols, each of which is to be regarded as a function of an agreed interval of time:

X—Precipitation.

Y_1—Runoff into river network.

Y_2—Water exchange with horizons not drained by the river network. (leakages or discharges of pressure water).

Z—Evaporation.

ΔW—Change in water storage over the agreed period.

All components are in millimetres of equivalent depth. The subscript "m" indicates that one of the components is considered only in relation to mire massifs, and the subscript "d" that it is considered only in relation to the unswamped part of the catchment. "Y_{1m}" stands for the equivalent depth of runoff from mires.

Taking the depth of precipitation falling in a given interval of time on the mire massifs and the whole catchment to be equal,[1] we obtain the following equations:

$$X = Z + Y_1 + Y_2 + \Delta W, \qquad (3.1)$$

$$X = Z_m + Y_{1m} + Y_{2m} + \Delta W_m. \qquad (3.2)$$

One set of symbols will be used for water storage ΔW and leakage Y_2 in the swamped part of the catchment, and another set of symbols for the same quantities in its unswamped part. If we indicate the total area of the catchment by F and the area of mire in it by ω, we may write:

$$\Delta W = \frac{F - \omega}{F} \Delta W_d + \frac{\omega}{F} \Delta W_m, \tag{3.3}$$

$$Y_2 = \frac{F - \omega}{F} Y_{2d} + \frac{\omega}{F} Y_{2m}. \tag{3.4}$$

The following relations can be deduced from (3.2)–(3.4):

$$Y_{2m} = X - Z_m - Y_{1m} - \Delta W_m, \tag{3.5}$$

$$Y_2 + \Delta W = X - Z - Y_1, \tag{3.6}$$

$$Y_{2d} + \Delta W_d = \frac{F(\Delta W + Y_2) - \omega(\Delta W_m + Y_{2m})}{F - \omega}$$

$$= \frac{1}{1 - \delta} [(\Delta W + Y_2) - \delta(\Delta W_m + Y_{2m})]$$

$$= \frac{1}{1 - \delta} [(X - Z - Y_1) - \delta(X - Z_m - Y_{1m})]. \tag{3.7}$$

These equations, in which $\delta = \omega/F$, are useful for two purposes. Firstly, they make it possible to determine movements of water in mire massifs between peat deposits and the subjacent soil. Secondly, they make it possible to determine the sum of losses into undrained horizons and changes of water storage in catchments and their unswamped parts. These components of the water balance are the most difficult to determine by an independent method.

Over sufficiently long periods of time the annual changes in water storage ($\sum\Delta W$, $\sum\Delta W_m$, $\sum\Delta W_d$) tend, as we know, to zero, and equations (3.5)–(3.7) make it possible to calculate the average water exchange of mire massifs (Y_{2m}), of catchments as a whole (Y_2) and their unswamped part (Y_{2d}).

Evaluation of the magnitude and direction (loss or pressure supply) of water exchange between mire massifs and subjacent soils is an important task not only for hydrological calculations and as a basis of schemes for draining mires and regulating their water regime, but also for determining the contribution that mires make to the maintenance of river systems. This last is a matter of great importance when mires are being drained and their water regimes altered over large tracts of territory. Prior calculations must then be made of how the irrigation and river systems of the area will be affected by the reclamation of mires and the transformation of their water regime, and plans have to be made to control it so as to avoid undesirable consequences.

The accuracy achieved in determining the average values of water exchange and changes in the water storage of mire massifs and catchments over yearly periods, as well as of the other terms in equations of water balance, is completely dependent on the accuracy achieved in measuring the other components. It is therefore advisable to use this method when independent measurement of all the components of equations (3.1), (3.2) and (3.4) is either impossible for lack of the necessary observations, or gives inaccurate results because the number of points of observation is too few. Water exchange between mire massifs and subjacent soils is the component that is most difficult to determine by direct methods. It cannot, of course, be done without a close network of piezometers with filters (for measuring capillary pressure) at different levels and a detailed survey of the hydrogeological structure of the place where the mire massif is situated. For this reason, independent measurement of the component Y_{2m} (and of the components Y_2 and Y_{2d} for river catchments) involves a great expense of resources and time. It is usually carried out only when other research work is in progress, and to check the accuracy of water balance figures.

Measurement of the other components—evaporation (Z_m, Z), runoff (Y_m, Y) and changes in water storage of undrained mire massifs (ΔW_m)— is less difficult. For these, methods of calculation have been worked out that are significantly more accurate and involve less expense of resources on field works. The accuracy of precipitation data depends on the closeness of the network of rain gauges in the catchment, on the geographical position and size of the area, and on the variety of its geophysical structure.

On the basis of 20 years of observation at a station of the State Hydrological Institute for studying mires, Rozhdestvenskaya (1973) has calculated the water balance of a swamped basin with a total area of 2.9 km^2. Observations were carried out on the runoff, precipitation, evaporation and water table. Use was made in the calculations of the results obtained from a study of the water yield of the acrotelm in five microtopes of the *Sphagnum*–shrub– pine and *Sphagnum*–*Eriophorum*–shrub groups.

This swampy catchment contains a convex mire massif covering an area of 1.83 km^2 with divergent flow and microtopes of the *Sphagnum*–shrub– *Eriophorum*, *Sphagnum*–pine and ridge–flark types. The pattern of water exchange conforms with that of the first case described at the beginning of section 3.2, and represented in the genetico-geotopic classification of mires by the mesotopes of insulated and effluent basins of the oligocentral type (I, 11, O-C and III, 12, O-C).

In the catchment, observations were made of the piezometric levels of the water table in the mineral soils under the peat deposit. By comparing the

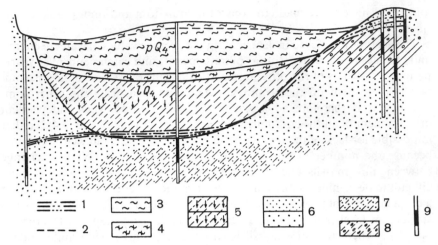

Fig. 24. Structure of a water catchment area converted into mire. 1—piezometric levels of groundwater in soil underlying peat deposit at different seasons of the year. 2—water table in peat deposit. 3—slightly humified (up to 25 %) *Sphagnum* and *Sphagnum–Eriophorum* peat. 4—compact, moderately humified peat containing remains of trees. 5—loam and sandy clay loam. 6—fine, intermediate and coarse sands. 7—mixture of silt or sand with clay interbedded with fine sand. 8—clay mixed with silt. 9—boreholes.

piezometric levels in the peat deposit located near the moss-covered surface with those in the subjacent water-permeable soils, it is possible to make immediate qualitative judgments about the direction of the vertical water exchange between them. As is obvious from the section in Fig. 24, the piezometric levels in the aquifer of the subjacent soil is significantly lower at all points of the mire massif than the water table of the mire, which practically coincides with its surface. The amplitude of seasonal fluctuations in the piezometric level is small, and, for that reason, the direction of vertical water exchange is the same at all seasons of the year. In this catchment therefore the convex massif is characterized by a constant vertical water exchange— an efflux from the peat deposit into the subjacent soil, which corresponds in the genetico-geotopic classification of mires to the case of insulated or effluent basins with a mesotope of the oligocentral type in its third phase (I and III, O–C, 3—see Fig. 19). In this case, the mire massif receives water from the atmosphere and through a surface influx from the surrounding slopes, usually observed only in the spring snow-melt, and loses water through horizontal and vertical exchange with the soil.

According to these calculations, which are based upon sufficiently reliable data, the following figures describe the water balance of a swampy catchment over a period of 20 years (1951–70):

Annual precipitation—801 mm

Annual horizontal runoff—222 mm (measured by hydrometric weirs on streams)

Evaporation—465 mm

Water exchange with subjacent soil—120 mm (including seepage into mire-free land in the catchment surrounding the mire massif)

It should be noted that in the spring, when snow melts, the main volume of melting snow descends quickly along the acrotelm from the central parts of the mire massif into hollows on the boundary between the peat deposit and the unswamped parts of the catchment (see Fig. 24). These hollows it floods and transforms into a marginal swamp of sluggishly moving water. As the water moves along this marginal depression to the weirs that enclose it, much of it seeps into the sandy soil of which the banks of the depression consist. For that reason $(Y_2 + \Delta W_d)$ almost always has a positive value in the winter half of the year, which includes the snow-melt, and its average multiannual value is also positive. In the summer half of the year, when the marginal hollows are not flooded and often dry up, horizontal runoff along the acrotelm from the mire massif either stops or is sharply reduced because of the meteorological conditions. Runoff into the streams that drain the catchment is maintained to a significant extent at the expense of the water storage of the unswamped part of the basin. In some years this term may be a negative quantity.

Changes in the water storage of the unswamped part of the catchment ΔW_d during winter and summer half-years taken separately and during whole-year periods can be calculated by taking into account the following considerations. The flux density of vertical water exchange into undrained horizons must be stable and is little affected by seasonal factors. This is demonstrated by the virtual constancy of differences of piezometric levels in the mire massif and the horizons below the peat deposit (see Fig. 24). It can therefore be assumed that the vertical exchange of water between the mire massif and lower horizons is the same in winter and summer and equal therefore to half the annual value. Then, using the same symbols as above, the average change in the water storage of the unswamped part of the catchment during annual and semi-annual (winter and summer half-year) periods can be obtained from the following relations:

$$\Delta W_d = (X - Y_1 - Z - \Delta W_m a_m - \overline{Y}_2) \frac{1}{1 - a_m},$$

where a_m is the proportion of catchment covered by mire expressed as a fraction, $\overline{Y}_2$ the average multiannual water exchange for single year and half-year periods, and the remaining components of the balance relate to

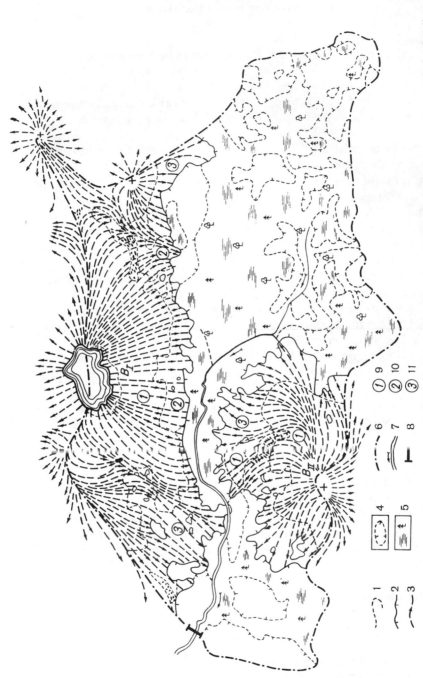

Fig. 25. Water-collecting mire with an area of 36·8 $\pm$ m². 1—boundaries of ridge–flark microtopes. 2—boundary of mire massifs. 3—flowlines on mire massifs. 4—unswamped lands. 5—swamped woodlands. 6—boundary of catchment area. 7—channel of river. 8—weir. 9—ridge–flark microtopes. 10—*Sphagnum–Eriophorum* and *Sphagnum–sedge* microtopes. 11—*Sphagnum–pine* microtopes.

corresponding periods. In the sample calculation considered the value of $\overline{Y}_2$ for annual periods is 120 mm, and, for semiannual periods, 60 mm.

Let us now consider the results of a calculation of the water balance components of a swampy catchment of a quite different structure (Fig. 25).

> Area of catchment—36·8 km^2
> Percentage of mire—43
> Percentage of wetlands—26
> Percentage of mire-free land—31

The boundaries of the catchment pass through the highest points of two mire systems of placodic type situated on a water divide, as can be clearly seen in the flow-net on the area of the massifs to be found in Fig. 25. The river flows between two mire massifs that are closely contiguous to it, both of which have a convex relief and microtopes predominantly of the ridge-flark type. The bed of the river is divided from the borders of the massifs by a narrow wooded water track covered by a variety of partly swamped timber. The sources of the river are situated among swamped woods. In this region there is a strip of land adjacent to the river bed which consists of much inundated meadowland.

The components of the water balance were calculated with the help of equations in the form of (3.5)–(3.7). The amount of vertical water exchange and alteration in water storage was calculated, like that of other items, for fixed intervals of time:

> $(Y_2 + \Delta W)$—for the whole basin;
> $(Y_{2m} + \Delta W_m)$—for the mire massifs;
> $(Y_{2d} + \Delta W_d)$—for the rest of the catchment, swamped and unswamped.

The chosen period of time was one month. Table 14 gives the calculated annual values of the components of the water balance.

The first fact to be noted is that over a period of 6 years the average values of the terms $(Y_2 + \Delta W)$, $(Y_{2m} + \Delta W_m)$ and $(Y_{2d} + \Delta W_d)$ have different signs. If we assume that over a period of many years the average annual changes in the water storage of the whole basin (ΔW), the mire massifs (ΔW_m) and the remaining, wooded part of the catchment (ΔW_d) tend to zero, then, as in the preceding case, the average values of these components must approach the average values of vertical exchange for the whole catchment, the mire massifs and the unswamped (wooded) part of the catchment. Here we find that over 6 years the catchment as a whole received an insignificant contribution from groundwater (on average 31 mm), that there was a vertical efflux or loss from the mire massifs into the soil below the peat deposit ($Y_{2m} = 27$ mm), and that an influx of groundwater was observed in the mire-free part of the catchment,

Table 14. Annual water balance (mm) of swampy catchment containing mire massifs situated on a water divide

Year	Precipitation X	Evaporation Z	Runoff from catchment Y_1	Horizontal runoff from mire massif Y_{1m}	$Y_2 + \Delta W$	$Y_{2m} + \Delta W_m$	$Y_{2d} + \Delta W_d$
1961	807	485	264	190	+55	+132	−4
1963	632	522	204	233	−93	−122	−70
1964	525	486	149	172	−110	−133	−93
1965	662	452	170	138	+40	+72	+16
1967	887	531	392	188	−36	+168	−190
1968	755	515	281	195	−42	+45	−107
6 Year Average	711	498	244	186	−31	+27	−75

which lies next to the river bed, is enclosed between the two mire massifs and occupies the lowest position in the catchment.

The runoff from the whole catchment Y_1 exceeds the runoff from the mire massifs Y_{2m} in years of heavy precipitation, but in years of low precipitation the position is reversed. This circumstance is explained by the fact that because of the structure of the catchment, the well-drained mire-free part of it is situated along the river bed and is immediately contiguous to it. As a result of this, the steeper slope of the water table in these places also produces a faster runoff in years when there is an abundance of water (through precipitation) than in the mire massif. Except during spring, when water rushes down in quantity over the aerotelm, the horizontal and vertical yield of mire massifs is extremely small.

3.3 Water Balance Methods of Calculating the Water Table Regime of Mires and Related Parameters

Knowledge of water table fluctuations in mires is indispensable in all cases involving the calculation of runoff, of water storage in the zone of aeration of mires that have been drained and are being put to some use, of the water storage conditions and irrigational requirements of the rooting layer of peat soils used for agricultural purposes, of the amount of water that must be drawn off drained mires to guarantee their standard of drainage and to plan the control of their drainage–irrigation network, and in many other matters involving the reclamation of mirelands and the conservation of the environment. Despite this, first-hand information about the water table regime of mire systems of different types and in different situations is extremely limited, both in respect of the number of points of observation maintained, and the length of time during which observations have been made. There are huge territories occupied by mire systems in the north-east of European Russia, in Western and Eastern Siberia and in the Far East, for which no systematic hydrological observations are available.

The situation is no better in regard to observations of the water table regimes of reclaimed mires. There are only a few stations where such observations are made, and the number of seasons they cover is not great. If one takes into account the fact that the water table regime of reclaimed mire massifs is also connected with the peculiarities of their systems of drainage and irrigation and the uses to which they have been put, it is easy to see that the present supply of data on this subject is in no way adequate for the planning of large-scale works of improvement, land development and conservation.

In these circumstances, great importance attaches to indirect methods of calculating the water table regime of mires, which enable one to compute its march and to recover data relating to long periods in its history. All water-balance methods of calculating water table take as their starting point equation (2.62), which describes a given part of a mire massif with an area ω bounded by fronts of influx and efflux L_1 and L_2.

The total change in water storage dW in the time dt, as described in equation (2.62), may be found from the alteration in the water table dz, the coefficient of water yield ξ_z in the area ω, and the alteration of water storage dW_{st} in the zone of aeration above the water table. Obviously, this last is numerically equal to the alteration in the storage capacity of the zone, which in turn is equal to the difference between the actual water content of the zone of aeration and the water content it would have, if capillary moisture were evenly distributed above the water table.

In the most general case, when one is dealing with any section of a mire massif in which the peat deposit is not uniform in its physical properties, the magnitudes dz, ξ_z and dW_{st} change across the area and are functions of the position of the given element $d\omega$ in the area ω. In these circumstances

$$dW = \int_\omega (\xi_z \, dz + dW_{st}) \, d\omega. \tag{3.8}$$

If we then choose a fragment which lies within the limits of a single microtope, and is accordingly uniform in the structure and physical properties of its acrotelm, equation (3.8) takes a simpler form:

$$dW = \xi_z \, dz + dW_{st}. \tag{3.9}$$

If one wishes to use equation (3.8) in calculations relating to drained mires, one must have data about the structure of the peat deposit, so that one can group together sections where the physical properties of the peat are the same. Therefore, in the case of parts of a mire massif where the structure of the acrotelm and peat deposit are uniform and are not subject to alteration through changes in the water table, equation (2.62) may be written thus:

$$\omega(\xi_z \, dz + dW_{st}) = \left[\oint_{L_1} q_{zn} \, dL - \oint_{L_2} q_{zn} \, dL + (p_p + p_{gr} - p_e)\,\omega \right] dt,$$

(3.10)

where the quantities $(\xi_z \, dz)$, W_{st}, q_{zn}, p_p, p_{gr} and p_e are functions of time. When the structure of the acrotelm and the peat deposit are uniform and unaffected by fluctuations in the water table, the following equalities obviously hold good:

$$\oint_{L_1} q_{zn} \, dL = q_{z1} l_1, \quad \oint_{L_2} q_{zn} \, dL = q_{z2} l_2,$$

where l_1 and l_2 are respectively the lengths of the equivalent fronts of influx and efflux. Then the expression for a change of level of the water table in a uniform section (microtope) of a mire massif takes the form

$$dz = \frac{1}{\xi_z} \left[p_p + p_{gr} - p_e + \frac{1}{\omega}(q_{z1} l_1 - q_{z2} l_2) \right] dt - \frac{dW_{st}}{\xi_z}.$$

(3.11)

To calculate the level of the water table at any given moment t, if the level z_n is known at an initial time t_n, use is made of the expression obtained by integrating equation (3.11) from z_n to z and from t_n to t:

$$z_t = z_n + \int_{t_n}^{t} \frac{1}{\xi_z} \left[p_p + p_{gr} - p_e + \frac{1}{\omega}(q_{z1} l_1 - q_{z2} l_2) \right] dt - \int_{t_n}^{t} \frac{dW_{st}}{\xi_z}.$$

(3.12)

For massifs in their natural state the quantity W_{st} in the zone of aeration is not great, especially in microtopes where the water table does not fall much below the acrotelm, as is usually the case in the zone of excess moisture. For that reason, this quantity can in most cases be disregarded. In improved mires, where the water table is at a relatively deep level, the storage capacity may reach very significant quantities and so break the close connection between alterations in the level of the water table and the levels of precipitation and evaporation. For that reason, allowance must be made for alterations in storage capacity when one is calculating changes in the water table over short intervals (hours, days and 5-day periods), and when there are frequent changes in weather conditions (short periods of precipitation alternating with rainless periods).

Different methods of solving equation (3.12) are suggested according to the aim for which calculation of the water table regime is undertaken, the data that form the basis of the calculation, and the relation of the phase of the regime that is being calculated to the existing state of affairs. All these methods agree, however, in their main objective, which is to use meteorological information and the known characteristics of mire massifs to discover how water levels change during certain given periods, or what the level will be at certain dates or critical moments in the water regime.

When we come to deal with reclaimed mires, we must add to these last particulars such important items as the type of drainage network, its structural elements (open, covered and vertical drains, etc.), the density of the open and covered network, the presence or absence of canals with embankments to intercept the horizontal flow of surface or ground water, etc.

As was said earlier, the main advantage of these methods is that they make it possible to lengthen the series of observed levels and of other hydrological quantities connected with them (e.g. seepage). With their help it is possible to produce computed forecasts of the pattern of water table movements, of how much water there will be in the zone of aeration and how it will move. With them one can also calculate the water regime of mires (including runoff) with the required degree of probability.

Let us now consider briefly the best ways of solving these equations. As a basis for calculating diurnal water levels in the warmer part of the year, when there is no water exchange with the subjacent soil ($p_{gr} = 0$), Novikov (1963, 1964, 1965) has proposed that the internal water supply ($p_p - p_e$) should be determined by means of equation (3.12) from data concerning the radiation absorbed by the surface of the mire. The difference between the radiation absorbed by the surface s_r and the heat lost through the evaporation of precipitation $l_e \times p_p$ (where l_e is the latent heat of evaporation) in a measured interval of time, divided by the latent heat of evaporation, obviously expresses the maximum quantity of moisture that can evaporate over and above that which has been precipitated, provided ($s_r - l_e p_p$) > 0. Now part of this surplus heat ($s_r - l_e p_p$) is transmitted to the acrotelm and must obviously be expended in turbulent exchange of heat with the atmosphere, in effective (or secondary) radiation and in heating the layer of peat and vegetation in the acrotelm. Let us call this part of the surplus heat ($s'_r - l_e p_p$). Then it is obvious that the quantity of heat that is spent on supplementary evaporation (i.e. in addition to the evaporation of what has been precipitated) will be expressed by the difference

$$(s_r - l_e p_p) - (s'_r - l_e p_p),$$

and the quantity of supplementary evaporation (i.e. in addition to that derived from precipitation) from the acrotelm will be expressed by the equation

$$p'_e = \frac{(s_r - l_e p_p) - (s'_r - l_e p_p)}{600}. \qquad (3.13)$$

If we suppose that for intervals of time of one day or more the storage capacity W_{st} of the acrotelm of undrained mires is equal to zero, we may reckon that the depth of additional evaporation p'_e is equal to the depth of moisture h_e removed by evaporation from the water table:

$$p'_e = h_e = -(p_p - p_e). \qquad (3.14)$$

Novikov has called these differences, $(s_r - l_e p_p)$ and $(s'_r - l_e p_p)$, the residual and absorbed radiation and symbolized them respectively by $s_{r, \text{res}}$ and $s'_{r, \text{res}, \Delta z = 0}$. As is plain from equation (3.13), when $s_r = s'_r$, $p'_e = 0$, and consequently there can be no change in the water table, i.e. $dz = 0$. If the absorbed radiation s_r is less than s'_r, then it follows from equation (3.13) that there has not been enough heat to evaporate all the moisture precipitated in the measured interval. In that case, the negative value of the equivalent depth p'_e stands for that part of the precipitation p_p that seeps into the acrotelm and raises the water table. Therefore, if we substitute the expression $(p_p - p_e)$ in equation (3.12), taking note of whether it is positive or negative, and then put $W_{st} = 0$, we obtain from equation (3.14) an empirical formula for calculating the water table of mires from standard meteorological observations:

$$z_t = z_n + \int_n^t \frac{1}{\xi} \left[\frac{1}{600} (s_{r, \text{res}} - s_{r, \text{res}, \Delta z = 0}) + \frac{1}{\omega}(q_{z1}l_1 - q_{z2}l_2) \right] dt, \quad (3.15)$$

or for finite (daily) intervals:

$$z_i = z_n + \sum_{i=1}^{i} \frac{1}{\xi_{zi}} \left[\frac{1}{600} (s_{r, \text{res}} - s_{r, \text{res}, \Delta z = 0}) + \frac{1}{\omega}(q_{zi}l_1 - q_{zi}l_2) \right], \quad (3.15')$$

where $s_{r, \text{res}}$ and $s_{r, \text{res}, \Delta z = 0}$ are in cal./day, z_i, z_n, l_1 and l_2 in cm, q_z in cm^2/day, and ω in cm^2.

Comparative calculations of daily levels carried out by Novikov showed good agreement with data from observations in mire stations. The greatest discrepancies were at the lowest levels of the water table (about 60 cm from the mean surface of the microtope) in *Sphagnum–shrub–Eriophorum* microtopes. This is explained by the inexactness of the calculations of the coefficients of water yield ξ_z, because the deviations had a systematic character. The calculations of $s_{r, \text{res}}$ for each day were based upon standard observations of cloudiness and precipitation. Radiation absorption was calculated by the formula of Braslavskiy and Vikulina (1954). Albedo for the mire surface was taken to be constant and equal to 0·16, as recommended by Romanov.

This very promising method of calculating the water regime and water balance of undrained mires permits one to investigate how much they are subject to change over long-term periods and to discover extreme conditions. It may therefore be widely used in the future, particularly to solve problems connected with the conservation of natural resources. For calculating the maximum spring runoff from undrained mire massifs with different degrees of reliability, Ivanov (1957b) has proposed a method of working out movements of the water table and the maximum height of water levels during the spring snow-melt, which is also based upon the solution of equation (3.12). In this, as in the preceding case, it is assumed that W_{st} does not change. No allowance is made for water exchange with the soil or evaporation, because during the snow-melt the water received by the acrotelm exceeds these many times over.

To deal with this case, equation (3.12) is written in the form:

$$z_t = z_n + \int_{t_n}^t \frac{1}{\xi_z} \left[a_t - \frac{1}{\omega} (q_{zi} l_1 - q_{z2} l_2) \right] dt, \qquad (3.16)$$

where a_t is the intensity of the snow-melt, which is a function of time and is calculated by the formula of Kuz'min (1961) or Popov (1968) from meteorological observations. The intervals of time for which calculations are made are taken to be single days.

Making use of equations (2.76) and (2.77) for equivalent mire massifs, one can write the relationship (3.16) in a simple form that is convenient for calculations:

$$z_t = z_n + \int_{t_n}^t \frac{1}{\xi_z} \left(a_t - \frac{2q_{rz}}{r_o} \right) dt, \qquad (3.17)$$

when there is no front of influx into mire massif, and

$$z_t = z_n + \int_{t_n}^t \frac{1}{\xi_z} \left(a_t + \frac{q_{z1} - q_{z2}}{B} \right) dt, \qquad (3.17')$$

when there is a front of influx. In these equations r_o is the radius of the equivalent mire massif (see (2.74)) calculated from the known area of the massif ω:

$$r_o = \sqrt{\frac{\omega}{\pi}},$$

and B is the equivalent breadth calculated by the formula (2.76'''):

Equation (3.17) was used as the basis for the calculation of the maximum runoff derived from snow and rain in mire massifs because of the absence of observational data regarding water levels (Ivanov, 1957b). This made it possible to draw isopleth maps showing the maximum spring and rain runoff from undrained mires with transit runoff (Ivanov, 1963) in the northern half of European Russia and Western Siberia, which are found in the official handbook (Anon. 1971c). Nekrasova (1969) has used equation (3.17) as the basis of a computer program for calculating the level of mire waters from meteorological data.

Equation (3.10) can also be used to solve problems about evaporation from individual mire microtopes of different types and from mire massifs as a whole, provided there is information about water table levels and atmospheric precipitation. Romanov (1961) and Ivanov (1953a, 1957b) have stated and proposed solutions for this type of problem. For calculations of evaporation from individual microtopes in undrained mire massifs, the values of L_1 and L_2 are taken to be equal to the length of the fronts of influx and efflux at the appropriate boundaries of the microtope. Then, on the basis of equation (3.10), the change of level in the acrotelm of the given microtope will be expressed thus:

$$\frac{dz}{dt} = \frac{\oint_{L_1} q_{zn}\,dL - \oint_{L_2} q_{zn}\,dL}{\omega\xi_z} + \frac{1}{\xi_z}(p_p + p_{gr} - p_e) - \frac{1}{\xi_z}\frac{dW_{st}}{dt} =$$

$$= \frac{1}{\omega\xi_z}(q_{z1}l_1 - q_{z2}l_2) + \frac{1}{\xi_z}(p_n + p_{nr} - p_n) - \frac{1}{\xi_z}\frac{dW_{st}}{dt}, \quad (3.18)$$

where in the given case q_{z1} and q_{z2} describe the seepage of the two neighbouring mire microtopes separated by the front of influx L_1, while l_1 and l_2 are the projected fronts of influx and efflux of the given microtope.

If p_p, p_{gr} and p_e be equal to zero and the storage in the acrotelm $W_{st} \approx 0$, then alterations in the water level of the microtope over a period of not less than one day are determined solely by the relation between influx and efflux, and, if we make $dt \approx \Delta t$, may be expressed as follows:

$$\frac{dz_*}{dt} = \frac{1}{\omega\xi_z}(q_{z1}l_1 - q_{z2}l_2). \quad (3.19)$$

The curve of the level's downward movement $z_* = f(t)$, as determined by equation (3.19), is called the normal curve of downward movement, and depends only on the seepage characteristics of the microtope itself and those of the microtope from which it receives an influx. Subtracting equation (3.19) from equation (3.18), we obtain an expression for the vertical water movement in the given microtope:

$$p_e - p_{gr} = p_p + \left(\frac{dz_*}{dt} - \frac{dz}{dt}\right)\xi_z \cong p_p + \frac{\Delta z_* - \Delta z}{\Delta t,}\xi_z. \qquad (3.20)$$

When there are no losses to the subjacent layers of soil, or they are insignificant in comparison with p_e,

$$p_e = \frac{(\Delta z_* - \Delta z)}{\Delta t}\xi_z + p_p. \qquad (3.21)$$

This last equation greatly simplifies calculation of evaporation from mire microtopes, when diurnal observations of water levels and precipitation are available. The accuracy of such calculations can always be increased by careful preliminary measurement of the seepage properties $k_z = f(z)$ and the layer coefficients of water yield $\xi_z = \xi(z)$ of the microtopes involved. In such conditions, equation (3.21) can be used as a reasonably simple method of checking by water balance the results of evaporation measurements made by other methods (by the method of thermal balance or with the use of evaporimeters) in the microtopes of undrained mires.

It is possible to use equivalent values for seepage and water yield when measuring by the above method the depth of evaporation from a given mire massif containing different types of microtope in a given interval of time Δt. In accordance with equation (2.75), the equivalent seepage of a mire massif bordered by N different microtopes is as follows:

$$q_{z_*} - \frac{q_{z1}l_1 + q_{z2}l_2 + \ldots + q_{zN}l_N}{l_1 + l_2 + \ldots + l_N}, \qquad (3.22)$$

while the equivalent average-adjusted coefficient of water yield ξ_{z_*} is:

$$\xi_{z_*} = \frac{\xi_{z1}\omega_1 + \xi_{z2}\omega_2 + \ldots + \xi_{zN'}\omega_{N'}}{\omega_1 + \omega_2 + \ldots + \omega_{N'}}, \qquad (3.23)$$

where N' is the number of different microtopes situated within the massif and $N' \geqslant N$.

There is a linear relationship between the water levels of the different microtopes such that

$$z_i = a_1 z_1 = a_2 z_2 = \ldots = a_{i-1} z_{i-1} = \ldots = a_{i+1} z_{i+1} = \ldots = a_{N'} z_{N'},$$

where the values of a_i are constant. Therefore the equivalent values q_{z_*} and ξ_{z_*} may be regarded as functions of the level z_i of any one of the N' microtopes:

$$\xi_{z_*} = \xi_*(z_i); q_{z_*} = q_*(z_i).$$

An analogous expression may then be used instead of (3.21) to calculate the amount of evaporation from the whole massif by water balance relations:

$$p_e = \frac{(\Delta z_{*i} - \Delta z_i)\xi_{z_*}}{\Delta t} = p_p, \qquad (3.24)$$

in which Δz_{*i} and Δz_i represent changes of level during Δt in the equivalent microtope, i.e. the microtope with whose levels the equivalent values of ξ_{z_*} and q_{z_*} are connected.

Taking account of the various processes involved and making allowances for peculiarities in the physical structure of the Byelo-Russian fens, Shebeko (1965, 1970) has solved equation (3.10) for drained mires planted with agricultural crops. In doing this, practical methods were worked out for calculating water movements in the zone of aeration and guaranteeing an optimal water supply for the rooting layer of agricultural crops. This was done by regulating the water regime in drainage systems in accordance with the current meteorological situation.

We shall not enter into a detailed exposition of these calculations, which are explained, not only in the works we have mentioned, but in official handbooks (Anon., 1972a, b), but devote time only to a discussion of the successive stages in the application of the water balance equation (3.10) to drained and undrained mires. For short intervals of time Δt (one day, five days, ten days or a month) used in these calculations, equation (3.10) is written in the form

$$\Delta z \xi_z = \bar{p}_p \Delta t - \bar{p}_e \Delta t + \bar{p}_{gr} \Delta t - \Delta W_{st} + \frac{\bar{q}_{z1} l_1}{\omega} \Delta t - \frac{\bar{q}_{z2} l_2}{\omega} \Delta t, \qquad (3.25)$$

where $\bar{p}_0$, $\bar{p}_e$, $\bar{p}_{gr}$, $\bar{q}_{z1}$ and $\bar{q}_{z2}$ are the average values for the given interval of time. The length of interval chosen Δt is determined, on the one hand, by the problems involved in the calculation, and, on the other, by the possibility of determining or directly measuring the different components of the water balance.

In the equations considered above, which dealt with undrained mire massifs, change in the storage of moisture in the zone of aeration of the acrotelm ΔW_{st} during intervals of time of not less than one day is insignificant and can be taken to be zero, allowing for the fact that over such long intervals of time the distribution of capillary moisture in the zone of aeration is on average stable. In drained massifs, however, ΔW_{st} may fluctuate greatly, even over quite long intervals of time. For that reason, the quantity ΔW_{st} and the distribution of moisture by depth in the zone of aeration as functions of time are often unknown in the case of drained mires, and are the most difficult of their properties to determine. To calculate them one must use the same equation of water balance (3.25), in which the known quantities (and those to be discovered) are the initial levels of the water table z_n, precipitation, evaporation and water exchange with the soil p_{gr}. This last is calculated by applying this same equation to periods during which runoff into the drainage system can be taken as zero. Calculations of the flow of moisture within the zone of aeration are made by application of the potential theory of the movement of moisture.

The quantity of runoff into the drainage system $(q_{z2}l_2/\omega)\Delta t$ is the second component of equation (3.25), and here also there are serious difficulties in determining it in the case of drained mires (open drains, main drains, canals and covered, underground drains). Here the total length of the front of efflux is equal to twice the length of all the open elements of the drainage network $2l_{2\,op}$ plus the length of the covered drainage $l_{2\,co}$:

$$l_2 = 2l_{2\,op} + l_{2\,co}.$$

Accordingly, the units of water discharge q_{z2}, which enter the drainage system (per unit length of drainage) and are dependent on the level of the water table z in drained mires, must be determined separately for the covered and open elements of the network, since the mechanism of efflux is different.

$$q_{z2} = q'_{z2} + q''_{z2},$$

where q'_{z2} is the runoff per unit length into open drains, and q''_{z2} the same for covered drains. The volume of water

$$Q'_{z2}\Delta t = 2q'_{z2}l_{2\,op}\Delta t$$

is the part of the runoff that passes straight into the open elements of the drainage network, and

$$Q''_{z2}\Delta t = q''_{z2}l_{2\,co}\Delta t$$

is the part that enters the covered elements. The last quantity is often described in the literature of the subject as the "drainage" or internal runoff of drained mires. It depends on the water table regime and the water supply of the zone of aeration, i.e. on the extent to which the zone of aeration is saturated with moisture and the extent to which the peat deposit conducts moisture at different depths and in different places.

The component $Q'_{z2}\Delta t$ must also include that part of the runoff that enters the network, not only by seepage, but by surface flow, as a result of the spring snow-melt or very heavy rainfall. The component of influx $(q_{z1}l_1/\omega)\Delta t$ in equation (3.25) need be taken into account only when the drained part of the massif is not divided off from the surrounding area by embanked canals which intercept the horizontal influx reaching it by flow or seepage from higher ground. For a direct estimate of this quantity, one must have data about the water table regime, the permeability of the soil and the gradients of groundwater flow in the areas surrounding the drained part of the massif.

It should be noted that, except for certain empirical formulae, whose use is limited to the conditions under which they were obtained, no direct methods have yet been worked out for measuring the discharges Q'_{z2} and Q''_{z2} as functions of the drainage network, the physical characteristics (hydraulic conductivity) of drained peat deposits and the changing meteorological conditions which determine the degree of saturation of the zone of aeration. This fact makes it impossible to measure the magnitude of changes in the water table Δz and to determine its regime $z_t = z(t)$, even when one has full information about precipitation (p_p), evaporation (p_e), vertical water exchange with the subjacent soil (p_{gr}) and the storage of moisture in the zone of aeration (W_{st}). To find Q'_{z2} and Q''_{z2} one must therefore return again to equation (3.25) and determine runoff $(Q'_{z2} + Q''_{z2}/\omega)\Delta t$ as the residual component of the water balance equation, but for this one must already know the values of Δz, ΔW_{st} and $p_{gr}\Delta t$ for chosen intervals of time Δt. As Shebeko rightly points out, there are difficulties of principle about this. To plan a drainage network that will guarantee a suitable water table regime $z(t)$ and the necessary water storage W_{st} in the zone of aeration, and will remove or supply the exact quantities of water required by the fields that are being drained, one must know beforehand the relation between the drainage potential of the system and the values of z and W_{st}. To know that drainage potential, however, one must ascertain through study of water table levels and meteorological conditions how the drainage system secures the removal of the necessary quantities of water, the maintenance of the prescribed water table levels and the moisture content W_{st} of the zone of aeration.

In the solutions proposed by Shebeko for solving this problem, use is made of certain special methods for finding the unknown components of the balance of moisture in the zone of aeration and alterations in the level of the water table. These are based on selecting periods during which some items in the water balance of drained mires can be taken as equal to zero. The values obtained for the unknown components in these periods are then used to calculate the water table regime and water storage at other periods. An equation due to Aver'yanov (1956) is recommended for estimating the equivalent depth of runoff into the drainage network $(h_{ro} = (q_{z2}l_2/\omega)\Delta t)$ for intervals Δt in periods when there is no surface runoff. This is used to find out how the downward curve of the water table moves under the sole operation of the ditches of the drainage network, since the other items in the equation are calculated by water balance methods. To simplify calculation of the values of h_{ro} Shebeko has compiled special nomographs which enable one to determine the daily fall of level from data about the water yield and seepage of the main water-bearing bed of peat, provided one has particulars about the distance between drainage ditches, their depth and their breadth at the bottom.

Despite the many assumptions that have to be made in these calculations and in the solution of the water balance equation (3.12), this is at present the only well worked out basis for regulating the water regime of reclaimed mires and providing the optimal supply of moisture for the rooting layer of agricultural fields on the basis of the best available meteorological information.

3.4 Measuring Water Exchange through Hydromorphological Relations

Our review of water balance methods of calculating water exchange has shown that the most difficult quantities to measure are always the exchange between the mire massif and subjacent soils and the external water supply at the border between the peat deposit and mire-free lands. All these methods regard losses by seepage or water supply from the soil (whether under pressure or not) as a residual item in the water balance equation to be determined after achieving the necessary accuracy in measuring the other items. Yet even when water balance has been measured with sufficient accuracy to determine water exchange as a residual element of it, there are serious deficiencies in this method. The most important of them is this, that the quantities to be measured and their sign (the loss or gain of moisture) are in no way related to any of the determinate physical parameters that characterise the structure of a mire massif. For that reason, the results obtained by this method cannot be extended to other analogous mire massifs, except for purely qualitative observations about the resemblances between this, that and the other mire massif. Consequently, this method, generally speaking, only permits solutions for a given case, and not general solutions and inferences. The same can be said of the results of measuring the components of water balance under field conditions in particular locations, and, above all, in swampy river basins, if runoff is determined by the usual hydrological technique of measuring discharges in streams and catchment-rivers, and if water exchange with subjacent strata is calculated with the help of a network of hydrogeological boreholes. As regards water exchange with subjacent soils, the results of such measurements only apply to the catchment area of that particular mire, and not to any definable class of natural formations. For that reason they cannot be generalized and extended to other examples.

Another deficiency is that the methods of calculation we have considered and the customary, widely-used field methods of measuring the components of water balance do not permit one to find out the distribution of the quantity and direction of water exchange over the area of a mire massif. In the case of simple mire massifs situated in a single morphological element and of relatively small dimensions, neglect of the variation of water exchange within the area of mire may be a matter of little importance. Some mire macrotopes, however, cover huge areas of many hundreds or thousands of square kilometres and have differences in their morphological structure. In some parts there may be a large influx of water from the soil, while in others this may be absent, or the flow may be in the opposite direction. In all such cases the distribution of the quantity and direction of water exchange throughout the area is a decisive factor.

If we accept as our basis the hydrological functions deduced in Chapter 2, it is possible to solve the problem of measuring water exchange between the peat deposits of mire massifs and underlying strata by a more general method and so explain the distribution of water exchange over the area of mire massifs. We shall begin with the equation for hydromorphological relations (2.80). Here, in the most general case, the values of the modulus of seepage $\overline{M}_s$, of the function of relief b_s and of internal water supply $\bar{p}_s$ are quantities that vary with position in the area of the mire massif and along any line of flow s. After substituting in equation (2.80) the itemized components of internal water supply $\bar{p}_s$ as found in equation (2.63), we shall adapt it to deal with two cases. The first is where a mire massif, or some fragment of it (see section 2.14), has both a meteoric and an internal soil-derived water supply, and the second is where the same massif has an exclusively meteoric water supply:

$$\frac{dy}{ds} = \frac{\bar{q}_0 b_0}{\overline{M}_s b_s} + \frac{1}{\overline{M}_s b_s} \int_0^s (\bar{p}_p - \bar{p}_e) b_s \, ds + \frac{1}{\overline{M}_s b_s} \int_0^s \bar{p}_{gr} b_s \, ds, \qquad (3.26)$$

$$\frac{dy_a}{ds} = \frac{\bar{q}_0 b_0}{\overline{M}_s b_s} + \frac{1}{\overline{M}_s b_s} \int_0^s (\bar{p}_p - \bar{p}_e) b_s \, ds. \qquad (3.27)$$

Subtracting the second equation from the first, we find that

$$\frac{dy}{ds} - \frac{dy_a}{ds} = \frac{1}{\overline{M}_s b_s} \int_0^s \bar{p}_{gr} b_s \, ds, \qquad (3.28)$$

or

$$\int_0^s \bar{p}_{gr} b_s \, ds = \overline{M}_s b_s \left(\frac{dy}{ds} - \frac{dy_a}{ds} \right). \qquad (3.28')$$

From these last equations, it is plain that, when the physical structure of the acrotelm and the form of flow in plan, as expressed by the functions $\overline{M}_s = \overline{M}(s)$ and $b_s = b(s)$, are the same, the internal soil-derived water supply (or the loss of water to the subjacent soil) of any given fragment is equal to the difference between the slope of a massif with a full water supply and one with an exclusively meteoric water supply multiplied by the product of $\overline{M}_s$ and b_s. If, using the same symbols as in equation (2.61), we designate $\overline{P}_{gr\,j}$ the average discharge of soil water for the whole of the jth fragment over a period of time, we obtain the expression:

$$\overline{P}_{gr\,j} = \overline{M}_s b_s \left(\frac{dy}{ds} - \frac{dy_a}{ds} \right), \tag{3.29}$$

where j is the ordinal number of the given fragment.

If the number of different fragments into which the whole massif is broken down is N, then the average quantity of water exchanged between the massif and the subjacent soil will obviously be the sum of the average quantities for each of these fragments:

$$\overline{P}_{gr} = \sum_1^N \overline{P}_{gr\,j}. \tag{3.30}$$

From expression (3.28) it follows immediately that at all points on the flow-line at a distance s from the beginning of the fragment, where $dy/ds = dy_a/ds$ (i.e. where the surface slopes of the massif are equal to those of a similar mire massif with an exclusively meteoric water supply), water exchange with the subjacent soil is equal to zero.

Putting equation (3.28) in the form

$$y - y_a = \int_0^s \frac{\int_0^s \overline{P}_{gr} b_s \, ds}{\overline{M}_s b_s} \, ds, \tag{3.31}$$

it is easy to see that the difference in the ordinates of the surface of the massif at a distance s from the chosen origin of the coordinates depends only upon the total water exchange along the whole length of the fragment s, and does not depend upon the way $\overline{p}_{gr}$ is distributed along the length s. Since the distribution of water exchange $\overline{p}_{gr}$ along any flowline is unknown, and is in this case the quantity to be determined, then to calculate graphically the quantity of water exchange within the limits of any section of a flowline, it is necessary to divide up the area of the mire massif into parts sufficiently small to ensure that water exchange $\overline{p}_{gr}$ and seepage $\overline{M}_s$ are constant within their bounds.

We shall look first of all at certain very simple cases, beginning with the class of mire massifs with normal profiles ($\overline{M}_s$ = const.), and a point or line within them from which flow diverges. For all such massifs, when $\overline{p}_s$ =

$\bar{p}_p - \bar{p}_e + \bar{p}_{gr}$ = constant, the general equation for the relief along the flow-line is (see Table 13)

$$y = \frac{\bar{p}_s s^2}{\beta \overline{M}} = \frac{\bar{p}_s s^2}{2(n+1)\overline{M}}, \tag{3.32}$$

where the values of the constants β or n are determined in accordance with Table 13 by the type of divergent flow. Where the shape of the massif in plan is round or symmetrical, the whole massif can be treated as a single fragment, since along any flowline s the law of divergence remains the same $(\beta = 4)$.

If a mire massif has a curvilinear divergent or a curvilinear convergent flow (see Figs 6 and 7), it must consist of two or more fragments with different values of the function $b_s = b(s)$. If, however, the modulus of seepage remains constant within the limits of each fragment, the mire massif can then be divided into several fragments with normal hydrodynamic profiles, for each of which equation (3.32) holds good with appropriate values of n and β.

Applying the same method as was used in deriving the relationship (3.28), we obtain from equation (3.32)

$$y - y_a = \frac{\bar{p}_{gr} s^2}{2(n+1)\overline{M}_s}, \tag{3.33}$$

or

$$\bar{p}_{gr} = \frac{2(n+1)\overline{M}_s(y - y_a)}{s^2}. \tag{3.34}$$

According to the conditions assumed in deducing equation (3.32), the value of $\bar{p}_{gr}$ within the limits of the chosen fragment is constant, and therefore represents the average amount of water exchange over the whole area of the fragment which has the given length s and the given difference between its ordinates y and y_a at the point s.

From equations (3.28'), (3.29) and (3.34) it follows that if any mire massif with a given degree of divergence and an unchanging modulus of seepage has a shallower relief than a corresponding massif with an exclusively meteoric water supply, it must have a negative water exchange with the soil $\bar{p}_{gr}$. Such massifs lose water by seepage to the horizons lying under their peat deposits. On the other hand, massifs with the same modulus of seepage and form of flow in plan $b = b(s)$, but a more developed relief (i.e. greater slopes at all points on the flowline) must have an internal supply from subjacent aquifers (a pressure supply). Table 15 gives two normal profiles of actual mire massifs with a radially divergent flow, where $\overline{M}_s = 10 \text{ cm}^2/\text{s}$ and $(\bar{p}_p - \bar{p}_e) =$

Table 15. Ordinates of the normal profile of a massif when $\overline{M}_s = 10 \text{ cm}^2/\text{s}$, $n = 1$, and $\bar{p}_p - \bar{p}_e = 200$ mm/year, (a) where no water is lost to the subjacent soil ($\bar{p}_{gr} = 0$) (b) where $\bar{p}_{gr} = -100$ mm/year.

s (m)	s^2 (m^2)	y_a(m)($\bar{p}_{gr} = 0$)	y_b(m) ($\bar{p}_{gr} = -100$ mm/year)
0	0	0	0
100	10^4	0·016	0·008
200	4×10^4	0·063	0·031
300	9×10^4	0·142	0·071
400	16×10^4	0·253	0·126
600	36×10^4	0·569	0·235
800	64×10^4	1·01	0·50
1000	10^6	1·58	0·79
1200	$1·44 \times 10^6$	2·28	1·14
1400	$1·96 \times 10^6$	3·10	1·55
1600	$2·56 \times 10^6$	4·05	2·02
1800	$3·24 \times 10^6$	5·12	2·56
2000	$4·00 \times 10^6$	6·32	3·16
2200	$4·84 \times 10^6$	7·65	3·82
2400	$5·76 \times 10^6$	9·10	4·55
2600	$6·76 \times 10^6$	10·68	5·34
2800	$7·84 \times 10^6$	12·40	6·20
3000	$9·00 \times 10^6$	14·20	7·10

200 mm/year. One of the calculated profiles was associated with losses ($\bar{p}_{gr} = 100$ mm/year), the other with no water exchange with the soil and a purely meteoric water supply.

In calculating the mean quantity of water exchange in such massifs, direct use is made of equation (3.34), if the profile of the actual massif $y = f(s)$ and its constant modulus of seepage $\overline{M}_s$ are known. By a completely analogous reasoning one can obtain relationships from the equations in Table 12 for calculating the water exchange with subjacent soils of mire massifs with a constant modulus of seepage, an external water supply and values of n equal to 1, 2, 3. From the equations in Table 11 one can obtain analogous functions for the water exchange with subjacent soil of mire massifs with a variable modulus of seepage along their flowlines and epicentres of divergent flow within their bounds.

There are many cases, however, where it is impossible to use these relationships to determine water exchange. When real mire massifs of complex structure are analysed into appropriate fragments, the functions that describe them, $b_s = b(s)$ and $\overline{M}_s = M(s)$, often cannot be expressed in terms of any integral or fractional power n, such as would permit integration of equation (2.80) in a finite form. The pattern according to which these functions change along their flowlines is more complicated. In such cases, it is easiest to make direct use of equation (2.100), applying it successively to each small interval Δs on the assumption that it is equal in length to the elementary fragment, i.e. to a section of the massif within whose limits the values of b_s and $\overline{M}_s$ may be taken to be constant. In this the length of the elementary interval s must be chosen with regard to the rate of change of b_s and $\overline{M}_s$ along the flowline, i.e. when divergence or convergence of flow is acute and $\overline{M}_s$ changes rapidly, the length of elementary sections must be reduced, just as they may be increased when changes of b_s and $\overline{M}_s$ are small.

To calculate water exchange by this method on the basis of equation (2.100), we shall first write the expression for change of the ordinate of the mire's surface in the section Δs in a form that is suitable for an exclusively meteoric water supply. In the general case, for any jth section, we find that

$$\Delta y_{aj} = \frac{\bar{q}_{j-1} b_{sj-1} + (\bar{p}_p - \bar{p}_e)_j b_{sj} \Delta s_j}{\overline{M}_{sj} b_{sj}} \Delta s_j. \tag{3.35}$$

Change in the ordinate of the surface along the flowline, when there is water exchange with the soil in the same section, will be expressed in the following form:

$$\Delta y_j = \frac{\bar{q}_{j-1} b_{sj-1} + (\bar{p}_p - \bar{p}_e)_j b_{sj} \Delta s_j + \bar{p}_{grj} b_{sj} \Delta s_j}{\overline{M}_{sj} b_{sj}} \Delta s_j. \tag{3.36}$$

Subtracting the first equation from the second and solving it for $\bar{p}_{grj}$, we find that

$$\bar{p}_{grj} = \frac{\Delta y_j - \Delta y_{aj}}{(\Delta s_j)^2} \overline{M}_{sj} = (i_j - i_{aj}) \frac{\overline{M}_{sj}}{\Delta s_j}. \tag{3.37}$$

This last equation makes it possible to calculate directly the quantity of water exchange with the soil in the given section of the mire massif s_j, if one knows the mean long-term modulus of seepage, the actual slope of the surface i and the slope i_a which it would have, if it had an exclusively meteoric water supply. It is therefore necessary to know the value of i_a for every jth section of the mire in order to calculate water exchange with the soil by equation (3.37). Knowing $q_{j-1} b_{j-1}$, this can easily be determined from (3.35). The influx into the jth section is obviously equal to

$$\bar{q}_{j-1} b_{sj-1} = \bar{q}_0 b_0 + \sum_{1}^{j-1} (\bar{p}_p - \bar{p}_e + \bar{p}_{gr})_j b_{sj} \Delta s_j. \tag{3.38}$$

This shows that the problem must be solved by calculating the values of $\bar{q}_{j-1}b_{sj-1}$, $i_{aj} = \Delta y_{aj}/\Delta s_j$ and p_{gr} for each section in succession from $j = 1$ onward. This is done for $\bar{q}_{j-1}b_{sj-1}$ by equation (3.38), for $i_{aj} = \Delta y_{aj}/\Delta s_j$ by equation (3.35) and for $\bar{p}_{gr}$ by equation (3.37). The following are the data required about each section dealt with in the calculations: the modulus of seepage $\bar{M}_{sj}$, the breadths of the fronts of influx and efflux b_{sj-1} and b_{sj}, the length of the sections Δ_{sj} and the slopes of the massif in these sections i_j. All these, as we said earlier, can be obtained directly from aerial photographs by drawing a flow-net and ascertaining the types and position of the microtopes in the massif.

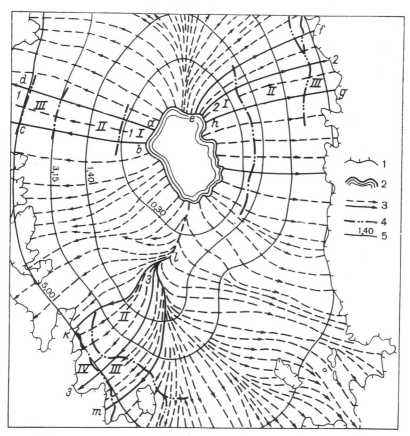

Fig. 26. A mire massif that followed the oligocentral path of development with a lake at the epicentre of its divergent flow. 1—boundaries of the massif. 2—edge of lake. 3—flowlines. 4 boundaries of mire microtopes. 5 contours of the surface of the mire. *I, II, III, IV*—types of mire microtopes (see note to Table 17).

We shall now consider the process of calculation in the actual example of a mire massif described in Fig. 26. We shall single out three fragments in this massif, calling them *abcd*, *efgh* and *klm*. We shall divide each fragment into sections, whose boundaries are those of the different types of microtope. As in Fig. 26, four different types of mire microtope are found in these fragments:

I. Heavily inundated ridge–flark complexes.

II. Ridge–flark complexes, with ridges occupied by *Sphagnum*, shrubs and pines, and flarks occupied by *Sphagnum* and *Scheuchzeria*.

III. *Sphagnum*–shrub–*Eriophorum* complexes.

IV. Pine–*Sphagnum*–shrub complexes.

In accordance with Table 8, we accept the following as their mean long-term moduli of seepage:

I. $45 \text{ cm}^2/\text{s}$; II. $15 \text{ cm}^2/\text{s}$; III. $16 \text{ cm}^2/\text{s}$; IV. $2·5 \text{ cm}^2/\text{s}$.

We shall use a flow-net to superimpose upon the plan of the massif contours reckoned downwards from the border of the lake, their heights being determined by ground survey along the profile 1–1. The numbers beside the contours marked on the plan of the massif show the difference of level between the given contour and the surface of the mire at the edge of the lake. In each of the three chosen fragments, we shall draw the boundaries of the microtopes in accordance with equations (3.35) and (3.37), taking as our basic intervals Δs_j the distances between the boundaries of the microtopes along the mean flowlines 1–1, 2–2 and 3–3. The length of b_{sj} is determined graphically as the length of the line drawn along the boundaries of the microtope between the extreme flowlines of the given fragment.

We shall compile two working tables for calculation. The first one is to determine by equation (3.35) the slopes of the surface i_a along the chosen fragments when the water supply is meteoric (Table 16). The second is to calculate by equation (3.37) the mean long-term water exchange with the subjacent soil $\bar{p}_{gr}$ (Table 17). The starting points for calculations are the values of s_j, Δs_j and b_{sj} derived from the map of the massif for each of the fragments. The quantity of the massif's meteoric water supply is taken to be the same for all types of microtope (differences in evaporation being reckoned insignificant) and equal to that of the region where the massif is situated, i.e. $\bar{p}_p - \bar{p}_e = 250 \text{ mm/year}$. The results of the calculation of water exchange for all three chosen fragments show that there are losses to the subjacent soil in the main part of the massif (Table 17). On the borders of the massif, seepage sharply increases in all the fragments. For example, in the third fragment on the boundary between the massif and mire-free land, where there is a pine–*Sphagnum*–shrub microtope, the loss is about 1400 mm/year. This means that here the greater part of the whole intake of moisture in that part of

Table 16. Table to assist in calculation of gradients when meteoric water supply of massif $(\bar{p}_0 - \bar{p}_e) = 250$ mm/year

s_j (m)	b_{sj-1} (m)	Δs_j (m)	$\overline{M}_s$ (cm²/s)	$\bar{q}_{j-1}$ (l.s⁻¹.km⁻¹)	$\bar{q}_{j-1} b_{sj-1}$ (l/s)	$(\bar{p}_0 - \bar{p}_e) b_{sj} \Delta s_j \times 10^{-4}$ (m³/s)	$[\bar{q}_{j-1} b_{sj-1} + (\bar{p}_0 - \bar{p}_e)_j b_{sj} \Delta s_j] \times 10^{-4}$ (m³/s)	$\overline{M}_s b_s$ (m³/s)	i_a (‰)
					Profile 1–1, fragment *abcd*				
0	165	0	45	1·6	0·254	0	2·54	—	0·36
362	255	362	45	—	—	6	8·54	1·15	0·74
1113	375	751	15	—	—	18·6	27·14	0·563	4·8
1513	410	400	16	—	—	12·3	39·44	0·656	6·0
					Profile 2–2, fragment *efgh*				
0	175	0	45	1·6	0·280	0	2·80	0·79	0·36
500	475	500	45	—	—	12·8	15·6	2·14	0·73
1375	687	875	15	—	—	40·3	55·9	1·03	5·4
1600	700	225	16	—	—	12·4	68·3	1·12	6·1
					Profile 3–3, fragment *klm*				
0	0	0	0	0	0	0	0	0	0
1250	1050	1250	15	—	—	52·0	52·0	1·58	3·3
1525	1040	275	16	—	—	22·7	74·7	1·67	4·5
1650	1040	125	2·5	—	—	10·3	85·0	0·26	32·6

NOTE Evaporation from water surfaces in the region of the massif is taken according to Braslavskiy and Vikulina (1954) as $\bar{p}_{ew} = 550$ mm/year. The area of the central lake $\omega_{lk} = 0.6$ km². The equivalent radius of the lake $r_{lk} = 2\pi r_{olk} = 2730$ m. The seepage from the lake across the projected front $\bar{q}_0 = \bar{q}_{j-1} = 1.61$ s⁻¹ . km⁻¹.

Table 17. Calculation by fragments of water exchange between a mire massif and subjacent soils according to the method of hydromorphological relations (see Fig. 26).

s(m)	y (m)	Δs (m)	Type of microtope	$\overline{M}_s$ (cm²/s)	b_s (m)	Δy (m)	$i = \dfrac{\Delta y}{\Delta s}$ (‰)	i_a (‰)	$i - i_a$ (‰)	$\dfrac{\overline{M}}{\Delta s} \times 10^{-4}$ (m/s)	$p_{gr} = (i - i_a)\dfrac{\overline{M}_s}{\Delta s}$ (mm/year)
Profile 1–1, Fragment abcd											
0	0	0			165			0·36			
362	0·30	362	I	45	255	0·30	0·83	0·74	+0·09	0·124	+35
1113	3·15	751	II	15	375	2·85	3·8	4·8	−1·0	0·02	−63
1513	5·00	400	III	16	410	1·85	4·6	6·0	−1·4	0·04	−177
Profile 2–2, Fragment efgh											
0	0	0			175						
500	0·85	500	I	45	475	0·85	1·7	0·73	+0·97	0·09	+275
1375	4·51	875	II	15	687	3·66	4·2	5·4	−1·2	0·015	−57
1625	5·91	250	III	16	700	1·40	5·6	6·1	−0·5	0·064	−100
Profile 3–3, Fragment klm											
0	0	0			0						
1250	3·37	1250	II	15	050	3·37	2·7	3·3	−0·6	0·012	−23
1525	4·34	275	III	16	040	0·97	3·5	4·5	−1·0	0·058	−183
1650	5·59	125	IV	2·5	040	1·25	10·0	32·6	−22·6	0·02	−1430

I—Flooded ridge–flark complex ($P_r = 30\%$, $P_f = 70\%$, $\overline{M}_s = 40$–50 cm²/s). II—Ridge–flark complex with *Sphagnum*–shrub ridges forested with pine and *Sphagnum–Scheuchzeria* flarks ($P_r = 50\%$, $P_f = 50\%$, $\overline{M}_s = 13$–18 cm²/s). III—*Sphagnum*–shrub–*Eriophorum* with small-hummock microrelief ($\overline{M}_s = 8$–16 cm²/s). IV—Pine–*Sphagnum*–shrub ($\overline{M}_s = 2·5$ cm²/s).

NOTE   The data accepted for precipitation and evaporation are as follows: $\bar{p}_o = 600$ mm/year, $\bar{p}_e = 350$ mm/year for raised-mire microtopes and $\bar{p}_e = 370$ mm/year for fenland microtopes.

the massif, which is derived from higher microtopes and from precipitation, is lost through seepage. Out of a total water supply of 85×10^{-4} m^3/s the amount lost through seepage is 59×10^{-4} m^3/s. In those very parts of the mire massif where there is an external influx from the central lake (profiles 1–1 and 2–2), the microtope adjacent to the lake, which is a much inundated ridge–flark complex, has a positive balance in its exchange of water with the soil. In this case, the positive character of this exchange indicates the presence of a significant amount of seepage, not only in the acrotelm of the given microtope, but also from the lake through the whole thickness of the peat deposit.

The accuracy and reliability of any calculation of vertical water exchange by the method of hydrological relations, as can be easily seen from the calculations we have made and from equations (3.35) and (3.37), depend mainly upon accurate identification of the types of microtope and a correct choice of the moduli of average seepage $\overline{M}_s$ for their acrotelms. Superimposing flow-nets, horizontal contours and microtope boundaries upon the map of the massif from which the values of s_j, Δs_j and b_{sj} are obtained can only introduce slight errors into calculations, since these parameters can be determined with complete certainty by aerial survey. The accuracy of the figures for water exchange can be increased in every case by reducing the gradations of change in the values of $\overline{M}_s$ for different types of microtope, i.e. by making finer distinctions between the structure of the plant cover and its indicator properties in relation to the hydrological characteristics of microtopes.

Analogous calculations have been carried out at a mire station of the G.G.I. on a mire massif catchment area of 2·9 km^2 (see Fig. 24). The results of a determination of the vertical water exchange of this catchment by the usual method of measuring all the other items in its water balance directly have already been considered in section 3.2. Here the average long-term loss for the whole catchment area of mire, as determined from the other items in the equation of water balance (3.6), amounted to 120 mm/year, while the loss calculated by the equations of water balance (3.35) and (3.37) amounted to 107 mm/year. If we remember that the losses into undrained aquifers from a whole catchment composed of permeable soils must exceed the vertical loss from the mire because of the massif's horizontal discharge into mire-free surroundings, it follows that the smaller vertical losses computed for the mire itself fully correspond to the accepted physical model of the process of runoff in a catchment area that is not insulated from its surroundings. This comparison justifies the inference that the order of magnitude and direction of water exchange with subjacent soils can be measured with a sufficient degree of reliability by the hydromorphological method, even with the relatively crude values given in Table 8 for the moduli of seepage $\overline{M}_s$ for the different microtopes.

3.5 Calculations of the Water Balance of Endotelmic Lakes

Lakes situated inside large mire systems are a very widespread phenomenon, particularly in the zone of excess moisture. In section 1.6 examples were cited of huge mire macrotopes in different regions of the West Siberian lowlands. These show quite clearly that endotelmic lakes are an inseparable part of large mire systems. Lakes may occupy a large part of the central part of mire systems situated on water divides (see Fig. 8). The formation of endotelmic lakes may be connected with ancient water bodies that already existed at the time of the first phase of mire formation (after the retreat of the glaciers of the last ice age), and also with later formations that arose as a result of the accumulation of peat and the development of a type of relief that is peculiar to mirelands. Following the more or less established terminology of telmatology (Galkina *et al.*, 1949; Ivanov, 1957b; Romanova, 1961, etc.), we shall call endotelmic lakes whose origin is connected with ancient lake basins primary lakes, and those which have been formed by the accumulation of peat and the development of mire massifs secondary. The formation of secondary lakes on mires in massive quantities is characteristic of the later stages in the development of mire systems, when they have entered the autogenic phase. Then, because of their convex surface, their main source of water supply comes to be meteoric, and other sources play a minor role.

The data that have now been accumulated on the structure of mire geotopes and endotelmic water bodies justify us in regarding the formation of lakes as one of the stages in the general development of mire systems (Ivanov, 1975), in which the relation between the area covered by vegetation and the area occupied by open water must go through different stages. These relations are determined by water balance relations and the physical conditions that affect the discharge of moisture from mires. In Chapter 4 it will be shown that, when peat accumulates and mire massifs increase in area, differentiation of the plant cover must lead to the formation of the most stable patterns of plant association, which are orientated ridge–flark and ridge–pool complexes (Ivanov, 1970). These last are transformed into lake–mire complexes (lake–mire geotopes), when the stability of the ridge–pool microtopes is disturbed by the erosion of the mire's internal hydrological network, which results in a spontaneous drying-up of the mire system. In these processes, the water exchange and water balance of endotelmic lakes and the disturbances of them by natural and artificial causes play a major part. The most important reason for studying them and making calculations concerning them is, therefore, to find out the criteria for the stability and transformation of mire systems when the reclamation of wetlands is being undertaken. Calculation of the water exchange of endotelmic lakes is no less important in order to decide how much water can be removed from them for industrial purposes

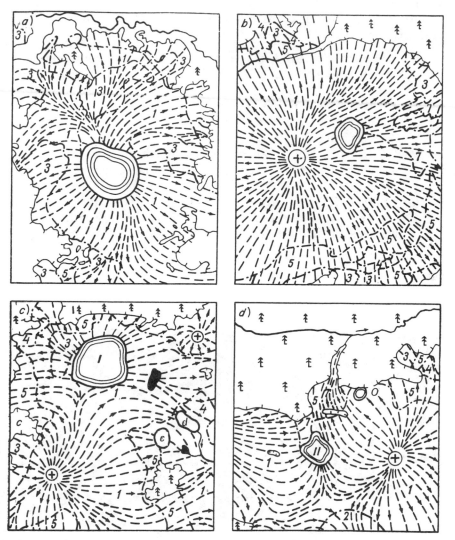

Fig. 27. Chief types of lake–mire complexes with isolated endotelmic lakes. a)—lake at epicentre of divergent flow. b)—lake in parallel-flowing stream on a sloping part of massif. c)—lake (I) in a divergent stream on a sloping part of massif. d)—lake (II) in a convergent stream on a sloping of massif with another lake (0) in contact with dry ground; + —epicentre of divergent stream. The symbols 1, 3–5, 7 and *c, d* represent different microtopes. For the other symbols, see Figs 7, 8 and 9.

and water supply. It is convenient to refer to all combinations of endotelmic water bodies (lakes) with their surrounding mire formations as lake–mire complexes. These combinations can be analysed into the following fundamental types:

(1) Convex mire massifs with a central lake at their epicentre (Fig. 27a).

(2) Mire massifs with a single large lake on a sloping part of the massif (Fig. 27b,c,d).

(3) Various forms of regularly orientated ridge–pool complexes, which are in reality ridge–pool microtopes or microtopes with an elongated ridge structure (Fig. 28a).

(4) Unorientated ridge–pool complexes, which are regressive stages in the development of the central parts of large mire massifs (Fig. 28c).

(5) Unorientated or slightly orientated lake–mire complexes with large lakes separated from each other by relatively narrow strips of peat with corresponding vegetation (Figs 8, 28b).

Among lake–mire complexes of the second type it is necessary to distinguish several varieties according to the hydrodynamic characteristics of

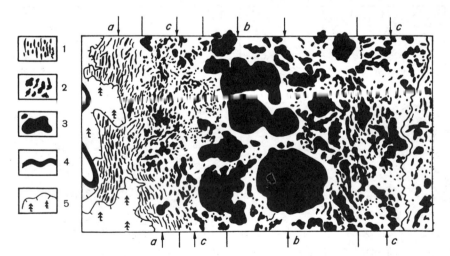

Fig. 28. Chief types of lake–mire complex with numerous lakes making up a single lake–mire system. a—orientated ridge–pool complexes with strip–ridge structure occupying the margins of the system. b—lake–mire complexes on a water-divide, which are the central part of the system, and are characteristic of the very large lake–mire systems in the north of the West Siberian plain. c—unorientated or weakly orientated ridge–pool complexes. 1—orientated ridge–pool complexes. 2—unorientated lake complexes. 3—large lakes. 4—river. 5—boundaries with dry ground.

water flow in their acrotelm. In some cases, the lakes that lie within them are situated in places where flow is divergent or parallel. In other cases, they are situated in places where flow is convergent. These two classes of lake have different water balance characteristics. There are instances of this second type where the lakes are situated on the borders of the mire massif, either where it abuts upon the surrounding mineral soil, or where there are endo-telmic islands of mineral soil (Fig. 27d). These complexes are due to the dam-ming up and accumulation of water flowing off the mire massif towards its boundary with the mire-free surroundings, and to the rise in the level of water caused by the growing thickness of the peat deposit and the raising of the surface of the mire. In some such cases, the lakes may have existed before peat began to form, and the only effect of the accumulation of peat is to increase the depth and change the shape of the lake. In other cases, the lakes only come into existence when the mire massif enters the autogenic phase, i.e. when the surface starts to assume a convex shape. This kind of lake is peculiar to mire massifs with a convex surface situated in a basin.

Lake–mire systems cover large areas in the northern regions of the wooded-mire zone of Western Siberia. This is one of its special peculiarities. In Figs 8 and 28 we show typical structures of a mire geotope with an unorientated lake–mire complex situated in the central part of a completely swamped expanse of the Surgut Polesie. As one passes from the central parts of the interfluves to areas adjoining the river courses, the endotelmic water bodies gradually acquire a definite orientation, and in the sloping part of the mire system they become elongated pools perpendicular to the flowlines, forming microtopes of the ridge–pool type.

In Table 18 there is a general description of the mire formations of the large river basins in the northern regions of Western Siberia, as well as particulars concerning the number of endotelmic lakes, their total area and their average sizes. Water bodies of less than 0·5 ha are not included in the number of endotelmic lakes, and the same is true of flarks with an open water surface in ridge–pool complexes. The proportion of open water surface is therefore higher than the percentage of lakes given in Table 18. It may amount to more than 50% of the area occupied by mire systems.

Analysis of the structure of lake–mire complexes shows that it is impossible to draw strict lines of demarcation between flarks with open water surfaces in orientated ridge–pool complexes and water bodies of larger dimensions with areas measured in tens or hundreds of hectares. These last are, in turn, situated in areas of mire among still larger water bodies, whose areas are measured in tens of square kilometres. At first glance, such lake–mire geotopes look like chaotic agglomerations of lakes of all sizes separated only by narrow strips of peat with vegetation of the raised mire type; but, when one studies the structure of such geotopes more carefully, it is not difficult

Table 18. Analysis of the amount of mire and lake in the mires of the northern part of the wooded-mire zone of the West Siberian Plain

Basin of river (to its outfall)	Area (km²)		Endotelmic lakes	Amount of mire in basin (%)	Amount of lakes in mires (%)	Total number of lakes of over 0·5 (ha)	Density of lakes (km⁻²)	Mean size of lakes (ha)
	Catchment	Mire						
I. Surgut Woodlands								
Trom-Yugan	56 300	35 000	6810	64	18·9	69 320	1·92	9·9
Agan	31 900	15 200	3230	57	17·8	40 490	2·46	8·0
Pim	11 600	9700	2460	84	25·4	22 330	2·30	11·1
Lyamin	15 900	12 200	2360	77	19·4	28 830	2·36	8·2
II. Basin of Rivers Nazym and Kazym								
Nazym	11 500	3740	300	33	8·0	3890	1·04	7·7
Kazym	35 600	10 500	1200	30	10·4	14 840	1·41	8·1
III. Left Bank of River Ob' to South of its West-flowing Section								
Bol'shoy Yugan	34 200	11 200	420	33	3·8	6660	0·60	6·3
Malyy Yugan	9970	2770	106	28	3·8	2020	0·73	5·2
Bol'shoy Salym	15 900	7450	340	47	4·6	4770	0·64	7·1
Turtas	12 700	5650	158	45	2·8	1740	0·31	9·1
Dem'yanka	34 400	18 500	800	54	4·3	11 690	0·63	6·8
IV. Basins of Rivers Konda and Northern Sos'va								
Konda—outfall	72 900	36 600	3200	53	8·3	22 020	0·57	15
Mulym'ya (Mutom)—outfall	7700	3200	418	41·5	13·0	3320	1·04	12
Supra—outfall	1660	460	18	28	3·9	300	0·66	6
Bol'shoy Teter—outfall	1100	800	113	72	14·1	470	0·59	24
Seul'—outfall	3760	1470	100	39·5	6·8	430	0·29	23
Endyr'—outfall	3940	1170	48	30	4·1	225	0·19	17
Northern Sos'va	97 300	12 500	343	13	2·7	3360	0·31	8·9
V. Basins of Rivers Vakh and Tym								
Tym—outfall	32 520	9270	241	28	2·6	3810	0·41	6·3
Vakh—outfall	75 360	29 030	2670	38	9·3	33 990	1·17	7·8

to see that the larger lakes tend to lie in the central parts of the interfluves. As one approaches the rivers, the size of the lakes becomes smaller and smaller, and near the rivers they assume a markedly elongated form with their long axis in a regular position (perpendicular to the general direction of flow), and then pass over into the usual ridge–pool mire microtopes. This principle is everywhere observed in the morphology of lake–mire complexes, in places where they are the predominating type of mire formation, particularly in the river basins whose characteristics are described in Table 18.

A study of the structure of lake–mire complexes, which was carried out by the West Siberian expedition of the G.G.I. in 1963–72, showed that the endotelmic lakes investigated, which were of the most diverse sizes, from a fraction of a hectare to tens of square kilometres, are in most cases very small water bodies, whose basin is completely contained in the peat deposit. Under them lie beds of raised-mire *Sphagnum* peat. Their thickness usually runs to several metres (2–3 m or more), while the average depth of the lakes is 1·5–2·0 m. The greatest depths (up to 4·5–5·0 m) are found only in small lakes and lake-like flarks.

The relief of the strata subjacent to the peat deposit that lies below the lake in no way reflects that of the basin in which the water body lies. As is plain from Fig. 29, the peat basin is a depression with an even, horizontal bottom and vertical walls of peat. The relief of the mineral strata under the lake is convex or slopes in one direction. There is therefore every reason to think that endotelmic lakes in similar lake–mire complexes are in most cases water bodies of secondary origin, which were formed while an organic stratum of peat was being accumulated on top of mineral soils. Consequently, the causes of such endotelmic lakes, their shapes, sizes and situations in mire systems, must be sought in the laws that govern the development of the mire systems themselves (see Chapter 4).

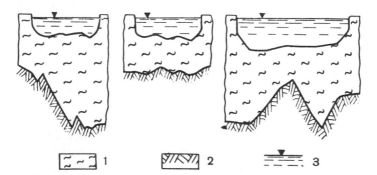

Fig. 29. Characteristic profiles of endotelmic lakes in large lake–mire systems. 1—peat deposit. 2—mineral soil. 3—level of water in lake.

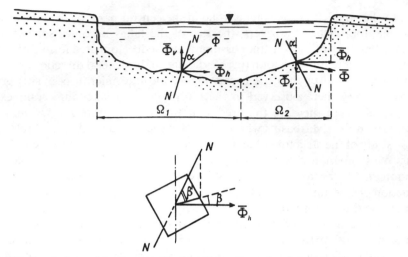

Fig. 30. Symbols used in the water balance equation of endotelmic lakes.

For any arbitrarily chosen lake (Fig. 30) in a stable condition the following water balance equation in its most general form must hold good over a sufficiently long interval of time[2]:

$$\bar{Q}_i + \bar{p}\omega = \bar{Q}_e, \tag{3.39}$$

where ω is the area of the lake, $\bar{Q}_i$ the total mean horizontal influx into the lake (or external water supply), $\bar{Q}_e$ the total mean horizontal efflux from the lake (the external efflux of the lake), and $\bar{p}$ the mean quantity of internal (vertical) water exchange per unit area of the lake, which is the algebraic sum of the mean quantity of precipitation $\bar{p}_p$, evaporation $\bar{p}_e$ and vertical water exchange over the surface of the bottom of the lake $\bar{p}_{gr}$ per unit of that surface:

$$\bar{p} = \bar{p}_p - \bar{p}_e \pm \bar{p}_{gr}. \tag{3.40}$$

We should note that equations (3.39) and (3.40) are in their own way analogous to equations (2.61) and (2.64), which represent the water balance of mire massifs.

Let us now agree that the sign "+" before $\bar{p}_{gr}$ will symbolize a vertical influx into a greater water body from the subjacent soil and the sign "−" a loss by seepage into the subjacent soil. Let us also analyse the meaning of the terms in equation (3.39) so as to cover the most general case of a lacustrine water body (see Fig. 30). The intensity of seepage (i.e. filtrational discharge per unit area, which we shall call the vector $\bar{\Phi}$) at each point of the bottom we shall analyse into a horizontal $\overline{\Phi}_h$ and a vertical $\overline{\Phi}_v$ component. Then the total vertical discharge over the whole surface of the lake bottom below the water line is expressed by the equation

$$\bar{p}_{gr}\omega = \int_{\Omega_1} \overline{\Phi}_v \cos\alpha \, d\Omega - \int_{\Omega_2} \overline{\Phi}_v \cos\alpha \, d\Omega, \qquad (3.41)$$

where Ω_1 is the area with a positive water supply through the lake bottom, Ω_2 the area with a negative supply (i.e. a loss through seepage), α is the angle between the vertical and the normal to the surface of the bottom at each point, and $d\Omega$ an element of the surface of the bottom. The values of $\overline{\Phi}_v$ and the angle α are functions of the position of a point on the lake bottom.

The total horizontal discharge over the bottom of the lake basin is expressed by the equation

$$\bar{Q}_i - \bar{Q}_e = \int_{\Omega'_1} \overline{\Phi}_h \cos\beta \cos\beta' \, d\Omega - \int_{\Omega'_2} \overline{\Phi}_h \cos\beta \cos\beta' \, d\Omega, \qquad (3.42)$$

where Ω'_1 and Ω'_2 are parts of the lake bottom across which there is respectively a horizontal influx and efflux of water, β is the angle between the vector of the horizontal component of seepage and the normal to an element of the bottom in the horizontal plane, and β' is the angle between the same vector and the normal to the element in the vertical plane.

We must note that the boundary dividing the parts of the bottom with a horizontal influx Ω'_1 from the parts with a horizontal efflux Ω'_2 does not generally coincide with that between the parts with a vertical influx Ω_1 and those with a vertical efflux Ω_2. Taking into consideration the relation (3.40), we substitute the expressions (3.41) and (3.42) in equation (3.39). We then find that

$$\int_{\Omega'_1} \overline{\Phi}_h \cos\beta \cos\beta' \, d\Omega + (\bar{p}_p - p_e)\omega + \int_{\Omega_1} \overline{\Phi}_v \cos\alpha \, d\Omega - \int_{\Omega_2} \overline{\Phi}_v \cos\alpha \, d\Omega =$$

$$= \int_{\Omega'_2} \overline{\Phi}_h \cos\beta \cos\beta' \, d\Omega. \qquad (3.43)$$

For shallow lakes with a sloping bottom, the submerged portion of the lake basin Ω differs little from ω, the area of the lake, which is a projection of Ω onto the horizontal plane. For that reason we take Ω as approximately equal to ω in the case of such lakes. Considering moreover that, at all points on the area of the bottom Ω where its slope is small (except round its shores), the angle α is nearly zero and $\cos\alpha$ nearly 1, it is possible to treat the areas of vertical water exchange Ω_1 and Ω_2 as nearly equal to ω_1 and ω_2. In the same parts of the surface of the lake (ω_1 and ω_2), the angle β' is nearly 90°

and cos β' nearly zero, and therefore the amount of horizontal water exchange can here be regarded as approximately zero. Moreover, the region of horizontal efflux and influx will be confined to the part of the lake bottom which is below the water-line and immediately adjacent to the shore line, where it has a steep slope and cos β' has correspondingly high values.

For lakes situated inside mire massifs, precipitous shores with vertical banks composed of peat and a flat bottom with gentle slopes are typical. In these circumstances, the zone of horizontal water exchange is the vertical bank of the shore (for which $\beta' = 0$ and cos $\beta' = 1$), while the surface of horizontal water exchange is approximately equal to the mean depth of the lake H_m multiplied by the length of its shore line L.

Taking into consideration these morphological peculiarities of endotelmic lakes and using L_1 for the front of horizontal influx and L_2 for the front of horizontal efflux, the equation of water balance (3.43) can in this case be presented in the following form:

$$\oint_{L_1} \Phi_h \cos \beta \, d(H_m L) + (\bar{p}_p - \bar{p}_e) + \int_{\omega_1} \Phi_v \, d\omega - \int_{\omega_2} \Phi_v \, d\omega =$$

$$= \int_{\omega_2} \Phi_h \cos \beta \, d(H_m L). \quad (3.44)$$

H_m is constant for the whole boundary, and therefore, if we suppose that

$$\cos \beta \, dL = dl, \quad \Phi_h = \bar{q}, \quad \text{and} \quad \int_{\omega_1} \Phi_v \, d\omega - \int_{\omega_2} \Phi_v \, d\omega = \bar{p}_{gr}\omega,$$

then we obtain the water balance equation in the following form:

$$\oint_{L_1} \bar{q} \, dl + (\bar{p}_p - \bar{p}_e + \bar{p}_{gr})\, \omega = \oint_{L_2} \bar{q} \, dl, \quad (3.45)$$

where $\bar{q}$ is seepage (or the discharge per unit length of the projected front) in the microtopes contiguous to the lake, which for the peat deposit of the mire is equal to the mean horizontal seepage of the acrotelm, and is in general a function of its position on the shore line of the lake. In this connection, it should be noted that the vertical water exchange of the lake $\bar{p}_{gr}$ is the total amount of vertical water exchange per unit area, without reference to the distribution of seepage over the lake bottom.

On the basis of equality (3.40), we may also write the last equation for endotelmic lakes in the form

$$\oint_{L_1} \bar{q} \, dl + \bar{p}\omega = \oint_{L_2} \bar{q} \, dl. \quad (3.46)$$

Written in this form, the water balance equation establishes a connection between the hydrological conditions that give rise to endotelmic lakes and their morphological properties. We shall begin by showing that this is the case in a few very simple examples.

Let the mean intensity of internal water exchange be $\bar{p}$, which, in the absence of any vertical water exchange with the bed of the lake, is completely determined by climatic conditions—the norms of precipitation and evaporation at the surface of the water. Let us first consider the very simplest case, where the whole shore of the lake is included in one and the same mire microtope. In this case, since $\bar{q}$ is constant, equation (3.46) can obviously be written in the form

$$\bar{q}l_1 + \bar{p}\omega = \bar{q}l_2, \tag{3.47}$$

from which it follows that the difference between the length of the projected fronts of influx and efflux on the margin of the lake must be determined by the relation

$$l_2 - l_1 = \frac{\bar{p}}{\bar{q}}\omega, \tag{3.48}$$

and the area of the lake correspondingly by the expression

$$\omega = (l_2 - l_1)\frac{\bar{q}}{\bar{p}}. \tag{3.48'}$$

From equations (3.48) and (3.48') it follows that a lake bounded by a uniform mire microtope in the zone of excess moisture must owe its existence to the fact that the front of efflux l_2 is greater than the front of influx l_1 by $\bar{p}\omega/\bar{q}$. As is plain from equation (3.48), the difference between the lengths of the fronts of efflux and influx on the margin of the lake grows with an increase in the internal water supply $\bar{p}$ (i.e. with an increase in the humidity of the climate), a decrease in the seepage of the surrounding microtope $\bar{q}$, and an increase in the area of the lake ω. Therefore the area of the lake, the relative lengths of its marginal fronts of influx and efflux and the type of microtope which surrounds it are unambiguously connected parameters defined by the relationship (3.48). This relationship we shall call *the water balance criterion for endotelmic lakes*, which in this case is written in a form that is suitable for the simplest possible conditions.

From equation (3.48') it is easy to see that for every size of lake (ω), situated in given climatic conditions ($\bar{p}$), in a definite type of microtope ($\bar{q}$), there must be a strictly defined relationship between the length of its marginal fronts of influx and efflux. Disturbance of this relationship must make the whole lake–mire system unstable. Either there will be a change in the seepage of the surrounding microtope, or in the size of the lake, or in the quantity of its internal water supply. This question will later be given special consideration.

Equations (3.45) and (3.47)–(3.48′) clearly also make it possible to solve the converse problem. The area of a lake and its projected fronts of influx and efflux can be directly measured by aerial survey. If the quantity of the internal water supply $\bar{p}$ is determined by climatic conditions and can be calculated from the difference between the norms of precipitation and evaporation for the given region and the size of the water body, then, by substituting these data in equation (3.48), it is easy to calculate the mean seepage $\bar{q}$ of the mire microtope in which the lake is situated. That is to say, if we know the morphological details of the lake (its area and the length of its marginal fronts of flow as indicated by its flow-net), it is possible to find the mean seepage of the surrounding mire microtope.

This is particularly important when the data obtained by aerial survey are used to analyse the conditions that give rise to lake–mire complexes and to study the physical characteristics of lake–mire geotopes situated in inaccessible wetlands, which have not been made subjects of research. In such cases, the seepage and other physical characteristics of the mire microtopes have not been directly (i.e. experimentally) studied, and it is not even known what types of microtope they contain. In these circumstances, endotelmic lakes serve as unique indicators by which one can determine the difference between the fronts of influx and efflux of a lake, the seepage of the surrounding mire microtopes (provided the balance of internal water supply $\bar{p}$ is known), or, from the known characteristics of the surroundings, the quantity of vertical water movement. Use is made for this purpose of data derived from aerial survey and general information about climate and hydrology.

The most important practical task is to find out the soil-derived water supply of the lake $\bar{p}_{gr}$, since this cannot be measured or determined by any direct method. If we try to calculate $\bar{p}_{gr}$ from the relationship (3.45) with the help of equation (3.40), we find that

$$\bar{p}_{gr} = \frac{\bar{q}(l_2 - l_1)}{\omega} + \bar{p}_e - \bar{p}_p. \tag{3.49}$$

This very simple example shows that the indicator properties of endotelmic lakes can be used to answer various questions, according to the problem posed, and also to analyse the conditions under which lake–mire complexes arise and develop.

Let us now consider a more complicated case, one that is most frequently encountered when the lake is situated among several different types of mire microtope. Here, if we decompose the fronts of influx and efflux into their different microtopes, we may replace the integrals in (3.45) by the corresponding finite sums and write:

$$\bar{p} = \bar{P}_p - \bar{P}_e + \bar{P}_{gr} = \frac{\sum_1^n \bar{q}_i l_i - \sum_1^m \bar{q}_j l_j}{\omega}, \tag{3.50}$$

where n is the number of different microtopes contiguous to the front of efflux, and m the number contiguous to the front of influx. We now introduce the concept of equivalent (or mean) seepage for the fronts of influx or efflux of the lake. On the basis of equation (3.22) we have:

$$\bar{q}_{if} = \frac{\sum_1^m \bar{q}_j l_j}{\sum_1^m l_j}, \qquad \bar{q}_{ef} = \frac{\sum_1^n \bar{q}_j l_j}{\sum_1^n l_j}, \tag{3.51}$$

where $\sum_1^n l_j = l_{ef}$ is the length of the projected front of efflux, and $\sum_1^m l_j = l_{if}$ is the length of the projected front of influx.

The relationship (3.50) can then be reduced to a simple expression analogous to (3.47);

$$\bar{p} = \frac{\bar{q}_{ef} l_{ef} - \bar{q}_{if} l_{if}}{\omega} = \frac{\Delta(\bar{q}l)}{\omega}. \tag{3.52}$$

When $\bar{p}_{gr} = 0$, we shall use $\bar{p}_*$ for the internal water balance and ω_* for the area of the lake. Then, according to equation (3.52),

$$\omega_* = \frac{\Delta(\bar{q}l)}{\bar{p}_*}. \tag{3.53}$$

When there is water exchange with the soil,

$$\omega = \frac{\Delta(\bar{q}l)}{\bar{p}}. \tag{3.54}$$

Dividing equation (3.53) by equation (3.54), we find that

$$\bar{p} = \frac{\omega_* \bar{p}_*}{\omega}, \tag{3.55}$$

or, since $\bar{p} = \bar{P}_p - \bar{P}_e + \bar{P}_{gr}$, that

$$\bar{P}_{gr} = \left(\frac{\omega_*}{\omega} - 1\right)\bar{p}_*. \tag{3.56}$$

If then the various values of the difference $\Delta(\bar{q}l)$ and of $(\bar{p}_p - \bar{p}_e) = \bar{p}$ have been calculated for a continuous series of sample lakes of various areas ω_*, it is easy to find the vertical water exchange with the soil for a lake of any given size by means of equation (3.56). In given climatic conditions, endotelmic lakes with an area $\omega > \omega_*$ must have a positive water exchange with the soil, i.e. a soil-derived water supply; but, when $\omega = \omega_*$, a negative one, i.e. a loss by seepage into the subjacent soil. Any area of lake ω_* having no water exchange with the soil $(\bar{p}_* = \bar{p}_p - \bar{p}_e)$ and a certain difference in its external water exchange $\Delta(\bar{q}l)$ may properly be said to represent a critical value, any deviation from which must be accompanied by the appearance of an internal water supply (in either direction), or the appearance of an external water exchange in the form of a channelled influx or efflux, or a change in the structure or composition of the plant associations in the microtopes surrounding the lake, i.e. a change in the types of mire microtopes and a resulting change in the hydraulic conductivity of the acrotelm.

It is obvious that, when it is known that there is no vertical water exchange with the soil $(\bar{p}_{gr} = 0)$ and no channelled water exchange with the outside, an endotelmic lake must satisfy the water balance equations (3.53) or (3.47), if it is surrounded by a uniform microtope. Deviation of the actual area of the lake from the critical value (ω_*), as for example in the direction of increase $(\omega > \omega_*)$, must signify that the given area of lake is insufficient to reduce by evaporation the quantity of precipitation to an amount that can be disposed of through the acrotelm of the surrounding microtopes at normal water levels. This means that the efflux from the lake through the acrotelm must in this case be greater than is normal in this type of microtope. Consequently, the conditions required for the existence and development of the corresponding plant associations will be disturbed. These last will be replaced by plant associations which produce a more permeable acrotelm. If, however, this is not possible and the vegetation degenerates continuously through over-saturation, the area of the lake will grow continuously, until a channel is formed for surface runoff, and the state of the whole system becomes stable.

Analogous processes take place in the opposite direction, when the area of lake proves less than the size required by the water balance criteria. The lake then begins to retreat rapidly from its banks, and its area contracts to the size necessary to give stability to the system. Calculations carried out in regard to endotelmic lakes in lake–mire systems of different types (see Table 19) show that in many cases, and particularly in convex mire massifs with lakes in the centre, the size of the lakes agrees with the critical one. If they have an exclusively meteoric water supply, such systems are in a meta-stable condition in relation to the climatic conditions and the microtopes that surround them. In an equal number of cases, however, we meet with endotelmic lakes whose area deviates markedly from the water balance criteria (3.52), particularly in the direction of excess. According to equation (3.56), such lakes, if they are in the zone of excess moisture, must lose much water through vertical seepage into the subjacent mineral strata or an external channel of water exchange (i.e. streams flowing out of them), or must be, at the given period of their development, in an unstable state, because the water table regime of the surrounding microtopes has been disturbed.

Table 19 gives the results of calculations relating to the water exchange of endotelmic lakes in different parts of the forest zone and in different positions within such systems. When lakes are situated at an epicentre of convexity in mire mesotopes, they have no influx from without. No figures for influx are therefore to be found in the column headed "Average horizontal water exchange". In all other such cases, the difference between horizontal influx and efflux is just another way of describing the total internal water exchange of the lake. The extent to which this disagrees with the difference between the norms of precipitation and evaporation expresses either the loss of the lake to subjacent layers of soil, or the water supply that it receives from them.

When we consider the results of the calculations given in Table 19 from this point of view, it is important to note that, in the European plain and the lowlands of Western Siberia, lakes which lose water to the soil under their peat deposits cover a very large area. This is particularly true in regions where mire massifs are situated on top of sand beds, as in the basins of the rivers Lyamin, Pim and Trom-Yugan. It occurs much less frequently when massifs are superimposed on soils of low permeability.

A simple review of the sources of error that may affect calculations based on equations (3.51), (3.52) and (3.56), which are mainly determined by the accuracy of the values used for the mean long-term seepage $\bar{q}$ of the various microtopes, suggests that values of water exchange below 40–50 mm/year (taken absolutely) are at the very limit of accuracy achievable in such calculations. For that reason, all the cases given in Table 19 where the mean annual water exchange with the soil was found to be less than 50 mm/year must be regarded as involving conditions in which it is difficult to establish the presence or absence of water exchange by this method with any degree of confidence. Looking at the results of calculations from this point of view, it is possible to refer lakes Nos. 1–3, 5, 8, 9, 11, 14–16, 35, 42, 43, 45–47 and 49–52 to the group of endotelmic lakes which have no water exchange with the soil. The others have a significant water exchange, and most of them show losses to the subjacent soil.

Nevertheless, there are some results relating to mires situated on water divides in a mire system which testify to the existence of a water supply derived from the subjacent soil. These are lakes Nos. 4, 6, 12, 20 and 21. Since it is very unlikely that there is an influx of pressure water from the soil

Table 19. Water exchange of endotelmic lakes in mire systems situated on water divides and inclined water divides in the zone of excess moisture

No. in order	Position of lake in lake–mire complex	Area of lake (measured) (km²)	Types of microtope adjacent to banks of lakes: Type	Ridges (%)	Flarks (%)	Mean value of seepage (l.s⁻¹.km⁻¹)	Mean horizontal water exchange of lake across acrotelm: Inflow	Outflow	Area of lake (calculated) (km²)	Divergence (%)	Mean annual water exchange of lake with bottom soil and peat (mm/year): loss	gain
1	2	3	4	5	6	7	8	9	10	11	12	13
						European part of Soviet Union						
1	In epicentre of convexity of massif (Fig. 27a)	0·6	I	—	—	1·35	—	4·35	0·68	+13	—	28
			II	60	40	3·10						
2	In epicentre of convexity of massif (Fig. 27a)	1·57	II	50	50	3·45	—	11·76	1·85	+18	—	36
			III	50	50	1·60						
3	In epicentre of convexity of massif (Fig. 27a)	1·08	II	50	50	3·45	—	6·63	1·04	−4	−7	—
			III	70	30	1·40						
			IV	80	20	1·85						
4	In epicentre of convexity of massif (Fig. 27a)	0·09	II	80	20	0·80	—	0·96	0·15			136
			IV	90	10	1·20						
5	In epicentre of convexity of massif (Fig. 27a)	0·68	IV	80	20	1·85	—	4·96	0·78	+15	—	30
			V	—	—	1·50						
6	In epicentre of convexity of massif (Fig. 27a)	0·08	IV	90	10	1·20	—	1·32	0·21	+162	—	320

No.	Description											
7	Single lake on sloping part of massif (Fig. 27b)	0·09	VI	—	—	1·75	0·49	0·72	0·04	−55	−120	—
8	Single lake on sloping part of massif (Fig. 27b)	0·09	IV	80	20	1·86	0·72	1·30	0·09	0	0	0
9	Single lake on sloping part of massif (Fig. 27b)	0·06	IV, VI	80, —	20, 10	1·85, 2·50	0·52	0·84	0·05	−17	−32	—
10	Single lake on sloping part of massif (Fig. 27b)	0·48	IV, I, VI	90, —, —	10, —, —	1·20, 0·70, 2·50	0·63	2·87	0·35	−27	−55	—
11	Single lake on sloping part of massif (Fig. 27b)	0·56	IV, VI	80, —	20, —	1·85, 2·50	0·54	3·68	0·49	−12	−24	—
12	Single lake on sloping part of massif (Fig. 27b)	0·06	IV, VI	90, —	10, —	1·20, 2·50	0·26	0·85	0·09	+50	—	100
13	Single lake on sloping part of massif (Fig. 27b)	0·16	I, VII	—, —	—, —	0·70, 2·50	0·18	0·58	0·06	−62	−121	—
14	Single lake on sloping part of massif (Fig. 27b)	0·03	II	50	50	3·45	0·31	0·52	0·03	0	0	0
15	Single lake on sloping part of massif (Fig. 27b)	1·28	IV, V	50, —	50, —	2·50, 2·50	0·38	7·85	1·18	−8	−16	—
16	Single lake on sloping part of massif (Fig. 27b)	0·10	II, IV	70, 60	30, 40	1·4, 2·25	0·62	1·18	0·09	−11	−24	—
17	Single lake on sloping part of massif (Fig. 27b)	0·69	VI	—	—	1·00	2·52	5·50	0·47	−25	−51	—
18	Single lake on sloping part of massif (Fig. 27b)	0·25	III, III	60, 40	20, 60	0·80, 2·00	0·38	1·56	0·19	−24	−51	—
19	Lake on the border of two convex mesotopes	0·03	IV, II	80, 50	20, 50	1·85, 3·45	0·56	0·69	0·02	−33	−63	—

Table 19—*continued*

No. in order	Position of lake in lake–mire complex	Area of lake (measured) (km²)	Types of microtope adjacent to banks of lakes			Mean value of seepage (l.s⁻¹ km⁻¹)	Mean horizontal water exchange of lake across acrotelm		Area of lake (calculated) (km²)	Divergence (%)	Mean annual water exchange of lake with bottom soil and peat (mm/year)	
			Type	Ridges (%)	Flarks (%)		Inflow	Outflow			loss	gain
1	2	3	4	5	6	7	8	9	10	11	12	13
	Western Siberia: Basins of rivers Lyamin, Pim, Trom-Yugan, Agan											
20	On water divides	1·62	VIII	50	50	6·05	—	20·0	2·52	56	—	139
21	On water divides	2·05	VIII	50	50	6·05	—	30·0	3·77	84	—	210
22	On slopes with divergent flow	0·69	VIII	50	50	6·05	6·54	7·08	0·07	−90	225	—
23	On slopes with divergent flow	0·56	VIII	50	50	6·05	5·20	6·05	0·11	−80	202	—
24	On slopes with divergent flow	0·14	VI / IV	— / 50	50 / 50	1·0 / 2·5	0·40	1·20	0·10	−29	70	—
25	On slopes with divergent flow	0·08	VIII	50	50	6·05	11·0	12·0	0·19	62	—	140
26	On slopes with divergent flow	0·09	VII / IV	— / 50	50 / 50	1·0 / 2·5	0·25	0·56	0·04	−56	142	—
27	On slopes with divergent flow	0·06	II	53	47	3·1	0·99	1·24	0·03	−50	119	—
28	On slopes with divergent flow	0·166	II	53	47	3·1	1·40	1·63	0·03	−81	205	—

29	On slopes with divergent flow	0·22	VIII	50	50	6·05	2·73	3·24	0·06	−73	177	—
30	On slopes with divergent flow	0·15	VIII	50	50	6·05	3·12	3·33	0·03	−80	206	—
31	On slopes with divergent flow	0·19	IV	80	20	1·75	1·05	2·02	0·12	−37	89	—
			II	53	47	3·10						
32	On slopes with divergent flow	1·44	VIII	50	50	6·05	10·6	18·3	0·97	−33	81	
33	On slopes with divergent flow	0·90	VIII	50	50	6·05	5·75	14·55	1·11	23		58
			II	53	47	3·1						
34	On slopes with divergent flow	0·28	II	53	47	3·1	2·23	3·09	0·11	−61	153	—
			VIII	50	50	6·05						
35	On slopes with divergent flow	0·47	VIII	50	50	6·05	3·94	6·95	0·38	−19	48	
36	On slopes with divergent flow	1·09	VIII	50	50	6·05	6·05	7·75	0·31	−81	201	
37	On slopes with divergent flow	0·12	VIII	50	50	6·05	2·72	3·02	0·04	−67	171	
38	On slopes with divergent flow	1·34	VIII	50	50	6·05	10·9	14·5	0·46	−66	165	
39	On slopes with divergent flow	0·38	VIII	50	50	6·05	6·05	7·56	0·19	−50	125	
40	On slopes with divergent flow	0·69	Ia	—	—	1·50	0·27	1·33	0·13	−81	200	
			III	80	90	0·80						
			II			4·0						
41	On slopes with divergent flow	1·39	VIII	50	50	6·05	8·77	16·77	0·95	−32	79	

Table 19—*continued*

No. on order	Position of lake in lake-mire complex	Area of lake (measured) (km²)	Types of microtope adjacent to banks of lakes — Type	Ridges (%)	Flarks (%)	Mean value of seepage (l.s⁻¹.km⁻¹)	Mean horizontal water exchange of lake across acrotelm — Inflow	Outflow	Area of lake (calculated) (km²)	Divergence (%)	Mean annual water exchange of lake with bottom soil and peat (mm/year) — loss	gain
1	2	3	4	5	6	7	8	9	10	11	12	13
Western Siberia Mire Massif of the Vasyugan and basin of River Konda												
42	On water divides	1·02	VI	—	—	1·75	—	4·82	1·01	−1	2	—
43	On the slope of a massif	0·69	I	—	—	1·0	1·72	2·98	0·40	−42	42	—
			IV	85	15	1·5						
			IV	90	10	1·2						
			Ia	—	—	2·0						
			IV	30	70	3·0						
44	On the slope of a massif	1·12	Ia	—	—	2·0	1·65	2·70	0·33	−70	68	
			V—VI	—	—	1·0						
			II	80	20	0·8						
			IV	40	60	3·0						
45	On the slope of a massif	0·47	IV	80	20	1·85	0·84	2·36	0·40			2
			V—VI	—	—	1·75						
			I	—	—	1·35						

No.	Location		Type							
46	On the slope of a massif	0·12	IV	85	15	1·30	0·71	1·18	0·15	23
			IV	60	40	2·25				
			Ia	—	—	2·0				
47	On the slope of a massif	0·36	IV	85	15	1·30	1·64	2·65	0·32	12
			Ia	—	—	2·0				
48	On the slope of a massif	0·12	Ia	—	—	1·75	0·74	1·37	0·20	65
			IV	60	40	2·25				
49	On the slope of a massif	0·10	IV	60	40	2·25	0·43	1·0	0·18	20
			I	60	40	1·35				
50	On the slope of a massif	0·09	VI	—	—	1·75	0·82	1·08	0·08	9
			IV	60	40	2·25				
51	On a slope near a water divide	0·30	IV	60	40	2·25	0·52	1·63	0·35	17
			V	—	—	1·75				
			IV	80	20	1·85				
52	On the slope of a massif	0·32	IV	60	40	2·25	1·41	2·45	0·32	0

NOTE The Roman numerals in Column 4 indicate the following types of mire microtopes

Ia—Pine–shrub with tree height of more than 6 m (from 15 to 20 m), Ib—Pine–*Sphagnum*–shrub and *Sphagnum*–pine–shrub with tree height of 4 to 6 m. II—Ridge–flark with *Sphagnum*–shrub ridges forested with pine and *Sphagnum*–*Scheuchzeria* flarks. III—Ridge–flark with *Sphagnum*–shrub ridges forested with pine and *Sphagnum*–*Scheuchzeria* flarks, some with open water surfaces. IV—Ridge–flark with *Sphagnum*–shrub ridges forested with pine and *Sphagnum*–*Eriophorum* flarks. V—*Sphagnum*–*Eriophorum* unforested, or thinly forested with dwarf pines of up to 3 m. VI—*Sphagnum*–shrub forested with pine. VII—*Sphagnum*–shrub–*Eriophorum*. VIII—Ridge–pool with *Sphagnum*–shrub forested with pine.

into endotelmic lakes on a water divide, one must conclude that these are lakes whose area has been altered in some way or other by erosion, and whose level has been lowered in this way, so that the horizontal runoff from them through the acrotelm is less than that calculated from the average seepage of the microtopes that surround them (see section 4.6). This very disagreement shows that the existing situation of such lakes is unstable, and that their surface area is in process of being changed.

4

Calculations of the Effects of Reclamation and Conservation on the Stability of Mire and Lake–Mire Systems

4.1 Statement of the Problem

In the preceding account (see Chapter 1 and section 2.12), mires were regarded as natural formations, dynamic geosystems, in which at the moment an extensive accumulation of organic material is going on, which in the course of time changes the biophysical properties of the mires themselves and determines the part they play in geophysical processes (Ivanov, 1972).

In the territory of our country, there are still large regions that have not been subjected to the intensive influence of man's economic activities. These include the vast wetlands in the north of European Russia, Western Siberia and many other regions of Russian Asia. Of all the country's natural land resources, mires, owing to their special peculiarities and inaccessibility, have so far remained the geotopic elements least affected by man's economic activities. Now, however, the progress of science and technology and of the means to bring influence to bear upon the environment have reached such proportions that any unwary or unscientific interference with geophysical processes may in a short time change their direction and produce irreversible deteriorations in the environment. In that situation, much attention must be devoted to the part that mires play in geophysical processes and to the evaluation of their usefulness to man. It must be possible to foresee any undesirable consequences and to avoid their appearance during the development and economic utilization of wetlands, treating this as an important aspect of the general problem of conserving and expanding natural resources.

In this chapter, attention is chiefly devoted to the role of hydrological factors and the processes of water exchange in the transformation of mire systems, since water, generally speaking, is the most active substance and the most important external factor in transforming the geophysical mantle of the earth, especially in the transformation of mire systems. In doing this, we shall base our argument on the patterns of relationship and adaptation that occur in complex geosystems (Anon., 1971b; Khil'mi, 1963, 1966), to which mires in all their forms must be referred, since their origin and development is determined by biophysical and geophysical processes. To achieve our end, we must select a limited number of the most important reciprocal relationships between a mire system and its environment, and between separate states and components within the system that determine the course of its development, the transformations of its structure and the alterations in its functions (Khil'mi, 1966). A block diagram of these relations was considered briefly in section 2.12 and presented in Fig. 20.

This approach makes it possible to compile suitable programs for calculating or estimating the effects of development or economic activities upon the water exchange of mires and upon the geotopes of natural mirelands and their surroundings. Drainage and artificial control of their water regime are, as we know, among the most radical methods by which man can affect the hydrological and thermal condition of mires. The character of these measures and the technical means of realizing them depend on the later use to which mires are put—for agriculture, peat production, building, afforestation, etc. In each of these cases, there is created on the transformed terrain an artificial geotope which is useful to man and has undergone appropriate modifications in its water regime and the biophysical properties of its components.

These, however, are by no means the only ways in which economic activities affect mirelands. Such measures as the occupation and urbanization of areas surrounding mires, the deepening of river-beds that collect water from mires, the construction of hydrotechnical works on river systems, the creation of reservoirs by filling up depressions (Ivanov and Shumkova, 1967), the laying of communications (conveyor pipes), road construction over mires, etc., lead to a fundamental change in the natural conditions of efflux from mires, to a change in the water balance of huge areas of mireland, and to corresponding changes in the condition of their plant cover and the existing processes of peat accumulation. In some cases, these changes may have a favourable effect on the natural resources of the area, but in others they may have unfavourable consequences that are irreversible.

When considering the processes of water exchange in previous chapters, it was assumed that mire formations (meso- and macrotopes), their structure and physical properties, their plant cover and its floristic composition remained unaltered in the processes of water exchange, and were not affected by changes in their external environment, the long-term course of meteorological phenomena, the mean annual influx and efflux of moisture and heat, by tectonic movements of the earth's crust or by alterations in natural drainage. In section 2.12, this was called the quasi-stationary condition of mire systems. This made it possible to disregard some external inputs into the system (input 27) and to treat others as unchanging external conditions (inputs 1–4, 15, 16), while we were considering the general interaction of mire systems and their elements with factors in the external environment (Fig. 20).

This approach is unsatisfactory, however, when we are considering the influence of changes of water regime on mire massifs. All changes introduced by man into the water regime of mire massifs must be regarded as external inputs into the system—as external influences that must evoke corresponding adaptations in the system. If these influences are quantitatively or qualitatively of such a nature that the system cannot sufficiently adapt itself to them (i.e. change its properties and structure to adapt itself to new conditions or actively change its external environment), then the system becomes unstable and is destroyed (Khil'mi, 1966). The chief aim in studying and evaluating the stability of natural formations under the influence of man's activities or natural causes is to discover these limiting conditions and how far the properties and structure of mire systems can be changed without destroying their general organization.

As we have not, at present, the means to solve such questions experimentally, it is necessary to choose another path—to study those adaptations and transformations of mire systems in natural conditions that are due to some definite combination of causes which is analogous to the influence of man's economic activities. This, as is obvious, may serve as a theoretical basis both for relevant quantitative calculations and for estimates of the consequences of artificial interference with nature—in this case, with the processes of water movement in mire systems.

4.2 Reversible and Irreversible Processes: the Stability of Mire Systems

The theoretical basis for forecasting changes in the elements or structure of nature as a result of change in the geophysical environment, and particularly of the hydrological or thermal regime of some particular area, is an understanding of the stability of natural systems and of the limitations of their power to adapt or regulate themselves in response to changes in their environment. Fundamental ideas about the stability or instability of physical systems, especially as applied to motion and to mechanical systems, have long been the subject of important research in the fields of mathematics, physics and mechanics. The rapid development of geographical science in recent years has moreover significantly extended our understanding of natural (geophysical) systems involving different levels in their structural organization. Besides this, we have acquired a much broader understanding of system stability as a result of the development of cybernetics as a scientific way of looking at how things interact in the organic world and how they can be controlled. By the stability of an organized biophysical system (Khil'mi, 1966) we must understand the degree to which its structure (or organization) and its fundamental functions and properties (qualities) are preserved, when, under the influence of external or internal factors, some of its functions and properties undergo serious alteration and are deflected from what is their normal (or average) condition.

The concept of system stability is closely connected with that of reversibility and irreversibility as applied to natural processes. In reality, every irreversible natural process can be regarded from the point of view of cybernetics as a succession of unstable states, in which none of the later states will repeat an earlier one. Any reversible process can be regarded as a stable state of a system which, under the influence of external or internal causes, is going through a closed cycle of successive states. Such a system must return to its initial state after passing through a series of intermediate states.

Let us consider some very simple examples of reversible and irreversible processes occurring in mire systems as a result of the activity of man. Suppose, for example, that a network of drains is laid to reclaim a mire massif. It is well known that a network of shallow open ditches laid in a deep peat deposit, which lowers the mean level of the water table, will exercise an important influence on the condition of a mire and the growth of vegetation in it. In oligotrophic microtopes of the moss group, the growth of pine and the development of shrubs will be enhanced, and a certain change will occur in the quantitative relations between the species of moss, herb and shrub of which their plant cover is composed.

If, however, such a network is not periodically cleared and renewed, its efficiency rapidly declines. Its ditches are grown over and blocked with peat, and in time the whole network disappears through the restoration of the original vegetation and the original and natural hydrological regime of the mire. This is a typical example of the stability of a mire system in relation to a once for all change in its state. The system reacted to the changes in such a way that the general course of later changes was directed to the restoration of its original state, and the system did not disintegrate. The course of development to which it was subjected proved to be reversible. To maintain such a system in an unchanged state, despite its stability in relation to the influences to which it is exposed, it is necessary to keep on exercising them— in this case, to clear out and renew the drainage network.

We shall now adduce another example. Let us suppose there is a shallow mire massif situated on a permeable sandy soil in the zone of deficient or unstable moisture. Its main source of water supply is an influx of groundwater (an external and internal supply derived from the soil). The massif is drained by deep drainage ditches, the bottom and part of the banks of which are situated in the same sandy soil as underlies the massif. If the banks of the drainage ditches are made steep enough to sink their channels by erosion still deeper in the sandy soil, the changes produced by this in the mire system cannot evoke reactions that would facilitate the restoration of the water supply of the mire and compensate for the influence they have exercised upon it. All the later changes ensuing as a result of draining will therefore prove irreversible. Consequently, a mire system subjected to such changed conditions will prove unstable. Its peat deposits will be rapidly oxidized, shrink in volume and grow denser. The whole system will disintegrate or achieve stability in a new form. There will then be no need to repeat the original action—to renew and clean out the drainage system—in order to maintain the new state. In this case, the changes introduced have set in motion an irreversible process.

An analogous case of the instability of a mire system in relation to a transformation effected upon it would be a fen massif dependent for its water supply upon a surface influx, whose water was completely intercepted and removed by building a system of high-banked ditches. In this case, the changes produced by draining would again be irreversible, and the system would be unstable in respect of them.

It is by no means always the case that changes in the state of a natural system are due to the influence or decisions of man. Any natural process in which an ecosystem (limited in space and time) arises and develops under the influence of a multitude of physical and biological factors may be regarded as a succession or alternation of stable or unstable states due to separate causes or to some combination of causes. From this it is easy to see that the basis of any scientific prediction of the changes in nature that will follow the action of any naturally or artificially produced causes, including hydrological factors, must in every case be a search for quantitative or qualitative criteria. It is these that permit us, firstly, to decide when the state of a system is unstable and changes irreversible, and, secondly, to determine what limits must be set to changes in the factors that affect the system, if the resulting changes are to be reversible and the system itself is to remain stable.

When we speak in this way of the scientific prediction of changes in nature due, let us say, to human agency, we must treat this last as an external factor acting upon certain definite functional and structural elements of the system, and evoking appropriate adaptations and changes in it. The reversibility or irreversibility of transformations depends on how far the system will be stable or unstable in relation to the changes brought about in its structure and functional organization. The concepts of invariance (stability) and reversibility as applied to the development of natural geotopes have no necessary connection with the influence of human activity upon them. Any complex natural system consisting of a multitude of components subject to the influence of internal changes or external causes unconnected with any human activity may be found to be in a stable or unstable condition, and as such undergo reversible or irreversible changes.

It must also be noted that in any final transformation of a natural complex by man the intended transformation will be achieved if the resulting process is irreversible. The changes produced in its state will make the system as a whole unstable and either transform it into something new or lead to its complete disintegration. If, however, the natural complex remains stable in respect to the changes produced in its components (i.e. the new development is reversible and the states of the system constitute a closed cycle), then the maintenance of the changed state demands periodic repetition of these same operations. Otherwise the intended aim of the transformation cannot be realised.

It is not difficult to see that all the general propositions that have been set forth also apply to methods of investigating the influence of human activity upon natural formations and on natural geotopes and processes, including the investigation of its effects on the state of water resources and the water regime. This applies in still greater degree to the devising of methods of deliberately changing natural complexes by introducing changes in their water regime and water exchange, which are, of course, the most important factors in the development of the environment. The problem of the stability of natural complexes and the reversibility or irreversibility of their processes is therefore directly connected with the problem of transforming nature and forms its theoretical basis.

In working out methods of developing terrains and transforming nature, we usually have to deal with a large number of different factors that are involved in the natural process. Quantitative evaluation of all the factors is literally impossible, both because many of the processes have not been sufficiently studied, and because of the difficulty of discovering the functional structure of complicated natural formations. On the other hand, if one considers separately the most important components of a process and discovers how they interact, that is often sufficient to explain the chief properties of a geotope as a natural system of a certain type and the conditions of its existence and development. In this context, it is important to distinguish between two fundamentally different groups of processes: those which are self-regulating and those which are not. Let us now consider certain properties of mire systems which entitle them to be regarded as self-regulating.

4.3 Self-regulation in Mire Systems

A self-regulating process in any natural system (in this case, a mire system) may be described as a process in which any externally or internally induced change in the state or functions of the system gives rise to a reaction which either restores the system to its original state, or changes it in such a way that it adapts the system to new conditions without destroying its fundamental properties and functions, i.e. without destroying the system. In the first case, we are dealing with a reversible, self-regulating process; in the second, with an irreversible or unidirectional process.

According to the thorough analysis of generalized schemes of self-regulation in the pioneering work of Khil'mi (1966), investigation of the phenomena of self-regulation must begin with the fundamental law of cybernetics concerning requisite variety. This says: "If the number of genuinely different states of an environment D be large, then the number of answering adaptations of a system S_d must be sufficiently large to enable the system S_d to respond with an appropriate adaptation to every state of the environment D." (Quoted from Khil'mi.) To put it in another way, the variety of states of the environment and of externally produced changes in a system which hinder the conservation of that system (i.e. its functions and properties) can only be neutralized by a sufficiently large variety of adaptations on the part of the system. In other words: "A variety of influences preventing a system from satisfying a condition can only be counteracted by a sufficiently large variety of reactions on the part of the system."

Thus the ability of a system to maintain a stable state (or the stability of a system in regard to the influences of the external environment) is nothing other than an ability to reduce or destroy each of the possible results of this variety of influences. As is demonstrated in theorems about requisite variety (Ashby, 1959), the variety of outcomes V_o in the state of the system cannot be less than the quotient resulting from dividing the number of disturbances V_d by the number of possible responses of the system V_r:

$$V_o \geqslant \frac{V_d}{V_r}.$$

If, for example, the variety of different disturbances of the system $V_d = 6$ and the variety of responses of the system $V_r = 2$, then the number of possible outcomes V_o under the influence of the external environment will be not less than 3. If these different resulting states are such that the most important properties of the system differ materially from its original properties, the system cannot be regarded as inviolate, or, consequently, as self-regulating. It is a necessary, if not a sufficient condition for a system to be self-regulating that the amount of variety $V_r \geqslant V_d$. The minimum amount of the system's variety V_r must be equal to V_d, in which case only one result can be guaranteed, since then $V_o = 1$. This unique outcome in a self-regulatory system must be the conservation of its original properties.

One of the clearest examples of the self-regulatory properties of mire systems, which is at the same time one of their fundamental characteristics, is the conservation of similarity between the relief of the lower tier of plant cover and that of the water table. This similarity is maintained throughout all stages in the process of peat accumulation and the modification of the relief of mire massifs. The mechanism of this self-regulatory process is as follows. Every significant and sufficiently prolonged lowering of the water table of a mire massif ought, in the normal course of events, to result in a change in its plant associations, an acceleration in the decay of moribund vegetation, and, in the last resort, a cessation of peat formation, i.e. of the growth and development of peat deposits. On the other hand, every significant and sufficiently prolonged raising of the water table ought to lead to a prolonged reduction or cessation of the aeration of the acrotelm and a retardation of the processes of decay. This would at the same time produce a deterioration in the growth of plants and a decrease in the annual increment of the mass of vegetable matter, as a result of which the plant cover would begin to decay and peat accumulation would cease.

Peat accumulation reaches its maximum in a mire when plant associations have achieved maximum development, and this occurs when they are in a stable state. From what has been said above, however, it is plain that this involves the maintenance of a certain minimal amplitude of fluctuation in water levels and the briefest possible deviation from their average position as a result of casual or seasonal changes in the weather. Consequently, this type of plant cover cannot maintain its stability, unless it possesses some physical property which restricts fluctuations of level to within the necessary limits and renders any such deviations as brief as possible.

The property in question is the pattern according to which hydraulic conductivity is distributed in the vegetation of the upper part of the acrotelm. It is an acknowledged fact that in the upper, very thin layer of the acrotelm, which is about 10–20 cm in thickness, hydraulic conductivity changes by 100–1000 times, i.e. by up to 2 or 3 orders of magnitude, and, if we consider the whole thickness of the acrotelm, by up to 4 orders (see section 2.7 and Ivanov, 1953, 1957b). This ensures that rain water and the spring snow-melt are rapidly disposed of without any significant rise in levels. When, on the other hand, precipitation is reduced or absent, this prevents the mire becoming dry, for horizontal seepage stops completely when there is the slightest fall in level.

For the above reason, fluctuations of level are small and relatively constant, despite the large seasonal changes in the quantity of precipitation descending on the acrotelm, a fact that is reflected in the long period during which it remains at the lower limit of the acrotelm and close to the mean long-term level. This self-regulative property of mire plant associations is also a fundamental condition of the existence and development of mires and guarantees their stability as ecosystems.

The maximum difference in mean long-term levels which does not lead to a change in the quantity or floristic composition of mire plant communities is very small (see section 1.5, Table 1). For several varieties of moss cover it is less than 4–5 cm. Changes of that magnitude in mean long-term levels are sufficient to produce important changes in the floristic composition of the moss cover.

Let us now consider another self-regulative property of mire systems. It is known that in the huge expanses of mire in the forest zone of Europe, Siberia, the Far East, Kamchatka and North America, there are vast territories occupied by mire microtopes with a strip-ridge type of plant cover, whose elements (ridges and flarks, ridges and pools) are at right angles to the flowlines and the direction of the maximum slopes of the mire surface (Ivanov, 1957b, 1970), i.e. to the direction of efflux. The ridge–flark and ridge–pool group of microtopes occupies more than 50 % of the area of all mires, and in selected zones in the temperate belt their area reaches 70 % of the whole. The wide extent of such complexes over the earth's surface and within every large mire system entitles one to think that it is probably the most stable form of plant cover under mire conditions, and ensures the best conditions for the adaptation of plants to changes in hydrological conditions.

Let us next consider why the strip-ridge structure of microtopes and the complexes of plant associations associated with it are the most stable form of organization and guarantee a mire system much wider opportunities of regulating and adapting itself to change in the external environment in comparison with a plant cover with a less complex structure. As explained earlier (see Fig. 20, section 2.12 and equation (2.79)), the one component of the water regime and, consequently, of the hydrology of a mire microtope which is almost independent of the composition and structure of its plant cover is its average seepage $\bar{q}_s$. The value of $\bar{q}_s$ along any flowline, according to equation (2.79), is determined by the area over which moisture is accumulated, the degree of divergence or convergence of flow b_s (i.e. by the relief of the massif), and by the external and internal water supply of the given section of the massif, $\bar{q}_0$ and $\bar{p}_s$. In the balance of internal water supply, $\bar{p}_s = \bar{p}_p - \bar{p}_e \pm \bar{p}_{gr}$, the one term dependent upon the composition and structure of the plant cover is evaporation ($\bar{p}_e$), since different plant associations, because they are adapted to habitats that differ in humidity and water table depth, differ also in their evaporative properties.

In consequence, preservation of the stability and continuity of the floristic composition of plant associations despite changes in seepage $\bar{q}_s$ along flow-lines (here regarded as an external factor) requires the plant cover to possess adaptive qualities such as enable it to allow different quantities of water through the acrotelm (as $\bar{q}_s$ increases along the flowline s) *without any change in the water table in each separate plant association*. By this means they pre-serve for themselves one and the same water and heat regime and the same degree of aeration. Therefore, of all structures that a plant cover can assume, the most stable must be the one that will best satisfy at least these two criteria:

(1) Its horizontal seepage $\bar{q}_s$ in the acrotelm must vary over the area of the mire.
(2) The mean depth of the water table $\bar{z}$ must be constant for every plant association within its area.

If the plant cover be uniform and consists of a single plant association or certain closely allied associations, the normal profile of a mire massif along a flowline satisfies these conditions. Along it the hydraulic conductivity of the acrotelm, as expressed by the modulus of seepage

$$M_s = \int_{z_0}^{\bar{z}_q} k_z \, \mathrm{d}z = \frac{\bar{q}_s}{i},$$

remains constant, and consequently the average level of the water table $\bar{z}_q$ also remains constant. Normal profiles can, however, only be formed when a mire massif happens to develop under favourable conditions, i.e. when the site has a suitable surrounding relief and hydrogeological structure (see section 1.6). That is how it comes about that normal profiles are usually met with only in mire mesotopes or limited sections of mire systems. Most mire systems and most large mire macrotopes situated on level or sloping water divides are characterized by flowline profiles with smaller gradients than the normal in such conditions, the stability of plant associations can only be guaranteed. If they have a structure which ensures that hydraulic conductivity of the acrotelm increases along their flowline, although the level of the water table remains constant. Making use of equation (2.80), we shall find the conditions that can ensure constancy of level along the flowline. To do this, we shall replace the modulus of seepage $\bar{M}_s$ by an expression derived from equation (2.56), and, solving the equation for $\bar{z}$, we find that

$$\bar{z} = z_0 - \frac{1}{i\bar{k}_0 b_s}\left[q_0 b_0 + \int_0^s (\bar{p}_p - \bar{p}_e - \bar{p}_{gr})b_s \, \mathrm{d}s\right]$$

$$= z_0 - \frac{\bar{M}_s}{\bar{k}_0} = z_0 - \frac{\bar{q}_s}{i\bar{k}_0}, \tag{4.1}$$

where $i = \mathrm{d}y/\mathrm{d}s$.

Some of the factors that affect a mire system in a semi-stationary state are climatic ($\bar{p}_p$) and some are morphological (b_s, b_0, i, $\bar{p}_{gr}$, $\bar{q}_0$). The last equation shows that, when these are constant, the average depth of the water table in any section of a mire system depends solely upon the mean hydraulic conductivity $\bar{k}_0$ of the acrotelm, the thickness of the acrotelm z_0 and the mean intensity of evaporation $\bar{p}_e$. It is impossible to guarantee the constancy of the average level $\bar{z}$, when seepage $\bar{q}_s$ changes along the flowline and is not proportional to changes of slope i, unless there is a corresponding change of $\bar{k}_0$, i.e. *unless the composition of the plant cover changes*. The constancy of level $\bar{z}$ required by a given plant association can only be reached by an increase in $\bar{k}_0$, but this can easily come about if the structure of the plant cover is an ordered complex of two alternating plant associations with markedly different levels of hydraulic conductivity $\bar{k}_0$. If an association possessing a low conductivity $\bar{k}_{0r}$ covers part, but not the whole, of the surface along the flowline, and alternates with another possessing a higher conductivity $\bar{k}_{0f}$, constancy of the level of the water table $\bar{z}$ can easily be achieved, not by a change in the type of association (i.e. in the floristic composition of the plant cover and the quantitative relations between its constituent species), but by a change in the ratio of the areas covered by one or other of the associations. When seepage $\bar{q}_s$ increases along the flowline without a proportional increase of slope i, associations of low conductivity must shrink in order to survive, and associations of greater conductivity must expand. Then both associations will be stable, and need not change their floristic composition to increase the hydraulic conductivity of the microtope. This is also observed in all types of ridge–flark complexes with a strip-ridge structure, whether the conditions be oligotrophic mesotrophic or eutrophic. There is an analogous process in ridge–pool complexes with this one difference, that the role of plant associations with high hydraulic conductivity is played by open water bodies situated between ridges.

The dependence of the acrotelm's conductivity $\bar{k}_0$ in microtopes of strip-ridge structure upon the conductivity of the plant associations in the ridges and flarks and on the relation between the areas covered by them takes the following form (Ivanov, 1957b, 1970) for ridge–flark complexes:

$$\bar{k}_0 = \bar{k}_{0r} \frac{1 + \dfrac{S_f}{S_r}}{1 - \dfrac{k_{0r}}{k_{0f}} \times \dfrac{S_f}{S_r}}, \tag{4.2}$$

where S stands for area, r for ridge and f for flark. For ridge–pool complexes the equation takes the form:

$$\bar{k}_0 = \bar{k}_{0r}\left(1 + \frac{S_p}{S_r}\right), \tag{4.3}$$

where p stands for pool.

Substituting these values of $\bar{k}_0$ in equation (2.57) for the seepage of a microtope q_z, we find that

$$\bar{q}_z = \frac{\bar{k}_{0r}\left(1 + \dfrac{S_f}{S_r}\right)}{1 - \dfrac{\bar{k}_{0r}}{\bar{k}_{0f}} \cdot \dfrac{S_f}{S_r}} i(z_0 - \bar{z}),\tag{4.4}$$

and

$$\bar{q}_z = \bar{k}_{0r}\left(1 + \frac{S_p}{S_r}\right) i(z_0 - \bar{z}).\tag{4.5}$$

From these expressions it is plain that, even when $\bar{q}_z$ changes along the flow-line and the level of z has to remain constant, the hydraulic conductivity of the ridges ($\bar{k}_{0r}$) and flarks ($\bar{k}_{0f}$) may remain unchanged (i.e. the components of the associations need not change, if the ratio of the areas S_f/S_r alters in the appropriate manner. The same is true of ridge–pool complexes, if the ratio between the areas of pools and ridges S_p/S_r changes similarly. At the same time, if we concede that the whole area of a mire massif, or any part of it, has a plant cover with a uniform structure and corresponding associations with known values of hydraulic conductivity $\bar{k}_0$, then a change of seepage without a change of level $\bar{z}$ (see equation (2.57)) must be accompanied by a corresponding change of $\bar{k}_0$ along the flowline, i.e. by continuous change in the floristic composition of the plant cover and of corresponding types of plant association.

The stability of the plant cover and of the associations of which it is composed is increased still further in strip-ridge structures, because here the growth of seepage $\bar{q}_s$ along the flowlines proceeds more slowly than when the structure of the plant cover is simple and uniform. As was also shown by Romanov (1961), evaporation from *Sphagnum–Eriophorum* and *Sphagnum–Scheuchzeria* flarks is greater than from pine–*Sphagnum*, *Sphagnum*–shrub and lichen–*Sphagnum* formations (groups of associations). This has been confirmed by subsequent researches into evaporation from ridges and flarks in the mires of the West Siberian plain by expeditions of the State Hydrological Institute (Bavina and Romanov, 1969). Comparison of evaporation from ridges with evaporation from flarks in the ridge–flark microtopes of the mire systems of the river Konda showed that over a whole season daily evaporation from flarks exceeds evaporation from ridges by 67%. Therefore increase in the area of flarks and decrease in the area of ridges, as well as increase in the area of pools in ridge–pool complexes, increases evaporation $\bar{p}_e$, and therefore decreases the internal water supply of the microtope

$\bar{p}_s$. According to equation (4.1), this decreases the modulus of seepage $\overline{M}_s$ along the flowline, and so helps to keep the level $\bar{z}$ constant along the flowline. Accordingly, changes in the ratios of coverage S_f/S_r or S_p/S_r ensure invariance of the level $\bar{z}$, both by increasing the hydraulic conductivity of the acrotelm and by decreasing the internal meteoric water supply.

From this it follows that ridge–flark and ridge–pool microtopes with a strip-ridge microrelief are the stablest forms for plant communities, i.e. they are a peculiar symbiosis ensuring the self-regulation of the mire system and the preservation of the floristic composition of every plant association through a wide range of changes in seepage and slope on the surface of a mire. In such cases the maintenance of favourable conditions for each plant association belonging to the ridge–flark complex is attained by an ordered change in the density of two plant associations that differ markedly in their floristic composition and physical properties. Mire systems consisting of microtopes with ridge–flark and ridge–pool complexes arranged in strips therefore possess the greatest range of possible adaptations to changes in external conditions, and, as a consequence, the greatest stability in relation to influences exercised upon their water regime by natural or artificial causes.

We have now considered the separate properties to be found in a self-regulating mire system, but practical methods of scientifically calculating the changes that may occur in mirelands, and the effects they will produce in their surroundings, must be based on quantitative estimates of the stability of mire systems and the limits of their capacity to adapt themselves to changes in external conditions. To make these calculations we must first of all establish the most general criteria of stability, both for mire systems as a whole, and for their separate components.

4.4 Criteria for the Stability of the Separate Components of Mire Systems

A general criterion for the stability of any part of a mire system may be obtained from the fundamental equation of hydromorphological relations (2.80), if we bear in mind that these relations make up the inner cycle of transformations portrayed in the general diagram of interactions between mire systems and their environment (see section 2.12 and Fig. 20). The main lines of connection making up this inner cycle in the diagram are 6–7, 11, 13, 15, 23 and 25. If there are no variations in the external inputs represented by 1–5 and 16, this cycle is closed. We can then obtain solutions that describe the stability of the components of the mire systems, taking as limiting conditions certain constant values for external inputs into the system.

Let us now substitute values derived from equations (2.54), (2.46), (2.63) and (2.82) for the terms of equation (2.80), and suppose that $\bar{p}_e = \bar{\alpha} R_b$, where

R_b is the radiation balance and $\bar{\alpha}$ the coefficient of evaporation (Romanov, 1962). Then, for any given part of a mire system whose position in space is determined by the value of the coordinate s, we obtain the equation in its explicit form:

$$\frac{dy}{ds} = \frac{(\bar{q}_{gr} + \bar{q}_{s,f})b_0 + \int_0^s (\bar{p}_p + \bar{p}_{gr} - \bar{\alpha}R_b)b_s\,ds}{b_s(z_0 - \bar{z}_q)\bar{k}_0}$$

$$= \frac{(\bar{q}_{gr} + \bar{q}_{s,f})b_0 + \int_0^s (\bar{p}_p + \bar{p}_{gr} - \bar{\alpha}R_b)b_s\,ds}{b_s \int_{z_0}^{\bar{z}_q} k_z\,dz}, \qquad (4.6)$$

where the terms not already introduced are explained below.

The distribution of the coefficient of filtration k_z through the depth z_0 of the acrotelm is connected with its other physical properties by the "partial seepage discharges" (Romanov, 1961). These other properties are the total and active porosity, the vertical distribution of porosity in each layer and the capillary characteristics. It follows that the modulus of seepage $\overline{M}_s$ is the fundamental attribute of the peat-producing layer incorporating, as it does, the average depth of the water table $\bar{z}_q$, which is an indication of the aeration of the rooting horizon.

Comparing the relationships that are dealt with by equation (4.6) with the system of direct and inverse relations in the diagram of interaction (see Fig. 20), we immediately establish the following important propositions. The external factors contributing to the origin and development of mires are: the input of solar energy represented by the term R_b in the formula for $\bar{p}_e$, atmospheric precipitation $\bar{p}_p$, soil-derived water supply represented by the terms $\bar{q}_{nn}$ and $\bar{p}_{gr}$, and surface influx represented by $\bar{q}_{s,f}$. The only external factors whose action produces important reactions are the soil-derived water supply and the surface influx (see 17–20 in Fig. 20), which may be altered by changes in the relief of the mire and the accumulation of peat. However, when we are considering only quasi-stationary conditions, i.e. short periods of time, this reaction is irrelevant, as are also Nos. 12, 21, 22, 24–26, since in these periods peat accumulation and change of relief can be ignored. For that reason, relief also counts as an external factor in quasi-stationary conditions, and is represented in equation (4.6) by the terms dy/ds and b_s (which express respectively the gradient and the form of flow in plan).

As has been pointed out earlier, in quasi-stationary conditions there is a closed cycle of interaction between evaporation, runoff, seepage, water levels, the composition and structure of the plant cover, the physical properties of the acrotelm (or peat-making layer), and the temperature regime of the acrotelm. This cycle in represented in Fig. 20 by Nos. 6–11, 13–15, 23 and 25, which are subject to no restrictions save those imposed by the external environment and the relief of the mire. In the equation of relationship (4.6), this closed cycle of interaction is represented by the expressions for the modulus of seepage $\bar{M}_s$:

$$(z_0 - \bar{z}_q)\bar{k}_0 \quad \text{or} \quad \int_{z_0}^{\bar{z}_q} k_z \, dz,$$

and $\bar{\alpha}R_b$, both of which vary along the flowline s, and are connected at every point on it both with each other and with the external environment by a relation that follows from equation (4.6):

$$(z_0 - \bar{z}_q)\bar{k}_0 + \frac{\int_0^s \bar{\alpha}R_b b_s \, ds}{b_s(dy/ds)} = \int_{z_0}^{\bar{z}_q} k_z \, dz + \frac{\int_0^s \bar{\alpha}R_b b_s \, ds}{b_s(dy/ds)} =$$

$$= \left[(\bar{q}_{gr} + \bar{q}_{sf})b_0 + \bar{p}_p \int_0^s b_s \, ds + \int_0^s \bar{p}_{gr} b_s \, ds \right] \frac{1}{b_s(dy/ds)}. \quad (4.7)$$

The terms on the upper line of equation (4.7), z_0, $\bar{k}_0$, k_z, $\bar{z}_q$, $\bar{\alpha}$, and others dependent on them, represent all possible changes in the physical properties of a mire's acrotelm, and are all connected with changes in the structure and floristic composition of its plant cover; but it is not difficult to see that the range of these changes is restricted by their need to satisfy this same equation, whose right-hand side consists exclusively of quantities that relate, not to the plant cover of the mire, but to the external factors that affect it.

From this it can be concluded that in any given section of a mire system, whose position in the system is fixed by the coordinate s, the only stable structures to be found in the plant cover are those whose physical basis is guaranteed by satisfying the condition

$$(z_0 - \bar{z}_q)\bar{k}_0 + \frac{\int_0^s \bar{\alpha}R_b b_s \, ds}{b_s(dy/ds)} = B = \text{const.} \quad (4.8)$$

Here B is an ascertainable function of the climate and surface relief of the mire. It is equivalent to the right-hand side (i.e. the bottom line) of equation (4.7), and has a constant value for any given value of s.

All other structures of plant cover for the given section of the mire system would be unstable, and must, in a comparatively short time, be replaced by another stabler structure which satisfies the condition B. It is important to note that for every value of B there may be not one, but several stable plant communities. We shall however confine our attention to those stable plant communities for which $\alpha R_b = \text{const.} = C$. Then all those communities and the mire microtopes formed by them will be stable, provided the relations between k_0, z_0 and $\bar{z}_q$ satisfy the condition

$$(z_0 - \bar{z}_q)k_0 = B - CA, \tag{4.9}$$

$$\text{where } A = \frac{\int_0^s b_s \, ds}{(b_s(dy/ds))_{s=s_0}} = \text{const.}$$

In other words, when there is a change in the external conditions of any section of a mire system, the composition and structure of its plant cover may be transformed in different ways, i.e. the process of transformation in the given case may prove indeterminate. Hence the probability of obtaining a particular plant community with a stable structure satisfying condition (4.9) cannot be determined without introducing supplementary criteria of stability.

In this way we reach a very important general conclusion. The process of peat accumulation and the stable existence and development of mire systems can only take place when changes of climate, the relief of the surface and external, anthropogenic influences are such as can still be compensated for by appropriate changes in the physical properties and structure of the active (peat-producing) layer, which will preserve the necessary ecological conditions for the existence of mire vegetation and peat accumulation. On the block diagram in Fig. 20, this is expressed by the functional relations 6–11, 14 and 15. These control dynamic equilibrium over short periods of time and represent an inner cycle of transformation. Their effects can be calculated, provided the external inputs are radiation and precipitation (Nos. 1 and 2), which are not affected by adaptations or transformations of the system, and the only other inputs are groundwater and relief (Nos. 3–5 and 16), which cannot be affected by the reaction of the system upon them in the relatively short periods covered by the calculations.

The fact that a mire system is in an unstable state need not lead to its destruction and disappearance as a natural formation. The usual course of development of mire meso- and microtopes, which was considered above (see section 1.6), may be regarded as a succession of metastable and unstable states. In this process, some microtopes are replaced by others, or their structure and position in the system changes, leading to a change in the structure of the system as a whole. The question whether the natural course of development of mires is in general reversible or irreversible is a very complex one, whose full treatment would take one far beyond the limits of the present work. There are, however, some aspects of it which are worthy of notice because of the new light that they throw upon the criteria of stability.

If we consider only the role that mires play in the march of physico-geographic processes on the earth's surface and in the globe as a whole, the development of mire systems seems to be an irreversible one. The direction in which their development moves and the transformations they undergo must follow the same course as the world's physico-geographic development. If, however, we consider separate parts of mire systems, such as certain groups of microtopes or certain types of mesotopes that are contained in such a system, the position is different. There it is possible to find real physical situations in the development of a system where, alongside the irreversible development of the whole system, there are microtopes forming part of the system whose changes of state are reversible, In other words, after a series of changes in the plant communities of a certain part of the system, the original plant community and the appropriate hydrothermal regime will be restored. In such cases, the process of development is itself an unbroken succession of unstable states. Unstable states, once they have appeared, are usually replaced by relatively stable ones, in which the plant cover hardly changes, or changes so slowly that the type of mire microtope and its component associations remains unchanged for a long period of time. Many examples can be cited where peat accumulation in a certain part of a system was not accompanied for a long period by any change in the floristic composition and structure of the plant cover. Suppose that it is the case that a mire mesotope, which belongs to the system, does not increase its area in plan and that the intensity of peat accumulation is practically uniform throughout it, so that the surface of the mire is raised equally everywhere without any change in its profile. Then, in these conditions, all the physical parameters which determine the intensity and conditions of water discharge in the acrotelm (gradient, internal water supply and the distribution of seepage and water table levels throughout the mesotope) will remain unchanged.

Letting this example suffice, we shall now give further consideration to the criteria of stability. As follows from what we have already said, criteria of stability must be thought of as a conjunction of conditions, expressible in quantitative terms, such as would enable us to answer two fundamental questions about the development of a system:

(1) Is the system, or any part of it, in an unstable state at the time in question, and must it therefore change its structure?
(2) How far can the chief physical parameters of the system change without destroying its basic functions and causing it to disintegrate, i.e. without putting an end to its existence as a natural formation?

Let us answer these questions so far as they apply to mire systems. The chief function of mire systems is the accumulation of peat and the annual renewal of the plant cover. The destruction of this function, whatever its cause, leads to its degradation and the cessation of the mire as a natural formation. But, in this case, the destruction of this function is the result of failure to meet another fundamental condition, upon which the existence of mire plant communities, and therefore of peat accumulation, depends. That condition is the maintenance of the water table (by the mire's self-regulative system) near the surface of the mire and within the permissible limits of long-term fluctuations. The violation of this condition, whether in the direction of constantly higher or constantly lower levels in comparison with the permissible limits, leads to the degradation and destruction of the plant communities of the mire. These are then replaced by other plant communities of a sort that is not typical of mires, and there is a change in the biophysical processes which had previously ensured the incomplete disintegration and conservation of the organic material accumulated from the moribund mass of plants. The destruction of a mire may therefore take place either by the desiccation or by the supersaturation of its peat deposit. Indeed these two forms of destruction are observed under natural conditions and also when mirelands are transformed during the development of natural resources.

Full definition of the criteria of stability entails the formulation of conditions that enable one to decide whether a system, or any of its separate parts, is at a given period in a stable or unstable state. These conditions can also be deduced from propositions of the highest generality concerning the reaction of plant cover to changes in ecological conditions, which, in the case of mire systems, are connected with their water supply. They can be reduced to the following:

(1) In every section of a mire massif delimited in plan by a boundary, the quantity of moisture flowing into and out of it must be such as is consistent with a regime of levels and rooting layer irrigation which corresponds to the optimal, stable state of the given plant community. The violation of this regime, whether by raising levels and increasing moisture, or by lowering levels and decreasing moisture, beyond the permissible ecological limits (Ivanov, 1970), involves either a complete change of plant associations, or a change in their structure or complexity, i.e. their distribution in space (in ridge–flark and ridge–pool complexes).

(2) Where water bodies (lakes) are enclosed within mires, the hydraulic conductivity of the acrotelm of the surrounding microtopes must correspond to the amount of water exchange that takes place between the lakes and the microtopes as a result of differences in their water budgets.

(3) Where there are no differences between the water budgets of endotelmic water bodies and the microtopes contiguous to them, the structure of the whole lake–mire system becomes unstable. This is

because ecological conditions do not permit any variation in areas occupied by the plant cover and open water surface in the lake–mire system.

(4) Plant communities in mires are only viable if their structure and floristic composition is such as to ensure that the plant cover has sufficient mechanical strength to resist external mechanical influences, such as the surface current of water, differences of water pressure at different points, seepage, water movements in open expanses of water and the fluidity of masses of peat that have been dispersed by swamping.

(5) The length of periods of deviation from the average values of the water regime must not be greater than the maximum length of time that the plants can endure without the appearance of irreversible changes in the composition of the plant cover.

The propositions that we have adduced to connect the existence and stability of the plant cover of mires with conditions in the external environment must obviously be particularized and expressed in quantitative form, before they can be used for calculation and prediction. It should, however, be noted that, although they may be insufficient to determine the behaviour of the system completely, they are absolutely necessary, i.e. their non-fulfilment must lead to changes in the structure of the mire.

It follows from what we have said that alterations in ecological conditions are chiefly due to change in the water balance of some section of a mire microtope, which in turn evokes a further chain of more or less complex transformations in the physical processes and structure of the system. In certain conditions, these transformations can lead to the disintegration of the whole system, but unstable states may also arise which, though they change its structure, may not lead to violation of its fundamental functions or complete destruction of the system.

These general propositions are illustrated by the processes that transform the structure of lake–mire systems as described by Ivanov (1969). To this question we shall return later for a brief review of these processes, but now we shall turn our attention to the relations which express in quantitative form the criteria of stability of certain important components of mire systems—endotelmic lakes.

In a uniform microtope surrounding a lake, the criteria of stability of the lake require fulfilment of the equality (3.48′):

$$\omega = (l_2 - l_1)\frac{\bar{q}}{\bar{p}}. \tag{3.48′}$$

When the lake is situated among different types of microtope, it must, for stability, satisfy the following equation:

$$\omega = \frac{\sum\limits_{1}^{n} \bar{q}_i l_i - \sum\limits_{1}^{m} \bar{q}_j l_j}{\bar{p}}, \tag{4.10}$$

or, written in another form,

$$\omega = \frac{\Delta(\bar{q}l)}{\bar{p}}. \tag{4.11}$$

From this it follows that an insulated, endotelmic lake is in a stable state if its area is equal to the ratio between the net internal and external water supply, the net internal water supply being the difference between the horizontal efflux from the lake and the influx which it receives through the acrotelm of contiguous microtopes. Non-fulfilment of this equality must lead to a change in the mean level of the water table in the contiguous microtopes. Lowering of the level results in the lake being overgrown from the banks and reduced in area. Raising of it brings about a change in plant communities and, when they are destroyed by inundation, an extension of the area of the lake.

4.5 The Destruction of Mire Systems

The destruction of mire systems comes about through one or other of two fundamental causes: a lowering of the water table which exceeds the ecological tolerance of the vegetation, or an inundation of the system which stops the normal growth and development of the chief microtopes. These phenomena, whose general features are well known and are described in telmatological literature, need in this case more detailed treatment. The process of degradation and disintegration is itself a series of complex and varied phenomena—a succession of different states of the system, which must each be taken account of to make correct quantitative calculations and predictions.

Intensive drainage and the lowering of the average water table below the peat deposit (i.e. below its interface with the subjacent soil) leads to the disintegration of mire systems through the desiccation of their peat. In these conditions, the capillary supply of moisture to the surface and the rooting layer either becomes too small to compensate for evaporation or stops completely. As a result, the main thickness of the peat becomes extremely dehydrated, its temperature rises and biological processes leading to the decomposition of organic material are activated. Decomposition reinforced by the pressure of the peat's own weight (which, after the lowering of the water table, is no longer suspended in water) and by capillary tension, also resulting from the lowering of the water table, leads to shrinkage of the whole peat deposit, a gradual increase in its mineral content and the disappearance of its organic components. When the natural plant cover is removed (or crops are harvested from agricultural fields of reclaimed peat), the desiccated peat is subject to wind erosion, which also accelerates its destruction and disappearance. The rapidity and extent of the shrinkage of peat deposits, especially in the period immediately after the lowering of the water table, depends largely upon their initial degree of saturation. Since supersaturation of peat deposits in their natural state is a characteristic of raised-mire peats, and therefore of oligotrophic mire systems, the most intensive shrinkage is found in raised deposits. That of fen deposits is less intense.

Existing literature shows that, according to observations in different countries and climates, the average rate of collapse of a peat deposit after drying over a period of 40–50 years varies widely—from 1–2 to 8 cm/year. In some cases, rates of 20–40 cm/year have been recorded in the first years after draining, when the water table was not lowered significantly (by not more than 80 cm). According to the data of Maslov (1970), in the Kal'skoye mire massif, situated on a raised terrace of the river Oka, where the peat deposit is from 1·5–2 m in thickness and is composed of wood-sedge peat in an intermediate state of decomposition, the rate at which the mire's surface fell, after it had been drained and its water table lowered to a depth of 140 cm, was 8·8 cm/year. The process of shrinkage slowed down in the following years. Research shows that if the average water table in a peat deposit is stabilized at some new depth after draining, then the speed of shrinkage, which is at its greatest in the first years after lowering, gradually slows down, and the thickness of the peat deposit tends toward some new limit.

If the lowered level of the water table remains within the deposit and the mire is not used as agricultural land or in some other way, the shrinkage and reduction in thickness of the peat deposit must eventually stop, when mechanical and biochemical equilibrium has been reached at the new level of the water table. If, however, a mire is exploited and its natural covering removed, the reduction in the thickness of the peat deposit will continue through the ceaseless processes of decomposition and the application of agricultural techniques. In the absence of renewal through the deposition of organic material, this process will continue until all the peat deposit has been transformed and there is no longer any organic soil composed of peat. In the first case, the process will prove reversible, if, when the water table is lowered, only part of the thickness of the peat is continuously aerated and its lower layers are located below the level of the water table. If a natural plant cover is preserved and there is an appropriate change in its composition and structure, peat accumulation may be gradually resumed at the new level and the mire system will survive.

In the second case, the process is irreversible, and in one way or another leads to the formation of a new type of geotope in place of the mire system. In those cases where the water table is lowered so far that the whole of the peat deposit is aerated, and where the capillary zone (when in equilibrium) is situated lower than the peat, it is expected that the thickness of the peat will decrease and that its disintegration will proceed at maximum speed, leading eventually to the complete disappearance of the organic stratum and a radical transformation of the geotope.

Other conditions being the same, the speed of the process depends absolutely on the climate. Maslov (1970) has processed and generalized the results of observations made in the USSR, the USA, Norway and some other countries. He found that the rate of shrinkage of a peat deposit ϵ_p (m/year) depends upon its initial thickness h_p (m), the average depth of the water table H (m), the time elapsed since the lowering of the water table T (years), and a climatic parameter α_p (°C/mm × 100). This function has the form

$$\epsilon_p = 0{\cdot}08H \frac{\alpha_p^{1{\cdot}4}\sqrt{h_p}}{e^{\beta T}}, \tag{4.12}$$

where the climatic parameter α_p is the ratio of the mean annual temperature of the atmosphere $\bar{t}$ °C to the annual precipitation $\bar{p}_p$ (mm) multiplied by 100:

$$\alpha_p = \frac{100\bar{t}}{\bar{p}_p},$$

and the coefficient β depends upon α_p and T:

$$\beta = 0{\cdot}1 + 0{\cdot}02\alpha_p - 0{\cdot}0025T.$$

The relationship (4.12) was obtained by a multiple correlation of the observational data, and for that reason the quantities entering into it must be substituted only within the prescribed limits. In Fig. 31, there is a graph of the dependence of the mean rate of shrinkage of a peat deposit $\bar{\epsilon}_p$ for periods of 40–65 years after draining upon the climatic parameter $\bar{p}_p/\bar{t}$, expressed in the form of a relation of the annual precipitation to the mean annual temperature of the atmosphere. These data are taken from Maslov (1970). As is clear from the relationship, the mean rate of shrinkage over long periods increases markedly with a decrease in the humidity of the climate, and changes relatively little in a wet climate.

The empirical relationship (4.12) is based on data concerning the peat deposits of fens. Further research is needed to decide how far this relationship applies to the rate of shrinkage of raised-mire deposits, particularly when their initial saturation is greater than normal. One important fact about this relationship is, however, that the rate of shrinkage, other things

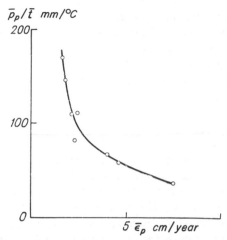

Fig. 31. Dependence of the mean rate of shrinkage of peat $\bar{\epsilon}_p$ upon the climatic parameter $\bar{p}_p/\bar{t}$ over periods of 40–65 years after drainage.

being equal, is directly proportional to the mean depth of the water table H after it has been lowered. Therefore, if the relief of the water table after lowering is not like the original relief of the massif, then, even if the peat deposit be homogeneous, its shrinkage at different points in the massif must be different. If again the relief of the lowered water table is horizontal, the original relief of the massif will be levelled off, since the amount of shrinkage in a given time will be proportional at each point to the difference between the level of the original surface of the mire and the horizontal relief of the lowered water table.

The disintegration and destruction of mire systems through desiccation of the peat deposit is rarely observed under natural conditions, and occurs chiefly in massifs of modest dimensions in the zone of deficient moisture. In the zone of excess moisture, the disintegration of mire systems through desiccation of the peat deposit rarely occurs. Even progressive denudation and the increased drainage of sections of mire resulting from tectonic movements of the earth's crust and changes in the drainage capacity of a river network (through the deepening of river channels) do not change the position of mire boundaries, nor decrease the area of mirelands (see for example Orlov, 1968). Such changes only lead to structural changes in mire systems and reduction in the rate of peat accumulation. The gradual swamping of areas in the zone of excess moisture over immense periods of time is, under unchanged climatic conditions, an irreversible process.

For this reason, the degradation and destruction of mire systems chiefly occurs as a result of artificial drainage. Much less study has been devoted to mire systems whose instability and disintegration are due to an excess of moisture, although, from the point of view of conserving natural resources, this process is of no less practical and scientific interest. If one wishes to explain the complex structures of lake–mire systems, which are very widely distributed, for example, in the north of the West Siberian lowlands (excluding the zone of permafrost), it is by no means enough to limit oneself to consideration of some processes of self-regulation based upon the adaptations of the plant cover to slow changes in the water regime, such as are described, in particular, by equation (4.8). The instability of these systems (Ivanov, 1969), which is due to a disturbance of the relation between the items in their water budget, both in individual endotelmic lakes and in the systems as a whole, is further complicated by many phenomena which arise as a result of the erosion of mire microtopes, whose development was made possible by the existence of a copious water supply. In some cases, erosion, by increasing internal drainage, may tend to increase the stability of lake–mire systems with an excessive water supply. In other cases, it may hasten their disintegration. In short, the natural development of such systems may follow different courses. These phenomena we shall consider in the following section.

4.6 The Role of Erosion in the Formation and Stabilization of of Lake–Mire Systems

Erosion in mires is a natural process of self-drainage. It is usually observed in mire macrotopes, and is a factor that disturbs the stability of lake–mire systems. That stability results from conformity with water balance criteria and the reaction of the plant cover to gradual changes in the water balance, which may be due to climatic changes, and sometimes to tectonic processes.

Endotelmic water bodies formed through an uneven accumulation of peat and a general raising of the surface of peat deposits dispose of their water (the excess which cannot be evaporated from the lake) through the acrotelm of the surrounding microtopes. When the area of a lake exceeds the critical value (see equation (3.39)), the influx of an excess of water and the raising of the water levels in the microtopes give rise to an uneven degradation of the plant cover and a network of internal streams, which take this water beyond the boundaries of the mire system. In these conditions, the streams within the mire join some of the lakes to each other (not all, but usually only the largest ones), forming a single lake–river system within the mire, along which a channelled stream runs out of the mire. The lake–mire systems of Western Siberia have more or less dense networks of endotelmic streams, which unite the larger lakes. They carry water away from the mires and lakes and convey it beyond the boundaries of the massif. Analogous mire macrotopes, but on a smaller scale, can also be observed in the large mire systems of European Russia.

When an endotelmic stream crosses the boundary of a mire (where the depth of the peat deposit becomes zero), a channelled stream emerges from the peat bed and enters a channel composed of mineral strata. At this point, there is a sudden change in the resistance of the stream bed to the erosive action of the current. Because of their peculiarities of structure (which is fibrous), peat soils in an intermediate or early stage of decomposition, even when fully saturated, are highly resistant to erosion in comparison with saturated mineral soils (especially fine-grained ones). This property of peat is responsible for the fact that in the channels of streams and brooks emerging from mires there is a sharp drop in the level of the bottom at the boundary between the mire and the mineral strata. The erosion and removal of the particles of mineral soil which make up the bed of the stream at the edge of the peat deposit is not compensated by a corresponding transport of organic particles from the peaty channel in the mire, from which the water emerges practically translucent and without any admixture of hard mechanical particles. Therefore, at the boundary of the mire and the mineral strata, sharp steps are formed in the streams that flow out of the mire. These steps often take the form of small waterfalls with a drop of 0·5–2·0 m.

The formation of such waterfalls at the edge of a mire (or peat deposit) deepens the bed of the stream and washes away some of the peat deposit. When the height of the stream is such that the falling stream has sufficient kinetic energy to carry the eroded material downstream, the eroded layer of peat collapses and the vertical peat wall of the waterfall retreats a certain distance upstream. There the same process is repeated, so that the waterfall cannot be stabilized and is continually displaced upstream. The speed of this displacement, according to the existing fragmentary data, sometimes amounts to 10–15 m/year. This displacement of a voluminous waterfall upstream in a peat channel inevitably leads after a period to the lowering of the level of water in the lake from which the stream flows, as soon as the waterfall in the channel reaches the lake. The lowering of the level of the lake is plainly a relatively short-lived occurrence, for the moment the waterfall reaches the edge of the lake, the transmissive capacity of the channel abruptly changes and the discharge of water increases, with the result that the water balance and the established regime of the lake are quickly destroyed.

The present level of water in endotelmic lakes that have gone through this process of lowering usually lies at 2–2·5 m below the level of the acrotelm of the surrounding microtopes. In such cases, it is easy to see the precipitous vertical walls of peat, which are laid bare by the lowering of the water level, as well as the abrupt downward slope of the mire towards the lake in the narrow marginal strip formed through the subsidence of the peat deposit as a result of the lowering of the water table in it. The sudden lowering of the lake gives rise to many new phenomena, which are due to the violation, not only of the lake's own water balance, but of the mechanical equilibrium of the lake–mire system. The first of these is a big gap between the level of water in the lake and that in the mire microtopes that are situated on its banks.

Another consequence of the lowering of the level of water in the lake is that waves begin to erode the banks of the lake. It is known that in endotelmic lakes that have not been lowered the level of water fluctuates within the limits of the acrotelm of the adjacent microtopes, and is always at the same height as the water table in its banks and in the adjacent microtopes. In similar fashion, the surface of the moss and grass vegetation on the banks of the lake rises to the same height above the mean level of the lake as it rises above the level of the water table in the mire. In these conditions, the mechanical action of waves on the banks is completely exhausted on the porous medium of the living and dead, but not decomposed, plant cover, which is thick enough to be highly resistant to the erosive action of waves. For that reason, the phenomena of erosion are not observed on the banks of mire-enclosed lakes that have not been lowered, and are in fact completely absent.

The lowering of a lake and the formation of vertical cliffs in banks composed of peat abruptly changes the action of waves upon the banks. The exhaustion of the waves in the plant layer of the acrotelm no longer occurs. The energy of the advancing waves erodes and destroys the vertical wall of peat, which slips down along with its plant cover into the lake. Through the lowering of the lake, the formation of a hydrostatic gap between the level of the lake and the water table of the adjacent mire microtopes and the erosion of the banks by waves, the banks of the lake begin to collapse and the area of the lake to increase. The last process manifests itself in very peculiar forms.

When the bank that divides the edge of a lake from a flark is eroded, a narrow bridge of peat is formed. Through horizontal pressure resulting from the big difference between the level of water in the lake and that in the flark, this bridge is broken down at its narrowest and weakest point. The severed ridge is then pushed forward into the lake by the pressure of the water behind it, sometimes bringing with it the whole thickness of the peat deposit, and the water in the flark then sinks to the level of the lake. The lowering of the water in a flark that has been merged into a lake gives rise to a new difference of level between this flark and the next one to it. The ridge that divides them is then subjected to the action of an increased horizontal pressure on one side and to wave erosion (abrasion) by the lake on the other. As a result, the process of destruction and lowering of water level is repeated in this next flark. The lowering of the lake therefore sets in motion a chain reaction of a special kind, which results in the successive destruction of ridges, the lowering of the level of water in flarks and an extension of the area of the lake. The process described is typical of lowered lakes situated in ridge–flark and ridge–pool microtopes. Judging by many indirect indications, it proceeds quite rapidly. In one season, several rows of flarks may be united to a lake and the shore may recede 10–30 m. But the destruction of banks and the extension of the surface of lowered endotelmic lakes take place in this way only in sections of the bank where the ridges and flarks are arranged in rows parallel to the line of the bank, or make only a small angle with it. In sections of the bank where they are perpendicular to the bank, or make a large angle with it (Fig. 32, direction *B*), the mechanism of destruction is different and the intensity of erosion much less.

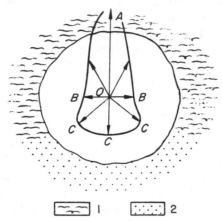

Fig. 32. The influence of differing types of adjoining microtope upon the direction in which the destruction of the banks of a lake is more or less intense. 1—ridge–flark microtopes with an indication of their orientation. 2—microtopes of the pine–*Sphagnum*–shrub group. *OA*, *OB*, *OC*—vectors of speed of destruction of banks.

When the flarks and ridges are perpendicular to the line of the bank, the lowering of the lake does not give rise to abrupt differences of level, nor to a horizontal pressure upon the ridge in the direction of the lake. The lowering of the lake in these parts of the shore line causes a free outflow from all the adjacent flarks that are open to the lake, a shrinkage through draining of the peat they contain, and the transformation of the system of flarks into a natural system of parallel ditches, which drain the ridges that lie between them. In this process, the surface of the flarks, and, to a lesser extent, the surface of the ridges, acquires a steep slope in the direction of the lake, owing to the progressive shrinkage of the peat in that vicinity. This gives rise to an intensive filtrational and surface flow of water along the flarks into the lake. At the lowest parts of the surface of the *Sphagnum–Scheuchzeria* and *Sphagnum–Eriophorum* microtopes which cover the flarks, streamlets arise and flow along the axis of the flarks. This phenomenon, like the previous one, is typical. In this case, however, destruction of the bank of the lake in the direction *B* (see Fig. 32) proceeds much more slowly. The removal of water through the lowering of the water table in ridge–flark microtopes does not in this case lead to abrupt differences of level between the flarks and the lake, but dries and solidifies the peat below both the ridges and the flarks at a considerable distance from the lake (hundreds of metres), raising the general resistance of the peat deposit to erosion and enhancing the stability of the bank. This is due in great measure to the fact that the long axis of the ridges is perpendicular to the bank, and that the gradual lowering of their surface to the level of the lake brings the living plant cover nearer to the edge of the water. In these parts of the shore line, this also prevents the formation of vertical faces of peat, which are of all shore lines the most susceptible to wave erosion.

The third process leading to the destruction of the banks of lowered lakes occurs when the shore line is occupied by microtopes of the pine–shrub or *Sphagnum*–shrub–pine group. A drop in the level of the lake in that case denudes the vertical face of the peat deposit, whose upper layers, in microtopes of this type, are protected by the roots of trees and shrubs. Whenever the level of the lake falls below the living plant cover and the acrotelm of the mire, the peat wall begins to be eroded by waves. The first parts to be washed away are the lower layers of peat, which are nearer the water's edge and therefore more susceptible to erosion. The upper horizons, which possess greater cohesion and are more resistant to erosion, form cornices which project above the water and then collapse slowly into the lake along with the living trees that grow in them. Here the surface of the peat deposit also sinks suddenly, and the surface of the mire on the shore line begins to tilt sharply towards the water's edge, following the sloping outline of the water table. This is accompanied by the formation of vertical cracks in the peat, which run parallel to the bank, and by breaks in the plant cover indicating slippage of the bank into the lake. The intensity of erosion in the banks of lakes with microtopes of the *Sphagnum*–pine–shrub group and others of close affinity to them is confirmed by many other phenomena described elsewhere (Ivanov, 1969).

The formation and lowering of endotelmic lakes are phenomena most often met with in mire systems that have reached the oligotrophic phase of development. For this reason, the chief groups of microtope on the banks of such lakes are complex moss (ridge–flark and ridge–pool) types and *Sphagnum*–pine–shrub–*Eriophorum* types with different modifications in the quantitative relations between the main species of plants. That is why the chief characteristic types of erosion affecting the banks of endotelmic lakes are in fact observed in these two groups of mire microtopes. Endotelmic lakes in the zone of unstable moisture, being situated among microtopes with eutrophic vegetation, are not as a rule exposed to erosion, since such lakes derive their water supply from mires and usually have a negative balance in their internal water supply. This applies still more to endotelmic lakes in the zone of deficient moisture, whose existence is necessarily connected with the presence of an external catchment area.

Let us now consider the case of a lake whose area has been increased after the reduction of its volume and the lowering of its average level. If the lake is situated in microtopes of the ridge–pool and *Sphagnum*–pine–shrub types (see Fig. 32), then, as we saw, the most intensive destruction of its banks must take place in the direction *OA*, in which ridges and lake-like flarks are parallel to the line of the shore. The erosion of the banks must be least intensive in the direction *OB*, in which the axis of the elements of the ridge–pool complex is perpendicular to the line of the shore. Lastly, in the direction *OC*, where microtopes of the *Sphagnum*–pine–shrub group adjoin the shore, the speed of destruction will be less than in the direction *OA*, but more than in the direction *OB*. The rate of extension of the area of the lake is then different in different directions, depending both on the orientation of the elements of its complex microtopes to the line of the shore, and on the type of microtope itself. To sum the matter up, any lake having at any time the shape and size depicted in Fig. 32 will change its shape at the same time as it increases its area.

As a result, every lowered lake in a ridge–pool complex, which has at first the form of a narrow strip perpendicular to the flowlines, will always have a tendency, through uneven shore erosion, to assume an oval, then a round, and finally an elongated oval shape with its long axis along the flowline of the mire's principal direction of seepage. Extensive materials obtained by aerial survey of lake–mire complexes containing ridge–pool or ridge–flark microtopes show that most lakes of considerable dimensions (of tens or hundreds of hectares) have a shape elongated along the flowline of the main filtrational movement of the mire waters, and are consequently elongated in a direction perpendicular to the elements of the ridge–pool and ridge–flark complexes. The smaller the lake (i.e. the nearer it is to its first state of existence as an element of a ridge–pool complex), the rounder its shape. Lakes that are even smaller than these take the form of elongated strips perpendicular to the general slope of the mire and have the same orientation as the elements of the ridge–pool microtope. This process is well portrayed in Figs 8 and 28. Investigations of this aspect of the morphology of lake–mire complexes containing microtopes of the ridge–pool, ridge–flark and *Sphagnum*–pine–shrub–*Eriophorum* types (Ivanov, 1969) show that endotelmic lakes always change their shape in the same way, whatever the type of lake–mire complex to which they belong.

Alongside these, the lake–mire systems of Western Siberia include widely distributed lake–mire complexes that at first glance seem extraordinarily chaotic in their shapes, their orientation, their combinations and the positioning of the large and small units within them. This is well seen in Fig. 28, zone *b*, and is connected with the fact that, along with the processes of erosion already described, other factors contribute to the transformation of the shapes of lowered lakes, delaying and changing the speed and direction of the enlargement of lakes by the erosion of their banks.

The most important of these processes are:

(1) The fusion of neighbouring lakes through enlargement into one lake.
(2) The shallowing of lakes through the destruction of their peat banks, followed by the displacement and re-deposition of the eroded material on the bottom of the lake, with the result that it is overgrown for a second time.
(3) The shrinkage of peat on the banks through the drainage of water into the lake at its new and lower level, which is accompanied by a lowering of the surface of the mire in the microtopes at the water's edge, an increased growth of wooded vegetation on the shore line, and, as a consequence, an increase in the firmness and stability of the banks.

From this it follows that the final shape of lakes of different sizes and their orientation with respect to the elements of ridge–flark and ridge–pool microtopes and to the general direction of flow of mire waters depends on the intensity and interaction of all the above processes. This greatly complicates the structure and development of lake–mire complexes. The role of all the three enumerated factors and the process by which individual lakes are enlarged and modified, so far as it depends on the type of mire microtope that surrounds them have all been systematically reviewed in an already mentioned work (Ivanov, 1969). These factors make it possible to explain the complex and apparently chaotic structure of the lake–mire macrotopes that are widely distributed throughout the northern half of the West Siberian lowlands. The formation of such structures is the result of two interacting processes: firstly, the formation of stable lake–mire complexes (including ridge–pool and ridge–flark microtopes) through the accumulation of peat and gradual changes in the relief of the mire, with appropriate reactions in the plant cover to the changing conditions of the water supply and the efflux of moisture from the mire; secondly, the continual disturbance of stable lake–mire formations as endotelmic erosion advances from one stage to another. The following are the stages through which it passes: erosion of the channels of internal streams, lowering of the level of endotelmic lakes, uneven erosion of their banks after erosion, increase of area and change of shape (in plan) of lakes, merging of lakes that have grown to great size, shallowing of lakes through increase of their area, renewal of overgrowth by vegetation after reaching the necessary shallowness, and resumption of mire formation. These phenomena and the chief phases in the causation and manifestation of unstable states in lake–mire systems and geotopes.

The phenomena we have considered show how great a role erosion plays in the formation of lake–mire systems and the occurrence of instability in their structure. These processes arise in mire systems that have acquired a high water content under natural conditions. In such cases, an increase in total water content causes an increase in the total area of open water and a decrease in the area occupied by plants, while a loss of water from the lakes with a lowering of their level and an extension of their area makes them shallow, and so leads to their being overgrown and converted into mire for the second time. Two opposing processes therefore operate in lake–mire systems and determine the speed at which organic material is accumulated: firstly, the enlargement of the water surface at the expense of the area occupied by plants, which reduces the annual accumulation of plant material and deposition of peat; secondly, the shallowing of the lake, leading to a resumption of mire formation and an increase in plant material and peat deposition. The final state of the system depends upon which of these two processes predominates. The disintegration and destruction of the system will obviously supervene, if the reduction in the increment of plant material (owing to the enlargement of the area of the lakes and the open water surface) predominates over the increase in its increment through the resumption of mire formation. This is because the fundamental function of the system—peat accumulation— will then be disturbed, and its peat deposits will begin to deteriorate. The opposite result will ensue, if the increment of plant material (owing to the lowering of the level of the lake by erosion and the resumption of mire formation) predominates over the decrease of that increment, owing to the contraction of the total area of the water body and the increase in the area of plant cover. Since the speed of plant renewal and mire formation, as well as the annual increment of plant material, depends on the hydrothermal regime, the quantitative relation between these two processes must be different in different climatic conditions. In a cold climate, the disintegration of lake–mire systems through an excess of water must supervene earlier and at a relatively lower water content than in a warmer climate. Keeping in view the processes described, we shall go on to consider the water balance criteria for lake–mire systems as a whole.

4.7 The Water Balance Criteria of Stability for Lake–Mire Systems

We considered above the water balance criteria for individual microtopes and lakes forming parts of lake–mire systems. Investigation of the laws that relate the external environment to the stability of lake–mire systems as a whole involves more than the establishment of criteria for the individual elements in them. A plurality of lakes which, along with the mire microtopes that surround them, forms a single interacting system, behaves like a qualitatively new natural formation, whose relations with the external environment cannot be reduced to the same laws as govern the interactions of its separate constituents. By this we understand not only the lakes and their adjacent mire microtopes, but any other surrounding microtopes whose water balance can be determined by purely climatic parameters. It is therefore essential, not only that individual lakes and microtopes should satisfy the criteria of stability, but that the system as a whole should conform to certain principles of water balance, whose violation from whatever cause may lead to the disturbance and disintegration of the system.

Let us indicate by $\omega_\Sigma = \Sigma\omega_i$ the total area of all lakes in a given lake–mire system, and express it as a fraction of ω, the area of the whole lake–mire system, ω_i being the area of the ith lake in the system. Let the projected length of the boundary that divides the given lake–mire system from the mineral lands that surround it be $l_\cap$. We shall symbolize the total area of all the mire microtopes in the system by $\omega_{\Sigma m} = \Sigma\omega_j$, where the suffix j indicates a type of mire microtope, and ω_j the area occupied by it in the system. We shall express the values of $\omega_{\Sigma m}$ and ω_Σ as fractions of unity, and their relative values by $\omega_\Sigma^* = \omega_\Sigma/\omega$, and $\omega_{\Sigma m}^* = \omega_{\Sigma m}/\omega$,

It is plain that, if the boundaries of the lake–mire system are stable, then whatever internal transformations the system may undergo through the instability of lakes and microtopes and through changes in the area of individual lakes, it must satisfy the relationship

$$\omega_\Sigma^* + \omega_{\Sigma m}^* = 1. \tag{4.13}$$

Let l be the total length of the projected boundary of the drainage network of the whole mire system, and $l_\cup$ the length of the projected boundary of its internal drainage (endotelmic streams and lowered lakes). The total length of the projected boundary of its internal and external drainage (along the boundary of the lake–mire system) will then be

$$l = l_\cup + l_\cap. \tag{4.14}$$

The boundary of internal drainage is created by internal streams flowing through the mire and the lakes joined up by them, provided their levels are significantly lower (by 0·8–2·0 m) than the water table in the adjacent mire microtopes. This is the so-called "lowered" lake–stream network, which coexists along with an "unlowered" lake–stream network. This last does not exercise any draining effect upon the mire system and its microtopes, and is not included, when making calculations, in the boundary of internal drainage. The mechanism by which a lowered lake–stream internal network is formed was briefly considered in section 4.6, and is expounded in more detail elsewhere (Ivanov, 1969).

The equivalent microtope in respect of evaporation for a given mire system is, we shall say, that which satisfies the condition

$$\bar{p}'_e = \frac{\sum\limits_{1}^{n} \omega_j \bar{p}_j}{\omega_{\Sigma m}}, \tag{4.15}$$

where $\bar{p}'_e$ is the average loss of moisture through evaporation from a unit area of the equivalent microtope, ω_j the area of microtopes of the jth type, $\bar{p}_j$ the evaporation from the same microtope, and n the number of different microtopes in the system.

The equivalent microtope in respect of the seepage of the acrotelm is, we shall say, a microtope that satisfies in the most general form the following conditions:

$$q'_1 = \frac{\sum\limits_{1}^{n_1} q_j l_j}{l_{\Sigma 1}} \tag{4.16}$$

$$q'_2 = \frac{\sum\limits_{1}^{n_2} q_j l_j}{l_{\Sigma 2}}, \tag{4.16'}$$

where q'_1 and q'_2 are the mean long-term values of seepage in the acrotelm adjusted to correspond with the fronts of efflux and influx of the microtopes, q_j and l_j are the mean seepage and boundary in plan of the jth type of microtope, n_1 is the number of different microtopes contiguous with the front of efflux, n_2 is the number of different microtopes contiguous with the front of influx, $l_{\Sigma 1}$ is the total projected front of efflux and $l_{\Sigma 2}$ the total projected front of influx of the whole system.

In lake–mire systems which are situated on level or inclined water divides and completely cover the interfluves (including, for example, all such systems in the West Siberian zone of excess moisture), there are no fronts of influx on the outer boundaries. In such cases, it is enough that the equivalent microtope for seepage should satisfy only one condition (4.16). It is then obvious that

$$l = l_{\Sigma 1} = l_{\cup} + l_{\cap}.$$

With the use of these symbols, it is possible to write the equation of water balance for lake–mire systems with no fronts of influx in the following form:

$$\omega_{\Sigma}(\bar{p}_p - \bar{p}_{e\,lk}) + \omega_{\Sigma m}(\bar{p}_p - \bar{p}'_e) = q'_1 l. \tag{4.17}$$

Since the total front of drainage l in every lake–mire system consists, generally speaking, of a front of inner drainage $l_{\cup}$ and a front of outer drainage $l_{\cap}$, the last equation may be written in another form:

$$\omega_{\Sigma}(\bar{p}_p - \bar{p}_{e\,lk}) + \omega_{\Sigma m}(\bar{p}_p - \bar{p}'_e) = \bar{q}_{\cup} l_{\cup} + \dot{q}_{\cap} l_{\cap}, \tag{4.18}$$

where $\bar{q}_{\cup}$ is the mean seepage for the equivalent microtope along the inner front of drainage, $\bar{q}_{\cap}$ is the same along the outer front of drainage ($\bar{q}_{\cup}$ and $\bar{q}_{\cap}$ may be different), and $\bar{p}_p$ is the norm of precipitation. Dividing both parts of the equation by ω, we find that

$$\omega_{\Sigma}^*(\bar{p}_p - \bar{p}_{e\,lk}) + \omega_{\Sigma m}^*(\bar{p}_p - \bar{p}'_e) = \bar{q}_{\cup}\frac{l_{\cup}}{\omega} + \bar{q}_{\cap}\frac{l_{\cap}}{\omega}. \tag{4.19}$$

Since $\bar{p}_p - \bar{p}_{e\,lk} = \bar{p}_{lk}$ and $\bar{p}_p - \bar{p}'_e = \bar{p}_m$ represent respectively the internal water supply of the lake and the equivalent mire microtope, dividing both parts of the equation by $\omega_{\Sigma m}^* \bar{p}_{lk}$ gives an equation of dimensionless quantities:

$$\frac{\omega_{\Sigma}^*}{\omega_{\Sigma m}^*} + \frac{\bar{p}_m}{\bar{p}_{lk}} = \frac{\bar{q}_{\cup}}{\omega_{\Sigma m}^*\bar{p}_{lk}} \times \frac{l_{\cup}}{\omega} + \frac{\bar{q}_{\cap}}{\omega_{\Sigma m}^*\bar{p}_{lk}} \times \frac{l_{\cap}}{\omega}. \tag{4.20}$$

Before considering the numerical value of the terms in these last equations, (4.19) and (4.20), for particular terrains occupied by lake–mire systems, we shall show what these equations give in the way of a general criterion for the stability of a lake–mire system. Fulfilment of condition (4.20) is obviously obligatory if the system is to be in a state of stable dynamic equilibrium. Change in any terms of the equation must therefore entail a corresponding change in some other terms, if the equation is to be satisfied and the system is to reach another stable state. During periods when this equality is not observed, the system is in an unstable state or is undergoing a change of internal structure.

Let us now consider what internal transformations may occur in a lake–mire system, allowing realistically for the known possibilities. The internal water supply of the lakes $\bar{p}_{lk}$, which is determined for any given terrain by the difference between the norms of precipitation and evaporation from the surface of the water, can be regarded (in the limits of a given climatic epoch) as independent of the distribution of water surfaces in a lake–mire system. $\bar{p}_{lk}$

therefore remains an unchanging quantity or invariant, whatever changes may take place in the other terms of equation (4.20). The evaporation from mire microtopes $\bar{p}'_e$ and, consequently, the internal water supply of mire microtopes $\bar{p}_m$ $(= \bar{p}_p - \bar{p}'_e)$ are terms whose variation is restricted. Evaporation, in particular, may vary from the slow evaporation found in the driest mire microtopes of the forest type (pine–*Sphagnum*–shrub and pine–cedar–shrub–*Sphagnum* in the case of Siberian mires), or, at the very limit, in sparsely stocked coniferous forests situated on dry sandy soils, to the rapid evaporation found in the most completely inundated mire microtopes, which is almost as great as from an open water surface. From this one estimates that the ratio $\bar{p}_m/\bar{p}_{lk}$ may vary from 2 to 1.

The length of the front of external drainage $l_\cap$ cannot change under natural conditions, since the boundary between mire geotopes and mire-free mineral lands is fixed by the level of drainage of the area, its river network and the climate in which the lake–mire system is situated (see section 1.2). Changes in these boundaries involving an increase in the area of mire (since in the zone of excess moisture the process of mire formation is irreversible and the area of mire does not contract when river beds are deepened) may occur through the artificial flooding of river systems. The length of the front of internal drainage may vary greatly, from a complete absence of it ($l_\cup = 0$) to lengths that significantly exceed that of external drainage ($l_\cup \gg l_\cap$). As already indicated, these changes are connected with the natural process of endotelmic erosion, which may take very complicated and peculiar forms (see section 4.6) considered in detail elsewhere (Ivanov, 1969).

Of the quantities mentioned in equation (4.20) only one $l_\cup$, the front of internal drainage, has a wide range of values (under the influence of natural processes or of human action). Immediate operation on the quantities $\bar{p}_{lk}, \bar{p}_m, \bar{q}_\cup$ and $\bar{q}_\cap$ is practically excluded (either in natural conditions or through the economic or technical activities of man). Artificial changes in the ratio of the area of lakes to that of mires (ω_Σ and $\omega_{\Sigma m}$) in the geotope (other than by improved drainage or other such measures, which change the water regime and runoff), though possible, are hardly practical propositions. In discussing transformations we shall therefore treat the ratio $\omega_\Sigma^*/\omega_{\Sigma m}^*$ as a dependent, and not an independent variable. In these circumstances, the only quantity in a lake–mire system that is susceptible to active change is the ratio of the front of internal drainage $l_\cup$ to the area of mire $\omega_{\Sigma m}$.

On the basis of equation (4.20), we shall consider to what consequences a change in the ratio $l_\cup/\omega_{\Sigma m}^* \omega$ may lead. It is obvious that change may occur through natural processes or through artificial measures, like the draining of mires. Let us suppose that enlargement of the lakes and of the length of internal water courses is going on through natural erosion. In that case, when the area of lakes ω_Σ is enlarged by the erosion of their banks (in which case the condition (4.13) must be fulfilled), the ratio $l_\cup/\omega^*_{\Sigma m}\omega$ increases through the increase of $l_\cup$, as well as through some contraction of the area occupied by mire microtopes $\omega_{\Sigma m}$.

If, however, the system remains stable and keeps its former boundaries, this must be compensated by a corresponding decrease of $\bar{q}_\cup/\bar{p}_{lk}$, or by an increase in the terms on the left-hand side of equation (4.20), i.e. of the ratios $\omega^*_\Sigma/\omega^*_{\Sigma m}$ and $\bar{p}_m/\bar{p}_{lk}$. But since $\bar{p}_{lk}$ is constant, the increase in $\bar{p}_m/\bar{p}_{lk}$ can only take place through an increase in the water supply of the mire microtopes $\bar{p}_m$. Decrease of seepage $\bar{q}_\cup$, which is possible if the microtopes are replaced by others with a lower water content, must be accompanied by a reduction in evaporation, so as to produce an increase in their water supply $\bar{p}_m$. These changes in the terms of equation (4.20) are therefore a coordinated transformation (as regards the direction of the changes in $\bar{q}_\cup$ and $\bar{p}'_e$). But absolute variations in the values of $\bar{q}_\cup$ and $\bar{p}_m$ may not be coordinated with changes in the microtopes. In that case, equation (4.20) cannot hold good and the system cannot be in a stable state, unless there is change in the ratio of open water surface to that occupied by mire microtopes $\omega^*_\Sigma/\omega^*_{\Sigma m}$.

The first thing to be decided is obviously how far a lake–mire system's internal front of drainage can change without changing the above ratio. To this end we shall make certain transformations in equation (4.20). Supposing that the equivalent seepages along the interior and exterior fronts of drainage are not materially different, we shall simplify the problem by accepting as a first approximation that

$$\bar{q}_\cup \cong \bar{q}_\cap = \bar{q}. \qquad (4.21)$$

Equation (4.20) can then be presented in the following forms:

$$\frac{\omega^*_\Sigma}{\omega^*_{\Sigma m}} = \frac{\bar{q}}{\bar{p}_{lk}\omega^*_{\Sigma m}}\left(\frac{l_\cup}{\omega} + \frac{l_\cap}{\omega}\right) - \frac{p_m}{\bar{p}_{lk}} = \frac{\bar{q}}{\bar{p}_{lk}\omega^*_{\Sigma m}} \times \frac{l}{\omega} - \frac{\bar{n}_{lll}}{\bar{p}_{lk}}, \qquad (4.22)$$

$$\bar{q} = \frac{\left(\frac{\omega^*_\Sigma}{\omega^*_{\Sigma m}} + \frac{\bar{p}_m}{\bar{p}_{lk}}\right) \times \bar{p}_{lk}\omega^*_{\Sigma m}}{\dfrac{l}{\omega}} = \frac{\omega^*_\Sigma\bar{p}_{lk} + \omega^*_{\Sigma m}\bar{p}_m}{\dfrac{l}{\omega}}, \qquad (4.22')$$

or

$$\frac{l_\cup}{\omega} = \frac{\bar{p}_m\omega^*_{\Sigma m} + \bar{p}_{lk}\omega^*_\Sigma}{\bar{q}} - \frac{l_\cap}{\omega}. \qquad (4.22'')$$

The last form of the equation makes it possible to decide when the system is stable, and how far $l_\cup/\omega$ may change without disturbing the ratio between the areas of lake and mire microtopes $\omega^*_\Sigma/\omega^*_{\Sigma m}$, i.e. without any change of the system in this respect.

Let us now consider the case where the external boundaries of a system's drainage have already been stabilized, and ω, the area occupied by the system, does not change. Since $\bar{p}_{lk}$ is constant for the region where the system is situated, and $l_{\cap}/\omega$, $\omega^*_{\Sigma m}$ and ω^*_Σ are also by hypothesis constant, the limits of change in the front of internal drainage and in the morphological coefficient of internal drainage $l_{\cup}/\omega$ are determined only by changes in seepage $\bar{q}$ through an alteration in the types of microtope, and changes in water supply $\bar{p}_m$ through an alteration in the amount of evaporation from them. The higher the values of $\bar{p}_{lk}$, ω^*_Σ and $l_{\cap}/\omega$, the less $l_{\cap}/\omega$ can change without disturbing the structure of the system (i.e. the ratio of the area of lake and mire). In the extreme case, when

$$\frac{l_{\cap}}{\omega} = \left[\frac{\bar{p}_m \omega^*_{\Sigma m} + \bar{p}_{lk} \omega^*_\Sigma}{\bar{q}} \right]_{\max},$$

which corresponds to the condition $\bar{q} = \bar{q}_{\min}$ and $\bar{p}_m = \bar{p}_{m\,\max}$, the range of possible change in the internal drainage $l_{\cup}/\omega$ without disturbance of the structure of the system is zero. Consequently, any increase in the front of internal drainage must be compensated by a contraction of the total area of lake and an expansion of the area of mire microtopes, since $\bar{p}_m > \bar{p}_{lk}$. If in the extreme case

$$\frac{l_{\cap}}{\omega} = \left[\frac{\bar{p}_m \omega^*_{\Sigma m} + \bar{p}_{lk} \omega^*_\Sigma}{\bar{q}} \right]_{\min},$$

which corresponds to the condition $\bar{q} = \bar{q}_{\max}$ and $\bar{p}_m = \bar{p}_{m\,\min}$, then the possible range of change in the internal drainage without destruction of the structure of the system is at its maximum through the replacement of the mire microtopes by types with a lower water content owing to a reduction of seepage $\bar{q}$. If

$$\frac{l_{\cap}}{\omega} < \left[\frac{\bar{p}_m \omega^*_{\Sigma m} + \bar{p}_{lk} \omega^*_\Sigma}{\bar{q}} \right]_{\min},$$

then the system will plainly be unstable through the inundation and destruction of the plant cover. Its existence may in this case be prolonged, if a front of internal drainage be formed by natural or artificial means, provided its length is sufficient to satisfy equality (4.22″), even though $\bar{q}$ may be at its maximum value for mire plant communities.

With the increase of the water content of the microtopes and the corresponding increase in seepage $\bar{q}$, their water supply $\bar{p}_m \to \bar{p}_{lk}$, since evaporation from them approaches the evaporation from an open water surface. In this case, as is plain from equations (4.13) and (4.20), changes in the ratio of the areas of lakes and microtopes $\omega^*_\Sigma / \omega^*_{\Sigma m}$ do not much affect fulfilment of the equality

(4.22). For that reason, when $\bar{q} \to \bar{q}_{max}$ and $\bar{p}_m \to \bar{p}_{lk}$, the system becomes unstable in respect of the relation between the areas of lakes and microtopes. If, in these conditions, a change of $l_\cap/\omega$ is produced by any external causes, the increase or decrease of $l_\cap/\omega$ cannot be compensated by corresponding changes of ω_Σ^* and $\omega_{\Sigma m}^*$ to satisfy equality (4.19). A decrease of $l_\cup/\omega$ may then cause the whole system to disintegrate, opening the way to various alternative sequels and later transformations (see section 4.2). From this also follows the important conclusion that the stability of a lake–mire system increases with an increase in the difference between the meteoric water supply[1] of lakes and that of mire microtopes, i.e. with the difference between evaporation from an open water surface and from mire plant communities.

It follows from what we have said that the water balance criterion for the stability of lake–mire systems, which limits the range of their variation, may be written in the following form:

$$\left[\frac{\bar{p}_{m\,min}\,\omega_{\Sigma m}^* + \bar{p}_{lk}\omega_\Sigma^*}{\bar{q}_{max}}\right]_{min} < \frac{l_\cup + l_\cap}{\omega} < \left[\frac{\bar{p}_{m\,max}\,\omega_{\Sigma m}^* + \bar{p}_{lk}\omega_\Sigma^*}{\bar{q}_{min}}\right]_{max}. \tag{4.23}$$

From this, as a special case, where $\omega_\Sigma^* = 0$ and $\omega_{\Sigma m} = 1$, one obtains a water balance criterion of stability for mire systems without lakes:

$$\frac{\bar{p}_{m\,min}}{\bar{q}_{max}} < \frac{l_\cup + l_\cap}{\omega} < \frac{\bar{p}_{m\,max}}{\bar{q}_{min}}. \tag{4.23'}$$

Finally, if we accept as a test of stability, not the ratio between the total areas of lakes and microtopes, but the disturbance of the fundamental function of the system, i.e. the cessation of peat accumulation and the disintegration of the system, the range of stable states permitting internal changes of structure is correspondingly enlarged, and on the basis of (1.23) and (4.13) will be expressed by the relation

$$\left[\frac{\bar{p}_{m\,min}\,\omega_{\Sigma m\,min}^* + \bar{p}_{lk}\omega_{\Sigma\,max}^*}{\bar{q}_{max}}\right]_{min} < \frac{l_\cup + l_\cap}{\omega} < \frac{\bar{p}_{m\,max}}{\bar{q}_{min}}. \tag{4.24}$$

On the left-hand side of this expression, the values of $\omega_{\Sigma\,max}^*$ and $\omega_{\Sigma m\,min}^*$ must correspond to some ratio of the areas of lakes and microtopes in the systems for which the increase of peat deposit relative to the whole area of the system would be practically zero. This condition begins to be fulfilled when

$$\frac{\omega_\Sigma^*}{\omega_{\Sigma m}^*} > 1,$$

which is equivalent to the condition $\omega_\Sigma^* > 0.5$ (since $\omega_\Sigma^* + \omega_{\Sigma m}^* = 1$), i.e. when the area of open water surface is greater than half the total area of the system.

Let us now consider the extreme case where there are no lakes in the system and the term which represents their area in equation (4.22″) is zero. Then, since $\omega^*_{\Sigma m} = 1$, in place of (4.22″), we have:

$$\frac{l_\cup}{\omega} = \frac{\bar{p}_m}{\bar{q}} - \frac{l_\cap}{\omega}. \tag{4.25}$$

We shall now explain within what limits the internal front of drainage $l_\cup$ and the value of the morphological coefficient $l_\cup/\omega$ may change, when the water supply $\bar{p}_m$ and the seepage $\bar{q}$ of the microtopes lie within known limits with which we are familiar. From equation (4.25) it follows that, if the coefficient of water supply $\bar{p}_m/\bar{q} \to l_\cap/\omega$, the length of the internal front $l_\cup$ must tend to zero. Otherwise, the mire system will be unstable and may disintegrate. If, on the other hand, the external front and the corresponding morphological coefficient are reduced ($l_\cap/\omega \to 0$), the morphological coefficient of internal drainage approximates to the value of the coefficient of water supply $\bar{p}_m/\bar{q}$. In that case, the extent to which the internal front $l_\cup$ can vary without disturbing the stability of the system is determined exclusively by the limits of the coefficient of water supply.

As is plain from equation (4.25), the smaller the coefficient of water supply, the smaller the value of the internal front of drainage for a mire system of the same size and the narrower the range within which it can vary for the same value of $l_\cap/\omega$. From this it follows that a mire system without any endotelmic lakes is stable only so long as the changes caused by the draining of water from the mire are sufficiently compensated by the development of its internal front and corresponding changes in the composition of its plant cover (i.e. in its microtopes).

From comparison of equations (4.25) and (4.22″) it is easy to see that, since $\bar{p}_m$ is greater than $(\bar{p}_m\omega^*_{\Sigma m} + \bar{p}_{lk}\omega_\Sigma)$, a lake–mire system is always less stable in regard to reductions of the coefficient of water supply $a = \bar{p}_m/\bar{q}$ than a mire system without lakes. This also explains the observed disappearance of lakes from mire systems, first of all in those latitudes where the deficiency in meteoric supply of the lakes $|p_{lk}|$ becomes equal to the surplus in meteoric water supply of the mire microtopes, and where therefore $(\bar{p}_m + \bar{p}_{lk}) = 0$. Beginning from these latitudes, lake–mire systems whose lakes have no soil-derived or external water supply (i.e. are without endotelmic or exotelmic catchments) prove unstable and cannot persist. We shall consider the bearing of these inferences upon the seepage of different types of mire microtope and the amount of meteoric water supply they receive in different latitudes through climatic differences.

4.8   Calculations Concerning the Stability of Lake–Mire Systems

We shall begin by setting realistic limits to the terms involved in equations (4.23), (4.23′) and (4.24). The limits of the coefficient of water supply of mire microtopes $p_m/\bar{q}$ are set by those of seepage $\bar{q}$ for different types of microtope and that of the internal water supply $\bar{p}_m$. An increase in the water content of the microtopes leads to an increase in their seepage and a reduction of their internal meteoric water supply, because an increase in water content produces an increase in evaporation. With a reduction of the water content of the microtopes, the above-mentioned quantities are changed in the opposite direction. Choosing from among all known types of mire microtope those with the greatest and the least water content and corresponding values of seepage and evaporation, it is possible to define the limits within which mire microtopes can exist and mire systems maintain their fundamental function of peat accumulation and avoid disintegration. The range of seepage of different types of mire microtope whose water supply is meteoric can be determined from the data in Table 8 (see section 2.8). It varies from $0\cdot5$–$1\cdot5$ $l.s^{-1}.km^{-1}$ for the driest pine–shrub microtopes to 11–15 $l.s^{-1}.km^{-1}$ for the wettest ridge–flark (with *Sphagnum–Scheuchzeria* flarks) or ridge–pool microtopes, in which flarks and pools occupy up to 90% of the microtope area, i.e. are the main element in the structure of the microtope. These limits really fix the range within which the average long-term seepage of microtopes $\bar{q}$ can vary without disturbing the biological and mechanical stability of their plant associations. They can therefore be accepted in calculations as extreme values, above or below which we now know that plant communities disintegrate or degenerate (see section 4.5) through excessive desiccation or inundation of the acrotelm and the peat deposit. We shall take 1 $l.s^{-1}.km^{-1}$ as the minimum value, because lower values may be already beyond the threshold of the system's stability. We shall take 15 $l.s^{-1}.km^{-1}$ as the maximum value.

Particular regions characterized by definite geophysical conditions must obviously be used for a quantitative evaluation and calculation of the limits of lake–mire systems. Taking account of the fact that the West Siberian plain is unique in the degree of swamping in its northern half, we shall carry out such calculations for this region. In doing this, we shall not consider the region of permafrost, because the necessary experimental data about the types, structure and physical properties of its mire microtopes are not available, and the morphology and structure of its mire formations have not yet been adequately studied.

We shall begin by carrying out some preliminary calculations for determining the water supply of mire microtopes $\bar{p}_m$ and endotelmic lakes $\bar{p}_{lk}$. For this we shall make use of accepted methods of calculating evaporation from a water surface and from mire microtopes. These last were considered in

Chapter 3. To determine the mean annual evaporation from a water surface use was made of Braslavskiy and Vikulina's map of evaporation (1954). To evaluate evaporation from mires use was made of equation (3.8) and corrected mean long-term values of $\bar{\alpha}$ for monthly evaporation (Bavina, 1967; Bavina and Romanov, 1969). The mean annual evaporation is reckoned to be the sum of the evaporation in the warm months of the year. Values of the radiation balance are calculated from the observations of the fifteen stations marked on the map in Fig. 33 and cover periods of from 35 to 45 years. A map of evaporation from mire microtopes was constructed on the basis of these figures.

Fig. 33. Map of the mean annual surplus or deficiency in the meteoric water supply of endotelmic lakes.

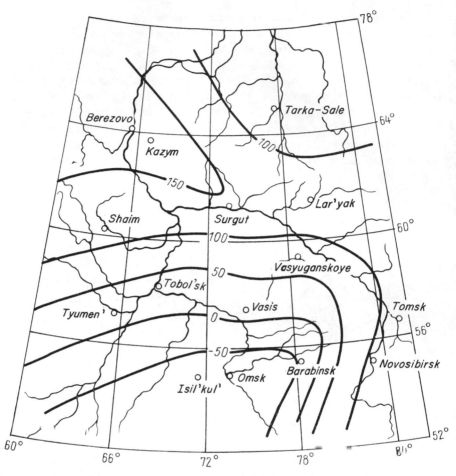

Fig. 34. Map of the mean annual surplus or deficiency in the meteoric water supply of the mire microtopes of Western Siberia.

The figures given in the National Geophysical Observatory's maps of long-term means of precipitation were used to calculate, as the differences between the norms of precipitation and evaporation, the amount of water gained or lost by endotelmic lakes and the amount of water gained by mire microtopes. From the figures so obtained, maps of the meteoric supply and loss of endotelmic lakes (Fig. 33) and mire microtopes (Fig. 34) were constructed. From these data, curves were drawn showing the change by latitude in the meteoric supply and loss of lake–mire systems between the longitudes 66° and 84°E. These will be found in Fig. 35. Each graph contains three

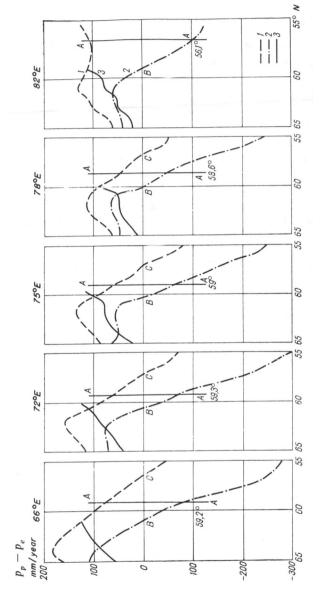

Fig. 35. Dependence of surplus or deficiency of meteoric water supply of the lake–mire systems of the West Siberian plain upon their latitude along the 66th, 72nd, 75th, 78th and 84th eastern meridians. 1—water supply of mire microtopes ($\bar{p}_m$). 2—water supply of lakes (p_{lk}). 3—difference between 1 and 2.

curves. Curve 1 gives the variation by latitude of the meteoric supply of oligotrophic moss microtopes (see section 1.8), curve 2 gives the variation of the meteoric supply of the lakes, and curve 3 gives the differences between water supplies of mires and lakes, when there is a positive balance. The vertical line AA is drawn at the latitude where the meteoric supply of mire microtopes is equal to the deficiency in the meteoric supply of the lakes, i.e. where

$$\bar{p}_m - \bar{p}_{lk} = 0.$$

It is obvious that in latitudes lying to the left of B (the point where curve 2 ($\bar{p}_{lk}$) intersects the axis of zero meteoric supply), lakes of all types may exist in lake–mire systems, including those at the epicentre of convex mire microtopes, which have fronts of efflux, but no fronts of influx (Types 1 and 4 of lake–mire complexes (section 3.5)). In such cases, the stable dimensions for lakes are determined by water balance criteria (3.53′) and (3.59). In the zone between the point B and the line AA there cannot be any lake without a front of influx or external water supply. Consequently, the lakes in this zone must be situated on the slopes of mire massifs, where the flow across their front of influx must be greater than the flow across their front of efflux. In these latitudes, the situation of lakes in lake–mire systems must therefore be of the second or third type. In such circumstances, there can rarely be lakes situated on sections of a slope with an extremely divergent flow, in which the influx across the outer front must usually be less than the efflux. From the line AA to C, the point where curve 1 ($\bar{p}_m$) intersects the line of zero meteoric supply, there is a wide zone in which endotelmic lakes must have a significant preponderance of influx (across the front of influx) over efflux (across the front of efflux). The whole deficiency in the meteoric supply of the lakes must be made good by their external supply from surrounding mire microtopes. Morphologically, this corresponds in practice with cases where lakes are situated on the slopes of mire massifs with an extremely convergent flow (see section 3.5). To the right of C there is situated a broad belt in which the existence of lakes dependent upon an external mire-derived water supply is impossible, because the microtopes here have a deficiency in their meteoric supply. Consequently, lake–mire systems in this zone can only exist because they have an external supply of ground or surface water, or an internal supply of pressure water. The inevitable result of this is that lake–mire systems are situated exclusively in depressions, basin-like hollows and other negative elements of relief, which ensure that the system has an external or pressure water supply. In these conditions, as was pointed out in Chapter 1, mire massifs must possess concave or flat reliefs sloping down towards the lakes that drain them.

On the basis of the relationships set out in Fig. 35 and the water balance criteria of the system (4.23) and (4.23'), it is possible to define the range of the morphological coefficient of drainage of a lake–mire system $(l_\cap + l_\cup)/\omega$, within whose limits variations will not produce a disturbance of its stability, nor a disintegration of the system. Accepting the limiting values given above for the seepage of mire microtopes, $\bar{q}_{min} = 1\,\mathrm{l.s}^{-1}.\mathrm{km}^{-1}$ and $\bar{q}_{max} = 15\,\mathrm{l.s}^{-1}.\mathrm{km}^{-1}$, we calculate the curves (Figs 36–38):

$$\left(\frac{l_\cup + l_\cap}{\omega}\right)_{max} = f_1(\delta) \quad \text{and} \quad \left(\frac{l_\cup + l_\cap}{\omega}\right)_{min} = f_2(\delta),$$

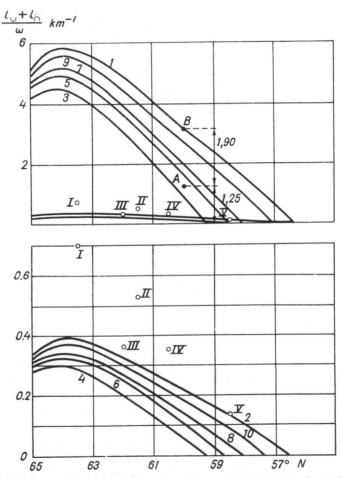

Fig. 36. Regions where mire and lake–mire systems are stable along the 66th eastern meridian. The curves below show the lower limit of stability with a magnified vertical scale. Roman numerals denote regions in Table 20.

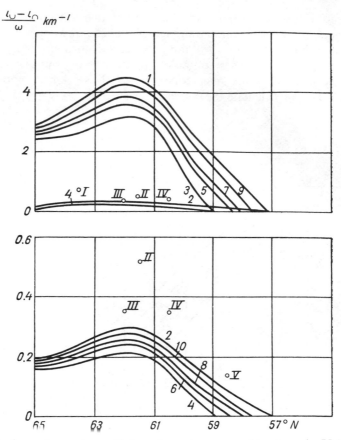

Fig. 37. Regions where mire and lake–mire systems are stable along the 75th eastern meridian. The curves below show the lower limit of stability with a magnified vertical scale. Roman numerals denote regions in Table 20.

which limit the range of stable states of lake–mire systems in different meridians, where δ is the latitude of the site.

All calculations relating to zones of stability are presented in Appendix 2. Curve 1 at the top of Figs 36–38 shows the change by latitude of the maximum values of the coefficients of water supply of mire microtopes ($a_{s\,max} = \bar{p}_m/\bar{q}_{min}$) and limits the range of stability of mire systems without lakes in respect of disintegration through desiccation. Increase of the value of the morphological coefficient of drainage $(l_{\cup} + l_{\cap})/\omega$ beyond the limits set by Curve 1 must lead to the appearance of a negative balance of organic material in the system and the degradation of the peat deposit, i.e. to a reduction in its thickness and

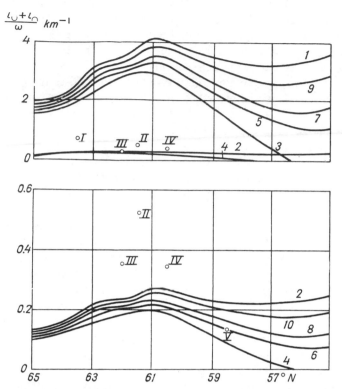

Fig. 38. Regions where mire and lake–mire systems are stable along the 84th eastern meridian. The curves below show the lower limit of stability with a magnified vertical scale. Roman numerals denote regions in Table 20.

the gradual disintegration of the mire system. Curve 2, lower down in Figs 36–38, shows the change by latitude of the minimum values of the coefficient of water supply ($a_{s\,min} = \bar{p}_m/\bar{q}_{max}$) and limits the range of stability of mire systems without lakes in respect of disintegration through excessive inundation, which, as was said, deprives plant communities of their biological and mechanical stability (section 4.5), diminishes the annual increment of biomass in the system and gives rise to erosion.

Degradation of mire vegetation at the upper limit of the values of a_s, i.e. from excessive inundation, takes place through a series of natural transformations by which mire systems without lakes are converted into lake–mire systems with a progressively increasing ratio of open water surface to the area of mire microtopes $\omega_\Sigma^*/\omega_{\Sigma m}^*$. Increase in the open water surface, accompanied by a development of the interior front of drainage $l_{\cup}$ and some decrease in water supply, goes on simultaneously with a reduction in the wetness of the microtopes, the emergence of small sections occupied by *Sphagnum*–shrub–pine microtopes (e.g. ridges in ridge–flark microtopes) and their coalescence into larger sections.

This in turn lowers the equivalent seepage $\bar{q}$ and raises the coefficient of water supply a_s. Thus the growth of the total area of open water surface in lake–mire systems raises their stability, as expressed in the graphs of Figs 36–38 by the downward displacement of the lower curves, which delimit the zone of stability when the open water surface is increased.

Curves 3, 5, 7, 9 and 4, 6, 8, 10, which delimit the region of stability, in the first cases through desiccation, in the second through excessive inundation, show the critical values of the function $(l_{\cup} + l_{\cap})/\omega = f(\delta)$ for various fixed ratios of the total areas of lakes and mire microtopes. In Figs 36–38, they are given for the ratios $\omega_{\Sigma}^{*}/\omega_{\Sigma m}^{*} = 1 \cdot 0, 0 \cdot 5, 0 \cdot 33$ and $0 \cdot 11$. The zones lying between Curves 1 and 3 and Curves 2 and 4 are conjunctions of these values of $(l_{\cup} + l_{\cap})/\omega$, in each latitude δ, where lake–mire systems must, without disintegration, change their structure, i.e. the ratio between the total areas occupied by lakes and mire microtopes. It is worth remarking that the zone of stable states is quite large for critical states where disintegration would be due to desiccation, and very small where it would be due to excessive inundation. It follows that changes in the structure of a lake–mire system when it is exposed to excessive inundation do less to increase its stability then analogous changes when it is exposed to desiccation.

Let us now consider the arrangement of the values of the hydromorphological coefficient l/ω in the graphs of Figs 36–38 relating to the actual lake–mire systems of the West Siberian plain (excluding the zone of permafrost). In Table 20, we cite the results of calculating the full morphological coefficient of natural drainage, both internal and external ($l/\omega = l_{\cup}/\omega + l_{\cap}/\omega$), for the lake–mire systems of the basin of the Northern Sos'va, the area between the rivers Vakh and Agan, the central part of the Surgut Polesie (the basins of the rivers Trom–Yugan, Pim and Lyamin, the northern half of the basin of the river Konda and the region of the Vasyugan'ye at the headwaters of the rivers Vasyugan, Parabel' and Chaya). Calculation of the morphological coefficients was based on a detailed interpretation of an aerial survey of lake–mire systems whose dimensions are specified in column 2 of Table 20. The processing was carried out by the usual method of interpreting and constructing flow-nets on aerial photographs, calculating the projected boundaries along the external margins of the lake–mire systems and along the internal fronts of drainage formed by endotelmic streams uniting lakes with channelled seepage and by lowered[2] endotelmic lakes. The data in Table 20 show that the external, internal and combined fronts of drainage of the lake–mire systems of the basin of the Konda and the basins of the

Table 20. Coefficients of complete, external and internal drainage of the lake–mire systems of the wooded-mire zone of the West Siberian plain

Physico-geographical region of mire systems	Total area of lake–mire systems studied (km²)	Relation of projected drainage to area of mire system (coefficient of drainage) km⁻¹				
		Combined coefficient of drainage l/ω	External drainage $l_\cap/\omega$	Internal drainage		
				Overall $l_\cup/\omega$	By internal rivers $l_{\cup r}/\omega$	By internal (lowered) lakes $l_{\cup lk}/\omega$
I Basin of northern Sos'va	339·2	0·70	0·58	0·12	0·08	0·04
II Region between the lower reaches of the Vakh and Agan	1992	0·53	0·17	0·36	0·23	0·13
III Region of central part of Surgut woodlands: basins of Rivers Trom-Yugan and Pim	6572	0·36	0·16	0·20	0·03	0·17
IV Basin of river Konda	6546	0·35	0·13	0·22	0·11	0·11
V Regions of Vasyugan'ye: the Ob'-Irtish watershed in the upper reaches of the Vasyugan, Parabel' and Chaya	7480	0·14	0·139	0·01	0·01	0·0

NOTE   All calculations were based upon the construction of flow-nets for lake–mire systems. They were verified on the ground by the West Siberian Expedition of the State Hydrological Institute (1964–69).

Surgut Polesie practically coincide; but as we move east to the basin of the Vakh the internal drainage of the systems increases, while the external drainage remains almost unchanged. As a result the combined coefficient of drainage grows by $1 \cdot 5((l_\cup + l_\cap)/\omega = 0.54)$. In the region of the Vasyugan'ye, the coefficient of internal drainage is almost zero, and the combined coefficient of drainage is equal to the coefficient of external drainage.

Let us now superimpose on the graphs of Figs 36–38 the values obtained for the combined coefficient of drainage. It is easy to see that the points indicated by the Roman numerals I, II, III, IV and V (Table 20) are almost all situated on the lower limit of the range of stability of lake–mire systems. For example, the value $l/\omega = l_\cap/\omega$ for the mire systems of Vasyugan'ye (see point V on the graph in Fig. 36) lies on the lower limit of the range of stability of mire systems with little or no area of lake. From this it is clear that for the existing lake–mire and mire systems of the West Siberian plain there is on the whole a large reserve of stability in respect of desiccation, which can be drawn on by an increase in their natural or artificial drainage. On the other hand, a relatively small increase in their wetness, or, what is the same, a decrease in the combined coefficient of drainage l/ω, will lead to a loss of stability and disintegration through excessive inundation.

Curve 1 (the upper limit of the stability of mire systems) shows that in the region of the Surgut Polesie (61–63°N) increases of drainage may reach as much as $l/\omega \approx 5 \, \text{km}^{-1}$ without risk of disintegration, while in the Vasyugan'ye region the greatest possible value is $2 \, \text{km}^{-1}$. In the latter region, the reserve of stability in regard to desiccation is generally speaking quite small, and necessarily involves an internal reconstruction of the system.

It must be remembered, however, that the values of l/ω and of the corresponding coefficients of water supply $\bar{p}_m/\bar{q}$, which we used in Figs 36–38 to calculate the limits of stability of lake–mire systems, are based on the equivalent values $\bar{p}_m$ and $\bar{q}$ (see equations (4.15), (4.16) and (4.16′)). Actual mire and lake–mire systems may incorporate different microtopes with values of $\bar{q}$ very different from the equivalent ones. For that reason, the actual range of stable states, which is delimited by the areas between curves 1 and 2, 3 and 4, 5 and 6, and so on, must be somewhat smaller. This entitles one to suppose that, when the value of l/ω approaches the curve that limits the area of stability, the states of the system can already be regarded as unstable.

The stability correlations presented in Figs 36–38 may be used directly to solve practical problems about the drainage and transformation of mirelands in different climatic zones. Indeed, if one knows the value of the natural coefficient of drainage l/ω for the system under review (e.g. $l/\omega = 1 \cdot 25$) and its situation (e.g. 60°N and 66°E), then by marking on the graph in Fig. 36 the corresponding point (A), one can determine directly the distance along the ordinate from A to Curve 1. It is plain that the magnitude represented by the segment AB and equal to 1.90 km^{-1} (according to the scale used for $(l_\cup + l_\cap)/\omega$) is the maximum value of the coefficient of supplementary internal drainage which can be achieved artificially by the building of a drainage network without risk of the disintegration of the mire system through desiccation. The development of an endotelmic drainage network producing the values $\Delta(l_\cup/\omega) > 1.90 \text{ km}^{-1}$ in a mire system located in the region under consideration (where its coefficient of natural drainage is 1.25) will lead to its rapid degradation. It will disturb the balance between the mean annual growth and decay of organic material, so as to raise the quantity of decaying material above the annual increment of biomass.

What has been said applies equally to the more general case, where the range of stability at every given ratio of the area of open water to that of plant cover is limited in the graphs of Figs 36–38 by curves 3 and 4, 5 and 6, etc. Here the only difference is that, when a mire system is being drained, it may pass through every stage in the gradual reduction of the total area of lake. Rapid lowering by artificial drainage of the level of endotelmic lakes, which were in a stable state and did not drain the system, may however lead to such a sharp increase in the internal drainage that it will disintegrate through desiccation, unless its structure changes.

We have now considered the conditions of stability of lake–mire and mire systems, making use for this purpose of the water balance criteria for lake–mire systems as a whole. In doing this, we endeavoured to find the physical limits within which mire microtopes and corresponding plant communities can exist without destroying the fundamental function of the system, which is peat accumulation. The maximum and minimum values of seepage were taken as these limits, because these are peculiar to the most saturated and least saturated of all the variety of mire microtopes encountered in natural conditions. Though seepage is a physical characteristic of the water conducting acrotelm of mire microtopes attributable to its plant communities, it is only an indirect indication of the limits of stability of these communities. Seepage by itself, as the quantity of water per unit of time flowing horizontally through a cross-section of the acrotelm of unit breadth, cannot be the immediate cause that determines the limits of the biological stability of the plant communities of mires. An increase in horizontal seepage leads to increased metabolism in the habitat of mire vegetation. It increases the quantity of dissolved nutrients fed to the root systems of plants, and, since the nutritional conditions of plants are thereby improved, there must also be an increase in the increment of plant material. Yet seepage must also be regarded as an indicator of other internal transformations taking place within the system, which directly affect the biological and mechanical stability of plant communities, and determine the limits within which they can exist. It is possible to show (Ivanov, 1975) that the seepage value $\bar{q} = 15 \text{ l. s}^{-1}. \text{ km}^{-1}$ corresponds approximately to a ratio of 9:1 between the surface of open water and that of the ridges in a ridge–pool complex (10% of the area of the microtopes is made up of ridges and 90% of open water surface). With this ratio and a slope in the surface of microtope along the flowline of $i_s \cong 0{\cdot}001$, the breadth of the ridges becomes very small, being at most 2–3 m. At this breadth the ridges prove mechanically unstable. Even the usual small reductions of water level in adjacent pools exert enough horizontal pressure on a ridge to deform and displace it. This leads in turn to the subsidence of ridges, the partial submersion of vegetation below the water table and its destruction through waterlogging. When there is also endotelmic erosion, as described in section 4.6, the horizontal pressure on ridges is increased and their destruction accelerated. Thus the accepted maximum value of seepage for a microtope acts in a given case as an indicator of a complex of characteristics determining the internal state of the system. A more detailed exposition of this question can be found elsewhere (Ivanov, 1970, 1972, 1975).

Conclusion

We have reviewed only a small part of a great problem—the role of mires as a component of our geophysical environment. The only questions touched on by us were concerned with the stability of these complex natural eco-systems in relation to artificial (man-made) or natural changes in their water regimes. It has been shown that with the help of what is known about the physical properties of mires as natural formations it is possible to predict the point at which changes in water regime will arrest the accumulation of organic matter and put an end to lake–mire and mire systems by progressive decay. It is a very different question whether this is a desirable process, and whether the rational use of land must involve irreversible processes leading to the destruction of mire systems and their replacement by other more highly valued types of land, or whether, on the contrary, measures should be taken to preserve them as, in many respects, a useful and valuable component of the environment. Probably there is no simple answer to this question. As a component of man's environment, mires have both a positive and a negative role, which depends upon what he needs to produce and how he has to live in different geophysical conditions. For that reason, decisions about the utilization of mires must be based upon a detailed evaluation of their role in this or that particular situation. Whatever role mires and mire microtopes may play in forming large or small ecosystems, it is important to consider in what measure mire systems can be useful to man in three principal ways: as a component of his environment, as a sphere of production, and as a useful natural resource.

It is now becoming increasingly obvious that there is little justification for regarding mire formations as elements of the natural environment that are bad for human life and activity, and must at all costs be transformed into lands and geotopic elements that are of greater utility to man. This question should be approached from a much wider scientific point of view and with a more liberal conception of man's economic needs.

It is here relevant to recall the principal ways in which mires are now being used, or may in future be used, as natural resources. They fall into three main categories.

(1) Ways of using mires that require the complete transformation of mire systems and the destruction of their fundamental function in geophysical processes, i.e. the arrest of peat accumulation in the areas they occupy and a complete transformation of the geotope, especially its conversion into agricultural land.

(2) Ways of using mires that involve the preservation of mire systems, either completely in their natural state, or with partial changes in their structure and plant associations, with the help of relatively mild technical measures aimed at making greater use of the natural produce of mires without disturbing their most valuable and important function—the accumulation of an organic material (peat) in the areas that they occupy.

(3) The use, or rather the preservation, of mires in their natural state as necessary components of the geophysical environment and the habitat of the human race, in order to maintain the equilibrium of the ecosystems in the biosphere, to maintain the quality of water supply and provide a good natural means of purifying water in the zone of excess moisture, to preserve hunting grounds, and, finally, to preserve and conserve mires as deposits of an organic material, whose future uses are still far from clear.

To the first category belong such uses of mires as peat production for industrial chemistry, for agriculture in the form of an organic fertilizer or cattle bedding, for various other needs, including the preparation of building material; the conversion of mires into agricultural land; the use of mires as sites for factories or houses, which is now attaining considerable proportions; the transformation of mires into forests by drainage.

To the second category belong all ways of using mires as plantations for producing useful wild plants and fruits—cranberries (*Vaccinium oxycoccus*), cloudberries (*Rubus chamaemorus*), crowberries (*Empetrum* spp.) and so on— and for the production of *Sphagnum* and other plants with valuable medicinal properties. It should be remarked that the value of mires in this respect is much underrated.

To the third category of use we must refer many functions performed by mires in geophysical processes which are important for the condition of man's environment (Aver'yanov, 1956), especially in water exchange and the preservation of the quality of water.

In this connection, the role of mires has not so far been adequately elucidated, although it is an established fact that mires, especially in the zone of excess moisture, are excellent natural filters. In them mechanical and biological pollutants are removed, and many elements are absorbed and retained by plants. Besides that, mires are an anti-erosional factor. Finally, account must be taken of the fact that mires are the habitat of many species and representatives of fauna, including many valuable species of migratory birds. Mire waters, being rich in humus, are also in many cases salubrious for man.

In deciding questions about the transformation and use of mirelands, account should be taken of the fact that mire systems are very diverse in their structure and properties, and in the functions they may perform in natural processes under different geophysical conditions. Whatever be the circumstances, however, the purposeful development of mirelands, their preservation and their transformation for specified objectives cannot be effected without appropriate calculations as to their future structure and estimates of how far they will retain their stability when exposed to this or that kind of interference. It is only in this way that one can plan controlled transformations and avoid the occurrence of unanticipated misfortunes as a result of destroying mire systems. In such activities, it should not be forgotten that in the present geological epoch mires are the only component of natural geotopes in which the accumulation of a valuable organic substance is taking place on a global scale upon the surface of the earth. That is why account should be taken of the fact that the area where this accumulation takes place is being diminished, whenever the exploitation of mires puts an end to this process.

It follows from this that natural resources will not be adequately conserved, nor land rationally utilized in any given case, unless it be taken for granted that the cessation of peat accumulation as a result of the exploitation of mires should not so exceed on a world scale the volume of organic matter that is annually accumulated as to lead to the gradual exhaustion of this resource. This should also be the guiding principle in determining the maximum area that is to be used in such a way as will bring to an end the accumulation of organic matter.

Appendix 1. Values of Modulus of Seepage and Coefficients of Filtration for Different Levels in the Acrotelm of Mire Microtopes

Group of microtopes: pine–*Sphagnum*–shrub

Levels z (cm)	With strongly-developed large-hummock microrelief[1] ($z_0 = 56$ cm, $\Delta y_{max} = 67$ cm, z from CSM)		With large-hummock microrelief[1] ($z_0 = 28$ cm, $\Delta y = 23$–34 cm, z from CSM)		With hummocky microrelief[2] ($z_0 = 36$ cm, $\Delta y = 24$ cm, z from CSM)	
	k_0 (cm/s)	A_z (cm²/s)	k_0 (cm/s)	M_z (cm²/s)	k_0 (cm/s)	M_z (cm²/s)
+20	151	11 480				
+16	86	6150				
+12	46	3120				
+8	27	1740				
+4	16	970	950	34 280		
0	10	580	86	2760		
−2	8·6	464	18·4	516		580
−4	7·3	382	10·7	278		233
−6	6·6	328	6·7	158	19·3	56
−8	5·6	267	4·6	101	8·3	44
−10	4·8	221	3·2	64	3·5	22
−12	4·1	182	2·1	37	1·85	13
−14	3·6	150	1·2	18	1·0	8·0
−16	3·0	121	0·61	8·0	0·66	5·4
−18	2·6	98	0·29	4·0	0·445	2·5
−20	2·2	80	0·20	1·8	0·34	1·4
−24	1·6	50	0·14	1·6	0·21	0·68
−28	1·0	29	0·04	0·20	0·175	0·0
−32	0·67	16	0·02	0·00	0·17	
−36	0·40	8·1				
−42	0·22	3·1				
−46	0·15	1·5				
−50	0·10	0·61				
−54	0·045	0·09				
−56	0·00	0·00				

Group of microtopes: *Sphagnum*–shrub–pine, *Sphagnum*–shrub and *Sphagnum*–shrub–*Eriophorum* forested with pine

Levels z (cm)	*Sphagnum*–shrub–pine ($z_0 = 60$ cm, $\Delta y_{max} = 50$ cm, z from CSM)		*Sphagnum*–shrub forested with pine ($z_0 = 48$ cm, $\Delta y_{max} = 50$ cm, z from CSM)		*Sphagnum*–shrub forested with pine ($z_0 = 32$ cm, $\Delta y_{max} = 20$ cm, z from CSM)		*Sphagnum*–shrub–*Eriophorum* sparsely forested with pine ($z_0 = 32$ cm, $\Delta y = 12$ cm, z from MSM)	
	k_0 (cm/s)	M_z (cm²/s)	k_0 (cm/s)	M_z (cm²/s)	k_0 (cm/s)	M_z (cm²/s)	k_0 (cm/s)	M_z (cm²/s)
+16	159	12 100						
+14	108	8 000						
+12	80	5 760	54	3 240				
+10	57	4 000	38	2 110				
+8	42	2 880	27	1 520	190	8 360		
+6	31	2 060	20	1 060	75	3 160	750	29 800
+4	22	1 380	15	800	40	1 580	245	9 280
+2	17	1 050	11	570	26	970	79	2 840
0	13	780	9.1	436	17	625	25	860
−2	11	640	6.7	308	13	440	8.1	258
−4	9.1	510	5.2	230	9.6	306	3.1	92
−6	7.4	397	4.1	174	7.4	220	1.93	54
−8	6.2	324	3.4	135	5.7	160	1.46	38
−10	5.3	263	2.7	104	4.2	110	1.12	27
−12	4.4	209	2.2	80	3.1	74	0.91	20
−14	3.7	171	1.86	63	2.5	56	0.75	15
−16	3.2	140	1.53	49	1.9	38	0.61	11
−20	2.35	94	1.00	28	1.44	26	0.52	8.3
−24	1.78	64	0.58	14	1.06	17	0.41	4.9
−28	1.34	43	0.33	6.6	0.49	5.9	0.31	2.5
−32	0.96	27	0.20	3.2	0.12	1.0	0.12	0.5
−36	0.62	15	0.12	1.5	0.05	0.2	0.00	0.0
−40	0.36	7.3	0.06	0.48	0.00	0.0		
−44	0.19	3.1	0.02	0.10				
−48	0.10	1.2	0.00	0.0				
−52	0.05	0.40						
−56	0.02	0.08						
−60	0.00	0.0						

Group of microtopes: sedge, *Sphagnum*-sedge, gramino-liceous

Levels z (cm)	Sedge with small-hummock microrelief ($z_0 = 32$ cm, $\Delta y = 6$ cm, z from MSM)		Sedge–*Sphagnum* forested with birch and pine with small-hummock microrelief ($z_0 = 32$ cm, $\Delta y = 9$ cm, z from MSM)		Unforested *Sphagnum*-sedge with even microrelief ($z_0 = 40$ cm, $\Delta y = 0$, z from MSM)	
	k_0 (cm/s)	M_z (cm²/s)	k_0 (cm/s)	M_z (cm²/s)	k_0 (cm/s)	M_z (cm²/s)
+20						
+16						
+12			3200	140 000		
+8			320	12 900		
+4			120	4480		
0	3100	>100 000	60	1920	35	1390
−2	116	3·00	43	1280	19	730
−4	0·79	22	34	940	12	440
−6	0·15	3·9	26	690	7·6	260
−8	0·05	1·2	20	472	4·7	152
−10	0·027	0·6	13	294	2·7	81
−12	0·015	0·3	8·6	173	1·2	34
−14	0·011	0·2	5·8	105	0·65	17
−16	0·011	0·2	4·2	68	0·35	8·5
−18	0·007	0·10	3·3	46	0·23	5·0
−20	0·006	0·07	2·5	30	0·15	3·0
−24	0·005	0·04	1·38	11	0·07	1·1
−28	0·002	0·01	0·50	2·0	0·04	0·48
−32	0·000	0·0	0·00	0·0	0·02	0·20
−36					0·02	0·80
−42					0·00	0·00
−46						
−50						
−54						
−56						
−60						

Levels z (cm)	Sphagnum–Eriophorum–sedge (including filiform sedge) with small-hummock relief (z = 32 cm, Δy = 26 cm, z from MSM)		Hypnum–sedge with small-hummock microrelief (z₀ = 60 cm, Δy = 25–30 cm, z from MSM)		Smallreed–birch with small-hummock microrelief and tree-stump protruberances (z₀ = 75 cm, z from MSM)	
	k_0 (cm/s)	M_z (cm²/s)	(k_0 (cm²/s))	M_z (cm²/s)	k_0 (cm/s)	M_z (cm²/s)
+20	2700	140 000				
+16	177	8490				
+12	78	3410	84	6000	35	3000
+8	42	1660	46	3160	19	1560
+4	21	740	10	670	4·4	345
0	10	330	1·66	100	0·33	25
−2	5·9	178	0·86	50	0·15	11
−4	2·9	81	0·39	22	0·10	7·0
−6	2·5	64	0·22	12	0·058	4·0
−8	1·34	32	0·15	8·0	0·030	2·0
−10	1·18	26	0·10	5·0	0·026	1·7
−12	0·85	17	0·08	4·1	0·024	1·5
−14	0·67	12	0·07	3·2	0·021	1·3
−16	0·46	7·4	0·05	2·7	0·020	1·2
−18	0·33	4·6	0·05	2·2	0·019	1·1
−20	0·24	2·9	0·05	1·9	0·019	1·1
−24	1·12	0·90	0·04	1·5	0·019	0·95
−28	0·05	0·20	0·04	1·2	0·018	0·85
−32	0·00	0·0	0·04	1·0	0·017	0·74
−36			0·04	0·9	0·017	0·68
−42			0·04	0·75	0·017	0·56
−46			0·05	0·50	0·017	0·42
−50			0·05	0·30	0·017	0·36
−54			0·05	0·20	0·017	0·33
−56			0·00	0·0	0·017	0·28
−60						

NOTE   The following symbols are used in this Appendix: y_{max}—maximum amplitude of the development of the microrelief; y—distance between mean levels of elevations and depressions of the microrelief; CSM—mean surface of microrelief; MSM—mean surface of microtope (see section 2.5); z_0—thickness of acrotelm; z—distance between the mean levels of its elevations and depressions.

Appendix 2. Calculation Table for Determining

Latitude in degree North	Water supply of mire microtopes P'_m (mm/year)	Coefficient of water supply of mire microtopes $Q_s = \bar{P}'_m/\bar{q}\,(\mathrm{km}^{-1})$		Water supply of endotelmic lakes P_{lk} (mm/yr)	Coefficient of water supply of lakes $Q_{lk} = \bar{P}_{lk}/\bar{q}\,(\mathrm{km}^{-1})$	
		When $\bar{q} =$ 1 l.s^{-1}.km^{-1}	When $\bar{q} =$ 15 l.s^{-1}.km^{-1}		When $\bar{q} =$ 1 l.s^{-1}.km^{-1}	When $\bar{q} =$ 15 l.s^{-1}.km
1	2	3	4	5	6	7
						Section along
65	90	2·84	0·189	65	2·05	0·136
64	105	3·32	0·221	52	1·64	0·109
63	125	3·95	0·263	55	1·74	0·116
62	133	4·46	0·297	58	1·82	0·121
61	138	4·11	0·273	50	1·58	0·106
60	90	2·84	0·189	−20	−0·63	−0·041
59	60	1·90	0·126	−60	−1·90	−0·126
58	20	0·63	0·042	−115	−3·63	−0·242
57	0	0	0	−1·60	−5·06	−0·334
						Section along
65	64	2·02	0·132	50	1·58	0·106
64	80	2·53	0·168	52	1·64	0·109
63	105	3·32	0·221	59	1·86	0·124
62	115	3·63	0·242	66	2·08	0·138
61	110	3·48	0·232	60	1·90	0·126
60	90	2·84	0·189	0	0	0
59	55	1·74	0·116	−30	−0·95	−0·063
58	35	1·11	0·072	−75	−2·37	0·158
57	10	0·316	0·074	−125	−3·95	−0·263
56	−35	−1·11	−0·072	−200	−6·32	−0·420
						Section along
65	60	1·90	0·126	40	1·26	0·084
64	70	2·12	0·147	45	1·42	0·094
63	100	3·16	0·216	50	1·58	0·106
62	110	3·48	0·232	60	1·90	0·126
61	130	4·11	0·273	55	1·74	0·116
60	120	3·79	0·252	40	1·26	0·084
59	110	3·48	0·232	0	0	0
58	105	3·32	0·221	−40	−1·26	−0·084
57	100	3·16	0·216	−75	−2·37	−0·158
56	105	3·32	0·221	−110	−3·48	−0·232
55	114	3·55	0·236	−120	−3·79	−0·251

Extreme maximum values of $(l_\cup + l_\cap)/\omega$ for different ratios $\omega_\Sigma^*/\omega_{\Sigma m}^*$, when $\bar{q} = 1\ \text{l.s}^{-1}.\text{km}^{-1}$					Extreme maximum values of $(l_\cup + l_\cap)/\omega$ for different ratios $\omega_\Sigma^*/\omega_{\Sigma m}^*$, when $\bar{q} = 15\ \text{l.s}^{-1}.\text{km}^{-1}$				
1	0·5	0·33	0·11	0·0	1	0·5	0·33	0·11	0·0
8	9	10	11	12	13	14	15	16	17
5°E Meridian									
2·44	2·57	2·64	2·76	2·84	0·162	0·172	0·176	0·184	0·19
2·48	2·76	2·90	3·15	3·32	0·165	0·184	0·202	0·210	0·22
2·84	3·22	3·40	3·72	3·95	0·190	0·214	0·226	0·248	0·26
3·14	3·59	3·80	4·20	4·46	0·209	0·239	0·253	0·279	0·29
2·84	3·28	3·48	3·85	4·11	0·190	0·218	0·231	0·256	0·2/
1·10	1·70	1·97	2·49	2·84	0·0735	0·113	0·131	0·166	0·19
0·0	0·65	0·95	1·52	1·90	0·0	0·0428	0·063	0·100	0·13
−1·50	−0·78	−0·44	0·20	0·63	−0 1	−0·0517	−0·029	0·0136	0·04
−2·53	−1·67	−1·26	−0·51	0·00	−0·167	−0·11	−0·0835	−0·0334	0·00
8°E Meridian									
1·80	1·88	1·91	1·98	2·02	0·119	0·123	0·126	0·129	0·132
2·08	2·24	2·31	2·44	2·53	0·138	0·148	0·153	0·162	0·168
2·59	2·84	2·96	3·07	3·32	0·172	0·189	0·197	0·211	0·221
2·86	3·12	3·24	3·48	2·63	0·190	0·210	0·216	0·232	0·242
2·69	2·96	3·08	3·32	3·48	0·179	0·197	0·206	0·221	0·232
1·42	1·90	2·13	2·56	2·84	0·0945	0·127	0·142	0·170	0·189
0·40	0·85	1·07	1·47	1·74	0·0265	0·0569	0·0662	0·0981	0·116
−0·63	−0·04	−0·24	0·76	1·11	−0·043	−0·0039	0·0145	0·089	0·072
−1·82	−1·09	−0·75	−0·11	0·316	−0·120	−0·0707	−0·0478	−0·0047	0·024
−0·87	−2·83	−2·41	−1·63	−1·11	−0·057	−0·0621	−0·0645	−0·107	−0·072
4°E Meridian									
1·58	1·69	1·74	1·84	1·90	0·105	0·112	0·116	0·122	0·126
1·78	1·89	1·94	2·05	2·12	0·120	0·130	0·134	0·142	0·147
2·37	2·64	2·76	3·00	3·16	0·161	0·180	0·188	0·205	0·216
2·88	2·96	3·08	3·32	3·48	0·179	0·197	0·205	0·221	0·232
2·92	3·33	3·52	3·87	4·11	0·194	0·221	0·234	0·257	0·273
2·52	2·96	3·16	3·54	3·79	0·168	0·196	0·210	0·235	0·252
1·74	2·33	2·61	3·13	3·48	0·116	0·155	0·174	0·209	0·232
1·03	1·81	2·18	2·86	3·32	0·0685	0·120	0·145	0·190	0·221
0·40	1·34	1·78	2·61	3·16	0·029	0·0926	0·122	0·179	0·216
−0·08	1·08	1·62	2·64	3·32	−0·0055	0·0725	0·108	0·176	0·221
−0·12	1·13	1·72	2·82	3·55	−0·0075	0·0753	0·114	0·187	0·236

Notes

Author's Introduction and Chapter 1, pages xxv–43

1. The author uses the Russian word "landshaft" to mean a limited part of the earth's surface with a distinctive morphology, climate, plant cover and water supply, and adds the prefixes "makro-", "mezo-" and "micro-" to indicate gradations of size. In this work, "landshaft" is translated by the word "geotope" from the Greek words γῆ (earth) and τόπος (place). Gradations in geotopic size are indicated without undue clumsiness by the use of the terms "macrotope", "mesotope" and "microtope". The word "landscape" has been avoided, because it is in origin an artistic, not a geographical term, and has not the same wide range of cognate forms as the Russian word "landshaft". (T)

2. Much thicker mantles of peat are found in blanket mires. These develop on sloping substrates under extremely oceanic, cool-temperate climates, for instance along the north-western seaboard of Europe. (T)

3. The solution that follows seems to have been first suggested by A. Colding in 1873. It is perhaps the best known instance in which the Dupuit-Forchheimer approximation has been used to solve a problem in groundwater flow without recourse to the Laplace equation (Childs, 1969). (T)

4. By the seepage or intensity of water exchange in a mire we understand the total quantity of water flowing per unit of time through a volume of peat 1 m^2 in area and equal in height to the depth of the peat deposit in that part of the mire massif.

5. The determination and calculation of the position of the mean surface of mires is considered in section 2.5.

6. The terms "acrotelm" and "catotelm" are used to denote what Ivanov calls the active and inactive horizons of mires. They are derived from the Greek words ἄκρος (topmost), κάτω (below) and τέλμα (marsh) (Ingram, 1978). (T)

7. Mire localities (*urochishcha*) or mesotopes and mire macrotopes.

8. In modern conditions, shallow areas in artificial reservoirs in river systems may also serve as the originating centres of mire formation.

9. Western telmatologists call them "lagg fens" or "marginal water tracks". (T)

10. By the index of dryness R_x is understood the ratio of the average total radiation to the average amount of heat expended on evaporating the annual norm of precipitation. (This is described by Budyko (1974, p. 322) as "the radiative index of dryness".—T)

11. These two different types of mire are described hereafter as "oligo-central" and "oligoperipheral". (T)

12. We cannot accept the view of certain scientists (Bradis, 1963) that mire vegetation (mire phytocoenoses) may only be classified in two ways. One school (G. I. Tanfil'yev, V. S. Dokturovskiy, V. N. Sukachev, P. I. Abolin, S. N. Tyuremkov, etc.) bases its classification of the phytocoenoses of mires upon the different ecological demands they make upon their environment, making a distinction between fenland, transitional and raised-mire vegetation in respect of the nutritional value of their environment. The other school (Yu. D. Tsinzerling, D. K. Zerov, I. D. Bogdanovskaya) takes plant life-forms as its basis of classification, distinguishing them into ligneous, graminoid, muscoid and other such categories. These two approaches to the classification of mires touch only upon certain aspects of these complex natural formations. The first approach focuses attention first of all upon the differences between the habitats of plants, as determined by the geomorphological conditions of the mire, the stages of its development and, in consequence, the mineral content of its water supply. The second approach, which classifies plants according to their biological nature, is not so much a classification of mires as of mire facies, i.e. of the elementary physico-geographical units which form some particular mire, for any particular mire massif may contain different facies with plants that differ in their life-form. This fact is clearly reflected in the classification of microtopes (Table 2), where variations in the mineral content of the water supply of the vegetation are tabulated lengthwise, and differences in the life-forms of the plants that make up different sorts of microtope are tabulated crosswise. (The implication of this footnote is that, in addition to the two systems of mire classification advocated by the rival schools of thought recognized by Bradis, there exists a third and superior system, namely the one used in this book, in which the other two systems are combined.—T)

13. The Russian method of analysing layered plant communities differs from that generally adopted in the west, in that it involves a wider interpretation of the term "dominant". It recognizes a dominant or chief species in each layer (the field layer, the shrub layer, the tree layer etc.). The term "edificator", from the Latin word "aedificator" meaning "builder", was introduced by J. Pavillard and J. Braun-Blanquet, and is used in Russian works for the species that determines the structure of the entire plant community. In a woodland, for example, this would normally be the dominant of

the tree layer. For further information, see Lavrenko (1947) and Aleksandrova (1978, p. 186–7). (T)

14. The noun *trava*, commonly translated "grass", is applied strictly to all plants with annual shoots that do not become woody. In the context of vegetation we have therefore rendered the adjective *travyanoy* as either "graminoid" (of grasses, sedges or rushes) or "herb-rich" (of herbose plant communities) depending on the context. (T)

15. *Flark* is a Swedish word which has exactly the same connotation as the Russian *mochazhina*, which means an elongated depression or furrow lying between the ridges of a mire. Flarks are often transformed by inundation into elongated pools. The author often calls these pools "lakes" (*ozyora*) or "lakelets" (*ozerki*), but in this context we have translated these words as "pools". (T)

16. Sectors in which the plant cover perishes and peat accumulation ceases because of the oversaturation of the peat deposit and the continuously high level of the water.

Chapter 2, pages 45–119

1. In Russian, as in English, there are many nouns to denote the passage of water through the soil, some indicating the process itself and others the capacity or disposition of the soil to transmit water in this way. The commonest of these nouns are *vodoprovodimost'* (hydraulic conductivity), *vlagoprovodimost'* (moisture conductivity), *pronitsayemost'* (permeability), *fil'tratsiya* (filtration) and *protochnost'* (seepage). (T)

2. The author's use of Cyrillic letters has obliged the translators to make changes in the writing, but not in the meaning of most of his equations. In this case however, not to avoid a confusion between Cyrillic and Roman letters, but between two different usages of the Greek letter Δ. Φ is here substituted for Δ, because Δ is also the letter used to symbolize a finite difference in some parameter, as in Δz. (T)

3. The coefficient of total porosity differs from the coefficient of active porosity, which is the ratio of the volume of the voids created by removing all moisture not bound to the peat matrix to the total volume occupied by the peat.

4. Here the author uses the symbol "w_T" for the weight/volume ratio of solid-phase peat, but he later uses it for the dead weight of the peat matrix. We have avoided this confusion by using "$_v G_{pm}$" in the first case and "G_{pm}" in the second. (T)

4a. The derivation of this expression is not explained. It appears to be adapted to a particular laboratory procedure for S_a, in which the units of Q are $cm^3 \ min^{-1}$, and is presumably derived from the basic Kozeny-Carman equation (see Marshall and Holmes (1979, p. 85)), by substituting appropriate values for Kozeny's constant, for the acceleration due to gravity and for the density and viscosity of water which depend on the temperature used. (T)

5. 1 poise $= 1 \, \text{gm cm}^{-1} \, \text{s}^{-1} = 1 \, \text{dyne s cm}^{-2}$.

6. This term has recently been proposed by Vorob'ev (1966). (Masing (1972) has proposed the term "mire microform" for what Ivanov calls "elements of microrelief" like hummocks, flarks and pool.—T)

6a. In (2.32) $\bar{\mathbf{i}}_1, \bar{\mathbf{i}}_2, \bar{\mathbf{i}}_3$ are unit vectors in the three mutually perpendicular directions of a Cartesian system of coordinates. (T)

6b. Grad Φ is dimensionless, but the dimensions of γh are those of pressure. (2.35) is therefore not dimensionally homogeneous. This causes further difficulty in (2.37), from which the dimensions of k are apparently not LT^{-1}, as demanded by convention, by Table 6 and by the author's subsequent use of this parameter. (T)

6c. It is usual to write expressions for Darcy's law with a minus sign on the right. This indicates a flux in the direction of diminishing potential and would seem to accord better with (2.33) and (2.35). Since the value of k is unaffected and the direction of flow is not normally in doubt in a one-dimensional analysis this departure from convention is unlikely to cause difficulty in simple systems. (T)

7. The accepted definition of the water table is that surface at which the water in the pores assumes atmospheric pressure, and this is the definition which the author generally uses. Owing to matric forces there is generally a zone above the water table in which the pores remain saturated, although they contain water at less than atmospheric pressure. This zone is known as the "capillary fringe". *Ceteris paribus*, its depth is greater in soils of finer grain. (T)

8. Figure 17 depicts the second case. Note that while fluxes are reckoned negative downwards, distances measured downwards from the line *Os* are here reckoned positive, both in accordance with equation (2.45). This sign convention for the flux $\mathbf{q}_y$ also accords with formulations of the water balance in equations (2.62) and (2.63), since an upward flux (positive) is recharged into the mire, while a downward (negative) flux would be a discharge from it. We are grateful to the author for clarifying this matter. (T)

9. In many types of mire microtopes, especially those of the herb-and-tree group, when water levels are high (in spring and in the rains of the late-summer, early-autumn period), it is normal for water levels to rise higher than the average surface of the microrelief. In consequence water movement at these periods is partly effected by surface current (*potok*). See equation (2.49) in Section 2.8.

10. The Russian words expressing this contrast are *liniya stekaniya* (line of flow) and *liniya toka* (line of current or streamline). The translator has tried to adhere to it throughout. (T)

11. Practical methods of interpreting aerial photographs of mires and the clues for different types of mire microtopes are set forth in textbooks (Kudritskiy, Popov and Romanova 1956, Anon. 1971c). The fundamental principles of hydrological calculations with the use of typological plans (or aerial photographs) of mires and flow-nets are explained elsewhere (Ivanov 1953a, 1957b, 1963).

12. Until this point the translator has used the letters W and w invariably and exclusively in terms denoting water, and the letters P and p invariably and exclusively in terms denoting peat. From this point onward, however, the author uses P and p for terms denoting internal water exchange and Q and q for terms denoting external water exchange. As the notation is clear and consistent, the translator has adhered to it in the hope that it will simplify the typography and avoid confusion. Those who would like to adhere to the earlier notation can do so by writing $_pW$ and $_qW$ for P and Q, and $_pw$ and $_qw$ for p and q. (T)

13. The word "placodic" is used to translate the Russian adjective *plakornyy*, which is here used as a technical term to describe the sort of vegetation that is characteristic of flat places. Visotskiy introduced the term "plakor", from the Greek words πλᾱξ meaning "something flat" and ὄσος meaning "mountain", to denote what we call an elevated plain or plateau. As Russian botanists use the adjective *plakornyy* of any flat water divide, this usage is not etymologically justifiable. It seems better therefore to eliminate the word ὄρος from the etymology of the words we use to describe such regions, and include in them the neutral word τόπος (place). The resulting terms are "placotopic" and "placodic", and what Visotskiy termed a "plakor" can be described as an elevated placotope. (T)

14. Gauss's Theorem is as follows: "Let the closed surface S enclose the volume P, and let X be a scalar or vector function of position, then, if dr is an element of the volume V, and dS an element of the surface S,

$$\int_{(P)} (\overline{V}) \, X \, \mathrm{d}r = - \int_{(S)} \mathbf{n} X \, \mathrm{d}S,$$

where $\mathbf{n}$ is a unit vector in the direction of the normal to dS drawn into the *interior* of the region enclosed by S." (C. F. Gauss, "Theoria attractionis", *Comm. soc. reg. Gott.*, Vol. II, Goettingen, 1813.) The above is quoted from Milne-Thomson (1968, p. 54). The author applies the theorem here to the relation of lines to areas, but it was originally applied to the relation of areas to volumes. (T)

15. Losses of moisture from the peat deposit into subjacent mineral strata located at separate points under the mire massif can hardly be taken seriously in view of the actual causes and original conditions that give rise to the process of mire formation.

16. The term "horizontal runoff" (*gorizontal'nyy stok*) is used to mean the quantity of external water exchange, i.e. the volume of water which flows from a mire massif to anywhere beyond its boundaries.

17. More precisely, what is taken as the horizontal axis is a projection of the streamline onto the horizontal plane, which we referred to earlier as the flowline (*liniya stekaniya*).

Chapter 3, pages 141–176

1. In the case of large mires and catchments, there may be a difference between the amount of moisture precipitated upon the part that consists of mire and the part that does not, but the network of gauges is not usually sufficiently close to enable one to take account of this difference.

2. It is not easy to decide what we should mean by a "sufficiently long" period of time. Generally speaking, the question is connected with the problem of the stability of endotelmic lakes in relation to the long (multi-annual) cycles to which periodic fluctuations of humidity are subject. For the present, we shall understand by average values the average multi-annual quantities for a period comprising several multi annual cycles of such fluctuations of humidity, or, in the extreme case, the average of these quantities (without considering the general direction of climatic changes).

Chapter 4, pages 228–238

1. In general this applies not only to differences in atmospheric water supply, but to differences between the internal water supply of lakes and that of mire microtopes.

2. For an account of lakes lowered as a result of the step-like erosion of endotelmic streams and rivulets, see section 4.6 and Ivanov (1969).

Bibliography

Aleksandrova, V. F. (1978). Russian approaches to classification. *In* "Classification of Plant Communities" (R. H. Whittaker, ed.), pp. 167–200. W. Junk, The Hague.

Allison, R. V. (1956). The influence of drainage and cultivation on subsidence of organic soils under conditions of Everglades reclamation. *Proc. Soil Crop Sci. Soc. Fla.* **16**, 21–31.

Anon. (1957). "Torfyanye mestorozhdeniya Zapadnoy Sibiri" (Peat deposits of Western Siberia). Glav. Uprav. torf. Fonda RSFSR i mosk. torf. Univ., Moscow.

Anon. (1971a). "Kolichestvennye metody analiza rastitel'nosti. Sbornik materialov tret'ego vsesoyuznogo Soveshchaniya 'Primenenie kolichestvennykh metodov pri izuchenii struktury rastitel'nosti'" (Quantitative methods of analysing vegetation. A collection of materials of the 3rd all-union Conference 'The application of quantitative methods to the study of the structure of vegetation'). Riga.

Anon. (1971b). "Topologiya geosistem—71. Resolyutsii simpoziuma, Irkutsk, 1971" (The topology of geosystems—71. Resolutions of the symposium, Irkutsk, 1971). Inst. geogr. Sibiri i Dal'nego Vostoka, Irkutsk.

Anon. (1971c). "Ukazaniya po raschetam stoka s neosushennykh i osushennykh verkhovykh bolot" (Directions for computing the runoff from undrained and drained raised mires). Gidrometeoizdat, Leningrad.

Anon. (1972a), "Metodicheskie ukazaniya po gidrologicheskim raschetam pri proektirovanii osushitel'no avtozhitel'nykh sistem Poles'ya. Chast' 1. Raschety po rezhimu pochvennoy vlagi pri osushenii bolot (Directions for hydrological calculations in planning the drainage and irrigation systems of the Polesie. Part 1. Calculations relating to soil moisture regime during the drainage of mires). Minsk.

Anon. (1972b). "Ukazaniya po opredeleniyu raschetnykh gidrologicheskikh kharakteristik, Stroitel'nye normy 435–72. Gosstroy" (Directions for determining computed hydrological characteristics, Building Standards 435–72. Gosstroy). Gidrometeoizdat, Leningrad.

Ashby, W. R. (1959). "An Introduction to Cybernetics". Chapman and Hall, London.

Aver'yanov, S. F. (1956). Fil'tratsiya iz kanalov i ee vliyanie na rezhim gruntovykh vod (Filtration from canals and its influence on groundwater regime). *In* "Vliyanie orositel'nykh sistem na rezhim gruntovykh vod", pp. 87–447. Izdat. Akad. Nauk SSSR, Moscow.

Babikov, B. V. (1970a). Stok i isparenie s osushennykh lesnykh bolot (Runoff and evaporation from drained forest mires). *Nauch. Trudy leningrad. lesotekh. Akad.* **142**, 28–39.

Babikov, B. V. (1970b). Vliyanie osushitel'noy seti na uroven' pochvenno-gruntovykh vod lesnykh bolot (The influence of a drainage system on the water table in the soil of forest mires). *Nauch. Trudy leningrad. lesotekh. Akad.* **142**, 56–64.

Babikov, B. V. (1970c). Kul'tura sosny obyknovennoy na osushennykh bolotakh Leningradskoy oblasti (Cultivation of the common pine on drained mires in the Leningrad region). *Nauch. Trudy leningrad. lesotekh. Akad.* **142**, 80–91.

Baden, W. and Eggelsmann, R. (1963). Zur Durchlässigheit der Moorboden. *Z. KultTech. Flurberein.* **4**, 226–254.

Bavina, L. G. (1967). Utochnenie raschetnykh parametrov ispareniya s bolot po materialam nablyudeniy bolotnykh stantsiy. *Trudy gos. gidrol. Inst.* **145**, 69–77; Refinement of parameters for calculating evaporation from bogs on the basis of observations at bog stations. *Sov. Hydrol.* (1967), 348–370.

Bavina, L. G. and Romanov, V. V. (1969). Isparenie s bolot bolotno-taezhnoy zony Zapadnoy Sibiri (Evaporation from mires in the taiga zone of Western Siberia). *Trudy gos. gidrol. Inst.* **157**, 66–77.

Bellamy, D. J. (1970). An ecological approach to the classification of European mires. *Proc. 3rd int. peat Congr.* (1968) 74–79.

Belousova, N. A. (1971). Geomorfologiya i rastitel'nost' bolot yuzhnoy chasti Onezhko-Belomorskogo vodozrazdela (The geomorphology and vegetation of the mires of the southern part of the Onega-White Sea watershed). *In* "Bolota Karelii i puti ikh osvoeniya", pp. 37–50. Petrozavodsk.

Bick, W., Robertson, R. A., Schneider, R. and Schneider, S. (1973). "Fachwörterbuch Moor und Torf Deutsch–Englisch–Russisch". Torfforschung, Bad Zwischenahn.

Bick, W., Robertson, A., Schneider, R., Schneider, S. and Ilnicki, P. (1976). "Słownik torfoznawczy niemiecko-polsko-angielsko-rosyjski". Państwowe wydawnictwo rolnicze i lesne, Warsaw.

Boch, M. S. (1972). O primenenii indikatsionnykh svoystv rastitel'nosti bolot pri ustanovlenii tipa pitaniya (The use of the indicatory properties of mire vegetation to determine the nature of the water supply). *In* "Osnovnye printsipi izucheniya bolotnykh biogeotsenozov," pp. 39–54. Nauka, Leningrad.

Boelter, D. H. (1964). Water storage characteristics of several peats in situ. *Proc. Soil Sci. Soc. Am.* **28**, 433–435.

Boelter, D. H. (1965). Hydraulic conductivity of peats. *Soil Sci.* **100**, 227–231.

Boelter, D. H. and Verry, E. S. (1977). Peatland and water in the northern Lake States. *For. Serv. gen. tech. Rep. U.S. Dep. Agric.* **NC-31**.

Bogdanovskaya-Gienef, I. D. (1963). "Zakonomernosti formirovaniya sfagnovykh bolot verkhovogo tipa na primere Polisto-Lovatskogo massiva" (The principles governing for formation of sphagnum bogs as exemplified by the Pola-Lovat' massif). Nauka, Leningrad.

Bradis, E. A. (1963). Prinpsipi i osnovnye edinitsy klassifikatsii bolotnoy rastitel'nosti" (Principles and fundamental units involved in the classification of mire vegetation). *Uchen. Zap. tartu. gos. Univ.* **7** (145), 9–20.

Braslavskiy, A. P. and Vikulina, Z. A. (1954). "Normy ispareniya s poverkhnosti vodokhranilishch pod redaktsiei A. I. Chebotarev" (Norms of evaporation from the surface of reservoirs (A. I. Chebotarev, ed.). Gidrometeoizdat, Leningrad.

Budyko, M. I. (1971). Energetika biofery i ee preobrazovaniya pod vozdeystviem cheloveka (The energy of the biosphere and transformations of it by human action). *Izv. Akad. Nauk SSSR, Ser. geogr.* **1**, 14–20.

Budyko, M. I. (1974). "Climate and Life" (trans. from Russian; D. H. Miller, ed.). Academic Press, New York.

Bulavko, A. G. (1971). "Vodnyy balans rechnykh vodosborov" (The water balance of river catchments). Gidrometeoizdat, Leningrad.

Buss, K. and Buss, H. (1971). Biologisko objektu klassifikacija ar komponent-analisi. *Jaunākais mežsaimniecībā*, Riga **13**, 3–5.

Byurig, R. F. and Kalyuzhnaya, I. I. (1965). Isparenie s sel'skokhozaystvennykh poley na osushennykh bolotakh Ukrainskoy SSR (Evaporation from farmlands on drained mires in the Ukrainian Soviet Socialist Republic). *Trudy gos. gidrol. Inst.* **126**, 132–152.

Childs, E. C. (1969). "An Introduction to the Physical Principles of Soil Water Phenomena". John Wiley, London.

Churaev, N. V. (1960). Metody issledovaniya vodnykh svoystv i struktury torfa s pomoshch'yu radioaktivnykh indikatorov (Methods of investigating the hydraulic properties and structure of peat by radioactive tracers). *In* "Novye fizikicheskie metody issledovaniya torfa", pp. 125–137. Gosenergoizdat, Moscow and Leningrad.

Churaev, N. V. (1963). Vliyanie strukturoobrazovatel'nykh protsessov na fil'tratsiyu vody v dispersnykh sistemakh (The influence of structure-forming processes on the filtration of water in dispersal systems). *Kolloid. Zh.* **25** (6), 718–721. *Chem. Abstr.* 1964 **60** 6247h.

Davydov, P. I. and Pisar'kov, Kh. A. (1970). Normy osusheniya (Drainage standards). *Nauch. Trudy leningrad. lesotekh. Akad.* **142**, 65–72.

Dittrich, J. (1952). Zur natürlichen Entwässerung der Moore. *Wass. Boden.* **4** (9), 286–288.

Dubakh, A. D. (1936). "Ocherki po gidrologii bolot" (Outlines of the hydrology of mires). Rechizdat, Moscow.

Dubakh, A. D. (1940). Gruntovaya voda v torfyanom bolote (Ground water in a peat mire). *Uchen. Zap. leningrad. gos. Univ., Ser. geogr.* **50** (2), 58–66.

Dubakh, A. D. (1944). "Gidrologiya bolot" (The hydrology of mires). Gidrometeoizdat, Sverdlovsk and Moscow.

Dubrovina, L. N. (1974). Raschet ispareniya s verkhovykh bolotnykh massivov Zapadno-Sibirskoy ravniny (Computation of evaporation from the raised-mire massifs of the West Siberian plain). *Uchen. Zap. leningrad. gos. Univ.* **376** (23), 82–89.

Dzektser, E. S. (1959). K opredeleniyu v polevykh usloviyakh koeffitsienta fil'tratsii torfyanoy zalezhi (Determining the coefficient of filtration of a peat deposit under field conditions). *Torf. Prom.* **1**, 27–30.

Eggelmann, R, (1978). "Subsurface Drainage Instructions". Parey, Hamburg.

Elina, G. A. (1971). Tipy bolot Pribelomorskoy nizmennosti (Types of mire in the low country of the White Sea). *In* "Bolota Karelii i puti ikh osvoeniya", pp. 51–79, Petrozavodsk. (cf. Elina, G. A. (1972). Types of swamps in Northern Karelia, USSR, *Proc. 4th int. peat Congr.* **1**, 59–74.)

Federova, R. V. (1971). Torfyanye bolota poluostrova Kanin (Peat mires of the Kanin penisula). *In* "Bolota Karelii i puti ikh osvoeniya", pp. 177–187. Petrozavodsk.

Ferda, J. and Pasák, V. (1969). "Hydrologic and Climatic Function of Czechoslovak Peat Bogs" (Czech with English summary). Výzkumný ústav melioraci, Zbraslav.

Galkina, E. A. (1946). Bolotnye landshafty i printsipy ikh klassifikatsii (Mire geotopes and the principles of their classification). *In* "Sbornik Rab. bot. Inst. V. L. Komarova Akad. Nauk SSSR.", pp. 139–156, Leningrad. (cf. Galkina, E. A. (1972). On bog territorial units. *Proc. 4th int. peat Congr.* **1**, 19–26.)

Galkina, E. A. (1959). Bolotnye landshafty Karelii i printsipy ikh klassifikatsii (The mire geotopes of Karelia and the principles of their classification). *Trudy karel. Fil. Akad. Nauk SSSR.* **15**, 3–48.

Galkina, E. A. (1963). Cherty skhodstva i otlichiya mezhdu klassifikatsiey torfyanykh mestorozhdeniy i klassifikatsiey bolotnykh urochishch (Resemblances and differences between the classification of the sites of peat deposits and that of mire localities). *Uchen. Zap. tartu. gos. Univ.* **7**(145), 35–46.

Galkina, E. A. (1964). Metody ispol'zovaniya aerofotosnimkov dlya tipizatsii i kartirovaniya bolotnykh massivov (Methods of classifying and mapping mire massifs by means of air photographs). *Uchen. Zap. pertrozavod. Univ.* **12** (2), 5–24.

Galkina, E. A., Gilev, S. G., Ivanov, K. E. and Romanova, E. A. (1949). Primenenie materialov aerofotos'emki dlya gidrograficheskogo izucheniya bolot (The use of air-survey materials for studying the hydrographic properties of mires). *Trudy gos. gidrol. Inst.* **13**(67), 5–25.

Galvin, L. F. and Hanrahan, E. T. (1967). Steady state drainage flow in peat. *Highw. Res. Rec.* **203**, 77–90.

Gerasimov, I. P. (1971). Chelovek i sreda. Sovremennye aspekty problemy (Man and the environment. Modern aspects of the problem). *Izv. Akad. Nauk SSSR. Ser. geogr.* **1**, 5–14.

Göttlich, K. (ed.) (1976). "Moor- und Torfkunde". Schweizerbart'sche, Stuttgart.

Hammond, R. F. (1975). The origin, formation and distribution of peatland resources. *In* "Peat in Horticulture" (D. W. Robinson and J. G. D. Lamb, eds), pp. 1–22. Academic Press, London.

Heikurainen, L., Päivänen, J. and Sarasto, J. (1964). Groundwater table and water content in peat soil. *Acta for. fenn.* **77**(1), 1–18.

Heinselman, M. L. (1963). Forest sites, bog processes and peatland types in the glacial Lake Agassiz region, Minnesota. *Ecol. Monogr.* **33**, 327–374.

Heinselman, M. L. (1970). Landscape evolution, peatland types and the environment in the Lake Agassiz Peatlands Natural Area, Minnesota. *Ecol. Monogr.* **40**, 235–261.

Holstener-Jorgensen, H. (1966). Influence of forest management and drainage on groundwater fluctuations. *In* "International Symposium on Forest Hydrology" (W. E. Sopper and N. T. Lull, eds.), pp. 325–333, Pergamon Press, Oxford.

Ingram, H. A. P. (1967). Problems of hydrology and plant distribution in mires. *J. Ecol.* **55**, 711–724.

Ingram, H. A. P. (1978). Soil layers in mires: function and terminology. *J. soil Sci.* **29**, 224–227.

Ingram, H. A. P. (in press). Hydrology. *In* "Swamp, Bog, Fen and Moor" (A. J. P. Gore, ed.). Elsevier, Amsterdam.

Ivanov, K. E. (1948). O fil'tratsii v poverkhnostnom sloe vypuklikh bolotnykh massivov (Filtration in the top layer of convex mire massifs). *Meteorol. i Gidrol.* (2), 46–59.

Ivanov, K. E. (1953a). "Gidrologiya bolot" (The hydrology of mires). Gidrometeoizdat, Leningrad.

Ivanov, K. E. (1953b). Issledovaniya vodoprovodimosti verkhnykh gorizontov bolotnykh massivov (Researches into the hydraulic conductivity of the upper levels of mire massifs). *Trudy gos. gidrol. Inst.* **39**, 50–59.

Ivanov, K. E. (1953c). Teoreticheskoe i eksperimental'noe obosnovanie metoda rascheta elementov vodnogo balansa bolotnykh massivov (The theoretical and experimental basis of a method of computing the water balance of mire massifs). *Trudy gos. gidrol. Inst.* **39**(93), 5–49.

Ivanov, K. E. (1957a). Organizatsiya punktov nablyudeniy nad urovnyami bolotnykh gruntovykh vod na gidrometeostantsiyakh (The organization of points from which to observe mire groundwater levels in hydrometeorological stations). *In* "Metodicheskie ukazaniya upravleniyam Gidrometsluzhby", No. 46, Leningrad.

Ivanov, K. E. (1957b). "Osnovy gidrologii bolot lesnoy zony i raschety vodnogo rezhima bolotnykh massivov" (Elements of the hydrology of forest-zone mires and calculations relating to the water regime of mire massifs). Gidrometeoizdat, Leningrad.

Ivanov, K. E. (1960). Voprosy dvizheniya vody v osushennykh torfyanykh zalezhakh i prichini ikh pereuvlazheniya (Questions concerning the movement of water in drained peat deposits and the causes of their over-saturation). *Trudy gos. gidrol. Inst.* **89**, 37–91.

Ivanov, K. E. (ed.) (1963). "Gidrologicheskie raschety pri osushenii bolot i zabolochennykh zemel'" (Hydrological calculations relating to the drainage of mires and swamps). Gidrometeoizdat, Leningrad.

Ivanov, K. E. (1965). Osnovy teorii morfologii bolot i gidromorfologicheskie zavisimosti. *Trudy gos. gidrol. Inst.* **126**, 5–47; Fundamentals of the theory of swamp morphology and hydromorphological relationships. *Sov. Hydrol.* (1965), 224–258.

Ivanov, K. E. (1969). Erozionnye yavleniya na bolotakh i ikh rol' v formirovanii ozero-bolotnykh landshaftov Zapadnoy Sibiri (Erosion phenomena in mires and their role in the formation of the lake-mire geotopes of Western Siberia). *Trudy gos. gidrol. Inst.* **157**, 78–97.

Ivanov, K. E. (1970). Nekotorye voprosy issledovaniya vzaimosvyasey rastitel'nykh soobshchestv i gidrologicheskogo rezhima zabolochennykh zemel' (Certain questions concerning research into the mutual relations between plant communities and the hydrological regime of swamps). *In* "Gidrolesomeliorativnye issledovaniya", pp. 129–145, Zinatne, Riga.

Ivanov, K. E. (1972). O torfonakoplenii i obrazovanii bolot kak fiziko-geograficheskom protsesse (Peat accumulation and mire formation as a physico-geographic process). *Vest. leningrad. gos. Univ., Ser. geol. i geogr.* **4**(24), 103–113.

Ivanov, K. E. (1974). Bolotnye-ozernye sistemy i ikh ustoychivost' pri preobrazovanii izbytochno-uvlazhennykh territoriy (Lake-mire systems and their stability during the reclamation of waterlogged areas). *Uchen. Zap. leningrad. gos. Univ.* **376**(23), 5–81.

Ivanov, K. E. (1975). Hydrological criteria of stability and reconstruction of bogs and bog/lake systems. *In* "Hydrology of marsh-ridden areas" Proc. Minsk Symp. (1972), pp. 343–353, IASH/UNESCO, Paris.

Ivanov, K. E. and Kotova, L. V. (1964). Voprosy dinamiki razvitiya i gidromorfologicheskie kharakteristiki ryamov Barabinskoy nizmennosti (The moss-mires of the Baraba lowlands—the dynamics of their development and their hydromorphological properties). *Trudy gos. gidrol. Inst.* **112**, 33–53.

Ivanov, K. E. and Romanov, V. V. (1965). Quantitative water budget criteria of evaluation of representativity of drainage areas in studying the influence physiographical factors upon hydrological regime elements. *In* "Representative and Experimental Areas", Proc. Budapest Symp. **2**, 669–675, Gentbrugge.

Ivanov, K. E. and Shumkova, E. L. (1967). Gidrologicheskoe obosnovanie i raschet vypadeniya lesov i rasshireniya ploshchadey estestvennogo zabolachivaniya pri podtopleniyakh v rechnykh sistemakh. *Trudy gos. gidrol. Inst.* **145**, 3–26; Hydrologic substantiation and computation of the reduction of forests and the expansion of naturally waterlogged areas after underflooding in river systems. *Sov. Hydrol.* (1967), 329–348.

Kalyuzhnyy, I. L. (1970). Otsenka variatsii ispareniya vnutri mikrolandshaftov verkhovykh bolot (Evaluation of variations in evaporation in the microtopes of raised mires). *Trudy gos. gidrol. Inst.* **177**, 39–58.

Kamenskiy, G. N. (1935). "Osnovy dinamiki podzemnykh vod" (Elements of the dynamics of subterranean waters). Ob'. nauchno-tekh. Izdat./Nat. Kom. torf. Prom., Moscow and Leningrad.

Kats, N. Ya. (1971). "Bolota zemnogo shara" (Mires of the world). Nauka, Moscow.

Khil'mi, G. E. (1963). Filosofskie problemy preobrazovaniya prirody (Philosophical problems relating to the transformation of nature). *In* "Vzaimodeystvie nauk pri izuchenii Zemli", Izdat. Akad. Nauk SSSR, Moscow.

Khil'mi, G. F. (1966). "Osnovy fiziki biosferi". Gidrometeoizdat, Leningrad; "Foundations of the Physics of the Biosphere" (O. Nakhimzhan and D. Page, trans.; A. P. Jacobson, ed.) (1967). Gidrometeoizdat, Leningrad.

Kil'dema, K. T. (1962). O printsipakh i metodakh vydeleniya bolotnykh landshaftnykh edinits (Principles and methods of distinguishing mire geotopes). *Ezhegodnik estonskogo geogr. Obshch.* (1960–1), 158–168.

Kiryushkin, V. N. (1964). K voprosu o razvitii bolotnykh massivov pologikh sklonov v usloviyakh raspredeleniya flyuvioglatsial'nykh otlozheniy (na primere yugo-vostochnoy Karelii) (The problem of the development of mire massifs with gentle slopes in association with fluvio-glacial moraines (for example, in south-eastern Karelia)). *Uchen. Zap. petrozavod.* **12**(2), 85–89.

Konstantinov, A. R. (1968). "Ispareniye v prirode". Gidrometeoizdat, Leningrad; "Evaporation in Nature" (Translation of 1st edn of 1963 by L. Shichtman). Israel Program for Scientific Translations, Jerusalem, 1966.

Konstantinov, A. R. and Sakali, L. I. (1967). Rol' sostavlyayushchikh teplovogo i vodnogo balansov v formirovanii landshafta (The role of heat and water-balance components in the formation of geotopes). *In* "Geofizika landshafta", pp. 40–52. Nauka, Moscow.

Korchunov, S. S. (1956). Opredelenie vlagokoeffitsientov torfa (Finding the moisture coefficients of peat). *Trudy vses. nauchno-issled. Inst. torf. Prom.* **13**, 74–88.

Korchunov, S. S. i drugie (1960). Izuchenie vodnogo rezhima osushennykh torfyanykh zalezhey (The water regime of undrained peat deposits). *Trudy vses. nauchno-issled. Inst. torf. Prom.* **17**.

Korchunov, S. S. and Mogilevskiy, I. I. (1961a). Mekhanizm ponizheniya vlazhnosti torfyanoy zalezhi pri osushenii (The mechanism of reduction of water content in peat deposits subject to drainage). *Trudy vses. nauchno-issled. Inst. torf. Prom.* **18**, 166–81.

Korchunov, S. S. and Mogilevskiy, I. I. (1961b). K voprosu ob istinnosti v izmereniyakh urovney gruntovykh vod v torfyanoy zalezhi pri pomoshchi smotrovykh kolodtsev (The reliability of water-table measurements in peat deposits by means of dip wells). *Trudy vses. nauchno-issled. Inst. torf. Prom.* **18**, 182–185.

Korchunov, S. S., Mogilevskiy, I. I. and Abakumov, O. N. (1961). Opredelenie vlagokoeffitsientov metodom postoyannogo raskhoda na poverkhnosti obraztsa (Determination of moisture coefficients by continuous loss from the surface of a sample). *Trudy vses. nauchno-issled. Inst. torf. Prom.* **18**, 156–165.

Korpijaako, M. and Radforth, N. W. (1972). Studies on the hydraulic conductivity of peat. *Proc. 4th int. peat Congr.* **3**, 323–334.

Kozlova, R. P. (1954). Bolotnye massivy stochnykh kotlovin slabo raschlennogo morennogo landshafta byvshego Tungudskogo rayona (Mire massifs in the perfluent basins of the slightly dissected moraine geotopes of the former Tungus region). *Trudy karel. Fil. Akad. Nauk SSSR*, **15**, 58–72.

Kudritskiy, D. M. (1973). N. G. Kell' i voprosy teorii deshifrirovaniya aerofotosnimkov (N. G. Kell' and questions concerning the interpretation of air photographs). *In* "Aerofotos'emka—metod izucheniya prirodnoy sredy", pp. 13–23. Nauka, Leningrad.

Kudritskiy, D. M., Popov, I. V. and Romanova, E. A. (1956). "Osnovy gidrogeograficheskogo deshifrirovaniya aerofotosnimkov" (The elements of the hydrogeographic interpretation of air photographs). Gidrometeoizdat, Leningrad.

Kulczyński, S. (1949). Peat bogs of Polesie. *Mem. Acad. pol. Sci.* B **15**.

Kuz'min, P. P. (1961). "Protsess tayaniya snezhnogo pokrova" (Thawing of the snow cover). Gidrometeoizdat, Leningrad.

Lavrenko, E. M. (1947). Ob izuchenii edifikatorov rastitel'nogo pokrova (The concept of edificators as applied to the plant cover). *Sov. Bot.* **15**, 1–16.

Lebedeva, N. V. (1959). Razvitie bolotnykh massivov podnozhiy sklonov i ikh vodoprovodyashchey seti na primere bolot Korzinskoy niziny (The development of mire massifs at the foot of slopes and of their water-conducting network as exemplified by the Korzinskaya depression). *Trudy karel. Fil. Akad. Nauk SSSR*, **15**, 49–57.

Lobell, R. (1953). Moorbruchkatastrophen. *Wass. Boden.* **5**(12).

Lopatin, V. D. (1949). O gidrologicheskom znachenii verkhovykh bolot (The hydrological significance of raised mires). *Vest. leningrad. gos. Univ.* **2**, 37–49.

Lundin, K. (1964). "Vodnye svoystva torfyanoy zalezhi" (The hydrological properties of peat deposits). Urozhay, Minsk.

Lykov, A. V. (1954). "Yavlenie perenosa v kapillyarno-poristykh telakh" (The phenomenon of transfer in porous bodies with capillary properties). Gosudarstvennoe Izdatel'stvo tekhniko-teoreticheskoy literatury, Moscow. (cf. Lykov, A. V. and Mikhaylov, Yu. A. (1961). "Theory of Energy and Mass Transfer" (W. Bigell, trans.). Prentice Hall, Englewood Cliffs, N.J.).

MacFarlane, I. C. (ed.) (1969). "Muskeg Engineering Handbook". University Press, Toronto.

Marshall, T. J. and Holmes, J. W. (1979). "Soil Physics". Cambridge University Press, Cambridge.

Masing, V. (1972). Typological approach in mire landscape study (with a brief multilingual vocabulary of mire landscape structure). *In* "Estonia: Geographical Studies", pp. 61–84. Acad. Sci. Estonian SSR—Estonian geogr. Soc., Tallinn.

Maslov, B. S. (1970). "Rezhim gruntovykh vod pereuvlazhnennykh zemel' i ego regulirovanie" (The groundwater regime of waterlogged lands and its control). Kolos, Moscow.

Milne-Thomson, L. M. (1968). "Theoretical Hydrodynamics". Macmillan, London.

Никанорова, I. V, (1969). Opyt programmirovaniya raschetov urovney bolotnykh vod po meteorologicheskim dannym na EVM (An attempt to compile a computer program for calculating the level of mire water from meteorological data). *Trudy gos. gidrol. Inst.* **157**, 138–147.

Neyshtadt, M. I. (1971). Mirovoy prirodnyy fenomen—zabolochennost' Zapadnoy-Sibirskoy ravniny. *Izv. Akad. Nauk SSSR, Ser. geogr.* **1**, 21–34; Natural world phenomenon—waterlogging of the East Siberian plain. *Sov. Hydrol.* (1971), 80–91.

Novikov, S. M. (1963). Raschety vodnogo rezhima i vodnogo balansa nizinnykh bolot i ryamov yuzhnoy chasti Zapadno-Sibirskoy nizmennosti (Computations of the water regime and the water balance of the fens and moss-mires of the southern part of the West Siberian lowlands). *Trudy gos. gidrol. Inst.* **105**, 5–44.

Novikov, S. M. (1964). Raschet urovennogo rezhima neosushennykh verkhovykh bolot po meteorologicheskim dannym. *Trudy gos. gidrol. Inst.* **112**, 5–32; Computation of the water-level regime of undrained upland swamps from meteorological data. *Sov. Hydrol.* (1964), 1–22.

Novikov, S. M. (1965). Raschet ezhednevnykh urovney gruntovykh vod na bolotakh po meteorologicheskim dannym. *Trudy gos. gidrol. Inst.* **126**, 48–64; Calculation of daily ground water levels in swamps using meteorological data. *Met. geoastrophys. Abstr.* (1965) **16**, 2755.

Novikov, S. M. (1966). K metodike rascheta izmenchivosti ispareniya s neissledo-
vannykh bolot s primeneniem metod kompozitsiy (In search of a means of computing the variability of evaporation from uninvestigated mires by the method of
composition). *Trudy gos. gidrol. Inst.* **135**, 172–80.

Orlov, V. I. (1963). Nekotorye zakonomernosti razmeshcheniya i formirovaniya
torfyanikov i bolot Zapadnoy Sibiri (Certain regularities characterizing the
distribution and formation of the peat deposits and mires of Western Siberia).
Uchen. Zap. tartu. gos. Univ. **7**, 216–229.

Orlov, V. I. (1968). "Khod razvitiya prirody lesobolotnoy zony Zapadnoy Sibiri
(The course of natural succession in the wooded-mire zone of Western Siberia).
Nedra, Leningrad.

Overbeck, F. (1975). "Botanisch-geologische Moorkunde". Wachholtz, Neumunster.

Pidoplichko, A. P. (1961). "Torfyanye mestorozhdeniya Belorussii" (The peat deposits
of Byelo-Russia). Minsk.

Pisar'kov, Kh. A. (1970). Vliyanie osnovnykh faktorov na intensivnost' osusheniya
lesnykh zemel' (The influence of fundamental factors on the intensity of forest
drainage). *Nauch. Trudy leningrad. lesotekh. Akad.* **142**, 9–27.

Pons, L. J. (1960). Soil genesis and classification of reclaimed peat soils in connection
with initial soil formation. *Proc. 7th int. Congr. Soil Sci.* **4**, 205–211.

Popov, E. G. (1968). "Osnovy gidrologicheskikh prognozov" (The elements of
hydrological prognosis). Gidrometeoizdat, Leningrad.

Radforth, N. W. and Brawner, C. O. (eds) (1977). "Muskeg and the Northern Environment in Canada". University Press, Toronto.

Ratcliffe, D. A. (ed.) (1977). "A Nature Conservation Review". Cambridge University
Press, Cambridge.

Romanov, V. V. (1953). Issledovanie ispareniya so sfagnovykh bolot (Research into
evaporation from sphagnum mires). *Trudy gos. gidrol. Inst.* **39**, 116–134.

Romanov, V. V. (1957). Isparenie s neosushennykh i osushennikh bolot (Evaporation
from undrained and drained mires). *Trudy gos. gidrol. Inst.* **60**, 20–42.

Romanov, V. V. (1961). "Gidrofizika bolot". Gidrometeoizdat, Leningrad; "Hydro-
physics of Bogs" (N. Kaner, trans.; Heimann, ed.) (1968). Israel Program for Scientific Translations, Jerusalem.

Romanov, V. V. (1962). "Isparenie s bolot Evropeyskoy territorii SSSR". Gidro-
meteoizdat, Leningrad; "Evaporation from bogs in the European territory of the
USSR" (N. Kaner, trans.; Heimann, ed.) (1968). Israel Program for Scientific
Translations, Jerusalem.

Romanova, E. A. (1960). O svyazi mezhdu rastitel'nost'yu, verkhnimi sloyami torfyanoy
zalezhi i vodnym rezhimon verkhovykh bolot Severo-Zapada (The connection
between the vegetation, the upper layers of the peat deposit and the water regime of
of the raised mires of the North-West). *Trudy gos. gidrol. Inst.* **89**, 92–122.

Romanova, E. A. (1961). "Geobotanicheskie osnovy gidrologicheskogo izlucheniya
verkhovykh bolot (s ispol'zovaniem aerofotos'emki)" (Radiation as studied by
air photogrammetry in relation to the geobotanical and hydrological elements of
raised mires). Gidrometeoizdat, Leningrad.

Romanova, E. A. (1965). Kratkaya landshaftno-morfologicheskaya kharakteristika
bolot Zapadno-Sibirskoy nizmennosti (A brief description in geotopo-morpho-
logical terms of the mires of the West Siberian lowlands). *Trudy gos. gidrol. Inst.* **126**,
96–112.

Rozhdestvenskaya, V. G. (1973). Vodnyy balans bolota Lammin-Suo (The water
balance of the Lammin-Suo mire). *Sb. Rab. Gidrol.*, Leningrad, **11**, 129–139.

Rycroft, D. W., Williams, D. J. A. and Ingram, H. A. P. (1975). The transmission of water through peat: I. Review. *J. Ecol.* **63**, 535–556.

Shaposhnikov, M. A. (1965). Osnovnye polozheniya dorozhno-stroitel'noy klassifi-katsii torfyanykh osnovaniy (The fundamental principles of the classification of peat foundations for the purpose of road construction). *Trudy tsentr. nauchno-issled. Univ. mat. Ekonomiki* **59**, 75–105.

Shaposhnikov, M. A. (1971). "Transportnoe osvoenie zabolochennykh lesov" (The development of adequate transport in swamped forests). Les. Prom., Moscow.

Shebeko, V. F. (1965). "Isparenie s bolot i balans pochvennoy vlagi" (Evaporation from mires and the balance of soil moisture). Urozhay, Minsk.

Shebeko, V. F. (1970). "Gidrologicheskiy rezhim osushaemykh territoriy" (The hydrological regime of territories undergoing drainage). Urozhay, Minsk.

Sjörs, H. (1948). Mire vegetation in Bergslagen, Sweden. *Acta phytogeogr. suec.* **21**, 277–290.

Smirnov, L. E. (1967). "Teoreticheskie osnovy i metody geograficheskogo deshifrir-ovaniya aerosnimkov" (Theoretical principles and methods for the geographical interpretation of air photographs). Izdat. leningrad. gos. Univ., Leningrad.

Smirnov, L. E. (1968). Informatsionnye svoystva aerosnimkov i otsenka ikh deshifrir-uemosti (The diagnostic value of air photographs and an evaluation of their decipherability). *Vest. leningrad. gos. Univ., Ser. geol. i geogr.* **1**(6), 94–107.

Sukachev, V. N. (1947). Osnovy teorii biogeotsenologii (Foundations of a theory of biogeocoenology). *In* "Yubeleynik sbornik posvyashchennyy 30-letiyu Velikoy Okmyabr'skoy sotsialisticheskoy revolutsii" **2**, Moscow and Leningrad.

Tsinzerling, Yu. D. (1938). Rastitel'nost' bolot (The vegetation of mires). *In* "Rastitel'-nost' SSSR", **1**, 355–435. Moscow and Leningrad.

Tyuremnov, S. N. and Vinogradova E. A. (1953). Geomorfologicheskaya klassifi-katsiya torfyanykh mestorozhdeniy na territorii RSFSR (Geomorphological classification of the peat deposits of the RUFSR). *Trudy mosk. torf. Univ.* **11**, 3–51.

Vinogradov, B. V. (1964). "Rastitel'nye indikatory i ikh ispol'zovanie pri izuchenii prirodnykh resursov" (Indicator plants and their use in the study of natural resources). Vysshaya Shkola, Moscow.

Vomperskiy, E. F. (1968). "Biologicheskie osnovy effektivnosti lesoosucheniya" (The biological principles of effective forest drainage). Nauka, Moscow.

Vorob'ev, P. K. (1963). Issledovanie vodootdachi nizinnykh bolot Zapadnoy Sibiii. *Trudy gos. gidrol. Inst.* **105**, 45–79; Investigations of the water yield of low lying swamps of Western Siberia. *Sov. Hydrol.* (1963), 226–252.

Vorob'ev, P. K. (1965). Issledovanie fizicheskikh kharakteristik deyatel'nogo gorizonta neosushennykh bolot. *Trudy gos. gidrol. Inst.* **126**, 65–96; Investigation of the physical characteristics of the active level of undrained swamps. *Met. geo-astrophys. Abstr.* **16**(11), 2755.

Vorob'ev, P. K. (1966). Privyazka resul'tatov eksperimental'nykh issledovaniy vodno-fizicheskikh svoystv torfa k poverkhnosti bolota (Application to the surface of a mire of the results of experimental investigations into the hydrophysical properties of peat). *Trudy gos. gidrol. Inst.* **135**, 210–222.

Vorob'ev, P. K. (1969). Opredelenie vodootdachi iz torfyanoy zalezhi estestvennykh bolot (Determination of the water yield from the peat deposits of natural mires). *Trudy gos. gidrol. Inst.* **177**, 59–80.

Weber, C. A. (1908). Aufbau und Vegetation der Moore Norddeutschlands. *Bot. Jb. Suppl.* **90**, 19–34.

Yaroshenko, P. D. (1961). "Geobotanika. Osnovnye ponyatiya, napravleniya i metody" (Geobotany. Fundamental concepts, aims and methods). Izdat. Akad. Nauk SSSR, Moscow and Leningrad.

Yurovskaya, T. K. (1959). Bolotnye landshafty rechnykh plesov Sredney Karelii (The mire geotopes along the river reaches of Middle Karelia). *Trudy karel. Fil. Akad. Nauk SSSR*, **15**, 84–93.

Index